# HIGH-PERFORMING SELF-MANAGED WORK TEAMS

D1319628

# HIGH-PERFORMING SELF-MANAGED WORK TEAMS

*A Comparison of Theory to Practice*

Dale E. Yeatts • Cloyd Hyten

SAGE Publications
*International Educational and Professional Publisher*
Thousand Oaks   London   New Delhi

*For information:*

SAGE Publications, Inc.
2455 Teller Road
Thousand Oaks, California 91320
E-mail: order@sagepub.com

SAGE Publications Ltd.
6 Bonhill Street
London EC2A 4PU
United Kingdom

SAGE Publications India Pvt. Ltd.
M-32 Market
Greater Kailash I
New Delhi 110 048 India

Printed in the United States of America

*Library of Congress Cataloging-in-Publication Data*

Yeatts, Dale E., 1952-
    High-performing self-managed work teams: A comparison of theory to practice / by Dale E. Yeatts.
       p.  cm.
    Includes bibliographical references and index.
    ISBN 0-7619-0469-7 (acid-free paper). — ISBN 0-7619-0470-0 (pbk.: acid-free paper)
    1. Self-directed work teams. I. Hyten, Cloyd. II. Title.
HD66.Y43 1997
658.4′036—dc21                           97-21091

This book is printed on acid-free paper.

99  00  01  02  03  10  9  8  7  6  5  4  3  2

| | |
|---|---|
| *Acquiring Editor:* | Marquita Flemming |
| *Editorial Assistant:* | Frances Borghi |
| *Production Editor:* | Diana E. Axelsen |
| *Production Assistant:* | Denise Santoyo |
| *Typesetter/Designer:* | Janelle LeMaster |
| *Cover Designer:* | Candice Harman |
| *Print Buyer:* | Anna Chin |

# Contents

# Preface and Acknowledgments

A *self-managed work team* (SMWT) is a group of employees who are responsible for managing and performing technical tasks that result in a product or service being delivered to an internal or external customer. Typically, the team consists of 5 to 15 employees who are responsible for managing all or most aspects of the work including, for example, planning and scheduling, monitoring, and staffing. Likewise, they are responsible for all the technical aspects of the work, whether it is assembling a computer board to be installed in a "smart bomb" or verifying claims and completing monthly reports so that recipients of government housing will continue to receive their housing subsidy. In addition, the team members of an SMWT typically rotate these management and technical responsibilities among themselves periodically (Goodman, Devadas, & Griffith Hughson, 1988; Johnson & Johnson, 1994; Wellins, Byham, & Wilson, 1991).

It should be noted that SMWTs are not work groups as defined by Johnson and Johnson (1994) because the interdependence among work group members is typically low, and the accountability for the work focuses primarily on the individual rather than the group as a whole. Likewise, SMWTs are not generally thought of as teams brought together for a short-term purpose, such as virtual teams or task teams. On the other hand, it is reasonable to suspect that many of the factors that are important to high SMWT performance will also be important to the performance of work groups and short-term teams.

The growing use of SMWTs appears to be the result of international competition in the last quarter of the 20th century, which has forced organizations in the United States to look for better ways of competing (Boyer & Pond, 1987). Growth in SMWTs is evident through national surveys that have documented the interest of corporations in teamwork and self-management (Lawler, Ledford, & Mohrman, 1989), through surveys of employees that describe their job characteristics (Fisher, 1986; Yeatts, Stanley-Stevens, & Ruggiere, 1992), through a growth in the participation at conferences on self-managed teams (Beyerlein, Flax, & Saiter, 1991), and through a growth in the membership of corporate networks on SMWTs (Yeatts, 1992).

The use of SMWTs has been found to result in higher performance at less cost (e.g., Cotton, Vollrath, Froggatt, Lengnick-Hall, & Jennings, 1988; Lawler, 1986; Macy, Peterson, & Norton, 1989; Pasmore, Francis, Haldeman, & Shani, 1982; Wellins, Byham, & Dixon, 1994). Unfortunately, social scientists have had difficulty substantiating this statistically, because of the difficulty in isolating the individual effects of self-management from the many other factors operating in the workplace (Nurick, 1982; Wagner & Gooding, 1987b; Wall, Kemp, Jackson, & Clegg, 1986). Consequently, it appears that the effects of SMWTs are best determined through methodologies such as case studies rather than quantitative analyses.

Case studies have shown that under the right circumstances, employees within SMWTs produce more at work than employees organized in a more hierarchical, traditional structure because they not only perform technical skills but management skills as well (Hackman, 1990; Hitchcock & Willard, 1995; Orsburn, Moran, Musselwhite, Zenger, & Perrin, 1990; Wellins et al., 1994; Yeatts, Hyten, & Barnes, 1996). Furthermore, case studies have shown that the decisions made by SMWTs are extremely effective because those making the decisions—the team members—are the most knowledgeable persons about the work (Buchholz, Roth, & Hess, 1987; Ray & Bronstein, 1995). SMWTs have also been found to produce more innovation and creativity because the team members can see the whole work process (Hitchcock & Willard, 1995).

Other performance improvements that can be attributed to SMWTs include the ability of team members to fill in for each other when a member of the team is absent, to help each other during times when important work has to be completed on a deadline, to schedule and assign the work to match the needs and strengths of team members, and to have more empathy for each other's problems because the team members understand what everyone is doing (Harper & Harper, 1989). Simultaneously, the number of first-line supervisors needed has been found to be less than in a more traditional work environment, because the SMWT members handle a large portion of the management responsibilities (Becker-Reems, 1994; Shonk, 1992). Thus, the employees within SMWTs have been found to perform at a higher level and at a lower cost than employees within more traditional work environments.

On the other hand, the ability of SMWTs to accomplish higher performance at less cost is dependent on a variety of factors, including the work and interpersonal processes, numerous environmental factors such as management support and employee training, the team's design, and characteristics of the employees themselves. When these factors have *not* been planned and implemented to support the SMWT, studies report little or no performance improvement and little or no cost advantage (Nurick, 1982; Tjosvold, 1986; Varney, 1989). The purpose of this book is to clarify the specific factors most important to an SMWT's success. This is accomplished by comparing those factors that have been identified in the literature with those actually found among 10 SMWTs that were carefully studied. These teams were selected from three different settings: manufacturing, public service, and health care.

## METHODS FOR IDENTIFYING FACTORS AFFECTING SMWT PERFORMANCE

Data for this book come from three sources. The primary source is 10 case studies of SMWTs funded by a 3-year grant (1994-1997) from the National Science Foundation. The purpose of the study was to identify those factors most important to SMWT performance. The case studies included both high- and low-performing SMWTs. Four case studies were selected from an international manufacturer of electronic equipment, two from a federal agency, one from a municipal agency, and three from a nursing home. We have chosen to keep their identities anonymous because we report on numerous problems of the low-performing SMWTs. Data collection included hour-long interviews with each team member, interviews with all relevant managers, observation of numerous team meetings, observation of the workplace and team members at work, a self-administered questionnaire completed by all team members, and, where possible, a review of organizational and team reports (see Appendixes B through E for survey instruments used). These data, with the exception of the self-administered questionnaire information, are reviewed in this book. Data collected from the self-administered instrument are not included due to difficulties found in comparing team member responses across organizations. In-person interviews and observations were found to be more valid. A more thorough description of the methods used is provided in Appendix A.

A second source of data is a 3-year study (1990-1993) funded by the Texas Advanced Research Program. The purpose of the study was to examine the effects of SMWTs on performance and employee attitudes. The study included 600 self-administered questionnaires and in-depth interviews with about 40 SMWT members. Participating organizations included Boeing Electronics, AT&T, the Department of Defense, and Valenite—a parts manufacturer.

A third source of firsthand information was the Network on Self-Managed Work Teams established by the authors in 1992. The network has met quarterly, with each meeting located at a different host site (e.g., Texas Instruments, Jostens, Lockheed). The host describes for the network members the SMWT program being used. The host typically has SMWT members describe their responsibilities, the problems they have encountered while working within an SMWT, solutions they have found, and successes they have enjoyed. Network members are given the opportunity to ask questions to learn how the host organization is handling various issues, such as performance evaluation and compensation.

The book also relies heavily on previous research findings and publications. Unfortunately, the breadth of existing research covering the many dimensions of SMWTs is greater than we have been able to cover. Nevertheless, we have attempted to include as many of the existing research findings as possible to help clarify the relationships between team dimensions and performance. We welcome input from readers who can lead us to additional literature that will further our development of one or more dimensions discussed here.

## ACKNOWLEDGMENTS

We wish to thank the many self-managed work team members and their managers who were willing to share with us both their triumphs and their blunders. These include employees at Texas Instruments (particularly Barry Johnson), the Department of Defense (particularly Janet Reardon), AT&T (particularly Jim Brennan), Good Samaritan Nursing Homes (particularly Julian Saxon), Boeing (particularly Ron Shenburger), General Services Administration (particularly Melanie DeSantis), Jostens (particularly Micky Kaehr and Marian Wagner), Denton Housing Authority (particularly Marian

Hamilton), and many others. Likewise, we wish to thank the many people at the University of North Texas who supported our efforts (particularly Drs. Susan Eve and Sigrid Glen), including providing faculty leave and assistance whenever requested. And we thank the National Science Foundation and Texas Advanced Research Program for their financial and other support. Finally, we wish to express our warmest thanks to the many graduate research assistants who worked with us in a team effort to complete the research, including Dr. Leslie Stanley-Stevens, Paul Ruggiere, Martha Hipskind, Debra Barnes, William Alexander, and Lisa Obsts.

# PART I

■                                                                                      ■

## Theoretical Frameworks for Understanding the Performance of Self-Managed Work Teams

■                                                                                      ■

Part I is presented in a historical context beginning at the turn of the 20th century, when the industrial revolution was beginning to have a major effect on how work was being performed. At this time, classical organizational theories such as scientific management were being developed. The shortcomings of this perspective gave rise to the human relations perspective, which placed far more importance on the connection between employee job satisfaction and performance. These were followed by the systems perspective, which took a broader view, including a focus on the environment outside the organization as well as inside it. Finally, the contingency approach is reviewed. Advocates of this approach believe there is no single perspective that can explain organizational performance because of the many different contingencies or situations that exist for organizations.

The theoretical assumptions underlying self-managed work teams (SMWTs) can be found in the classical, human relations, systems, and contingency perspectives. Classical theorists believe that it is the work procedures and technical

1

tools that are of primary importance to organizational performance—SMWTs are designed so that the most appropriate technical procedures are followed. It is believed that those with firsthand knowledge of the technical work—the team members—are in the best position to determine the most appropriate technical procedures.

Human relations theorists believe that employee participation in decision making allows the employee to satisfy higher-order needs, such as self-actualization and autonomy, as described by Maslow (1954/1970). Furthermore, theorists believe that participation contributes to the employee's positive self-image and the opportunity for positive interactions with management. SMWTs provide employees extensive involvement in, and identification with, the organization for which they work through participation in decision making. This allows employees to satisfy higher-order needs and develop a positive self-image.

Advocates of systems theory and, in particular, the sociotechnical systems perspective, believe that SMWTs provide a tool for achieving the best match between the technical and social systems (Pasmore et al., 1982; Trist & Bamforth, 1951). In SMWTs, team members are given the authority to make all or most decisions related to their work. The team members are believed to be in the best position to identify and make decisions about the relevant technical and social factors because they have firsthand knowledge of the work and employees involved. A good match results in a more effective use of technology and in an "enriched" work environment, where employees have increased responsibility, task variety, and so on.

Finally, advocates of the contingency perspective believe that high organizational performance is contingent on a variety of employee, technological, and environmental factors. The SMWT allows those in direct contact with the technology and environment to make decisions about the work. Proponents believe that the SMWT is able to respond quickly to contingencies that present themselves at the employee, technological, or environmental levels.

# 1

■

# The Classical and Human Relations Theories

■

## THE CLASSICAL ORGANIZATION PERSPECTIVE

In the early 1900s, organization theorists worked to develop a view of managing organizations that would enable organizations to function as rationally and efficiently as possible—sometimes referred to as the classical organization perspective or theory. It was believed that organizational efficiency could be best achieved with the application of rational administrative procedures (Hackman & Oldham, 1980). This required clear and unambiguous channels of authority to allow for centralized command and control of the organization (Scott & Mitchell, 1976). Perhaps the single most important principle underlying this view was division of labor. It was believed that maximum work efficiency is achieved when jobs are simplified and specialized to the greatest extent practicable. This allows workers to become experts at their special skills and abilities. It was explained that specialization requires less overall knowledge to become an expert, reduces distractions because fewer different tasks are performed, and avoids wasting time changing from one task and/or workstation to another.

The views of classical organization theorists were implemented through the emergence of *industrial engineering*. A primary goal of industrial engineering was (and still is) to increase the productive efficiency of organizations. This included designing work so that the quickest and most efficient methods were standardized for all employees performing the same basic tasks. Industrial engineers explained that the efficiency of the whole organization would be maximized to the extent that the subparts were designed to work efficiently. Industrial engineers also held that simplifying and routinizing jobs would increase the interchangeability of employees, which, in turn, would reduce time needed for training and allow for easy replacement of problem employees.

Perhaps the most famous of the industrial engineering theorists is Frederick W. Taylor (1911), who developed the principles of *scientific management*. These principles include scientifically studying the technical aspects of the work, matching employees to the technical demands of the jobs, being sure that employees perform the work exactly as specified by prior scientific analysis, and providing bonuses to employees who successfully complete a day's work. Thus, rather than the traditional craft model, where workers were responsible for doing a total job, Taylor proposed that jobs be broken into discrete tasks. He believed that efficiency could be gained by standardizing repetitive tasks that were broken into minute parts.

To accomplish this plan, Taylor initiated time and motion studies. These were to analyze tasks of the work, reorganize tasks with efficiency in mind, and subsequently, improve performance. In addition, the economic self-interest of the workers was to be satisfied through various incentive work plans (e.g., pay based on the number of units assembled). Furthermore, it was believed that, with these studies and the reorganization of tasks, training time would be brought to a minimum.

The function of the manager under scientific management or classical theory was to set up and enforce performance criteria to meet organizational goals. The main focus of a manager was on satisfying the needs of the organization and not on the needs of the individual (Hersey & Blanchard, 1988; Klein, 1994; Taylor, 1911).

Other traditional organization/management approaches include what has been referred to as bureaucratic theory and administrative management. *Bureaucratic theory*, originally developed by Max Weber (in the Gerth & Mills, 1958, translation), outlines a rational approach for structuring productive organizations. According to Weber, the *bureaucracy* was needed because the state of management was in disarray. Managers needed advice to overcome practices of management by favoritism, nepotism, and intuition. Morgan and Hiltner (1992, p. 15) have outlined what Weber believed to be the most important qualities of bureaucracy:

1. A strict chain of command (each person reports to only one supervisor)
2. Selection and promotion based on interpersonal and technical skills (not nepotism, favoritism, or intuition)

3. Detailed rules, regulations, and procedures for each job to make sure it is accomplished
4. Strict specialization, which matches competence and job responsibility
5. Centralization of power at the top of the organizational structure

Thus, Weber's bureaucratic theory calls for well-defined positions, a clear division of labor, explicit objectives, and a clear chain of authority.

The *administrative management* approach included detailed descriptions of what the general duties, or functions, of managers should be. These were provided through clearly articulated guidelines or principles. Fayol (1949), a contemporary of Frederick Taylor, originally presented 14 principles, which have undergone numerous revisions and refinements. These have been distilled into at least four primary functions of management, including planning, organizing, leading, and controlling.

Today, many of the concepts that were inherent in the works of the classical theorists, such as Taylor, Weber, and Fayol, are used to manage organizations. The scientific management, bureaucratic, and administrative management theories have provided the guidance needed to implement what Lawler (1992) refers to as the *control-oriented approach*. This approach appears to have reached its greatest popularity in the 1960s, when many people assumed that it gave American industry a competitive advantage in the world. Companies, such as Exxon, Kodak, IBM, AT&T, and General Motors, produced sophisticated organizational charts, trained managers to direct and control employees, and developed elaborate information systems to support a control-oriented philosophy. This approach has maintained its dominance, but, as international competition has grown, an increasing number of organizations have begun looking for more competitive approaches for getting the work done.

## THE HUMAN RELATIONS MOVEMENT

During the late 1920s and 1930s, experiments at the Western Electric Hawthorne plant by Roethlisberger and Dickson (1939) and their associate Mayo (1946) were showing that organizational performance was more than the sum of technical improvements in how the work was done. As Perrow (1986) has explained, Roethlisberger (an industrial psychologist from Harvard) and Dickson (a manager at the Western Electric plant) took two groups of workers doing the same kinds of jobs, put them into separate rooms, and kept careful records of their productivity. One group (the test group) had the intensity of its lighting increased. Its productivity went up. For the other group (the control group), there was no change in lighting. But, to the amazement of the researchers, its productivity went up also. Even more puzzling, when reversing the stimulus so that the degree of illumination in the test group was continually lowered, it was found that output still continued to go up. It was not until the lighting was barely above moonlight conditions that productivity stopped rising. After continued studies over many years, including attitude surveys of "what's on the worker's mind" and group studies on how employees influenced each other's attitudes and behavior, the researchers began to draw conclusions about the importance of human relations to the performance of the organization. For example, Roethlisberger and Dickson (1939), in their book *Management and the Worker,* state,

> The study of the bank wiremen showed that their behavior at work could not be understood without considering the informal organization of the group and the relation of this informal organization to the total social organization of the company. The work activities of the group, together with their satisfactions and dissatisfactions, had to be viewed as manifestations of a complex pattern of interrelations. (pp. 551-552)

During this period, other researchers also began to investigate this "human relations" perspective (Barnard, 1938; Parker, 1984). This included examining the relationship between morale/satisfaction and productivity and between management leadership and productivity. Advocates of this approach believed that in addition to finding the best technological methods to improve output, it was beneficial to create positive human relations within the organization. Early contributors to this perspective believed that employee satisfaction was directly related to employee performance and subsequently the performance of the organization. However, subsequent research has been inconclusive with regard to the relationship between satisfaction and performance (Iaffaldano & Muchinsky, 1985, provide an extensive review of this research in their meta-analysis).

The human relations advocates also contended that high performance could be achieved if employees were treated fairly, with respect, and were allowed some participation in the decisions related to their work. Consequently, managers were encouraged to be more cooperative with workers, to upgrade the social environment at work, and to reinforce individual employees' self-images. It was explained that "good" management was democratic rather than production-centered and concerned with human relations rather than with bureaucratic rules. Barnard (1938), a major contributor to this view, advocated conciliatory management relations that would enhance cooperation between employees and supervisors. Parker (1984), another major contributor, contended that managers were responsible for motivating employees to pursue organizational goals enthusiastically, not simply to obey orders. She rejected the notion that managers should be groomed to give orders, believing instead that they should be trained to work with employees toward the attainment of common objectives.

Several perspectives have emerged out of these initial works. Two perspectives particularly relevant to SMWTs are the human resource perspective and the participative-management/high-involvement perspective.

## The Human Resource Perspective

Advocates of the human resource perspective, like those of the broader human relations movement, believed that employees should be treated fairly and with respect and that cooperation with management should be encouraged. The human resource advocates distinguished themselves by focusing attention on employees as valuable resources that should be developed by the organization (Miles, 1965). They explained that when employees have input into decisions, better solutions are developed. They contended that organizations should make a long-term commitment to the development of employees because it would make them more valuable to the organization. Furthermore, it was believed that employees desire to participate fully, to resolve their "higher needs" for autonomy and self-actualization, and to identify with the goals of the organization.

The work of McGregor (1960) has provided the human resource advocates with a conceptual model similar to their own. McGregor has theorized that management takes either of two views of the employee. If managers take the *Theory X* perspective, they view employees as hating their work, avoiding it, and being indifferent to organizational needs and goals. If managers take the *Theory Y* perspective, they assume that employees want to take responsibility for their work, desire the opportunity for personal development within their job, and want to help achieve organizational goals. The human resource advocates argued that the Theory Y approach is the appropriate one. They explained that managers should view employees as valuable resources and arrange the work so that the employees' personal goals and those of the organization are in support of one another.

The work of Maslow (1954/1970) also helped human resource advocates to clarify their view. Maslow believed that there is a hierarchy of needs in all individuals. Once the lower-order needs, such as physiological and safety needs, are satisfied, the higher-order needs, such as self-actualization and autonomy, become important to the individual. When applying this perspective to organizations, the human resource advocates explained that employees need extensive involvement in, and identification with, the organization in order to satisfy their higher-order needs.

## The Participative-Management, High-Involvement Perspective

More recently, the *participative-management* or *high-involvement* perspective has grown within the human relations school of thought. Advocates of this perspective agree with the views of the human relations movement as well as the human resources perspective but distinguish themselves by placing even more emphasis on the importance of employee participation in decision making related to their work (Anthony, 1978; Hackman, 1978; Lawler, 1986; Susman, 1979). Proponents believe that employees can be trusted to make important decisions about their work, that they can develop the knowledge needed to make these decisions, and that the result of employee participation in decision making is greater organizational effectiveness. More specifically, advocates of this view believe that high employee involvement in decision making has a direct positive effect on the employee's social and psychological states, which, in turn, affect the employee's performance.

In addition, advocates of this view have explained that employees, when provided the authority to make decisions about their work, can typically consider both social and technical factors more effectively than can management or engineers. In more traditional settings, it is explained, decisions are often made by engineers or managers, who either do not consider social factors or are less familiar with the social factors than are the people actually performing the work. Similarly, engineers and managers are sometimes less familiar with the technical aspects of the work because they often lack the advantage of firsthand knowledge.

In our own examinations of SMWTs, we have seen a good example of this. At Texas Instruments, a high-technology organization, managers and engineers had been making decisions about the layout of the employees' work for years. Once employees were given the opportunity to make these decisions, the employees decided to rearrange several large pieces of equipment. This resulted in hundreds of thousands of dollars being saved because the new arrangement allowed employees to better coordinate their efforts, and this resulted in considerably more time spent actually performing the work.

Advocates of participative management are *not* in complete agreement regarding the amount of authority that should be provided to employees. The application of participative management in the workplace can be found to range from soliciting employee opinions only, as in quality circles, to allowing them to make most or all decisions related to their work, as in the case of SMWTs (Lawler, 1986; Myers, 1991).

## SUMMARY

The classical organizational approach has emphasized a concern for technical aspects of the work and focused on formal authority and centralized structure. The human relations approach has focused on the interrelations between employees and the relationship between management and the employee. The classical and human relations perspectives have continued to be a focus of organizational researchers. However, empirical results have been less than clear, and conclusions have tended to support the view that high organizational performance is dependent on a myriad of qualifiers and conditions that have to be taken into account, with neither theoretical perspective adequately explaining organizational performance in all types of organizations and all performance situations.

# 2

■

# Systems Theories and the Emergence of the Sociotechnical and SMWT Perspectives

■

In the latter half of the 20th century, a growing number of organizational theorists began turning their attention beyond employees and their immediate work environment and toward groups within and outside the organization. These theorists began examining how groups, such as departments and branches of the organization, interact with one another as well as how one organization interacts with another. Theorists subsequently began to view the organization as a *system* or collection of interrelated and interdependent parts. As Holt (1990) has noted,

> Just as the human body is a system with organs, muscles, bones, a nervous system, and a consciousness that links all the parts together, an organization is a system with many interdependent parts that are linked by the social dynamics of human beings working together. (p. 50)

Advocates of the systems approach have pointed out that many managers have defined their roles within singular parts without viewing the whole organization or the larger system within which the organization operates. They have noted that managers should not only pay attention to activities

10

within their organization but also pay close attention to decisions made outside their organization. They have explained that such attention is necessary in order for managers to anticipate future effects the environment might have on their part of the organization as well as on the organization as a whole. Prior to the systems perspective, organizational researchers gave little attention to the broader organization or the environment surrounding it.

Application of the systems perspective can be illustrated by taking as an example a nursing home and its admissions office, where decisions are made to admit or reject applicants. Whereas classical and human relations theorists would focus their attention on the behaviors of the employees in this office, systems theorists would examine how this office is related to other offices and departments within the nursing home, as well as how it is related to people and organizations outside the nursing home. That is, systems theorists might focus their attention on how decisions made by the admissions office affect other groups within the nursing home, such as the various nursing stations and laundry and cafeteria sections. Likewise, they might examine how the admissions office and nursing home affect organizations and individuals outside the nursing home, such as hospitals, adult day care centers, and families. Furthermore, they might examine those organizations in the broader environment that make decisions directly affecting the admissions office and nursing home as a whole, such as Medicare and Medicaid reimbursement policies for nursing homes passed by the U.S. Congress. Thus, systems theorists focus their attention on the interrelationships of parts within the organization, as well as conditions outside the organization that affect it and that it affects.

Theorists who have studied primarily those systems within the organization have been referred to as *closed systems* theorists. The closed systems approach was the initial focus of most of the first systems theorists. As the studies of systems within organizations grew, some theorists noted that the closed systems approach, as well as classical and human relations theories, tended to ignore relationships between factors in the environment and the *focal* organization, that is, the organization being studied (Katz & Kahn, 1966). Study of the broader environment came to be known as the *open systems* or *environmental perspective*. Open systems researchers have addressed a myriad of important environmental factors, including changing technology, political conditions, economic and demographic factors, social and cultural variations, and environmental stability and flexibility (Banner & Gagné, 1995; Zey-Ferrell, 1979).

Many of the researchers who take a closed systems approach acknowledge the importance of the organization's relationship to its surrounding environment. These researchers explain their relative lack of emphasis on open systems factors by pointing out several methodological problems associated with them. They explain that many of the variables studied in the closed systems approach, such as employee motivation, satisfaction, and performance, can be relatively easily measured by questioning employees, examining organizational records, and observing. On the other hand, many of the open system factors, such as culture and social change, are broad in scope and difficult to operationalize and measure (Zey-Ferrell, 1979).

Examination of open and closed systems research shows that, at best, closed systems researchers include a few of the most theoretically important open systems factors within their research frame. Similarly, open systems researchers tend to consider only those closed systems factors believed to be most salient to their focus of study.

A major criticism of the systems model has been its treatment of conflict within the organization. Systems theorists generally view conflict as an aberration from the general tendency of organizational parts to work interdependently. Critics have argued that conflict should be treated as an inevitable and normal condition of an organization's functioning. For example, they have explained that the organization should be viewed as one that has multiple goals that are not necessarily in agreement with one another. When goals are not well defined, it is natural for the organization to experience internal conflict as groups within the organization compete for dominance. Critics have argued that the systems model largely ignores these competing groups, their conflicting interests and values, how the competing interests contribute to change within the organization, and how some groups are able to gain advantage over others.

Provided below is a review of the systems theory, as it has been applied to an organization's broader environment. This is followed by a review of systems theory from a more closed perspective—the sociotechnical systems theory and several subtheories that have emerged from it.

## OPEN SYSTEMS AND THE ENVIRONMENTAL PERSPECTIVE

The open systems theorists first began distinguishing their views from the more general systems model by focusing specifically on the exchange process between the organization and its environment. Consequently, the environment became the central focus for these theorists. They have explained that as the focal organization interacts with the environment to secure resources, it becomes dependent on the environment. Reciprocity is established as the focal organization provides resources back to the environment. Cooperation and conflict are found at varying degrees between the organization and its environment to the extent that reciprocity is or is not achieved (Zey-Ferrell, 1979).

Perrow (1986) has explained that initially the environment was viewed by systems theorists as anything "out there" of interest to the researcher. These researchers progressively began to catalog things that we should look for out there. The first step was the analysis of two or three interacting organizations, initially labeled *interorganizational analysis,* with the emphasis on the effect of the other organizations on the focal organization. Then, the idea of a *set* of organizations began to gain interest among researchers and, from there, the idea of a network of organizations, focusing on the properties of the networks rather than any one organization in it.

Advocates of the environmental perspective typically have focused on the complexity of an organization's environment, ranging from the organization's interaction with immediate customers and suppliers to systems of government, ecological systems, and cultural beliefs. It is explained that these varying complex environments must be understood by those managing the organization in order for the organization to survive and prosper. Furthermore, it is explained that this complexity has often resulted in the environment going unstudied altogether, because of the difficulties in measuring environmental complexity and change.

Systems theorists who have studied the environment often highlight the constant state of environmental change and the consequent effects on organizations. Emery and Trist (1965) have described a "turbulent field" in which the environment is changing independently of organizational actions but in ways that are often threatening to organizational survival. Pasmore (1988) has noted that for some organizational executives, continual environmental change is viewed as a persisting threat to the organization and something that must be continually dealt with. For other executives, environmental change is viewed as a recurring opportunity to gain competitive advantage. This has led some systems theorists to concentrate their research on how organizations change with turbulent environments and how environments change due to the manipulations of organizations.

General Motors provides a good example of an organization responding to and, at the same time, manipulating its environment. It responded to international competition by changing its technologies and implementing new management practices to better match those of its competition. At the same time, it attempted to manipulate the environment by placing pressure on U.S. legislators to establish tougher automobile import quotas.

## SOCIOTECHNICAL SYSTEMS THEORY

The sociotechnical systems theory is primarily a closed systems approach that emphasizes the interrelationship of the social and technical systems within an organization (Kelly, 1978; Pasmore et al., 1982; Trist & Bamforth, 1951; Trist, Higgin, Murray, & Pollack, 1963). The focus is on the work system, as opposed to the more traditional focus on individual jobs (Manz & Sims, 1989). Trist and Bamforth (1951), in their study of British coal mines, showed that the business of coal mining could best be understood in terms of two systems—the technical system, including machinery and other equipment, and the social system, including the social relationships and interactions among the employees. The *social system* of an organization has come to be seen as the people who work in the organization and the relationships among them (Emery, 1959; Pasmore, 1988) and the *technological system* as the tools, techniques, procedures, strategies, skills, knowledge, and devices used by members of the social system to accomplish the tasks of the organization (Cummings & Srivastva, 1977; Emery, 1959; Woodward, 1958).

Advocates of this perspective explain that the most effective organizations are those where the social and technological systems are integrated and supportive of one another (Emery, 1959). The term *joint optimization* or *best match* is used to describe the relationship between the social and technological systems of the organization, where each is sensitive to the demands of the other (Pasmore et al., 1982).

Fisher, Rayner, and Belgard (1995) have explained the importance of considering both the social and technical systems in relation to an organization's work teams:

> There are two basic types of needs or issues that arise on a team—task and [social] relationship. Task issues relate to the actual work that the team must accomplish. Relationship issues relate to how well the people on the team get along and work together. A team that is too heavily focused on task may find itself overlooking important relationship issues. As a result, tension may rise and tempers may flare. A team that overemphasizes relationships may find that important tasks do not get done or that quality begins to slip. As a result, the team may lose credibility as expectations are not met, motivation of team members may decline, and individuals may begin to point fingers. (p. 209)

The sociotechnical systems theory is described as having clear advantages over both classical theories and human relations perspectives. As noted above, the classical approach largely ignores the personal needs of the employees carrying out the work. The human relations perspective gives little attention to the operation of the technical aspects of the work. Advocates of the sociotechnical systems theory explain that this approach examines the technical and social systems simultaneously, with the end goal of joint optimization of the two—high task productivity and fulfillment for employees (Hackman & Oldham, 1980).

Argyris (1990) has noted that the military bureaucratic organization is a good example of the lack of joint optimization. He has explained that in the military organization, the following assumptions are made: People will perform most effectively when assigned to highly specialized repetitive tasks; there is one best way to perform any job; differences among people should be ignored; leaders are fair-minded and unemotional; and all goals and decisions should be determined by superiors for their subordinates. Argyris has explained that these assumptions create an environment where employees are expected to be passive, dependent, and respectful of authority figures. The assumptions do not recognize what Argyris has explained are common employee needs and desires—to be active, independent, experiencing variety in the workplace, equal, and able to make decisions and control one's actions. By not recognizing the needs within the social system, the military has created a technical system that frustrates employees rather than accommodating their needs and desires. The result has been described as less than optimal organizational performance (Pasmore, 1988).

Attempts to implement the sociotechnical systems perspective have included the redesign of the workplace to "enrich" jobs, such as providing work variety, and the reorganization of employees into SMWTs. Each of these sociotechnical approaches is discussed further below.

## The Job Enrichment/Characteristics Theory

Advocates of job enrichment theory, also referred to as job characteristics theory, believe that the technical system, in terms of the work design, has large effects on the employee's satisfaction, motivation, and performance. The better the match between the design of the work and the personal needs of the employee, the higher the employee satisfaction, motivation, and performance. Turner and Lawrence (1965) brought attention to five important job design characteristics: (1) variety in the work, (2) employee autonomy in performing the work, (3) social interaction provided by the job, (4) knowledge and skill, and (5) responsibility entrusted in the employee. Hackman and Oldham (1975, 1976, 1980) have expanded and developed this work by adding several additional job characteristics and by proposing a causal relationship between the job design characteristics, the employee's psychological state, and employee motivation, satisfaction, and performance. They believed that by enriching the job through redesign (e.g., providing skill variety, allowing the employee to undertake a "whole" piece of work, emphasizing the importance of the work, and providing autonomy and feedback), employees would experience increased feelings of responsibility for the work, meaningfulness of the work, and knowledge of the results of the work. It was explained that these, in turn, would affect the employees' motivation, satisfaction, and performance.

Advocates of job enrichment theory have stressed that the joint optimization between the job's design and the employee is dependent on the needs and desires of the specific employees. That is, different employees may respond differently to the same job. For example, whereas one employee may prefer to "grow" in his or her job through increased job variety, responsibility, and autonomy, another employee may prefer much less growth in the job or prefer no growth at all. In this latter case, a common response from the employee might be: "Just let me come to work, do my task, and go home at 5." The consequence of this realization has been that the characteristics of the individual employee must be identified prior to identifying the best sociotechnical match and subsequent redesign of the job (Aldag & Brief, 1979; Evans, Kiggundu, & House, 1979; Hackman & Oldham, 1980; Hersey & Blanchard, 1982; Hogan & Martell, 1987; Lawler, 1986).

Unfortunately, research has not clarified the employee characteristics that should be considered prior to determining how to redesign a job. Undoubtedly, the most widely studied characteristic is growth need, that is, the difference between employees with regard to their need for growth within their jobs. It has been contended that employees desiring growth can be expected to prefer jobs providing high skill variety, autonomy, and responsibility, whereas those not preferring growth will prefer less of these characteristics (Hackman & Oldham, 1980; Loher, Noe, Moeller, & Fitzgerald, 1985). Consequently, a highly enriched job would be most appropriate for an employee with a high growth need. However, studies that have examined this relationship have been inconclusive (Aldag & Brief, 1979; Evans et al., 1979; Kelly, 1992; Kemp & Cook, 1983; Lawler, 1986).

## The SMWT Approach

As noted above, an SMWT consists of employees who are responsible for managing and performing the technical tasks that result in a product or service being delivered. Team members are typically responsible for managing all or most aspects of the work and performing all the technical tasks involved. Technical tasks are typically rotated among team members, as are management responsibilities, such as monitoring the team's productivity and quality.

The SMWT approach to managing staff is described by Cummings (1978) as a direct outcome of sociotechnical systems theory and design. SMWTs are intended as a tool for achieving the best match between the technical and social systems. Team members are given the authority to make all or most decisions related to their work. They consider both the technical needs and social concerns prior to making decisions and are believed to be in the best position to identify the relevant technical and social factors because they have firsthand knowledge of the work and employees involved (Harper & Harper, 1989; Manz & Sims, 1989).

SMWTs can be thought of as providing an "enriched" work environment. As Cummings (1978) has explained, the SMWT provides group members with the opportunity to use different skills, to complete a meaningful piece of work, to perform tasks that affect other team members, to make important work-related decisions, and to learn how well they are doing. The combination of these is likely to satisfy those employees who have needs for autonomy, responsibility, and meaningful tasks.

The social needs of employees are addressed as team members get to know and understand one another (Larson & LaFasto, 1989; Lawler, 1986; Plunkett & Fournier, 1991). The team environment allows employees to keep in touch with those around them and recognize when a coworker has job-related or non-job-related needs and/or problems. Team members are believed to be most knowledgeable about the social needs of others on the team and how to best structure the technical work so that each employee's needs and preferences are considered.

Similarly, SMWT members are believed to be most knowledgeable of the technical system directly related to the work. Team members are able to regularly share with each other technical information and feedback on job-related matters (Hackman, 1990; Larson & LaFasto, 1989; Lawler, 1992). Furthermore, information sharing occurs with management at all hierarchical levels of the organization. This satisfies the important technical need for transferring information up as well as down the hierarchical chain of authority (Honeycutt, 1989; Pearce & David, 1983; Thomas & Griffin, 1983) and satisfies the social need for knowing and understanding those at varying hierarchical levels.

Thus, advocates of the SMWT approach have explained that it provides the greatest opportunity for identifying the best match between the technical and social systems, assuming the team members are provided the authority to modify their technical work and their day-to-day social behaviors (Orsburn et al., 1990).

# 3

■

# Contingency Theories

The Importance of Individual, Technical,
and Environmental Differences

■

The theories developed within the classical, human relations, and systems schools of thought were described by their proponents in a universal sense— there was one primary factor or focus that explained organizational and employee performance. The focus of classical theorists was the work procedures: It was believed that high organizational performance was directly the result of "scientifically" determined procedures for doing the work. The focus of the human relations theorists was the morale and satisfaction of the employees: It was explained that the highest performance could only be obtained when employees were satisfied and morale was high. The focus of systems theorists was the subsystems within the focal organization and the systems within which the focal organization was located: High performance was the result of the varying subsystems working well together and the organization as a whole having a "good fit" with the larger systems of which it was a part.

Advocates of contingency theory have explained that there is no *one* factor—including the work process, employee satisfaction, and the system— that alone determines high organizational performance (Galbraith, 1973). Instead, high organizational performance is achieved by continually altering the organization's characteristics to best match the organization's specific situations or contingencies. The situations or contingencies that have been examined by these theorists fall into at least three major areas: individual, technological, and environmental.

## EMPLOYEE CHARACTERISTICS AS CONTINGENCIES

Advocates of the contingency approach have pointed out that organizational performance is directly related to the performance of the employees making up the organization. They have explained that, because of this fact, management should implement those factors within the organization that cause employees to work at a high level. They have explained further that the factors that cause one employee to work at a high level may not be the same that cause a second employee to work at a high level. Consequently, the factors that should be implemented within an organization are contingent upon the particular characteristics of the employees within the organization.

They have explained, for example, that some employees are best motivated by economic rewards, whereas others have a greater need for challenging work, and still others for meaningful work. Moreover, the same individual may be motivated by different things at different times and in different situations. If this is true, the implication is that the motivating factors to be implemented within the organization will depend upon the particular characteristics of the employees and how the employees respond to motivating factors in varying situations and at varying times.

Substantial support for this view comes from research showing that management methods used in one circumstance do not often work the same way in other circumstances. Fiedler (1967), an early advocate of this view, proposed that high organizational performance would be obtained if managers identified the varying circumstances under which the employees worked and then implemented the most effective factors for each circumstance—the most effective factors being contingent upon the characteristics of the employees and, in particular, their view of management. Vroom and Yetton (1973) have also supported a contingency view by concluding that the effectiveness of any factors implemented by management to improve performance will be contingent upon the manager's personal attributes, such as experience and communication skills.

Critics of this perspective have taken the view that there is no systematic way of classifying employee characteristics, organizational circumstances, and appropriate organizational responses to each circumstance that would be meaningful and usable. Critics have generally agreed that the appropriate response to varying organizational circumstances is contingent to some extent upon employee characteristics. However, the idea of trying to derive a model that includes all employee characteristics and organizational circumstances and their appropriate responses is believed to be too cumbersome and difficult to apply.

## TECHNOLOGICAL CONTINGENCIES

Advocates of this approach have explained that the organizational design that will produce the highest level of organizational performance is contingent upon how the work must be technically carried out. Some types of work are complex in nature, whereas others are simple and repetitive. Some types of work are routine whereas others are continually addressing new situations. Some types of work require employees to have little interaction, whereas others require a great deal of interdependence among employees. In sum, the advocates of the contingency approach have explained that the most effective organizational design for high performance is contingent on the technical aspects of the work. For some, the most important technical characteristic is complexity; for others, it is the routineness of the work, and for others, it is the level of interdependence.

### Complexity of the Task

Woodward (1965) classified technologies according to their level of complexity. She explained that *high technical complexity* exists when the work can be programmed in advance and fully automated—it can be standardized and predicted accurately. Such technologies include large batch and mass production operations (e.g., the production of automobiles), as well as continuous process operations, where the most complex technologies are found (e.g., the production of oil-based products and chemicals). In these situations, Woodward found that the organizational design used was hierarchical in nature. Top management made all important production decisions because there was little variability in how the work was to be accomplished.

On the other hand, Woodward (1965) has described *low technical complexity* as existing when the work processes depend primarily on people and their skills and knowledge and not on machines and automation. The work activities cannot be programmed in advance, and the quality of the product depends on the skills of those employees directly producing the product.

Such technologies include small batch and unit technology, where one of a kind, customized products are made. This would include, for example, a furniture maker who constructs furniture designed to suit the tastes of a few individuals or a printer who supplies engraved wedding invitations for specific couples. Woodward found that work of low technical complexity required workers to have flexibility to adapt to the orders of individual customers and that this flexibility was made available through decentralized organizational designs.

Thus, Woodward (1965) concluded that the most effective organizational design is contingent upon the technical complexity of the work. Work requiring high technical complexity is performed best when the organization uses a more traditional hierarchical authority structure. Work requiring low technical complexity is performed best when decision making is in the hands of the employees actually making the product.

## Routineness of the Task

A second focus taken by contingency theorists has been on the routineness of the organization's work. Perrow (1967) found that an organizational design that included well-established rules and procedures was effective if the tasks of the organization were routine. It was explained that such tasks have low variability. *Low task variability* exists when the task is highly standardized or repetitious and the employee routinely encounters the same situations. With low variability, the employees need only to learn the procedures for performing the task effectively while top management makes all important production decisions.

In contrast, nonroutine tasks were characterized by high variability. *High task variability* exists when the employees continually encounter new situations or problems to be overcome. It was explained that nonroutine tasks require employees to be able to make decisions about the work, develop new procedures, and handle new problems (Argote, 1982). Consequently, Perrow (1967) concluded that the most appropriate organizational design for nonroutine tasks includes a relatively flat and decentralized structure, where employees have the authority and autonomy to make decisions about the work quickly. Thus, advocates of this perspective have contended that the most effective organizational design for high organizational performance is contingent upon the routineness and subsequent variability of the technology.

Interdependence of the Task

Whereas Woodward (1965) focused on task complexity and Perrow (1970) on a task's variability, Thompson (1967) has been concerned with *task interdependence.* Thompson believed that the most appropriate organizational design for producing high performance is contingent upon the interdependence of tasks, that is, the manner in which different organizational tasks are related to one another. When task interdependence is low, employees and departments are individually specialized and work separately and independently. High interdependence is found where employees and departments are jointly specialized and depend on one another for supplying the inputs and resources needed to get the work done. Whereas high interdependence requires an organizational design that accommodates interaction and coordination, low interdependence (e.g., piecework) does not. Thus, here again, the most appropriate organizational design for producing high organizational performance is contingent upon a characteristic of the technology used—the interdependence of the tasks.

## ENVIRONMENTAL CONTINGENCIES

Theorists supporting the environmental contingency perspective believe that high organizational performance is achieved by continually altering the organization's design to best match the organization's environment. Perhaps the environmental characteristic receiving the greatest attention among theorists has been environmental *uncertainty* or *instability.* Lawrence and Lorsch (1967) have studied three different industries, which they believe represent three levels of uncertainty, as measured by variables such as rate of change in the environment. They selected a set of companies representing each industry and then, for each company, examined three departments—production, research and development, and sales. Of the three industries, the plastics industry was believed to have the most uncertain environment, because of the rapid pace of technological and product change. An examination of the three departments within each of the plastics companies showed that the departments tended to have their own design, which matched the part of the company's environment that each was dealing with. Furthermore, the departments of the highest-performing plastics companies tended to have designs that were informal, decentralized, and unstandardized.

Lawrence and Lorsch (1967) determined that the industry with the most certain or stable environment of the three industries they considered was the container industry. An examination of organizations and their departments in this industry showed that the highest-performing ones were centralized, formalized, and standardized. The food-processing industry was the third selected because it was perceived to have an environment less certain than the container industry but more certain than the plastics industry. The organizational design of the high-performing food-processing industries was found to be in between the other two with regard to formality, centralization, and standardization.

Similar results have been reported by Burns and Stalker (1961). Like Lawrence and Lorsch (1967), they found that high-performing organizations in uncertain, unstable environments tended to have designs that were relatively informal, decentralized, and unstandardized. On the other hand, high-performing organizations with relatively certain, stable environments tended to be much more formalized, centralized, and standardized. The reasoning was that uncertain, unstable environments require that employees make unique, on-the-spot decisions relatively quickly. This was only done effectively by those organizations that gave lower-level employees the authority to make such decisions. On the other hand, where the environment is relatively certain and stable, the decisions to be made are relatively routine and can be anticipated by top management. Rules and standards can be developed by top management and used by employees to guide their decisions.

Thus, Burns and Stalker (1961), like Lawrence and Lorsch (1967), concluded that the best organizational design for creating high performance is contingent upon the organization's environment and, in particular, the environment's degree of certainty or stability.

# 4

■

# Contemporary Theories
# Explaining SMWT Performance

■

The majority of theoretical models that have been presented in the literature to explain the performance of teams have focused on *work teams* rather than the more specific *self-managed work teams* (SMWTs). Work teams, in general, are typically thought of as intact and identifiable groups of employees (even if small or temporary) working within an organization, that are perceived as such by members and nonmembers, that have differential roles, and that have one or more tasks to perform that result in a product, service, or decision (Hackman, 1990; Hackman & Oldham, 1980).

SMWTs are uniquely different in that the team members have the authority, as a team, to make decisions about the work and to handle internal processes as they see fit to generate a specific team product, service, or decision (Hackman & Oldham, 1980). Consequently, there are a variety of factors important to *self-managed* work teams that do not apply to all work teams. These include, for example, factors that help SMWT members develop effective decision-making procedures, obtain relevant information related to decision making, and work with customers and suppliers. Provided below are theories specific to SMWT performance, as well as several that were developed to explain performance of the more general work team. The theories are presented for the most part in chronological order, as they have been introduced in the literature, beginning with McGrath's (1964) impressive attempts to organize information known at that time about work teams into a theoretical model.

## McGRATH'S INPUT-PROCESS-OUTPUT MODEL

One of the first and most influential models of work team performance was introduced by McGrath (1964; see Figure 4.1). He used an input-process-output model to organize the salient factors he identified from his extensive review of previous studies of work teams. The input factors include individual-level factors, group-level factors, and environment-level factors. The output factors are divided into two groups: *performance outcomes,* such as quality and number of errors, and *other outcomes,* such as satisfaction and group cohesion.

Researchers found McGrath's (1964) theoretical model to be particularly useful because it provided a framework for organizing and systematizing the research findings on work team performance existing at that time. Furthermore, McGrath provided an impressive, thorough review of the existing research.

## GLADSTEIN'S MODEL OF SUBJECTIVELY RATED EFFECTIVENESS

Gladstein (1984) provided one of the first empirical examinations of *self-managed* work team performance. With a sample of about 100 sales teams, a variety of sophisticated multivariate procedures were used to test aspects of a theoretical model of SMWT performance.

Perhaps Gladstein's (1984) single most important finding was that factors in the model were good predictors of self-reported performance but *poor* predictors of actual performance, as measured by sales revenue. She states, "It appears that individuals have implicit models of how certain modes of group process 'should' benefit performance and attribute good outcomes to the group when the appropriate process has been instituted" (p. 551). That is, team members have a preconceived notion of the input and process factors that are most important to high performance. If their team has these characteristics, then the employees rate team performance as high, regardless of actual performance, such as sales revenue.

As a result of her analysis, Gladstein (1984) presented a theoretical model for explaining subjectively rated performance (Figure 4.2). She did not

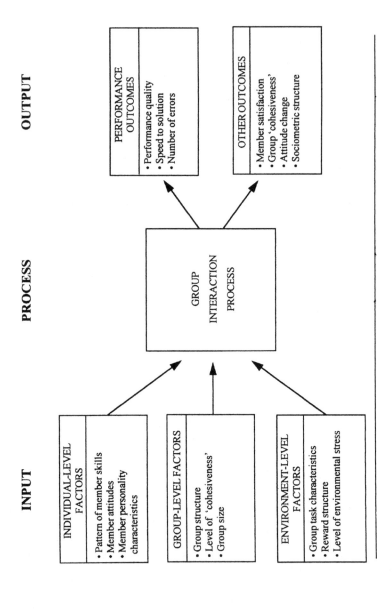

**Figure 4.1.** Summary of McGrath's Input-Process-Output Framework for Analyzing Group Behavior and Performance. SOURCE: Hackman, 1988.

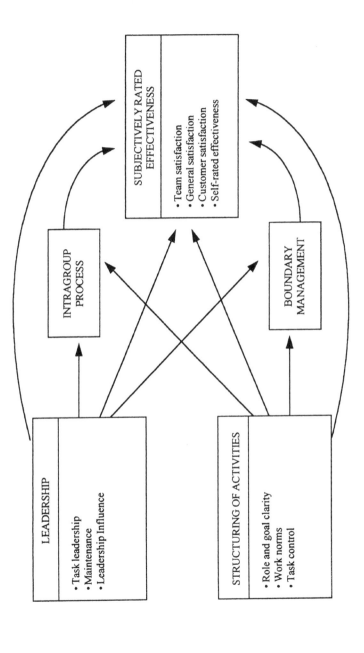

**Figure 4.2.** Gladstein's Model of Factors Affecting Subjectively Rated Effectiveness.
SOURCE: Reprinted from "Groups in Context: A Model of Task Group Effectiveness," by Deborah Gladstein, published in *Administrative Science Quarterly*, 29(4), December, 1984. p. 509; used by permission of *Administrative Science Quarterly*.

provide a model for explaining the teams' actual sales performance because the factors measured in her study could shed almost no light on these. Gladstein speculated that the actual performance of the sales teams studied may have been affected by environmental factors beyond the teams' control, such as the size of the sales teams' potential markets in their target areas.

In her theoretical model, Gladstein (1984) identified two input factors important to subjectively rated performance—leadership activities and structuring of activities. Leadership activities were measured in terms of how rewards were distributed and high performance encouraged. Structuring activities were measured in terms of role and goal clarity, norms for doing the work, weighing of each team member's input during decision making, and team control over the team's tasks. Team members were more likely to perceive their team's performance as high if they had a clear understanding of their team's roles and goals, felt that each team member's amount of influence on decision making was in proportion to the member's knowledge of the issue, and believed that the team had sufficient control over its tasks to perform at a high level.

Gladstein (1984) found two process factors to be important to subjectively rated performance—boundary management and intragroup process. Boundary management was defined as the degree of misunderstanding with individuals and groups outside the team. Intragroup process included factors such as open communication, supportiveness, and discussion of appropriate work strategies. Gladstein found that team members who perceived their team as working well with those outside the team and working well together perceived their team to be performing at a high level. She explained that the teams under study needed effective boundary management and intragroup process to procure resources and information, manage interdependencies, and transfer team output to others.

Gladstein (1984) also proposed that the team's tasks, in terms of how much information processing was needed to complete them, would moderate the effects of the process criteria on team performance. She suspected that the importance of boundary management and intragroup processing to team performance would be influenced by the level of information processing needed. Her subsequent study found no significant moderating effects, so she did not include this as a moderating factor in her revised theoretical model. However, she did note that the variation among the teams with regard to information processing was relatively low, which may have prevented any noticeable effect.

As will be seen below, the input and process criteria identified by Gladstein (1984) have received increasing attention among work team theorists and researchers since Gladstein first reported her findings.

## THE PEARCE-RAVLIN MODEL

Pearce and Ravlin (1987) have presented a theoretical model of SMWT performance (referred to by them as self-regulating work group performance) based on their review of past research examining factors affecting SMWT performance, as well as research on the more general work teams. Their model contains four groups of factors (Figure 4.3). The most exogenous are *precondition* factors, believed to be necessary for an SMWT to have any chance of being implemented successfully. Pearce and Ravlin concluded that one set of preconditions is related to the tasks to be performed: The tasks must allow for the exercise of autonomy and, as a whole, must be meaningful to the team members. A second precondition is related to the broader organization: Management must be supportive of SMWTs and the expectations for the teams must be well defined and reasonable. The third precondition is that all the team members themselves regard SMWTs and the autonomy and responsibility associated with them as desirable.

Pearce and Ravlin (1987) proposed that the preconditions directly affect the *design* of the team. This includes a host of design factors, including open communication, minimal status differences, flexible coordination, a heterogeneous composition, autonomy over the task assignments, and rewards at both the group and individual levels. These, in turn, have important positive effects on the SMWT's *activation* and *process criteria.*

*Activation* refers to instituting ongoing activities or functions that will break down workplace norms that do not fit the SMWT environment and, instead, will encourage the types of employee behavior necessary for high SMWT performance. Such activities include explicit and publicized support from management for SMWTs. Pearce and Ravlin noted, for example, the importance of praising team members in interdepartmental communications, the company newsletter, and bulletin board memos. Other activation functions described are the provision of training to improve team skills, incentives to encourage teamwork, and team "coaches" to stimulate open communication and job rotation within the SMWTs.

The process criteria are described as being affected by the team's activation functions and design. Pearce and Ravlin (1987) identified three process criteria: variety of inputs, coordination, and commitment. They have explained that a variety of inputs from team members are needed for effective decision making. As they have stated, "The broader the variety, the greater the chances of developing creative ways of reducing uncertainty and improving on traditional production methods" (p. 773). Coordination is viewed as central to the team's performance because of the multiple skills and interrelated tasks that SMWT members typically perform. Finally, commitment is

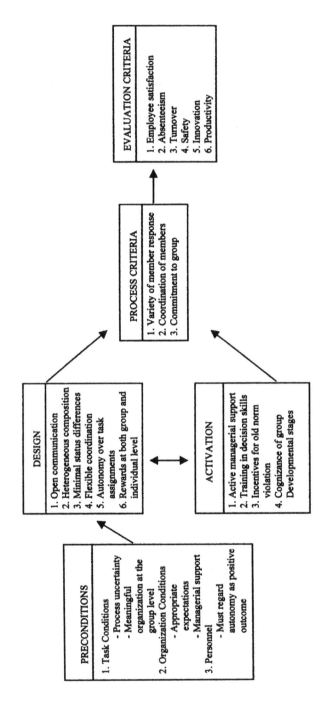

**Figure 4.3.** The Pearce-Ravlin Model of Self-Regulating Work Group Performance.
SOURCE: Pearce & Ravlin, 1987; used by permission.

viewed as essential because of the need for team members to be self-motivated to accomplish team goals.

Pearce and Ravlin's (1987) review of the literature found an array of factors that had been used to represent team performance or, as they termed them, *evaluation criteria.* These included employee satisfaction, productivity, absenteeism, turnover, safety, and innovation. They viewed these as being directly affected by only the process criteria, with the other factors (i.e., preconditions, design, and activation factors) having indirect effects on performance via the process criteria.

## HACKMAN'S MODEL OF SMWT PERFORMANCE

Hackman (1988, 1990) and his colleagues (Hackman & Oldham, 1980) have presented perhaps the most thorough theoretical model explaining SMWT performance (Figure 4.4). They measure performance, or in Hackman's words, *effectiveness,* in three ways. First, the task output is measured in terms of its acceptability to those who receive or review it. Hackman (1988) has explained that performance is low if the task output does not meet the specifications of the customer—even if the quality of the output is very high or productivity is high. He has noted, for example, that if the quality of the output is higher than desired by the customer, it is likely to also be more expensive and, consequently, cost the customer more. Second, team performance hinges on the capability of the team members to work together in the future. The current output of the team may be extremely satisfactory to the customer, but if this cannot be sustained over the long term, then performance as a whole is (or will eventually be) low. Finally, the needs of the team members must be more satisfied than frustrated by the team.

Hackman's (1988, 1990) theoretical model, like most others, uses an input-process-output approach to explain SMWT performance. Unlike most other theoretical models, however, Hackman's is found to differ substantially with regard to the factors treated as process criteria. Most other theoretical models focus primarily on interpersonal factors such as communication and coordination. Hackman's model, on the other hand, treats these interpersonal factors as characteristics of the team's composition and, subsequently, as input factors. Hackman includes as process factors level of effort placed directly on doing the work, amount of knowledge and skill applied to the work, and appropriateness of the work strategies used. In support of his view, Hackman explains that the process criteria in his model focus on those aspects of interaction that relate directly to doing the work. The interpersonal process factors used in most other models are important to SMWT performance because they enhance these work process criteria.

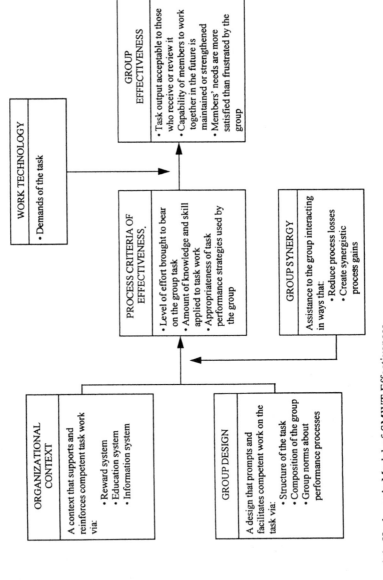

**Figure 4.4.** Hackman's Model of SMWT Effectiveness.
SOURCE: Adapted from Hackman, 1988, and Hackman & Oldham, 1980.

Hackman's (1988, 1990) theoretical model includes two sets of input factors, those at the organizational level and those at the team level. For each process criterion, Hackman has identified crucial organizational and team factors. The process criterion *level of effort* is believed to be affected at the organizational level by positive consequences (rewards) for high team performance and clear, challenging goals. *Knowledge and skill* are affected at the organizational level by the educational resources available to team members and the ease with which team members can access these resources. These include technical consultations and training. *Appropriate performance strategies* are influenced at the organizational level by the existing information system. Hackman explained that strategy selection requires information about the task's requirements and constraints, available material resources, the customer's expectations, and the consequences of alternative strategies. The better the information system, the more easily this information can be obtained by the team and appropriate performance strategies selected.

When considering the effects of team inputs on the process criteria, Hackman (1988, 1990) proposed that the *level of effort* is affected by the team's job characteristics, including skill variety, task significance, and task identity (i.e., ability to see how one's work relates to a "bigger picture"). These job characteristics are believed to have positive effects on the team members' motivation and subsequently the level of effort applied directly to the work. The work process factors *knowledge* and *skill* are believed to be affected by the team's composition, including task-relevant skills among the team members, interpersonal skills, team size, and heterogeneity among the team members.

The work process factor *use of appropriate strategies* is believed to be affected by group norms. Hackman (1988, 1990) has explained that at times, teams follow little structured planning or discussion about how the work of the team will be carried out. Consequently, there is a need for team norms that encourage the seeking of alternative strategies and that routinely consider the advantages and disadvantages of these before selecting one. Hackman explained that group norms are also valuable when they result in team members regulating each other's behavior so that the strategies selected will be carried out.

Hackman's (1988, 1990) theoretical model includes two sets of moderating factors: work technology and group synergy. Like Gladstein (1984), Hackman reasons that the work technology or type of work performed moderates the effects of the process criteria on the team's performance. In other words, the extent to which the process factors can affect the team's performance is determined by the type of work and, in particular, the demands of the work. For some types of work, all three of the process criteria play important roles for achieving high team performance. For other types of work, only one or two of the process criteria are important to team performance. For example, in the case of a team using production technology, the achievement of high team performance may require great effort, a good deal of knowledge and skill, and a sophisticated performance strategy—all three process criteria are important to high performance. On the other hand, for a relatively simple service job, such as the maintenance of parking lots, much less knowledge and skill are required because the work basically involves only picking up debris and sweeping. Furthermore, there is little need for complex performance strategies. Only the level of effort plays an important role in achieving high team performance. Thus, Hackman explains that the type of work is a moderating factor that determines the importance of the process criteria for team performance.

Group synergy is viewed by Hackman (1988, 1990) as moderating the effects of the input factors on the process factors. Hackman explains that a highly coordinated and cooperative team can produce synergy, or results that are more effective than the sum of the individual team member contributions. Group synergy can result in team members finding innovative ways to avoid process losses and subsequently minimize waste and misuse of members' time, energy, and talent. Group synergy can create process gains by increasing coordination, commitment, and motivation that likewise result in more effort, energy, and talent applied to the work. Hackman viewed group synergy as the result of a team culture that finds everyone committed to the team, proud of it, and willing to work hard to make it one of the best. As Hackman (1988) has explained, "When individuals value their membership in the group and find it rewarding to work collaboratively with their teammates, they may work considerably harder than they would otherwise" (p. 326). Hackman included within his model group-building activities that are proposed to increase members' commitment to the group and subsequently their willingness to work hard on the group task. He has recommended activities such as encouraging members of a team to give the team a name, to decorate their work area, and to participate in an athletic league as a team.

## SUNDSTROM–De MEUSE–FUTRELL MODEL OF TEAM EFFECTIVENESS

Sundstrom, De Meuse, and Futrell (1990) have provided perhaps the most creative model of work team performance. They have presented it as a means of analyzing the performance, or, in their terms, effectiveness of work teams.

They chose not to use the input-process-output format for displaying the factors believed to be most crucial to work team performance because they felt such a format implies that performance is an end state rather than a continual process (Figure 4.5). Instead, they have attempted to present their model in such a way as to avoid temporal dynamics and highlight the interrelationships between the major sets of work team factors, including the organizational context, team boundaries, and team development.

In their presentation of their model, Sundstrom et al. (1990) did not clearly distinguish whether the model applies to work team performance or *self-managed* work team performance. They defined work teams as "inter-dependent collections of individuals who share responsibility for specific outcomes for their organizations" (p. 120). This suggests that their focus is on those teams that have at least some level of self-management. Further-more, in their review of the literature, they referred to studies of SMWTs, as well as those focused on work teams more generally.

Sundstrom et al. (1990) used two factors to represent team performance. One (referred to by them as performance) mirrors what Hackman (1988) used: the customer's assessment of the team's output. Sundstrom et al. have explained that work team performance can be measured as the "acceptability of output to customers within or outside the organization who receive team products, services, information, decisions, or performance events (such as presentations or competitions) (p. 122). The second measure of work team performance is team viability. Generally, the authors have referred to viabil-ity as the team's ability to avoid burnout and stay together over the long term. They include here team members' satisfaction and willingness to continue working together.

The Sundstrom-De Meuse-Futrell (1990) model includes three major sets of factors that affect performance. These are focused on external conditions and internal processes of the work team. The organizational context includes organizational culture, characteristics of the task, mission clarity, autonomy, feedback, rewards, training, and the physical environment. The authors have explained that these factors can augment team performance by providing resources needed for performance and providing continued viability as a work unit. The organizational context is viewed as having ties to the team via team boundaries and having direct ties to the team's performance.

The second set of factors is labeled team boundaries and has been defined as those conditions that both separate and link work teams within their organization. Included here are factors that differentiate the team from others; pose real or symbolic barriers to the access or transfer of information, goods, or people; and allow for external exchange with other teams. Sund-strom et al. (1990) have described the team's boundaries as mediating be-

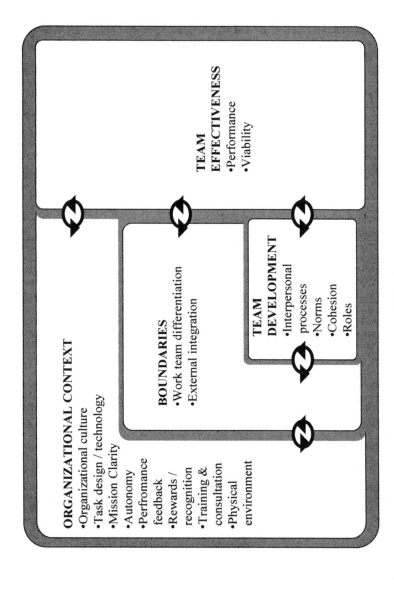

**Figure 4.5.** Ecological Framework for Analyzing Work Team Effectiveness
SOURCE: Sundstrom et al., 1990; used by permission.

tween the organizational context and the team's development and as having direct ties to the team's performance. In their discussions, they have noted that if the boundary becomes too open or indistinct, the team risks becoming overwhelmed and losing its identity. At the same time, if it is too closed or exclusive, the team might become isolated and lose touch with suppliers, managers, peers, or customers.

The third set of factors included in the Sundstrom et al. (1990) model of work team performance is team development. Their main idea here was to emphasize the fact that, over time, teams change and develop new ways of operating as they adapt to their contexts. Factors included here are interpersonal processes, norms, cohesion, and roles. The authors have viewed these as factors to be addressed in efforts to aid team development and process interventions.

## THE TANNENBAUM AND SALAS MODELS OF TEAM PERFORMANCE

Tannenbaum, Salas, and their colleagues have worked together to produce two similar models of work team performance (Salas, Dickinson, Converse, & Tannenbaum, 1992; Tannenbaum, Beard, & Salas, 1992). Both models are presented here because each contributes unique ideas (Figures 4.6 and 4.7). Both Tannenbaum and Salas have defined the work team as "a distinguishable set of two or more people who interact dynamically, interdependently, and adaptively toward a common and valued goal/objective/mission, and who each have some specific roles or functions to perform" (Tannenbaum et al., 1992, p. 118; see also Salas et al., 1992). Thus, they have not focused specifically on SMWTs and, instead, their models are designed to explain the performance of work teams in general.

The Tannenbaum and Salas models (Salas et al., 1992; Tannenbaum et al., 1992) are similar to most previous models by using an input-throughput-output format. The Tannenbaum and Salas models both treat work team performance in terms of quality, quantity, errors, and on-time deliveries. The Tannenbaum model also includes costs. Both also explicitly show the impacts of feedback resulting from team performance. Feedback is viewed as ultimately influencing two sets of inputs: task characteristics and individual characteristics. This suggests, for example, that feedback may influence the task characteristics by causing the work to be assigned differently and influence individual characteristics by demotivating or motivating the team members. Although most theorists acknowledge the importance of feedback, most have not explicitly included it in their theoretical models.

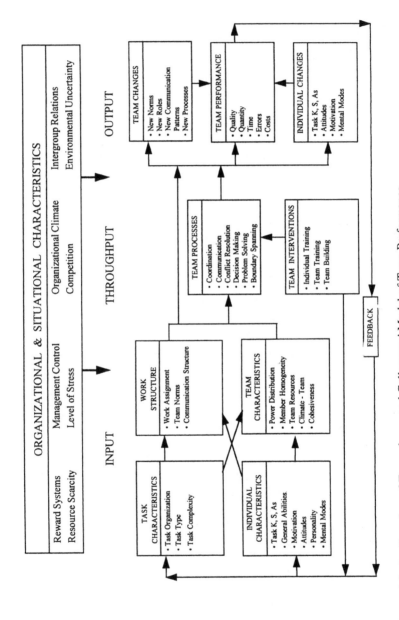

**Figure 4.6.** An Overview of Tannenbaum and Colleagues' Model of Team Performance.
SOURCE: Reprinted from *Issues, Theory, and Research in Industrial/Organizational Psychology,* edited by K. Kelley, 1992, p. 121, with kind permission from Elsevier Science, NL, Sara Burgerhartstraat 25, 1055 KV Amsterdam, The Netherlands.

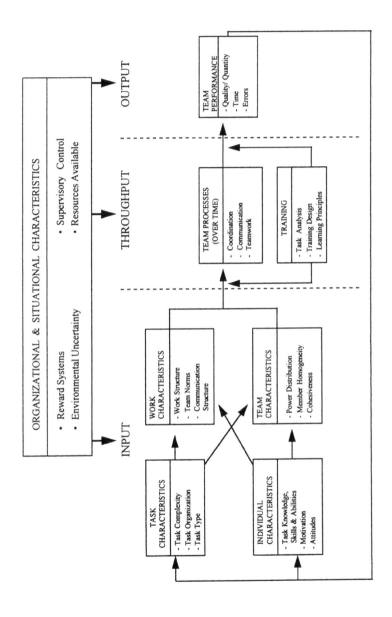

**Figure 4.7.** An Overview of Salas and Colleagues' Model of Team Performance
SOURCE: Salas et al., 1992; used by permission.

Furthermore, the Tannenbaum model (Tannenbaum et al., 1992) includes two additional sets of outputs: team changes and individual changes. These occur as a result of team processes, the work structure, and team characteristics and contribute to the feedback affecting the task and individual characteristics. This uniqueness of the Tannenbaum model explicitly suggests that work teams experience constant change in team characteristics such as norms, roles, and processes and in individual characteristics such as knowledge, skill, attitudes, and motivation.

Like most models of work team performance, the Tannenbaum and Salas models (Salas et al., 1992; Tannenbaum et al., 1992) treat interpersonal or team processes as the throughputs that have direct effects on the team's performance. However, the Tannenbaum and Salas models largely differ from previous models in their identification of the salient inputs. Their models suggest that two sets of inputs, task and individual characteristics, influence two additional sets of inputs, work structure and team characteristics. These latter two, in turn, influence the team's processes, and in Tannenbaum's model, they also have direct effects on the output factors. The Tannenbaum and Salas models are somewhat unique here by giving more prominence or importance to the task characteristics than do most other models of work team performance.

An additional uniqueness of the Tannenbaum and Salas models (Salas et al., 1992; Tannenbaum et al., 1992) is their explicit inclusion of training in their models. Tannenbaum views training as having a direct effect on the team processes as well as the task and individual characteristics. Salas treats training as moderating the effects of the process factors on performance and moderating the effects of the input factors on team processes.

## CAMPION AND COLLEAGUES' THEMES RELATED TO WORK GROUP EFFECTIVENESS

Campion, Medsker, and Higgs (1993) conducted an extensive review of the literature focused on the relationship between work team design and performance (referred to by them as effectiveness). They subsequently identified five major themes that included 19 design characteristics believed to affect work team performance. An empirical assessment of these led them to conclude that each of these 19 factors did indeed contribute to a work team's performance. Their empirical analysis included work teams generally rather than SMWTs specifically, although they did include the level of self-management and participation in decision making as two design characteristics in their empirical assessment.

The model they subsequently presented distinguishes the five themes and 19 design characteristics as well as the effectiveness criteria used (Figure 4.8). Campion et al. (1993) did not intend this to represent a formal theory. Their model does not attempt to show interrelationships between the identified themes and design characteristics. Instead, their focus was to identify the most important design characteristics, with the idea that many of these could be manipulated by human resource managers to improve team performance. Their effectiveness criteria included productivity, satisfaction, and manager judgments of team performance. The five major themes are job design, interdependence, composition, context, and process.

Job design included five characteristics originally identified by theorists emphasizing the importance of job enrichment and sociotechnical systems. Those found to be the most important in their analysis were self-management and participation. Campion et al. (1993) suspected that this may have been due in part to the influence of these on "the motivational quality of members' jobs" (p. 840).

A second theme, interdependence, was found to be important to employee satisfaction. When team members were interdependent for rewards and feedback, interdependence was particularly important. It had much less effect on employee satisfaction if the interdependence was due to the task or team goals.

The third theme, team composition characteristics, had the greatest impact on manager perceptions of performance. Campion et al. (1993) attributed this to the manager's influence in determining the team's composition. Managers may have been more likely to report positive effects of composition because they were most likely to have established the existing composition. An examination of the composition characteristics shows that heterogeneity had almost no effects, and this was attributed to a lack of variation in the data. Preference for "group work" likewise had little effect, and flexibility was found to be important only in the case of management judgments. On the other hand, relative size was important to all the performance criteria, with larger groups performing at a higher level.

An examination of the fourth theme, context characteristics, showed that managers generally perceived training as highly important to team performance, whereas employees felt that manager support was highly important (Campion et al., 1993). No effect was found in the case of intergroup communication and cooperation, and this was attributed to the nature of the work, because the work for the teams studied did not require them to rely on one another.

Finally, the process characteristics were found to be most highly associated with the performance criteria: productivity, satisfaction, and manager

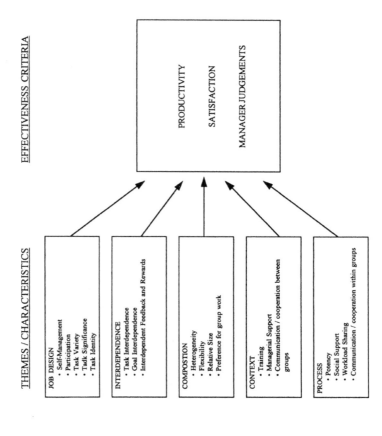

**Figure 4.8.** Campion and Colleagues' Themes and Characteristics Related to Work Group Effectiveness
SOURCE: Campion et al., 1993; used by permission.

judgments. The characteristic, potency, or the belief of a team that it can be effective was highly related to all measures of work team performance. Workload sharing and communication and cooperation were important to productivity and manager judgment but not to employee satisfaction, whereas social support was found to be only important to productivity with no effects on employee satisfaction or manager judgments.

## COHEN'S MODEL FOR EFFECTIVE SMWTs

Cohen (1994) has drawn on a variety of existing organizational theories and research on SMWTs to develop a theoretical model for explaining SMWT performance (Figure 4.9). Her model deviates somewhat from the more traditional input-process-output models by treating process as an input, resulting in an input-output model. Her rationale for this approach is that process criteria have a reciprocal relationship with input criteria and that both affect SMWT performance. Although her model does not display reciprocal or feedback relationships, she has explained that they are to be understood as existing.

Cohen's (1994) model displays three sets of outputs that are described collectively as effectiveness: team performance (i.e., costs, productivity, and quality), member attitudes (e.g., satisfaction), and withdrawal behaviors (i.e., absenteeism and turnover). She has noted that performance and attitude criteria mirror those found in many previous theoretical models, whereas withdrawal behaviors are much less common. Few models have treated absenteeism and turnover as outputs, with the closest concepts including team viability or the ability to continue working as a team.

Cohen's (1994) four sets of input factors are task design, group characteristics, supervisory behaviors, and the organizational context. Cohen has acknowledged the possibility of moderating effects but chose not to include them in her model for reasons of parsimony and ease in testing. Cohen noted that the importance of the first set of factors, those associated with task design, was originally presented by researchers who developed the job enrichment/characteristics theory (Hackman & Oldham, 1980; Turner & Lawrence, 1965), as well as those who have presented the sociotechnical theory (Pearce & Ravlin, 1987). The premise is that enriched tasks will allow for variety, significance, autonomy, and feedback and that these will ultimately result in high meaningfulness, responsibility, motivation, satisfaction, and performance.

A second set of input factors, group characteristics, includes group composition, group beliefs, and group process (Cohen, 1994). The group com-

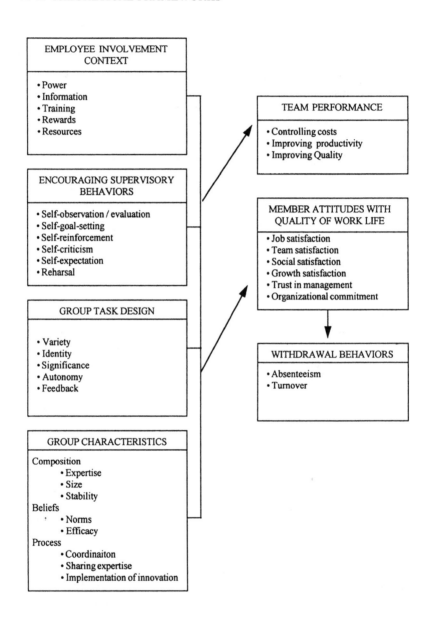

**Figure 4.9.** Cohen's Full Model of Self-managing Team Effectiveness
SOURCE: Cohen, 1994; used by permission.

position factors include the team members' level of appropriate technical and interpersonal skills, the size of the team, and the team's instability, that is, degree of turnover that is occurring within the team. This latter factor—instability—has been largely ignored by most SMWT theorists, at least explicitly. However, it is reasonable to expect that, when team members are constantly changing, a variety of effects will occur, including difficulties maintaining high coordination and communication as well as a consensus regarding team norms.

Group beliefs include the team's norms and efficacy. Norms are defined as "standards that are shared by group members which regulate group behavior" (Cohen, 1994, p. 85). It is noted that the greater the consensus regarding team norms, the better the team can control member behaviors. Team efficacy is defined as "the shared belief among group members that a group can be effective" (p. 85). Cohen has explained that team confidence, or efficacy, contributes to the team's ability to perform at a high level. This is similar to Campion et al.'s (1993) construct, potency, or the generalized belief among team members regarding the group's capability to accomplish particular tasks (see also Sims & Lorenzi, 1992).

Cohen's (1994) definition of group process includes team coordination and caring, sharing of expertise, and implementation of innovation. As she has explained, coordination and caring involve working together without duplicating or wasting efforts and doing so with energy and team spirit. Sharing of expertise means that team members share and listen to each others' knowledge and expertise. Implementation of innovations describes a team's ability to invent and implement new and better ways of doing its tasks. These process factors are viewed as being affected by other team characteristics and, in turn, affecting team performance, much like that found in other theoretical models that use an input-process-output format. The factors are viewed differently from other models in that they are believed to have reciprocal relationships with the other team characteristics.

A third set of factors included in Cohen's (1994) theoretical model are described as those that encourage team members to display supervisory or leadership behaviors. Here, Cohen has highlighted the work of Manz and Sims (1987), who have identified six *supervisory* behaviors that SMWT members should display to enhance team member performance. These behaviors are termed supervisory or leadership behaviors because they are the behaviors that are more traditionally viewed as being performed by a supervisor (see Figure 4.9). Cohen has explained that when team members internalize self-leadership behaviors, there will be positive effects on team performance because team members will be focusing their individual attention on those behaviors important to team performance. These include establishing their own performance goals, conducting self-evaluations to determine their progress toward reaching these goals, and establishing self-regulating behaviors to assist in reaching their goals. It is explained that it is management's role to facilitate the internalization of these leadership behaviors within the team members.

Cohen's (1994) final set of input factors are those at the organizational level. She used the work of Lawler (1986, 1992) to clarify four major dimensions at the organizational level important to SMWTs. These include decision-making authority that is given to SMWT members, availability of needed information for decision making, rewards that are linked to team performance results, and team member training that enables team members to develop the knowledge required to contribute to organizational performance. Cohen has added to Lawler's four dimensions a fifth, resources. This emphasizes the importance of adequate raw materials, equipment, tools, and space. These five organizational dimensions are viewed as interdependent. It is explained that, when only one or several of these are present, high team performance will not occur. For example, having all the available information, training, and authority needed to perform a task will not result in high performance if the team lacks the necessary resources to accomplish the work or cannot see the link between the team's rewards and high performance of the task.

# 5

■

# Development of a Theoretical Framework to Explain SMWT Performance

■

A synthesized theoretical model was initially developed that drew upon the work team theories reviewed in Chapter 4. The primary purpose for developing this model was to provide a theoretical framework that could be tested. A multicase, multimethod replication design (Yin, 1989) was used to test and revise the synthesized model (see Appendix A for a detailed description of the methodology). Such a methodological approach requires that multiple case studies be conducted in order to evaluate the accuracy of an existing theory and to modify the theory as necessary to reflect what is found in the case studies. Provided below is first, a presentation of the synthesized model, followed by a presentation of the final theoretical model resulting from the multiple case studies, that is, studies of 10 SMWTs from manufacturing, government, and health organizations.

## A SYNTHESIS OF THEORIES AND THE INITIAL MODEL TESTED

A synthesis of the theories described above resulted in an input-process-output framework (Figure 5.1). The primary criteria used for including or

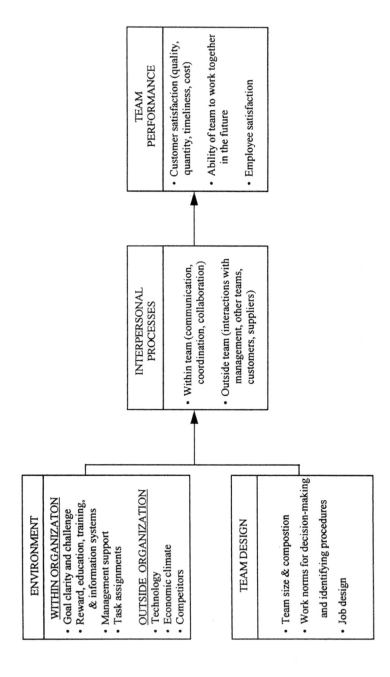

**Figure 5.1.** A Synthesis of Theoretical Models Explaining Work Team Performance

excluding a factor was (1) its frequency of use in previous theoretical models, (2) the amount of empirical evidence supporting inclusion of the factor, and (3) theoretical rationalizations that provided well-thought-out and explained support for inclusion of the factor.

The primary groups of factors in the model include interpersonal processes, the environment surrounding the team, and team design. *Team performance* was organized into three primary factors: customer satisfaction, ability of the team to work together in the future, and employee satisfaction. Customer satisfaction relates more specifically to the quality, quantity, timeliness, and costs of the product or service.

The *interpersonal processes* were treated as the intermediate factors between inputs and outputs. Internal processes include factors such as communication, coordination, and collaboration within the SMWT. External processes include team member interactions with management, other teams, customers, and suppliers.

The *environment surrounding the team* is divided into environmental factors within the organization and those outside the organization. Influential factors proposed to exist within the organization but outside the SMWT include the reward, education, training, and information systems; management support; goal clarity and challenge; and task assignments to the team. Environmental factors outside the organization have not been studied as extensively. However, open systems theorists explain that factors such as new technologies, the economic climate, and competitors have important influences on the organization, and it is reasonable to expect that this effect would extend to SMWTs (Beyerlein & Johnson, 1994; McEnery & Lifter, 1987; Pasmore, 1988).

*Team design characteristics* have been included in all the theoretical perspectives reviewed above. These include factors such as team size and composition, work norms for making decisions and identifying best procedures, and the design of the team's jobs (e.g., skill variety, significance)

There were a host of variables not included in the initial theoretical framework, variables that were identified by one or more theorists or consultants as important to SMWT performance. Many of these factors were included in our methodology and, more specifically, in our instruments designed to measure characteristics of both high- and low-performing teams (Appendix B). For example, we specifically examined the effects of Hackman's (1988) work process factors—effort, procedures for doing the work, and knowledge and skill. We examined whether these factors were able to discriminate between high- and low-performing teams and whether they, or team process factors, were most directly linked to the team's performance. We included an examination of the importance of team resources as highlighted by Cohen (1994), an examination of the effects of leadership behavior as identified by Manz and Sims (1989), and the possible moderating effects of work technology as suggested by Hackman and referred to by Gladstein (1984), Cohen (1994), and others.

## A THEORETICAL MODEL EXPLAINING SMWT PERFORMANCE

The most dramatic revisions to our initial theoretical framework came as a result of our first six case studies—two government SMWTs (within a federal agency) and four manufacturing SMWTs. Only minor revisions were made as a result of the remaining four case studies—one government SMWT (within a municipal agency) and three health SMWTs (within a nursing home). Provided below is, first, a discussion of the measures we chose for SMWT performance. This is followed by an overview of the revised theoretical framework that resulted from our in-depth case studies of SMWT performance.

### Measures of SMWT Performance

Developing an accurate theoretical model to explain SMWT performance requires first establishing a clear, measurable definition of SMWT performance. Factors can then be identified that influence the measures. As Cohen (1994), Hackman (1988), and others have observed, establishing empirical measures of SMWT performance is difficult. Cohen (1994) has stated, "In many cases, no good objective measures of team performance exist. If good objective measures exist, they may not be comparable across teams and across organizations" (p. 69). Hackman (1990) has noted that outside of the laboratory setting, it is typically difficult to identify what "good" team performance is.

The measures we used for SMWT performance included customer satisfaction and the team's economic viability. We did not include employee satisfaction or the team's capability to continue working together in the future—two measures that are often included in theoretical frameworks explaining SMWT performance. We concluded from our examination of the literature and initial examination of employee attitudes that the factors affecting employee satisfaction and team viability are not necessarily the same as those that affect customer satisfaction and economic viability. Similar conclusions have been researched by other theorists as well (Kelly,

1992). Therefore, we concluded that a single model to explain all four measures would be less accurate than limiting the performance measures to only two. Furthermore, we felt that customer satisfaction and economic viability provided more accurate and valid measures of team performance as described in specific SMWT theoretical models. Each of these measures is described in more detail below.

### Customer Satisfaction

Hackman (1990) has explained that outside of the laboratory setting, it is difficult to identify what good team performance is. This holds true, even when we can measure specific outputs, such as the number produced or served, the number returned for rework, the number of complaints, or the amount of time required to do a task. Nevertheless, these have been commonly used performance measures (see, for example, Gladstein, 1984; McGrath, 1964; Nieva, Fleishman, & Rieck, 1978). However, the questions that must be asked when considering these measures include: Is team performance higher when one team produces more than another? And if one team serves more clients in less time, does that constitute higher performance? The answer to these is clearly "no" in cases where the customer is dissatisfied with the product or service received or if the cost of the product or service is not profitable. Are teams that produce a higher quality product or service higher-performing teams? Again, the answer is clearly "no" in cases where the quality of the product exceeds that desired by the customer or client and obtaining the excessive quality adds to the cost of producing the product or service.

Thus, the use of quantitative measures that simply measure levels of productivity or quality are not necessarily good measures of the team's performance. That is, simple quantitative measures may not validly indicate how well a team has done its work because such measures do not consider the preferences of the team's customers—those receiving the team's product or service, nor the economic viability of the team.

It is interesting to note that an examination of the SMWTs we studied showed that most were generally focused on their customers' satisfaction. For example, one memorandum from a manager overseeing a group of SMWTs stated,

> It is critical that each team take responsibility for satisfying their customers. We will be encouraging them to visit their customers, whether that means other teams, engineers, managers, etc., to learn their customers' 'care-abouts.' Measuring customer satisfaction is a challenge. We will help the teams explore

alternatives for measuring and improving this important metric. (Meeker, 1993, p. 5)

### Economic Viability

Few researchers or theorists studying SMWTs include economic viability as a measure of SMWT performance, and this measure was not originally included in our theoretical model. However, in our initial discussions with managers, to identify high- and low-performing teams, it was suggested that the economic viability of the team be included as a measure of performance. It was explained that a situation can easily exist where the SMWT's customers are highly satisfied, but the team is not economically viable. That is, it is costing the organization more resources than the team ultimately produces. In this case, the team becomes overly burdensome to the organization and will eventually be disbanded.

Mohrman, Cohen, and Mohrman (1995) have noted the important point that the team's economic viability can be applied at two levels, both the team and business unit levels. The SMWT can be economically viable at the team level but, simultaneously, cause other parts of its business unit to have economic problems. For example, we observed a situation where an SMWT was producing a high volume of a particular product and then passing the product on to an internal customer within its business unit. This resulted in the team producing the product at a relatively low cost but also producing a stockpile of the product for the internal customer and, subsequently, creating a high cost for the business unit as a whole.

### Overview of the Theoretical Framework

The major revisions included the addition of two groups of factors: work process factors and team member characteristics (Figure 5.2). The work process factors have replaced the interpersonal factors as those having direct effects on SMWT performance. In the revised model, the interpersonal process factors are viewed as having effects on performance through the work process. Also included in the revised theoretical framework is work technology, in the form of *demands of the tasks*. It is treated as a moderating factor between work process and team performance. Two other major revisions were the inclusion of recursive arrows and feedback as an output factor. Finally, additional factors have been added to the interpersonal processes, the team design characteristics, and the environmental characteristics.

A review of the data indicated that Hackman's (1988) work process factors, described above, had direct effects on the teams' performance.

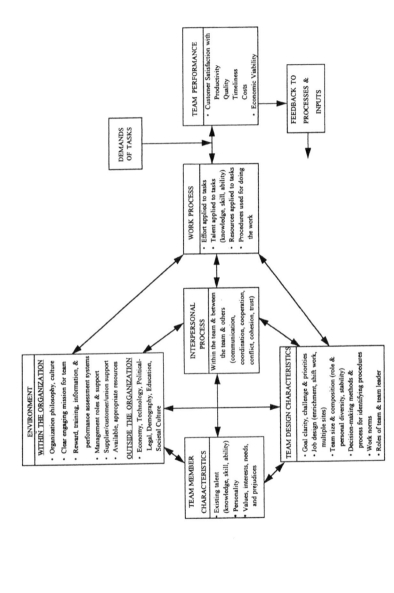

**Figure 5.2.** Factors Affecting Self-Managed Work Team Performance

53

Hackman's work process factors include team effort, knowledge and skill, and procedures for doing the work. We found a fourth essential work process factor to be the resources applied to the work, including materials, equipment, tools, and space.

We concluded that the team's interpersonal process, which is most often treated as having direct effects on team performance, was affecting the team's performance via the work process factors. For example, within one SMWT, we found that the interpersonal processes were affecting the work process factor *knowledge and skill* and this in turn was having negative effects on performance. In this case, poor interpersonal processes were preventing team members from applying all the knowledge and skill needed to satisfy the team's customers. Thus, the poor interpersonal processes had negative effects on team performance via the team's work process factor—knowledge and skill.

Several of the theoretical models explaining SMWT performance have treated *team member characteristics* as a separate group of factors affecting team performance (e.g., McGrath, 1964; Salas et al., 1992; Tannenbaum et al., 1992). We chose not to include these factors separately in our initial theoretical framework because the majority of theorists had proposed that such factors should be considered in the context of the team's composition. However, our case studies clearly indicated that team member characteristics contributed a great deal to the team's performance. Individual characteristics include the knowledge, skill, and ability that the person brings to the team; the values, interests, needs, and prejudices of the team member; and the personality of the team member.

*Work technology* has been considered by some researchers as a moderating factor between team process and output. Gladstein (1984) has provided one of the few empirical studies testing for this moderating effect and found no significant relationship in her study of sales teams. However, she concluded that this could have been due to a lack of variability in the sales teams' work technology. Hackman (1988) has emphasized the importance of work technology as a moderating variable and has included it in his theoretical framework of SMWT performance. Cohen (1994) has also noted the importance of work technology as a moderating variable but chose to leave it out of her model for reasons of parsimony and ease of analysis. One advantage of the case study approach is that it allows for a direct examination of moderating factors while avoiding difficult statistical problems associated with such relationships. In our study of 10 SMWTs, we found that work technology, in terms of the demands of the work, did moderate the effects of the work process factors on SMWT performance. For example, in several health care SMWTs studied, teams primarily made up of nurse's aides, team effort was found to be the most important work process factor affecting these teams' performance. Knowledge and skill, appropriate strategies, and resources definitely affected these teams' performance. However, because the demands of the work required intense face-to-face relationships between the team members and customers (residents of the nursing home), it appeared that team member effort was most important.

Almost all SMWT theorists have referred to the importance of *feedback* as an output factor. However, few have included it in their theoretical models (e.g., Campion et al., 1993; Cohen, 1994; Gladstein, 1984; Hackman, 1988; Pearce & Ravlin, 1987). Likewise, we chose to leave it out of our initial theoretical framework. However, conclusions from our analyses indicated that feedback is a crucial factor that should be explicitly included. For example, feedback from customers was found to have direct effects on a team's strategies for doing the work and on the knowledge held by team members.

Still another change in our model was the inclusion of recursive relationships among the input factors, and between the input and the process factors. It was clear that inputs had effects on one another and that team and work processes had effects on inputs, as well as vice versa. For example, when considering the high-performing manufacturing teams studied, the interpersonal process factor, *communication*, influenced the organization's information system, an environmental factor. Effective communication resulted in modifications to the organization's information system that resulted in the system's improved ability to meet the SMWT's information needs. Simultaneously, an effective information system was found to have positive influence on the quality of communication occurring between team members and between the team members and others outside the team. Such findings led us to include recursive arrows in our model to demonstrate the importance of such relationships. Here again, the case study approach provides an advantage over more quantitative approaches because it allows the researcher to observe recursive relationships. More quantitative approaches have difficulty deciphering recursive relationships, and in some cases, it becomes impossible to do so, resulting in this important dimension being ignored or treated superficially.

Finally, our revised theoretical framework includes several environmental, team, and interpersonal process characteristics not initially included in our model of team performance. Within the environmental group of factors, we felt it was important to include additional factors outside the organization that affect the team's performance, including the political-legal and education systems, social demographics, and societal culture. Additional environmental factors within the organization include the organization's philosophy and culture; a clear engaging mission for the team; supplier, customer, and union support; available appropriate resources; and characteristics of team tasks. Additional team design characteristics include goal clarity, challenge, and priorities; decision-making methods and processes for identifying best procedures; and roles of the team and team leader. Finally, additional interpersonal processes include cooperation, conflict, cohesion, and trust. Provided in the remaining chapters is a review and discussion of these many factors that were found to be important to SMWT performance.

# PART II

## The Work Process
Actually Doing the Work With Effort,
Talent, Procedures, and Resources

The work process refers to the factors that are applied directly to accomplishing the team's work. This includes effort placed directly on doing the work, the procedures used for doing the work, the talent applied to the work (knowledge, skill, and ability), and the resources used to accomplish the work. These have direct effects on the team's performance. As one figure of speech would describe it, the work process is "where the rubber hits the road," that is, where the employees actually do the work.

Most previous theoretical frameworks have treated the team's interpersonal process, rather than the work process, as having direct effects. However, we found that the interpersonal processes, such as communication and coordination, were enhancing the work process factors and that these work process factors were, in turn, directly affecting the team's performance.

In the following section, there is a discussion of each work process factor and an introduction to some of the most influential factors found to affect them, including environmental, team design, interpersonal, and team member characteristics. The section concludes with a discussion of the SMWT's task demands and how these moderate the influence of the work process factors.

# 6

■

# Effort Placed Directly on the Work

■

*Effort* refers to the amount of human energy expended directly on doing the  work. Employee effort is closely tied to motivation and commitment. A highly motivated and committed team member is likely to place a high degree of effort on the work itself. However, this is not necessarily the case if circumstances divert the team member's energies away from actually performing the team's tasks. For example, a highly motivated and committed team member might be forced to spend large portions of his or her energy on overcoming coordination problems with other team members or people outside the team. The result could be very little effort placed directly on doing the team's tasks.

Katerberg and Blau (1983) have reemphasized the importance of focusing employee energy directly on the work by stating,

> Individuals have a reservoir of energy that can be allocated among a variety of activities, some of which are productive and some of which are not. . . . Regardless of one's overall arousal level or level of available energy, the allocation of energy between relevant and irrelevant activities can make the difference between success and failure. (p. 250)

We found this to be the case among the SMWT members we interviewed A variety of factors were found to prevent team members from placing all ' energies on the work itself, including environmental, team design, member characteristics, and interpersonal process factors.

A particularly influential environmental factor found to affect employee effort was management support. In several federal government SMWTs studied, the managers working most closely with the SMWTs did not support the team concept. This resulted in team members focusing much of their energies on their own personal well-being and less on the tasks of the team. A second reaction was to expend their energy on confronting management by constantly taking their concerns to higher management levels, where more support was available. In either case, team member effort was diverted from doing the work itself.

Team design factors found to affect effort included the size of the team and team norms. The team members on the smaller teams showed a greater level of effort by spending less time feuding among themselves and by holding themselves personally responsible for the team's performance. Large teams were found to develop factions within the teams that spent energy vying for control of the team. Furthermore, large teams caused reduced feelings of personal responsibility and were found to increase the likelihood of social loafing and shirking behaviors, all of which reduced effort and ultimately team performance. These types of behaviors have been discussed in detail by Kidwell and Bennett (1993), as well as others.

Our examination of team norms found them to have both positive and negative effects on effort. If the team's norms included placing high levels of effort directly on the work, team members were found to try to adhere to this, even if it meant spending time after work completing a project. On the other hand, if team norms included placing only moderate effort on the work, team members were found to adhere to this behavior and encourage it in new team members. For example, in a high-performing manufacturing SMWT, one of the team members, "Tom" explained to us that soon after he joined the team he chose to reduce his work effort at the request of another team member. This team member pointed out to Tom that his performance on his machine was exceptionally higher than the performance of the team member who had been working on the machine previously. Furthermore, if Tom's performance continued to be higher, management would begin inquiring why performance on this machine had not always been so high. It was suggested to Tom that he lower his effort and only over time increase it. It was explained that, in this way, the team's performance would adhere nicely to the organization's push for gradual continuous improvement. Tom agreed, and he reduced his work effort.

Hackman and Morris (1975) have described how team norms can develop to influence the amount of effort placed on doing specific tasks:

For example, if members find the task activities frustrating and unpleasant, they are likely, after some time, to notice the adverse attitudes of others in the group—and perhaps to share these reactions verbally. Gradually, through such interaction, group members may come to an implicit or explicit agreement that the best way to minimize the unpleasantness they experience is to minimize the energy invested in doing the work. If, on the other hand, members find their work on the task exciting, fulfilling, or otherwise rewarding, these experiences also are likely to be shared with one another, and a norm of high effort may be the result. (p. 79)

Interpersonal processes were likewise found to affect level of effort, including coordination, communication, and trust. Hackman (1975, 1988, 1990) has highlighted the influence of interpersonal processes on effort, noting that coordination, in particular, can greatly reduce effort. Johnson and Johnson (1994) have addressed effort and described strategies for using interpersonal processes to increase effort. Our data showed that in highly coordinated teams, team members spent relatively little time determining who would do what and when, leaving more time for team members to do the work itself. Furthermore, high trust and open communication channels resulted in team members being able to obtain information they needed quickly and being willing to reveal errors so that they could be fixed as quickly as possible and team members could get on with accomplishing the work.

Team member characteristics found to have particularly obvious effects on effort were found among new team members who lacked knowledge, skill, and ability to accomplish one or more team tasks. These members were found to devote a high proportion of their energies to on-the-job training rather than to the tasks themselves. A second team member characteristic that was not as obvious but appeared to reduce effort was found where interest in the work was particularly low. In one case, a team member confided that the work had become boring over the years. Although he did not link this to a reduction in his effort, interviews with managers suggested that his effort was lower than most employees, leaving open the possibility that his lack of interest contributed to his lower effort.

As noted above, studies have suggested that the amount of effort placed on doing the work is closely tied to motivation and commitment (Hackman, 1988; Katzenbach & Smith, 1993a; Pearce & Ravlin, 1987). Without high motivation and commitment, the team member will not have a great deal of energy to place directly on doing the work. On the other hand, a high level of motivation and commitment does not necessarily mean that there will be a high level of effort placed on doing the work—high levels of energy resulting from motivation and commitment can be diverted from the actual work and to other concerns. Because of the importance of motivation and commitment to employee effort, each is reviewed below.

## WORK MOTIVATION

*Maslow*

There are literally dozens of theories that have been developed to explain what motivates the employee (for reviews of these, see Ilgen & Klein, 1988; Katzell & Thompson, 1990). Perhaps one of the earliest theories can be found within the scientific management school of thought. Here, it was believed that motivating employees was a simple matter of offering them higher pay. The higher the pay, the more motivated the employee. The human relations perspective had its own view of what motivates employees—the more satisfied the employee, the more motivated the employee. Later, Maslow (1954/1970) suggested that people are motivated by much more than just money or job satisfaction. More recent motivation theories, such as expectancy theory, appear to be built on Maslow's basic principles.

### Maslow's Hierarchy of Needs

Maslow (1954/1970) concluded that there are five categories of human needs that can be ranked or ordered according to how basic the need is:

| | |
|---|---|
| *Physiological needs* | were described as most basic and include the need for food, water, air, shelter, and sex. |
| *Security needs* | include personal safety, job security, and economic maintenance. |
| *Social needs* | include the need for love, affection, and a sense of belonging. |
| *Esteem needs* | refer to the need for self-esteem, respect by others, recognition for accomplishments, and prestige. |
| *Self-actualization* | refers to the need for self-fulfillment, personal growth, creativity, and the like. |

Maslow (1954/1970) explained that unmet needs in any of these categories will potentially motivate a person, whereas needs that are already met will not. That is, if a person perceives herself or himself as being deprived of a particular need, this perception will create a desire to perform those behaviors that will result in fulfilling that need. Likewise, if a particular need is perceived as being met, the person would not be motivated to perform behaviors related to satisfying the need. When applied to the workplace, this suggests that money will be a strong motivator to the extent that it is viewed as a means of satisfying categories of needs, such as physiological needs and security needs. However, if these needs are perceived as being met, the employee will no longer be motivated to satisfy them and instead will look for means of satisfying higher-order needs such as social needs, esteem needs, and self-actualization.

Thus, Maslow (1954/1970) believed that there is a step-by-step process in which lower-order needs are recognized, met, and replaced by higher-order ones. Maslow's theory suggests that what motivates team members will depend on the needs that they are attempting to satisfy and what they perceive will help them to satisfy those needs. Maslow's perspectives on the influence of unmet needs can be found within more recent motivation theories, such as expectancy theory—one of the most developed theories of employee motivation.

## Expectancy Theory

Much like Maslow, Vroom (1964/1995) has also suggested that it is the desire to satisfy an unmet need that motivates a person—the individual makes a conscious decision to perform those behaviors or tasks that are perceived or "expected" to satisfy an unmet need. Vroom has explained that the individual will be most motivated when he or she expects that he or she can accomplish the required behavior or task, the resulting rewards will be forthcoming, and the rewards will satisfy needs. Thus, Vroom has identified three major components in this theory:

1. *Expectancy* or the degree of confidence that a person has with regard to his or her ability to successfully accomplish the required behavior
2. *Instrumentality* or the degree of confidence a person has that if the behavior is performed successfully he or she will be rewarded appropriately
3. *Valence* or the value a person places on the expected rewards

If any one of these conditions does not exist, then the individual's motivation will be greatly reduced. In-depth reviews of expectancy theory have been provided by many theorists, including Ilgen and Klein (1988), Landy and Becker (1987), and Lawler (1973).

Applying expectancy theory to the motivation of SMWT members suggests that high motivation will exist where desirable rewards are available to the team members, the team members believe the rewards will be provided to them if they achieve specific tasks, and the team members believe the specific tasks can be achieved. Our study of SMWTs confirmed this. In particular, we found team members to be highly motivated in those teams where the team had clear, measurable goals that team members perceived to be attainable and also believed would result in desirable rewards.

Where motivation was low, we found team members to be frustrated because one or more of the three conditions of motivation were reported to be lacking. For example, in a government SMWT studied, the team did not have clear, measurable goals. As a result, team members were unsure what behaviors or tasks needed to be accomplished in order to achieve the rewards being offered. In a nursing home SMWT, where motivation was high, team members knew that monetary rewards would not accompany the achievement of specified goals. However, in this case, the team members believed that achieving the goals would result in satisfying higher-order social, esteem, and self-actualization needs—all reported to be highly valued by the team members.

### Other Motivation Theories

Katzell and Thompson (1990) have categorized the dozens of theories that have been introduced to explain motivation into two groups: exogenous and endogenous. The exogenous theories focus on factors external to the individual that can be changed to increase motivation. These include, for example, organizational incentives and rewards and social factors such as leader behavior and employee participation. Examples of exogenous theories include reinforcement theory, goal theory, and material resource theory.

Endogenous theories deal more with the relationship between mental processes and motivation. These are believed to be influenced only indirectly in response to variation in one or more of the exogenous variables. Examples of endogenous theories include attitude theory and equity theory.

## COMMITMENT

Employee commitment has been viewed as existing in several different forms (see, for example, Halaby & Weakliem, 1989; McGee & Ford, 1987; Meyer, Paunonen, Gellatly, Goffin, & Jackson, 1989; Mottaz, 1988; Reichers, 1985; Snizek & Little, 1984). One form has been labeled *affective commitment* and refers to the employee's emotional attachment to and identification with the organization or team. It is this form that is most commonly thought of when speaking of commitment. A second form has been referred to as *continuance commitment* and focuses on the employee's perceived costs associated with leaving the company (Meyer et al., 1989). In this latter form, commitment is not so much the result of emotional attachment as it is the perceived need to have one's job.

Researchers have found that affective or emotional commitment can increase and direct the employee's energy and subsequently result in more effort being placed on doing the work (Comer, 1995; DeCotiis & Summers, 1987; Lee, 1971; Mowday, Steers, & Porter, 1979). Larson and LaFasto (1989) have described this commitment as

> a sense of loyalty and dedication to the team. It is an unrestrained sense of excitement and enthusiasm about the team. It is a willingness to do anything that has to be done to help the team succeed. It is an intense identification with a group of people. It is a loss of self. (p. 73)

Highly committed team members can be expected to find ways of overcoming differences between each other, as well as with those outside the team, to place more of their energies directly on accomplishing the team's goals. On the other hand, low commitment can result in team members exerting less energy, with much of the energy they do exert being directed to concerns other than the work itself. Becker-Reems (1994) has reported such cases in her study of health care SMWTs. She found that low committed team members sometimes attempted to make team performance fall below an acceptable level or started a smear campaign against specific team members. Fisher, Rayner, and Belgard (1995) have reported similar effects of low commitment, noting that it can result in team members focusing their energies on blaming one another for team failures rather than searching for solutions (see also Tjosvold, 1986).

Our study supported these conclusions. For example, one government SMWT we studied had recently lost a team member, who was described by the remaining members as having been highly uncommitted to the team. "Bill" had constantly focused his energies on displaying his knowledge and highlighting the lack of knowledge of others. It was explained that his lack of commitment to the organization began to grow as the SMWT was established. The reason for establishing the SMWT, at the time that it was established, was because the group's supervisor had decided to leave the organization. Bill had expected to become the supervisor for the group and was very disturbed to learn that the group would not have a supervisor and, instead, would operate as an SMWT. His subsequent lack of commitment to the team resulted in much of his energies being placed in behaviors that were not focused on the actual work. Furthermore, his behavior affected others by diverting their energies from the team's work. As a result, the performance of the SMWT was low. And, after Bill's departure, it was found that he had neglected to perform a variety of tasks that placed the whole organization in jeopardy with federal regulators.

A second case study revealed a manufacturing team, all members of which were highly committed. Their primary focus was on accomplishing their team's tasks, which they perceived to be very important. Differing views among team members were encouraged, to increase the pool of possible solutions to various work problems. Highly energized discussions were routine. The team members' high level of commitment appeared to be related to several factors, including the members' perception that the work was extremely important, that they were personally responsible for the team's performance, and that the other team members, whom they highly respected, were extremely committed to the team.

An examination of the factors that are believed to increase commitment appears to link them to explanations of motivation. Pearce and Ravlin (1987), for example, have suggested as causes of commitment (1) autonomy over decision making, (2) meaningful tasks, (3) desired rewards, and (4) an appraisal system that recognizes the individual's contributions. These can all be easily viewed as factors that can produce motivation as well as commitment. Unfortunately, researchers have not untangled the relationship between motivation and commitment. Nevertheless, it is clear that both can increase an employee's level of energy and, subsequently, contribute to more effort being placed directly on doing the work.

# 7

■ '

# Talent, Resources, and Procedures for Doing the Work

■

## TALENT—KNOWLEDGE, SKILL, AND ABILITY

The performance of the teams we studied was directly affected by the amount and kind of *talent* applied to the work—that is, knowledge, skill, and ability. The highest-performing teams were characterized by team members who applied all the knowledge, skills, and abilities needed to do the tasks. In relation to effort, we found that the teams that demonstrated a high level of talent but displayed low effort performed low. Similarly, if effort was high but the application of talent was insufficient, performance was low.

An examination of the teams we studied showed that the low-performing teams typically had responsibility for certain tasks that no one on the team had the talent to accomplish. In several low-performing teams, these tasks were found to have been previously performed by a supervisor. For example, on one team, the scheduling of the work had been turned over to the team but with no accompanying education or training. Consequently, the knowledge applied to developing the team's work schedule was lacking, and as a result, the team's performance suffered.

Teams found to perform adequately, that is, not low but not high either, were found to have at least one team member who could perform any one of the team's tasks. Teams with this level of existing talent have been referred to as *balanced* teams and have been evaluated positively by some researchers and practitioners. However, we found that in these teams, there tended to be multiple team tasks that only one or a few team members had the talent to accomplish. Consequently, if the right person wasn't available when a particular task needed to be accomplished, the team's performance suffered.

The highest-performing teams, on the other hand, were characterized by team members, each of whom could perform all of the team's tasks. Thus, the findings did not support the view that a balance of talent is optimal and, instead, indicated that performance is highest where all team members possess the talents needed for doing all the team's tasks.

There is no doubt that the most important factors affecting the team's amount and kind of talent applied to the work were team member characteristics: existing knowledge, skills, and abilities. Without these, there was no possibility that team members could apply them to the work (see also Varela, 1971). Closely linked to this was the environmental factor: training and education provided to team members by the organization. Talent required for the work was most likely to be applied to the team's tasks where continual and appropriate training and education were obtained by team members.

When considering the team design characteristics, composition of the team—in terms of the team members' combined talents—was found to affect the kinds of talents that could be applied to the work. As noted above, team performance was highest where all team members had all the talents needed to accomplish the work.

Another important team characteristic affecting the amount of talent applied to the work was the norms practiced by the team. These included openness in pointing out perceived talent insufficiencies and willingness to provide and accept cross-training. For example, during the team meetings of one high-performing manufacturing SMWT, team members would periodically discuss the quality of the work being performed. In some cases, certain operating procedures would be questioned or the appropriate procedures for preparing a machine for use would be reviewed. This would sometimes result in some team members questioning the existing procedures or preparations being used by one or more other team members. A lively discussion would ensue, and all team members appeared to learn something from the discussions.

Still another important team characteristic affecting the talent applied to the work was the decision-making procedures used. In the high-performing teams, the decision-making process included giving extra weight to the opinions of those team members who had the most talent with regard to the particular problem being considered. Consequently, which team member's opinion got the most weight depended on the particular topic under review. On the other hand, on low-performing teams, some team members were typically found to dominate team decision making, even where other team members had more talent with regard to the particular subject being considered. Furthermore, other team members tended to shy away from participation in decision making, even when they were among the most talented members regarding the subject. Similar findings have been reported by Hackman (1975).

## RESOURCES APPLIED TO THE WORK

The *resources* applied to the work are typically the materials and space needed to accomplish the work and include, for example, tools, supplies, equipment, and work space (Ilgen & Klein, 1988; Katzell & Thompson, 1990; Zander, 1994). This definition of resources has sometimes been used to describe *technology,* as when Bettenhausen (1991) used the term *technology* to refer to "the equipment, materials, physical environment, and programs involved in acting on and/or changing an object from one state to another" (p. 352). It is reasonable to expect that when the most appropriate resources are applied to the work the SMWT's performance will be higher than when less appropriate or a lack of appropriate resources are applied. Our case studies confirmed this proposition. The high-performing teams we studied appeared to use the most appropriate resources available during the work process, whereas the low-performing teams were less likely to be doing so.

For example, when considering the most appropriate use of space, one high-performing team was found to have rearranged its equipment so that several machines could be operated simultaneously by a single team member. This resulted in the organization saving hundreds of thousands of dollars. On the other hand, in a low-performing government SMWT, the office space available to the team members did not appear to be used in the most appropriate way. In this case, the most senior members had their choice of offices, and they chose offices based on the comforts they offered rather than on how the offices could best be used to enhance team performance. The importance of applying the most appropriate resources while doing the work has, in general, been implicitly understood by many of the SMWT theorists and researchers but not included explicitly in their theoretical models.

A variety of factors were found to affect the SMWT's use of the most appropriate resources. No doubt the most important was the environmental factor: available appropriate resources. If the most appropriate resources were not available, the SMWT could not use them during the work process. An examination of our data shows that the high-performing teams had all the resources needed to do the work and were constantly evaluating the quality of their resources (e.g., tools and equipment, computer software) to be sure that they were using the most appropriate resources available within their budgetary limitations. All the low-performing teams studied also had resources available to accomplish the work. However, some of these teams did not appear to always have the most *appropriate* resources available. For example, a low-performing manufacturing team had tools that were difficult and time-consuming to use. Furthermore, the tools had caused several team members to experience wrist injuries. This team did eventually obtain more appropriate tools. However, prior to the new tools becoming available, the team was not applying the most appropriate resources to the work, and this negatively affected the team's performance.

Additional environmental factors affecting the application of appropriate resources included the development of new technologies; the education, training, and information systems; and management support and encouragement. Each of these was found to be interrelated. The high-performing teams were found to periodically review new technologies, such as new equipment, introduced by vendors. Those identified as more cost-effective than the ones they were currently using were adapted and used during the work process. This was most often observed in the case of tools where technological improvements in metals were continually improving the durability of the tools. Several high-performing manufacturing teams were found to periodically compare the cost and durability of their existing tools with those becoming available through new technologies.

Closely linked to the use of new technologies were the education, training, and information systems. These provided the team members with up-to-date information on new technologies being introduced in the marketplace that could enhance the team's resources. Furthermore, high-performing teams were found to routinely assign team members to training so that they could learn how to use the most appropriate resources during the work process.

On the other hand, low-performing teams were more likely to have team members who lacked adequate training to use the most appropriate resources. For example, in one of the lower-performing teams that we studied, some team members were uncomfortable using the available computer software and consequently did their tasks laboriously with paper and pencil. It appeared that training and education in the use of the computer software could have resulted in more team members using the computer—the most appropriate resource available for their work—and, subsequently, increasing the team's performance.

Also important were management support and encouragement. Teams were not able to adopt new technological resources unless management was willing to support the change. Similarly, teams were not likely to look for or attempt such changes unless management encouraged the teams to continually consider alternative resources. This was particularly evident in several low-performing teams we studied, where managers were not encouraging team members to consider alternative resources. Furthermore, when the low-performing teams did propose changes, management provided little support for the request. In one low-performing manufacturing SMWT, this was due to the manager's lack of confidence that the team members could make a good decision about the available resources. In another, it was likewise due to management's lack of confidence in the team's decisions and, in addition, to a more basic desire that the SMWT be disbanded altogether.

The effects of applying appropriate resources on SMWT performance are closely tied to the other work processes, employee effort, and talent. To the extent that the most appropriate resources are unavailable, team members will be unable to apply their efforts and talents most effectively on the work. If ample resources are available, they will be of little use without sufficient employee effort and talent.

## PROCEDURES FOR DOING THE WORK

It has long been established that the particular procedures used for doing the work can have significant effects on a team's performance (e.g., Davis, 1973; Maier, 1963; Shiflett, 1972). For example, a team that is using the best procedures available will keep to a minimum the amount of time and number of people needed, as well as expenses, in performing the work. On the other hand, less successful procedures may result in the team using excessive staff and taking longer to complete the work, which may result in inaccuracies in the work itself.

There are a variety of characteristics within and outside the team that were found to affect the particular procedures chosen for doing the work. When considering the team design characteristics, perhaps the single most important factor was the methods and tools used for determining the best work procedures. We found that the high-performing teams were methodical in evaluating the procedures used, whereas low-performing teams were more likely to simply rely on doing the work the way it had always been done. Furthermore, high-performing teams were more likely to welcome cooperative conflict among team members as various possible procedures were considered; they then selected those procedures that appeared best. The tools used by high-performing SMWTs for selecting procedures included, for example, process mapping or flowcharting to clarify how existing work was being done and how future work might be done, brainstorming to identify all possible ways of improving existing procedures, and feedback from management and customers to identify areas for improvement.

Closely tied to the tools used for selecting best procedures were the team norms related to work procedures. We found that effective team norms included periodically evaluating existing work procedures. Low-performing teams, on the other hand, were less likely to include this as a normal part of their activities. For example, a low-performing manufacturing team was unaware of the need to periodically evaluate its procedures. This eventually contributed to the team's low performance. Consequently, management stepped in and began working with the team to evaluate and improve the procedures being used.

Still another important team design characteristic is the establishment of measurable team goals. A team is less likely to be using the best procedures possible if it is not clear what the procedures should be designed to accomplish. In one low-performing government SMWT, team members lacked measurable goals. Consequently, the team was less clear what effect its procedures were having, or whether one procedure was better than another. On the other hand, the high-performing teams we studied had very specific measurable goals and, when these were not met, these teams reevaluated their procedures to look for ways to improve.

Important team member characteristics affecting the procedures used included talent—the knowledge, skills, and abilities held by team members. Teams with more talent tended to consider more different possible procedures for doing the work and subsequently were more likely to chose effective procedures. Furthermore, they were more likely to have team members that saw the advantages of periodic evaluations of procedures and were knowledgeable in how to conduct such evaluations.

Influential environmental characteristics included training and education, clarity of team purpose and objectives, and management encouragement. Just as the talents of team members positively affected the team's development of best procedures, training and education were found to provide the needed talent to team members. For example, in one low-performing SMWT, we found that management was attempting to enhance team member talent through daily 1-hour training sessions on evaluation techniques.

A second environmental characteristic found to be important was clarity of team purpose and objectives. One of the teams we studied did not have a clear purpose or clear objectives. Consequently, the team members were unable to derive clear, measurable goals. And, as noted above, without these, the team was unable to determine the best procedures to use.

Finally, management encouragement of team process mapping, flow-charting, and other methods for identifying effective work procedures was found to be routine among high-performing teams. These managers encouraged the SMWTs to take the lead role in evaluating their work procedures. On the other hand, encouragement was rarely found among the lower-performing teams, where procedures were determined more by existing norms and habit.

## THE DEMANDS OF THE TASKS: A MODERATING FACTOR

It has been suggested by a variety of theorists that the effects of the process factors on work team performance may not always be equally important (Blumberg & Pringle, 1982; Gladstein, 1984; Hackman, 1978). However, researchers have been reluctant to draw firm conclusions because of the difficulty in testing this proposition statistically (e.g., Cohen, 1994; Gladstein, 1984).

Hackman and Oldham's (1980) observations are particularly relevant here, because they focus not only on the work process but also specifically on SMWTs. The authors concluded from their research that some work process factors may be more important than others, depending on the demands of the particular task being performed:

> The importance of the intermediate [work process] criteria varies from task to task. For some, such as the assembly of grain driers at Butler, all three of the intermediate criteria need to be high. Producing large quantities of high-quality driers requires great effort, a good deal of knowledge and skill, and a relatively sophisticated performance strategy that efficiently sequences and coordinates the work of members. In other cases, only one or two of the intermediate criteria are salient in determining how effectively the group performs. Consider, for example, a group of park workers who have responsibility for maintaining a specified section of the park grounds. No complex knowledge or skill is required for satisfactory performance, as the work basically involves only picking up debris and raking. (p. 185)

In the cases we studied, we did not find the demands of the tasks to moderate the importance of the work process factors. We found all four factors to always be important, regardless of the task. However, we did find that the demands of the tasks moderated the *amount* of a work process factor that was needed to achieve high performance (or the *sophistication,* in the case of work procedures).

In the case of the park workers, described by Hackman and Oldham (1980), we would conclude that the amount of knowledge and skill needed to accomplish their task is relatively low, whereas the amount of effort needed is relatively high. However, knowledge and skill are no less important than effort. Without the knowledge and skill to do the work, it could not be accomplished, just as without any effort, the work would not get done.

When considering our case studies, the task demands of most of the SMWTs were found to require a high amount of all four work process factors in order for the teams to perform at a high level. For example, in one high-performing manufacturing SMWT, the team members performed multiple tasks on multiple machines and were continually receiving new tasks and completing old ones. The team members were constantly needing to increase and apply new talents as new tasks were received. Resources were continually changing as machines were removed or brought in to complete tasks. New procedures for doing the work were continually being considered as new tasks arrived. Greater effort on the tasks resulted in products being produced to customer specifications in a more timely fashion than when effort was less. In sum, all the work process factors were important to the SMWT's performance, and a high amount and sophistication of each was needed to produce high team performance.

In a second example, we studied a nursing home work team that was made up of nurse's aides and a registered nurse serving a section of a nursing home. The tasks consisted of going from room to room, providing personal care to the nursing home residents in their section. Here we found that three of the work process factors needed to be at a relatively high level or amount to positively affect team performance. More specifically, we found that a high amount of team member effort on the tasks was necessary to positively affect customer satisfaction—high effort resulted in the "little" things being done that made the difference between a satisfied resident or an unhappy resident. A high amount of talent was likewise needed. High performance required knowledge in a variety of areas, including federal regulations, and a variety of skills and abilities, such as those associated with transferring residents from a bed to a wheelchair without causing harm to the team member or resident. Likewise, it was found that a large variety of resources were needed to obtain high performance. These included, for example, the availability of wheelchairs and other personal care devices. Finally, the procedures used were likewise important to the team's performance. However, it was found that the amount or level of procedural sophistication needed was relatively low. There appeared to be a limited number of procedural variations available to the team. That is, there were four team members and a section of residents. Team members had little choice but to go room to room repeatedly during the day—first in the morning and then at lunch time. This consumed the large portion of their workday. Therefore, the level of procedural sophistication was relatively low. However, the importance of the procedures to achieving high team performance was still very high. Without using the most appropriate procedures, regardless of how simple they might be, the team's performance would be low. Thus, in our case studies, we found that all four work process factors were equally important to the SMWT's performance, but that the level or amount needed of each factor varied, depending on the particular demands of a team's tasks.

# PART III

■                                                                              ■

## The Interpersonal Process
The 6 Cs Plus Trust Within and
Outside the Team

■                                                                              ■

The interpersonal processes that occur among team members and between them and people outside the team have received much attention by theorists and researchers of SMWT
performance. Interpersonal processes include communication, coordination, cooperation, collaboration, conflict,
cohesion, and trust—all of which are highly interrelated.
Traditional theories of work team performance have viewed
the interpersonal processes as having the most direct effects
on a team's performance and as being affected by a variety
of inputs (e.g., McGrath, 1964). Our data indicated that the
influences of the interpersonal processes permeated all areas,
including the work process factors, characteristics of the
team, the team's environment both within and outside the
team's organization, and even the characteristics of the team
members themselves. Its greatest influence on the team's performance was found to occur through its influence on the
team's work process, including team member effort, talents,
available resources, and procedures applied to the work.

Although the interpersonal processes are highly interrelated within the workplace, each is discussed separately below to help clarify their importance to SMWT performance.

# 8

■

# Communication and Coordination

■

## COMMUNICATION

In a government SMWT we studied, one of the team members perceived himself to be more "experienced" than the others on his team. Whenever he communicated with others on his team, he was perceived by them to flaunt this fact in an arrogant manner. As a result, team members chose to avoid communicating with him whenever possible. This had a negative impact on the team's work processes and ultimately on team performance. More specifically, it was found that communicating with him was distracting to team members and reduced their effort on the team's tasks. The talents applied to the work were negatively affected because team members refused to ask him for assistance or to be cross-trained (taught) by him—and in this case, he had valuable computer knowledge that he could have taught team members. Similarly, what were perceived to be the best procedures for doing the work were continually being modified so that the arrogant team member could be avoided. Again, the lack of communication and ineffective communication between the most talented team member and the rest of the team had negative effects on the team's work process and subsequent performance.

The importance of communication cannot be understated. As two highly respected organizational theorists, Katz and Kahn (1966), have noted, "Communication is . . . a social process of broadest relevance in the functioning of any group, organization, or society" and is "the very essence of a social system or an organization" (pp. 223-224).

The concept of communication has been defined in dozens of ways (Johnson & Johnson, 1994). Although these all differ to some extent, there does appear to be agreement that *interpersonal communication* is a process that includes the following sequence of steps:

1. *Encoding*—the sender encodes a message in such a way that it can be understood by the receiver.
2. *Channeling*—the message is transmitted through selected channels, such as face-to-face communications, the telephone, a memorandum, or a conference.
3. *Decoding*—the receiver interprets the message and in so doing gives it meaning.
4. *Feedback*—the receiver responds to a sender's message with an understandable return message.

A clear example of this process was provided to us by a machine operator of a manufacturing SMWT, who reported that on one occasion, he received a written message attached to the machine he was about to set up for operation. The message stated that 3 hours had been "charged" to the machine; that is, although the machine had not actually been in operation, another team member had charged the customer for 3 hours of machine operation. An interview with the sender of the message indicated that the encoding of the message was intended to inform the machine operator that he would need to double his efforts to make up for the 3 hours that had been charged. The channel of the communication in this case was a note written on a piece of paper and left on the machine. The message was decoded by the receiver to mean he needed to increase his efforts on the machine to make up for the 3 hours charged. He subsequently did so, and this was evident to the sender (feedback) because the output produced by the machine operator for 8 hours of work was what the customer expected for 11 hours of machine operation.

Thus, communication is more than simply transmitting a message. It includes the complete cycle of encoding a message by a sender, transmitting it through a medium, decoding the message by a receiver, and then acknowledging receipt and understanding of the message by a receiver through feedback (Holt, 1990). Communication within the team, as well as communication between the team and others outside the team, was found to be related to the team's work process, environment, design, and the team member characteristics. These relationships are discussed below.

## Communication and the Work Process

As noted above in the case of the arrogant team member, infrequent and insulting communication was found to result in negative effects on all aspects of the SMWT's work process. In another case, regarding a manufacturing SMWT that we studied, the communication observed within the team was very different—it could be described as honest, frank, continual, and regular. Team members met briefly and informally every morning on the shop floor to review the day's work. They also held regular 1-hour weekly meetings to review and discuss team progress. Furthermore, two or more members would meet as needed during the day on the shop floor. These informal, impromptu meetings occurred frequently and whenever the team needed to respond to a customer, supplier, specific work-related problem, or new information from management. Whenever new information came to a team member, it was quickly disseminated among all the team members. Finally, team members communicated any problems they were having and freely solicited advice—there appeared to be no "holding back" when it came to revealing problems. There was no evidence of blame or scolding when a team member informed the others that he had made an error. Instead, team members solicited ideas from one another to identify the best approach for correcting the mistake and keeping any repercussions of the mistake to a minimum.

Not surprisingly, this team was the highest-performing team of those we studied. Communication had direct positive effects on the team members' talents applied to the work, as they continually learned from each others' mistakes and freely asked for help when it was needed. Through communications, they identified the machine-operating preferences of team members, as well as who was most talented with the various machines, and used this information when assigning team members to machines.

The communication among team members was found to positively affect their effort on the tasks because their time away from producing the product was kept to a minimum—team members were not distracted from their work. And, with regard to resources, the continual and regular communications resulted in the team quickly identifying resources that were inappropriate, not working, or likely to be insufficient to do the work, as well as resources that appeared to be working best.

## Communication and the Team's Environment

Traditional theories of work teams have proposed that the team's environment, design, and team member characteristics affect the team members' communication. Our data support these propositions. Furthermore, the data suggest that the effects are reciprocal; that is, communication affects the team's environment, design, and team members.

Particularly relevant environmental factors related to communication include the organization's culture, resources available to the team, the training and information systems, and relations with management. Neuhaus (1990, p. 95) has noted that the organizational culture can influence the opinions and ideas of the team members and subsequently how they communicate. The culture may be one that supports a trusting environment where team members are encouraged to communicate freely, honestly, and often, or it may encourage team members to question the motives of others and never let others know what is really being thought.

Simultaneously, communication within the team can affect the team's culture. Unclear, inaccurate communication can result in misunderstandings that lead to mistrust. Clear communications can avoid misunderstandings and enhance the opportunity for trust to develop. Trust can, in turn, foster a supportive team culture that can "spill over" into other parts of the organization and affect the culture of the broader organization.

In one of the organizations participating in our study, a conscious effort was being made to place those employees who had worked within an effective SMWT into other SMWTs that lacked an effective team culture. The hope was that these employees would communicate to those on their new teams the characteristics of an effective team-based culture. Furthermore, it was hoped that this would eventually affect the broader organizational culture. In this case, communication played a key role in transferring ideas from the employees to their new teams and allowing a more team-based culture to spread. Presently, it is unclear whether this technique of moving employees will accomplish its goals.

Available resources are another environmental characteristic that can influence the team's communication. A lack of telephones, linkups to computer mail systems, or other supplies can reduce the channels available for communicating. Physical location of team members can also enhance or inhibit communication. In one low-performing government team studied, several team members were located in offices secluded from the rest of the team as well as from available telephones. This inhibited their ability to communicate with other team members, as well as with people outside the team.

Perhaps the single most important environmental factor affecting communication is the training available to develop communication skills. It was clear that most of the team members of SMWTs needed to communicate much more when working within SMWTs than they did prior to joining an

SMWT. Consequently, some of the team members initially lacked the personal experience and formal training in communication needed to communicate effectively. In some organizations, training in communication skills was used to improve communication. This included training in listening as well as in learning to express oneself clearly.

Finally, our data showed that communication within the team and between the team and those outside the team affects the ability of the organization's information system to disseminate important information. Communication between team members and those outside the team is the means by which the team requests and obtains information. Poor communication can result in the information system transferring information that is inaccurate or doesn't match the customer's request.

Also related to communication and information gathering is "scouting" or "scanning" the environment within and outside the organization for any information that could assist the team. This might include information helpful in identifying new technologies that could help the team, new competitors that could threaten the team, and new markets for the team, and developing philosophies of management that could influence the team. Communication is a key in obtaining much of this important information. Ancona and Caldwell (1992) have noted that "individuals carrying out this activity show high levels of communication with marketing, sales, and research and development" (pp. 641-642).

The close tie between communication and information exchange was seen in a low-performing manufacturing SMWT we studied. Very little communication existed between the SMWT and its primary supplier, which was also an SMWT within the same organization. The result was a poor exchange of information so that the supplier provided too much of some supplies and not enough of others. This affected all aspects of the SMWT. It affected the team's interpersonal processes negatively, as conflict with the supplier increased and coordination with others, including its customers, decreased. And, the SMWT's work process was negatively affected as effort on the task was reduced in order to revise the task assignments and procedures for doing the work.

In another manufacturing SMWT, communication between the SMWT and others was much more plentiful, resulting in more complete, useful information. The team kept in constant communication with engineers who were periodically revising the product that the team was assembling. Constant communication included the engineers periodically visiting the team and demonstrating for the team members some of the new revisions to the product. This high level of communication greatly enhanced the team's information. It allowed the team to plan for the upcoming changes in the product in terms of needed training, task assignments, and revised procedures. The result was a positive effect on the team's work process as more effort was placed on the task, procedures were improved, and the most appropriate knowledge, skills, and abilities were applied to the work.

### Communication and Team Design

Particularly relevant team design factors include the norms of the team, team size, the composition of the team, and the team leader. *Team norms* are those practices and procedures within the team that occur without conscious planning and often develop and evolve during the course of the team's existence. For example, team norms may have developed to determine how often and regularly team meetings occur. This will subsequently affect the amount of communication that occurs. Furthermore, during the team meetings, norms may dictate that all team members communicate freely and often, or that the team leader and/or a few team members dominate discussions and communications that occur (Neuhaus, 1990).

Team norms may include the use of effective communication techniques during the team meeting, or communication may occur in such a way that team members are confused, are misunderstood, or simply receive false information. Similarly, the norm may be that clear, comprehensive notes are recorded so that everyone can review what was said or that there is no recording of the meeting of any kind and only those who were at the meeting know what was said. Thus, the team's norms establish expectations of how communications will occur, their quality, and their frequency.

Simultaneously, it is typically through communication that norms evolve. Clear, regular communications can help a team, as team members share with one another ideas for improving. This can result in new ideas being adopted and team norms changing to reflect the new ideas.

Team size was also found to affect communication. A team with a size of about six to eight members appears to be best for high-level communication—in our study, the highest-performing team had six team members. Research suggests that at this size, all or most members are encouraged to communicate, and communication among team members is relatively frequent (Brightman, 1988). Our study supports this conclusion. For example, the largest team we studied had 17 members spanning three shifts. In this team, there was little encouragement for team members to communicate. The team leader was selected by the team members and expected to participate highly in communications that were needed. The team also informally selected several other people who did much of the communicating within, as well as outside, the team. Several other people, who appeared to be highly extroverted, self-selected themselves to communicate freely and participated in most team decision making. Still other team members were expected to communicate very little and received few communications from others. Interviews with these people suggested that they self-selected themselves for this role and preferred to keep communications to a minimum (with the exception of one team member). Furthermore, they worked primarily on the 10 p.m. to 6 a.m. shift, where communication with the whole team was more difficult.

It is interesting to note that whereas team size was found to greatly influence the communication that occurred within this team, there did *not* appear to be a subsequent negative effect on the team's work process or performance. In fact, the team was performing at a high level. However, a review of all our cases suggests that the potential for communication problems was greater for larger teams. As Neuhaus (1990) has noted, "In teams where there are several people involved, the communication process can be quite complicated. . . . The opportunity to misinterpret information, ideas, and messages is great" (p. 94). As the number of people increases, the opportunity for miscommunication also increases.

Another team design characteristic important to SMWT communication is the role of the team leader. We found that communication was more prevalent where team leaders encouraged communication. Brightman (1988) has identified some of the team leader characteristics that can encourage communication, including careful listening, summarizing ideas and feelings frequently, avoiding being overly critical, encouraging team members to speak, encouraging and protecting minority views, and dealing with disagreements openly.

Finally, communication that was honest and continual was found to positively influence the SMWT's decision-making process. Our data suggest that, when communication was open and nonthreatening, various alternative procedures were more likely to be discussed by all team members and their combined talents to be brought to bear on the issue of what procedure to use. Subsequently, more complete information was brought to bear on decision making, which enhanced the likelihood of selecting the best procedure available for doing the work and increasing the team's performance.

## Communication and Team Member Characteristics

The characteristics of the team members make up another group of factors that were found to affect communication within the team. These included the team members' knowledge and skills, interests in the work, and personality of the team members. Not surprisingly, team members who joined an SMWT had varying degrees of communication skills. To the extent that all team members possessed such skills, communications that occurred were more frequent and appeared to be more clearly presented and understood. On the other hand, team members who lacked communication skills were more likely to produce misunderstood communications and negative results that accompany poor communication.

A team member's knowledge about the work was also found to affect his or her amount of communication. Knowledgeable team members typically communicated more often and were typically listened to more closely. On the other hand, less knowledgeable persons appeared to communicate less often. Knowledge also affected communication when the information communicated was not understandable to the less knowledgeable team members. In these cases, the communications were not meaningful at best and could be misinterpreted and result in unintended consequences at worst. Similarly, Buchholz, Roth, and Hess (1987) have noted that problems in communication can occur when the team is composed of people from varying knowledge backgrounds or professions. This can result in professional jargon being misunderstood by those not trained in the particular profession.

Team members who had lost interest in the team's work or had become bored showed less interest in communicating with others regarding the work. In one case, a team member who had worked at the same type of job for many years reported himself to be bored with the work. He was found to communicate with managers and other team members less often than most team members.

The team member's personality also appeared to affect the frequency and type of communication. Team members who were well liked and outgoing were more likely to be involved in communications than team members who were not. Although we did not conduct personality tests, it was clear that those who appeared more extroverted were also much more likely to communicate with others. Of course, increased communications alone did not result in positive influences on the work process, and, where too much or inaccurate information was communicated, it noticeably reduced the amount of effort on the task because of the time wasted in these communications. Furthermore, as noted above, insulting communication had negative effects on the work process. Buchholz et al. (1987) have noted that "communicating a feeling of superiority in position, power, or ability implies the other person can't be right because of his/her inadequacies" (p. 80). Such communications from one team member to another were found in our study to reduce or eliminate communication.

## COORDINATION

Coordination has received much less attention than communication in the literature but was also found to be extremely important to an SMWT's performance. *Work coordination* refers to the act of performing two or more steps of a work process in a proper order. Hackman (1988, 1990) has perhaps brought the most explicit attention to coordination by discussing its direct effects on the team's work process. If the work is not well coordinated between team members, then the steps or procedures used for doing the work will not be carried out well. Hackman has noted that this can, in turn, reduce the amount of effort placed on doing the work because the employees' energies must be concentrated on overcoming the coordination problems. Thus, both the work procedures and team effort are negatively affected.

An example to support this was found in a government SMWT we studied. In this team, two and sometimes three team members would periodically travel to a predetermined location in one of the southwestern states of the United States in order to auction off government supplies and equipment no longer needed (e.g., government automobiles). The auction was advertised weeks in advance, and typically there were many potential buyers at these auctions. The procedures that were followed in carrying out the auction ranged from securing the airplane tickets for the trip to collecting the money and recording the sales. For such a trip, a great deal of coordination was needed, not only between the team members going on the trip but also with people at the sale site. Team members reported that, for some auctions, coordination became a problem. When a coordination problem occurred, it sometimes resulted in team members having to spend an extra day at the auction site to finish up business. Thus, poor coordination resulted in less effort spent directly on the tasks because energies had to be expended on activities that could have been avoided had the coordination been better. Furthermore, the poor coordination left the team members with less time to perform other tasks, once they returned from the auction, because of the one-day delay.

Coordination has been found to affect other factors as well. When considering the team's environment, coordination was found to affect the training received. For example, well-coordinated teams planned their activities in such a way that team members were available to take needed training classes on the days they were offered. Less coordinated teams found that team members had to skip needed and desired training classes because the team's most critical tasks had been scheduled to be performed at the same time as the training classes.

Other environmental factors affected by coordination include team suppliers and customers. We found that poor coordination can frustrate suppliers because the SMWT is more likely to miscalculate needs. This can demotivate the suppliers, resulting in them being less responsive to the team's requests and ultimately resulting in the team not having available to it in a timely fashion the resources it needs to conduct its work. Similarly, poor coordination can result in the team losing customers, as the customer seeks to work with others who are better coordinated and subsequently predictable.

When considering factors affecting coordination, the team design characteristics of norms and size, were observed to have large effects. The norms of the team were found to greatly affect the team's practices and procedures, including their emphasis on coordination. Size of the team was also found to affect coordination, with larger teams often having more difficulty coordinating their efforts.

It appeared that coordination was also affected somewhat by team member characteristics. Some personalities seem to be more inclined to carefully coordinate all details of a task, whereas others prefer to leave room in the work process for adjustments as they go along. Differences in approaches can be particularly problematic when they result in fundamental disagreements regarding how to coordinate the work. This was found to result in one team member carrying out the work one way and another team member carrying it out a different way and the performance of each being reduced to the extent that their efforts were not coordinated.

# 9

■

# Cooperation,
# Collaboration, and Conflict

■

Cooperation and collaboration are concepts that are highly related and are sometimes treated synonymously. For example, in Larson and LaFasto's (1989) excellent book on teamwork, a chapter devoted to a "collaborative climate" appears to use the terms *cooperation* and *collaboration* interchangeably. A review of the literature suggests that most writers choose to use one of the two terms and ignore the other. For the purposes of the following discussion, *cooperation* and *collaboration* are viewed synonymously and are defined as the act of two or more people working together for a common purpose.

The term *conflict* has not gone without its own variety of definitions. Traditionally, *conflict* was defined as disagreements between two or more people that leads to mistrust, poor communication, and lack of cooperation. During the late 1960s, behaviorists began viewing conflict as a natural occurrence that can lead to either problems and dysfunctional behavior or to beneficial behavior. *Beneficial conflict* has been termed *cooperative conflict* and refers to those situations where two or more employees have opposing ideas and interests but are motivated to explore and understand the views and interests of the other. Tjosvold (1986) has explained that

they understand the shortcomings in their own perspective, appreciate the desires and requirements of others, try to integrate other ideas and aspirations, and develop a fresh viewpoint that responds to the reasoning, perspective, and needs of others. Then they can reach mutually satisfactory decisions based on the ideas and interests of several people. Their relationships also are strengthened, and they are confident that they can resolve conflicts in the future. Throughout the conflict, people emphasize their cooperative dependence. (p. 117)

On the other hand, dysfunctional conflict has been termed *competitive conflict* and described as a relationship where the disagreeing persons choose to define their own positions vigorously and attempt to win over others. Tjosvold (1986) has described it this way:

They try to understand the other to find weaknesses in his arguments, not to modify their own conclusions. They want to counterattack, undercut other positions, and make their own views and interests dominate. They may conclude that they must use superior authority or other means to impose their solutions. (p. 117)

In this way, conflict results in a failure to reach an agreement and, in its place, a solution may be imposed by the more powerful. This has been described as leading to personal ill will and little confidence that future problems can be solved (Ephross & Vassil, 1988; Tjosvold, 1986).

More recently, Jehn (1995, p. 257) has described conflict in the context of the social and task environments. In the context of the task, conflict is based on different views of the team's tasks. In the context of the social environment, conflict is based on poor interpersonal relations (Guetzkow & Gyr, 1954; Pinkley, 1990; Priem & Price, 1991; Wall & Nolan, 1986). Similarly, Amason (1996) has referred to these as *cognitive conflict* and *affective conflict*. Not surprisingly, our study found cooperation and conflict to have a variety of effects on the SMWT. Simultaneously, a variety of SMWT characteristics were found to enhance or diminish cooperation and conflict. These relationships are discussed below.

## COOPERATION, CONFLICT, AND THE WORK PROCESS

Conflict can result in large amounts of time spent in disagreements among team members, subsequently reducing the amount of time left to focus on actually doing the work. Conflict has been found to result in avoidance tactics among team members that directly reduce the amount of effort placed on the work and alter the procedures used for carrying out the work (Bettenhausen, 1991; Ephross & Vassil, 1988). This was supported by our research and shown in Chapter 8's example of an arrogant team member. Conflict has also been reported to cause apathy (Ephross & Vassil, 1988) as team members are unable to reach decisions and take actions. This again results in less effort placed on doing the work.

Cooperation, on the other hand, can reduce the amount of time spent on activities away from the work and subsequently can increase the amount of effort placed directly on doing the work. Furthermore, cooperation can enhance team member motivation and, subsequently, effort, as team members believe that cooperation will allow them to achieve tasks and reach goals that could not be accomplished otherwise. Thus, during the work process, conflict has negative effects, whereas cooperation has positive ones. However, as we shall see, the effects of conflict and cooperation are sometimes reversed.

## COOPERATION, CONFLICT, AND THE ENVIRONMENT

The SMWT's environment has been found to have large effects on team member cooperation and conflict. The reward system of the organization is particularly influential. If it is designed so that rewards are received for high *team* performance, then team members will be motivated to cooperate with one another to achieve the team goals. On the other hand, if the rewards are based on *individual* performance, conflict is more likely to occur as team members struggle to make themselves look good, regardless of the effects on the team's overall performance (Johnson & Johnson, 1994; Kouzes & Posner, 1987).

The organization's culture, training, and coaching greatly influence whether and how conflicts are resolved. Most theorists and researchers agree that conflict is inevitable and can have positive influences on the SMWT, for example, by increasing the number of differing ideas available to choose from when making decisions. However, for such positive effects to occur, the organization's culture and the team's norms must be such that conflict is openly addressed and managed cooperatively.

Training and coaching can provide team members with the skills to study conflict and learn how to discuss it productively. It is reasonable to expect that when cooperative conflict is not taught, it is less likely to be used, and, consequently, conflict is more likely to have negative effects on the work process. Cooperative conflict is characterized by team members who express friendliness, mutual concern, and respect. This allows team members to be more prepared to discuss conflict and to believe that conflict can be resolved for mutual benefit (Jandt & Pedersen, 1996; Tjosvold, 1986).

A poor information system can also lead to negative or competitive conflict. A poor information system can result in team members receiving different and incomplete information that results in conflicts as team members come to different conclusions about how to handle work situations and tasks. Team members will not understand why others have made the decisions they have unless all team members have all the relevant information available.

Low management support can also result in competitive conflict. Managers who do not support the SMWT concept can easily sabotage the team's information system. Likewise, managers who have not been trained to understand their roles in managing and encouraging SMWTs can unknowingly damage the information system. This, in turn, can increase the likelihood of competitive conflict.

In a government SMWT studied, we found that first- and second-line managers were not transferring information to the team through the team's designated liaison member. Instead, the managers were providing information to "Sue"—one of the team members who had been the group's supervisor prior to the SMWT being established. The first-line managers did not believe the team could make good decisions and felt that giving the information to Sue would increase the chances that good decisions would be made. This practice resulted in constant conflicts between the team members and Sue and between the team members and the first- and second-line managers. Team members felt that Sue was not discouraging the managers from transferring information through her, and they felt that managers were purposely ignoring the designated team member liaison. Furthermore, they felt that Sue kept certain vital information to herself until it was to her advantage to share it with the rest of the team—such as when she needed to bring into question the credibility of another team member who was questioning a proposal of hers. Sue described herself as being stuck in the middle, sympathizing with the managers and their concern that the team make the best decisions possible and with the team in that it was not being respected by management. Thus, in this case, a lack of management support and a poor information system contributed to competitive conflict within the SMWT.

Just as conflict and cooperation are highly susceptible to influences from the information system and management, the reverse can be true as well—the information system can be affected by team cooperation and conflict. When cooperation is high among team members, the information system is much more effective—team members are more likely to share all available information with their teammates readily. On the other hand, when conflict is high, team members may keep information to themselves, use it to support their own agendas and proposals, and choose to give misleading information to sway members to agree with their side.

## COOPERATION, CONFLICT, AND TEAM DESIGN

A variety of team design factors can heighten cooperation and conflict. As noted above, team norms that encourage team members to share information, listen to each other's ideas, exchange resources, and respond to each other's requests through positive interdependence will enhance cooperation (Ephross & Vassil, 1988).

Closely tied to norms are goals of the team that stress cooperation. With cooperative goals, people realize that they are personally successful only when their team members are also successful. This encourages team members to help each other perform effectively (Tjosvold, 1986). As Kouzes and Posner (1987) have noted,

> Shared visions and values bind employees together in collaborative pursuits. Group tasks, complementary roles, and shared rewards also play a role. Tasks that require people to exchange ideas and sources reinforce the notion that participants have cooperative goals. As individuals jointly work together, seeing that they need information from each other in order to be successful, they become convinced that everyone should contribute and that by cooperating they can all accomplish the task successfully. (p. 135)

Although norms that encourage cooperative goals have been found to be beneficial, the positive effects of norms that encourage cooperative conflict should not be understated or overlooked. Ideally, when attempting to achieve cooperative goals, team members do not always initially agree on how the goals are to be achieved. Instead, a variety of ideas are offered, some of which may conflict. These are initially presented in an atmosphere of cooperative conflict, and after careful consideration of them, the best *cooperative decision* is made. In this way, the best work procedures are selected and, in turn, there are positive effects on the team's performance. Norms of cooperative conflict are used in this process as ideas on how to do the work or solve a problem conflict and employees work together to determine which are best.

Janis (1988) has coined the term *groupthink* to refer to group norms that produce too much cooperation. That is, team members are unwilling to offer alternative choices from those already offered by one of their teammates. As a result, the team may not consider all possible alternatives, may not make the best possible decision, and, in the case of the work process, may not apply the best procedures to the work. Thus, cooperative conflict is preferred to groupthink because it will produce a variety of choices from which the team can select. Furthermore, because it is cooperative in nature, the team members will be open to other ideas and willing to change their decisions if discussions and facts reveal a better alternative.

When considering the effects of team size on cooperation and conflict, we found that other team design factors such as norms of cooperative conflict were more important. As the team's size increases, we found the likelihood of factions or subgroups to develop within the team. These subgroups would occasionally reach different conclusions with regard to the best decision or procedures to follow. However, when the team had strong norms of cooperative conflict, our data showed that the factions were able to cooperate, overcome their differences, and make what appeared to be the best decisions. The large size did not prevent the best decision from being selected. On the other hand, if cooperative conflict was not the norm, the factions arising from the large team size can be expected to compete with one another and use a more competitive conflict approach, resulting in a variety of negative effects.

These relationships were evident within several large manufacturing SMWTs. We observed a high-performing team of 17 members that held clear, strong norms supporting cooperative conflict. This team was able to use cooperative conflict to consider the pros and cons of various alternatives and make informed decisions that were agreed on by all the factions within the team. The second manufacturing SMWT of 13 members was low-performing and displayed a norm of competitive conflict. Some team members displayed a disrespect for others on the team and continually blamed them for the team's performance. In this team, a sense of security and personal safety was lacking, with some team members feeling threatened by others and feeling that serious harm could come to them if they were not cautious in what they said. In this low-performing team, factions were very suspicious of each other. Our interviews with team members suggested that biases for or against certain factions played an important part in the team decisions that were made. Consequently, decisions were not made solely on the facts regarding the best alternative available but instead were influenced by biases regarding the factions. Subsequently, the data suggest that for this second team the best decisions and procedures were not always the ones selected. Thus, it appears that the size of the team was not as important to the existence of cooperative conflict as were other factors such as team norms.

Other team design factors found to produce cooperation and conflict included the job's design and the composition of the team. In designing the work, the team will typically identify a variety of special skills, resources, and knowledge that are needed to do the tasks. The team must decide who is going to do what in order to accomplish these tasks. Conflict will often arise if several team members want to do the same tasks. In our study, teams that practiced cooperative conflict were found to be successful at identifying good fits between the tasks and the talents of the team members. On the other hand, if the teams practiced competitive conflict, the best fits between the tasks and team members were not always selected. In either case, the job's design produced conflict that was handled either cooperatively or competitively.

When considering the composition of the team, the combination of team member characteristics can be expected to be produce conflicts and cooperation. This is perhaps most evident where differing personality types come together within the team and are found to inherently cooperate or conflict. When considering our case studies, we found the composition of the team to have very large effects on the level of conflict. This was particularly evident on a low-performing government SMWT. On this team, its composition of members included a person who had been a supervisor prior to establishing the team. This appeared to invite competitive conflict, as team members attempted to demonstrate that their viewpoints were as "correct" as the past supervisor's. Simultaneously, the supervisor periodically created competitive conflict by attempting to demonstrate her superior knowledge and connections with management.

## COOPERATION, CONFLICT, AND TEAM MEMBER CHARACTERISTICS

We found cooperation to be high to the extent that team members were similar in their job status, values, prejudices, and talents. Although these similarities reduced conflict, they created problems by not providing enough variety of ideas. On the other hand, if the team members were very different, the opposite effect occurred. There were a variety of different ideas available, but the team had difficulty reaching agreements acceptable to everyone.

We found this latter problem when studying a government SMWT that had a wide range of status ratings among its members, from GS-5 (typically requiring a high school degree) to GS-13 (often requiring a master's degree). This team was experiencing a high level of conflict. Those with the lower ratings generally felt threatened by those with the highest ratings and were suspicious of the decisions recommended by them. Those with the highest ratings tended to downplay the recommendations of the lower-status team members and described them as generally less knowledgeable and inferior. These attitudes, stemming from large status differences, created a high level of conflict and resulted in questionable decisions being made by the team.

As noted above, personality differences can also contribute to cooperation and conflict. When personalities come together that complement one another, cooperation is often the result. When two personalities come together that seem to inherently clash with one another, conflict can be expected to result.

# 10

■

# Cohesion and Trust

■

## COHESION

*Cohesion* is the degree to which members of a team feel attracted to their team and compelled to stay in it (Bettenhausen, 1991; Holt, 1990; Organ & Hammer, 1950). Cohesion has been viewed as being based on either of two attractions—one being the tasks of the team and the other being the team members themselves (Mikalachki, 1969; Seashore, 1954). Cohesion was found to be related to the team's work process, environment, team design, and team member characteristics.

In one nursing home SMWT we studied, the team was made up of four managers of a nursing home, including the nursing home administrator and the directors of nursing, social work, and mental health. All members displayed a high level of both task-oriented and team-oriented cohesiveness. When considering task-oriented cohesion, all team members expressed a deep concern for the residents they served and perceived their job tasks as a means of addressing these concerns. They were reluctant to miss a day of work because they believed that residents would suffer as a result. In the case of team-oriented cohesion, all team members expressed a deep personal admiration and respect for the others on the team. They expressed a strong desire to be with and work with each other. This was the most cohesive team of those we studied.

At the other extreme was a government team that purchased and sold products for the government. Team members reported that their tasks were important functions that needed to be done. However, they displayed much less passion or commitment to their tasks than the health care SMWT. For example, team members routinely took days off from work to "use up" their sick days—including taking off Fridays to give themselves a long weekend. They reported that it would be OK if their tasks did not get done until a later time. This was not the attitude of those in the health care SMWT, who felt that if they missed a day of work, residents would suffer. When considering team member attractiveness to one another within the government SMWT, feuds and enemies were the norm. Cohesiveness in terms of team member attractiveness was almost nonexistent.

## Cohesion and the Work Process

Task-oriented cohesiveness has been reported to positively affect a team's level of effort placed directly on the work due to its influence on the team members' commitment to the work (Bettenhausen, 1991; Zaccaro & Lowe, 1988). Team-oriented cohesiveness has also been viewed as affecting effort through its positive influences on the team members' commitment to one another. However, team-oriented cohesiveness has also been found to decrease effort due to time spent among team members discussing non-work-related subjects (Zaccaro & Lowe, 1988).

Our data supported these previous findings. For example, in the highly cohesive nursing home SMWT we studied, high task-oriented cohesiveness appeared to positively influence the team members' efforts on the work. Furthermore, team-oriented cohesiveness resulted in the SMWT members being committed to one another and providing extra effort to please their teammates. On the other hand, team-oriented cohesiveness could also be attributed to the team members, who met socially to discuss personal concerns both during and outside of working hours, and this reduced their effort on the work. Overall, however, it was concluded that the high cohesiveness within this SMWT positively influenced effort on the work, given that the high cohesiveness (both task- and team-oriented) resulted in team members routinely working beyond their scheduled hours without additional pay.

A second work process factor found to be affected by task-oriented and team-oriented cohesion was the extent of team member talents placed on doing the work. With high cohesion of either type, team members were more likely to ask for assistance or defer to others who had more talent with regard to the particular tasks being performed. On the other hand, in low-cohesive teams, such as one of the government SMWTs we studied, team members were less willing to ask for help or seek out those who were most talented with regard to a particular task.

## Cohesion and Team Design

Research has suggested that team-oriented cohesiveness facilitates decision making because the communication among team members is more open—team members feel "safer" in expressing differing views and ideas (Lott & Lott, 1961; Mickelson & Campbell, 1975). However, team-oriented cohesiveness can also lead to *groupthink* (a practice of agreeing with others rather than disagreeing), which, in turn, can lead to a reduction in the number of alternative work procedures that are considered by the team as it attempts to identify best work procedures (Jewell & Reitz, 1988). Jewell and Reitz have described the research findings:

> Members of cohesive groups do feel freer to express opinions, especially unpopular opinions, than members of less cohesive groups but only up to a point. Studies consistently suggest that, once cohesive groups begin to achieve a certain degree of likemindedness, additional information important to the best solution of the problem is likely to be rejected if it is inconsistent with the developing consensus. (p. 254)

Our data show some support for these conclusions. Team members of the most cohesive SMWT were comfortable during the decision-making process, and interviews suggested they felt free to offer alternative suggestions during the initial stages of the decision-making process. However, it did appear that these team members did not want to introduce alternatives, once a degree of "likemindedness" was detected.

Cohesiveness has also been reported to influence the norms of the team (Holt, 1990; Jewell & Reitz, 1988), and this was supported by our data. Teams high in cohesiveness were found to more rigorously adhere to the team's norms. Team members did not want to upset others or to be ostracized by the team. Consequently, they were more willing to adjust their behavior to match the norms of the group. On the other hand, team members within low-cohesive SMWTs were less concerned about upsetting others or being ostracized because their relationships with most of the other team members were valued much less.

Team design factors found to affect SMWT cohesiveness included goal clarity and the team's size. Task-oriented cohesiveness was directly related to goal clarity. Team members had difficulty developing task-oriented cohesiveness to the extent that they had difficulty identifying the team's primary goals. A lack of goal clarity contributed directly to a lack of task clarity, which, in turn, contributed to multiple perceptions of what the team's primary tasks were. Without a clear understanding of the tasks, task-oriented cohesion was less.

An examination of team size showed that smaller teams generally had higher levels of team-oriented cohesiveness because team members were able to have more interactions with each other and to get to know each other better. This allowed them to learn about and be sensitive to each other's concerns. In large teams (roughly 10 or more), team members had difficulty getting to know others to the same extent. This contributed to the development of factions within the group and a reduction of team-oriented cohesion. On the other hand, the size of the team did not appear to affect the level of task-oriented cohesiveness.

### Cohesion and the Environment

A variety of environmental factors within the organization have been reported to affect an SMWT's cohesion. The culture of the organization can be one that encourages the team members to work together in a collaborative, respectful manner or in a competitive manner. The former can naturally lead to increased team-oriented cohesion, whereas the latter is likely to do the opposite. This was supported by our data. The nursing home SMWTs were located in a culture that emphasized caring for others. The government SMWT was located in a culture that did not support or encourage collaboration between workers of varying status.

Simultaneously, cohesion can also affect the culture. In our study, where cohesion was particularly high within a manufacturing SMWT, other teams and people within the organization appeared to take notice. Once they saw what it was like to work within a cohesive SMWT, they also wanted to work in a cohesive environment. Although wanting to develop a cohesive environment and actually being able to do so are very different, the highly cohesive team appeared to influence the broader organizational culture to work in this direction.

Another environmental factor that can affect cohesion is the physical location of team members. Physical location can be a barrier to cohesion if team members are located in separate areas where they seldom cross paths. Without contact between members, team-oriented cohesion will be more difficult to develop. Furthermore, the potential for this cohesion will be reduced if some work locations are more desirable than others and competition is the means used to determine who gets the choice locations.

A government SMWT provided examples of the effects of physical location. A few team member offices were located in more desirable parts of the building, where there were fewer disturbances and no telephones for performing the undesirable administrative duties. The team members in these offices were largely cut off from the rest of the team members, which inhibited team-oriented cohesion. Furthermore, team members competed among themselves to obtain these offices, and this competition appeared to have additional negative effects on the cohesiveness of the team.

Still another environmental factor affecting cohesion is the reward system. In the above example, the desirable office space could be thought of as a reward. By providing *individual* rewards, competition between team members is encouraged, and cohesiveness can be expected to be less. Rewards that focus on *team* achievements, on the other hand, are likely to encourage team members to work out their differences so that they can achieve the rewards. Of course, this requires that the rewards are valuable to the team members. A token team bonus was not found to be a valued reward.

When considering environmental factors outside the organization, Ancona and Caldwell (1992) suggested that the SMWT's cohesion is reduced to the extent that the external environment introduces a variety of new ideas and information to the team. They have noted the similarity here with Homans's (1950) observation that complexity and conflict in the external environment will be replicated within the group when information from the environment is imported into the group. Our data appear to support this proposal. For example, within a manufacturing SMWT we studied, as external information increased, the team had a larger number of different choices available, compared with a second manufacturing SMWT that received far less input from the external environment. This subsequently appeared to influence the cohesiveness of the teams, with the first being clearly less cohesive than the latter. However, other factors were also contributing to the differences in cohesiveness between these two teams, particularly team size. Consequently, it is difficult to decipher the extent to which variety of external information was influencing cohesiveness.

## Cohesion and Team Member Characteristics

Our data suggest that those SMWTs composed of people who were similar in work status tended to have higher levels of team-oriented cohesion than those teams with members having a wide range of work status. Where status differences were small, team members appeared to have more in common, which contributed to the cohesion.

When considering gender differences, no effects were detected on cohesion. Some of the SMWTs we studied were almost exclusively male or female. Among these teams, some showed a very high level of cohesion, whereas others showed the opposite. In these SMWTs, gender did not have a noticeable effect.

Other team member characteristics that did have noticeable effects on cohesion included the interests and values of team members. Team members had positive feelings toward those who held similar values and had more to talk about with those who had similar interests. Furthermore, it is reasonable to expect that any negative prejudices held by one team member regarding another would reduce team-oriented cohesion. However, in our case studies, no prejudices became apparent.

## TRUST

*Trust* can be defined as a belief held by one team member about another that (1) the behavior of the other can influence whether one gains or loses something, (2) one has no control over the other's behavior, and (3) that the other will behave in such a way that the gains will result (Deutsch, 1962; Johnson & Johnson, 1994). Researchers have treated trust as a multidimensional concept including honesty, truthfulness, loyalty, competence (i.e., technical or interpersonal skill and knowledge), and consistency (Butler & Cantrell, 1984; Schindler & Thomas, 1993).

Trust has received relatively little attention when compared with most of the other interpersonal process factors. Larson and LaFasto (1989) have reported that trust is positively related to several of the work process factors, including the amount of effort placed on doing the work and the talents applied to the work. Our data support their findings. Where trust was reported to be high, team members spent less energy worrying about what others were doing or thinking and more energy directly on doing the work. Furthermore, team members who trusted one another were more willing to ask for assistance or allow a more talented team member to perform tasks they were less skilled at doing. Consequently, the optimum talent was applied to doing the work.

When considering the SMWT's team design, Kouzes and Posner (1987) have reported that trust results in team members being more willing to consider alternative viewpoints during the decision-making process. The authors have also reported that high trust positively influences the team members' willingness to let others exercise influence over them. Our data support these observations. Where high trust was reported, team members were willing to offer alternative choices that were received by other team members in a constructive, nonthreatening way. Team members experiencing low trust tended to believe that the alternatives offered by others were designed to benefit only certain others, rather than the team as a whole. They also thought that those presenting alternatives had other ulterior purposes, such as punishing certain team members.

When considering team norms, trust has been found to affect the kinds of team norms that develop. For example, Larson and LaFasto (1989) have noted,

> The first team norm that's supported by trust is that members of the team must be willing to share information with each other, especially when that information is negative. If a team member is having problems figuring something out or making a decision, this is the kind of information that must be shared. Hiding negative information and not being willing to listen to negative information are norms that can be ruinous to team outcomes. (p. 91)

Our data support their findings. Trust appeared *to affect* the team's norms. Furthermore, we found that trust *was affected by* the team's norms. For example, in a high-performing, manufacturing SMWT, the six team members had been working together as a team for more than 5 years. Trust had become high among these people. This trust appeared to affect the development of team norms, such that open communications existed and included freely sharing mistakes and lack of knowledge.

In another example, trust appeared to be affected by the team's norms. In this case, trust was negatively affected where competition between team members was the norm. In a government SMWT we studied, it was the norm for an arrogant team member to display his superior knowledge and highlight the lack of knowledge of other team members. This norm destroyed any trust between this team member and those he insulted.

The environmental factor reported to have perhaps the largest association with trust is the information system. As noted above, without trust, the information system is likely to be inaccurate and incomplete. Kouzes and Posner (1987) have explained it this way:

> What happens when people do not trust each other? They will ignore, disguise, and distort facts, ideas, conclusions, and feelings that they believe will increase their vulnerability to others. Not surprisingly, the likelihood of misunderstanding and misinterpretation will increase. . . . When we encounter low-trust behavior from others, we in turn are generally hesitant to reveal

information to them and reject their attempts to influence us. . . . All of the behavior that follows from a lack of trust is deleterious to information exchange and to reciprocity of influence. (p. 147)

We likewise found that low trust negatively affected the information system, with the information shared among team members being distorted and inaccurate. Furthermore, we found the relationship between trust and the information system to be reciprocal; that is, to the extent that the information received from another was found to be inaccurate or distorted, it appeared to reduce the level of trust.

# 11

■

# Interpersonal Processes
# Between the Team and Others

■

The importance of the 6 Cs—communication, coordination, cooperation, collaboration, conflict, and cohesion—along with trust is not limited to interpersonal relationships among team members. Interpersonal relationships between the team and others within the organization, as well as between the team and those outside the organization, are also very important to the team's performance and have more recently begun to receive attention from theorists and researchers.

The SMWT often must interact with other teams and individuals within its organization. These teams and individuals may provide services, supplies, and resources to the SMWT, or they may be the SMWT's customers in the sense that they receive services and products that the SMWT produces. Likewise, the SMWT may deal directly with suppliers and customers outside its organization. Furthermore, the SMWT must interact with a variety of managers. These typically include those managers who are overseeing the SMWT, as well as other managers who can assist the SMWT. And there are sometimes individuals and organizations that provide assistance or support to the SMWT. This support can range from technical assistance provided by an engineer or lawyer outside the SMWT's organization to administrative help from the personnel department within the SMWT's organization.

Ancona and Caldwell (1992), in their study of a variety of teams, have organized these interpersonal relationships with others outside the team into ambassadorial activities, external task-coordination activities, and scouting activities. Each is considered below.

## AMBASSADORIAL ACTIVITIES

*Ambassadorial activities* include those that assist the team in interacting with its organization's power structure and, in particular, its immediate managers. These activities include promoting the team, securing resources, and requesting help. They rely primarily on effective communication and cooperation with managers and others outside the team.

An examination of our data shows that the high-performing teams routinely engaged in ambassadorial activities. For example, the team leader of a high-performing manufacturing team met routinely with the team's immediate manager to highlight positive statistics on the team's performance. Other team members participated in these ambassadorial activities by publishing a monthly team newsletter and charting team performance to highlight the team's successes and progress. These were shared with the manager and others who interacted with the team and were displayed prominently on a wall adjacent to the team's location. Such communications built a positive image of the team, which appeared to influence the managers' attitudes toward the team. Furthermore, when an opening for a new team member occurred, it was reported that the team received a higher than normal number of applications from other people within the organization. It was explained that the team's extremely positive image, enhanced by its ambassadorial activities, attracted people throughout the organization who were looking for a new position.

### The Interpersonal Process and Management

Interactions with management are of particular importance to the SMWT. Managers typically provide vital information to the team, including keeping the team informed of changing organizational policies and the organization's mission for the team. Managers working most closely with the SMWT are typically consultants to the team as well as evaluators of the team's performance. The SMWT may also have periodic contact with other managers who can provide assistance to the team. The interpersonal processes between managers and the SMWT can affect the team's work process, including the procedures and effort applied to the work; the environment surrounding the team, such as the resources available to the team; and the team's design, including the size of the team and its roles.

Perhaps the most important single interpersonal factor affecting the SMWT's relationship to management is communication. Good communication between the SMWT and managers was found to facilitate the accurate transfer of information to and from the team and management, which, in turn, directly affected the team's work process. It is typically managers who inform the team of its purpose and mission. When communication is poor, the team may misunderstand these. This can have a variety of negative results on the work process. For example, the team members may spend time on activities that do not address the team's purpose and, subsequently, effort is reduced on those activities that do achieve its purpose. The team may not seek out the training it needs, not realizing that it is needed, and, consequently, not apply all the talent needed to do the work. And the team may not apply the appropriate resources or procedures for accomplishing the objectives set out for it by management.

Good communication is necessary in cases where the team wants to influence management's definition of the SMWT's purpose and goals. For example, team members may have discovered new markets or a sellable variation of the team's existing product or service through its scouting activities. Good communication between the team and management is needed to convey these discoveries and clarify the advantages of altering or expanding the team's purpose and objectives, and the team's product or service. If the team is successful in convincing management of such changes, this will, in turn, affect the team's work process.

Likewise, the team may want to make major changes in how it carries out its work and needs management's approval to do so. Here again, good communication is needed to accurately convey information about the change. For example, the team will need to clearly define the change, provide a well-thought-out description of what the team will gain by implementing the change, explain how it fits the company's strategy, and describe the cost trade-offs, potential risks, and benefits to the change.

Finally, as noted above, ambassadorial activities are important for the SMWT to gain management support. These include efforts to communicate team strengths to convince management that the team's ideas and proposals should be seriously considered, to promote the team, and to secure resources for the team. Such activities require clear communications with management to be successful. (see also Burgelman, 1983; Dean, 1987; Dutton & Ashford, 1992).

An examination of our data shows that these activities and various means of communicating with management did appear to positively influence the manager's willingness to support the SMWT. For example, in the case of a high-performing manufacturing SMWT, the team's manager was willing to allow the team to take over the operation of several machines that another team had been operating, but not at an optimal level. Also, the manager approved the team's proposal to add a new member to the team. Thus, effective ambassadorial activities resulted in the team being able to alter its work process to accommodate new machines and its team design to add a new member.

Several researchers have reported that ambassadorial activities are not effective in the long run in influencing management, if the team does not perform at a high level. Our data also provide support for this conclusion. It was only the high-performing teams that were able to persuade management to follow team recommendations and preferences. The low-performing teams had little or no hard evidence that could be presented to management in an attempt to win management support for team initiatives. Furthermore, low-performing teams were more likely to be bogged down in more basic concerns, such as meeting customer demands, with little time left for ambassadorial activities. In low-performing teams, communications with management were more likely to involve defending and explaining the team's performance, rather than promoting the team's performance.

## EXTERNAL TASK-COORDINATION ACTIVITIES

*External task-coordination activities* refer to those coordination activities with others outside the team that assist the team in obtaining needed resources from suppliers, feedback on the team's performance from customers, and coordination with others outside the team that is necessary to successfully perform team tasks. We found that the high-performing teams successfully coordinated activities with others outside the team. The team leader was the focal point for these activities, although by no means the only person on the team involved. In the high-performing teams, all team members were responsible for coordinating activities with others outside the team, to the extent that their technical responsibilities within the team could be more effectively performed by such activities. For example, in a second high-performing manufacturing team, the team members who operated a particular machine coordinated their activities routinely with suppliers to be sure the machine would be in constant use. The team leader was typically informed of such coordination activities as they occurred, and the whole team was informed at least once a week during the team's weekly meeting.

An examination of a low-performing government SMWT, on the other hand, found a lack of effective task-coordination activities. One of the team members, who had been the supervisor of the team members before the team was established, routinely interacted with people outside the team and committed the team members to perform activities on specific days without the team members' knowledge or involvement. In this case, the coordination of tasks with people outside the team was poorly executed because the affected team members had not been involved in the decision-making process and, consequently, did not always carry out the commitments made. In a second case, a low-performing manufacturing SMWT was poorly coordinating its activities with an internal customer, another SMWT. As a result, the low-performing team was providing its internal customer with more units of certain products than were wanted. This lack of coordination with its customer resulted in a stockpile of products that became an unwanted expense to the organization.

## SCOUTING ACTIVITIES

*Scouting activities* refer to those that provide the team with access to information that can assist the team in better achieving its goals. Such information might include facts about new machines or tools related to the team's work, customer needs, supplier abilities to meet team needs, or new technical work that the organization is planning but has not yet assigned to a team.

A review of our data indicates that the high-performing teams spent more time on scouting activities. For example, a high-performing manufacturing team was found to be continually scouting for any new technical work that had not yet been assigned to a team. When the team learned of such new technical work, several team members would investigate the requirements of the work and whether the work could be fit into the team's schedule. The result of these activities was that when an existing team task was completed, such as the assembly of 5,000 missile parts, the team had new work to replace this finished work. Consequently, the team members rarely feared that the team would run out of work to do, once completing their current technical work; that is, they were less fearful that, once completing the team's current work, the team members would be released from the organization due to a lack of available work for them. These scouting activities required effective communication with others outside the team, as well as effective coordination of the work flow, as existing tasks were completed and new tasks were sought and obtained.

In another case, a high-performing nursing home team appeared to have difficulty successfully performing scouting activities, and this appeared to reduce the team's work process and performance. In this case, one of the team's responsibilities was maintaining the financial solvency of the nursing home. This required that the team continually scout the environment for existing sources of revenue and, in particular, for changes in government reimbursement rates related to health care and nursing homes. The difficulty in scouting occurred because the periodic changes in government reimbursement rates were difficult to predict. Consequently, the team was less able to determine which services would be most profitable to provide or even which would be reimbursed at all. This has become a common problem for the nursing home industry.

In sum, the SMWT typically has many interpersonal interactions that occur between the SMWT and those inside its organization, as well as between the SMWT and those outside its organization. These interpersonal processes can be organized into ambassadorial activities, external task-coordination activities, and scouting activities. Each group of activities is important to the team's work process and performance, as well as other team dimensions.

# PART IV

■                                                                    ■

## The Environment Surrounding the SMWT Within and Outside the Organization

■                                                                    ■

The environment surrounding the SMWT was found to have numerous effects on the team's performance through its influences on the team's work process, interpersonal process, design, and team member characteristics. We begin by focusing on the philosophy of the organization. High-performing SMWTs were located within environments that held philosophies and a culture conducive to SMWTs. They were located within environments that were specifically designed to advance and sustain SMWTs through a variety of systems, including those for rewarding employees, performance appraisal, education and training, and information exchange. Furthermore, the high-performing SMWTs were more likely to obtain support from managers, suppliers, customers, and the culture within which they operated. Other environmental factors associated with high-performing SMWTs were found outside the organization, including the market demands for the team's products or services, the development of new technologies, and the demographic, sociological, and cultural characteristics of the SMWT's surrounding area. The next nine chapters address these many environmental factors.

# 12

■

# The Organization's Philosophy, Culture, and Mission for the SMWTs

■

The highest-performing SMWTs were located within organizations that had developed a philosophy and culture that supported the use of *self-managed work teams* and had developed a clear mission for each of its SMWTs.

## THE PHILOSOPHY OF THE ORGANIZATION

The *organizational philosophy* is the body of stated beliefs and values that guide all aspects of the organization, such as how employees are to be managed and what factors are to be considered during the decision-making process. At one extreme, a traditional philosophy can be viewed as support- ing scientific management; that is, this organizational philosophy supports the belief that employees can be expected to place little value on their work and to be indifferent to the organization's needs and goals. It is believed that managers of the organization should be the decision makers and take a control-oriented approach. Employees are told what to do and are given no opportunity to participate in decision making. With this philosophy, a well-defined, hierarchical power structure is the norm. This philosophy supports McGregor's (1960) Theory X.

At the other extreme is a philosophy that supports high employee involvement. This philosophy believes that employees want to take responsibility for their work, desire the opportunity for personal development within their job, and want to help achieve organizational goals. It is believed that employees can be trusted to make important decisions about their work and that employee decision making will result in greater organizational performance (Lawler, 1986; Shonk, 1992). Employees are viewed as an integral part of the organization, and managers are accountable not only to those in higher positions but also to the employees they manage. This philosophy supports McGregor's (1960) Theory Y.

The SMWTs we studied were located within organizations that fell somewhere between these two extremes. Our data show that an organization's "official" philosophy did not necessarily reflect the beliefs and values actually held by management and the employees, and that the beliefs and values held by one part of the organization were not necessarily the same as those held by another. For example, in a manufacturing organization we studied, we found two high-performing SMWTs located in the same division and surrounded by beliefs and values that supported employee decision making. Within this same organization, we also studied two low-performing SMWTS, located in a different division of the organization and experiencing beliefs and values that were somewhat more traditional. The official philosophy of the manufacturing organization, as outlined by official publications and top management, was one of employee empowerment and involvement. However, it was the managers at all levels of the organization who determined the extent to which the official philosophy was the basis for how employees were managed and decisions made. Tjosvold (1986) has pointed out this discrepancy and its potential effects:

> If managers talk about common effort but reward competitors, and if they talk about trust but do not truly trust workers, then employees are apt to conclude that the corporate philosophy is comprised of empty words intended to confuse and perhaps exploit them. (p. 55)

## Organizational Philosophy and SMWT Performance

It was clear that the stated philosophy of the organization when practiced had large effects on the SMWT's work process and, in turn, performance. A philosophy that supported employee involvement was found to facilitate and encourage the development of organizational systems and supports that enhanced SMWT performance, including reward, training, and information systems. A high-involvement philosophy was found to allow for extensive employee decision making and to attract new employees who held values and beliefs that were conducive to the functioning of SMWTs. Furthermore, a high-involvement philosophy was found to encourage cooperation and cooperative conflict, which, in turn, had positive effects on the SMWT's work process and performance.

On the other hand, where the stated philosophy supported a more traditional work environment and this philosophy was practiced, the SMWT's performance was negatively affected. We found that in this environment, the SMWTs lacked support from the organizations' systems, including those related to rewards, training, and information exchange. The SMWTs lacked support from managers, and their team designs had problems that prevented the teams from making the best decisions possible. Furthermore, the interpersonal processes were more likely to include competitive conflict and less likely to encourage high levels of cooperation, as team members struggled among themselves over how to gain and maintain support from those outside the team.

Several of the government SMWTs we studied provide good examples of the effects that more traditional organizational philosophies can have on an SMWT's environment, design, team member characteristics, and, subsequently, the SMWT's work process and performance. The philosophy of the federal government agency, as expressed by official internal employee policy and practiced by its managers, was a belief that an individualistic work environment was most effective. The philosophy was that decision making is best when it occurs at the top levels of the management hierarchy. This philosophy was supported by the agency's existing civil service reward system—one that did not encourage teamwork. Similarly, the philosophy was supported by an education and training system that was designed to address individual needs and included relatively little focus on team building, collaborative decision making, cooperative conflict, or the like. Managers did not attempt to nurture or assist the SMWTs and, in fact, directed their efforts at undermining the teams.

Without a stated philosophy that supported employee involvement in decision making, the SMWTs lacked sufficient system supports and management supports. The SMWT members struggled to identify goals, interact among themselves, interact with those outside the team, and make decisions that would enhance the work process and performance. More specifically, when considering the work process, effort on the job was reduced to respond to management concerns. Furthermore, the most appropriate procedures identified by the team were not always used because management would not allow the teams to implement the work procedures they had selected.

When examining the influence of organizational philosophy on team member characteristics, we again found it to be large. Organizations that stated and practiced a participative management philosophy attempted to hire employees who had worked in an SMWT previously or had personalities, values, and interests that appeared to be conducive to a work team environment. For example, in one organization, we found that applicants were screened by placing them in a room and having them construct something from materials in the room. The applicants were observed through a one-way viewing mirror to judge how well they interacted and cooperated with others. Furthermore, we found that employees self-selected into organizations that held either an employee involvement or a traditional philosophy. Where the philosophy changed to employee involvement, some employees who preferred the traditional philosophy left the organization.

## THE CULTURE OF THE ORGANIZATION

*Organizational culture* can be defined as a set of basic assumptions and norms that guide employee behavior within the workplace, are learned by new employees, and evolve (Banner & Gagné, 1995; Sackmann, 1991). Varney (1989) has described culture as "a social energy that can move people to act" and "a hidden yet unifying theme that provides meaning, direction, and mobilization for the organization" (p. 128). Schein (1984) has provided a more complex but comprehensive definition of culture as

> the pattern of basic assumptions that a given group has invented, discovered, or developed in learning to cope with its problems of external adaptation and internal integration, and that have worked well enough to be considered valid, and, therefore, to be taught to new members as the correct way to perceive, think, and feel in relation to those problems. (p. 3)

The culture of the organization and the philosophy of the organization have been treated by some theorists as synonymous. However, the majority appear to treat organizational philosophy as an explicit set of values and beliefs that may or may not be practiced, whereas organizational culture is treated as an implicit set of assumptions and norms that are being applied by the existing employees. To the extent that the explicit philosophy is actually practiced, it may reflect the organizational culture. For example, in one organization we studied, the published philosophy stated that the employees' knowledge and abilities were the backbone of the organization, that employees could best be used within SMWTs, that managers should be "coaches, trainers, and coordinators," and that the employees should be responsible for traditional management roles within their teams, such as "work scheduling, training, quality control, material ordering, defect analysis" and so on. In one division of the organization, this stated philosophy was found to be practiced. The result was a culture where SMWTs and teamwork were highly respected by managers and employees alike. Team members had grown to assume that their teams could always expect to receive the supports they needed to perform at a high level. Thus, the existing culture within this division of the organization reflected the organizational philosophy—one that highly supported teams. However, in another division of the same organization, interviews with team members suggested that the stated philosophy was not practiced by managers, and the organizational culture of the division also did not reflect the stated philosophy. In this culture, team members were less likely to assume that management would support the team and that the team had the authority to make decisions related to the team's work. Thus, within this division, the explicit philosophy and implicit culture were different.

Researchers have studied culture at the organizational level as well as the existence of multiple cultures within the same organization (Hackman & Oldham, 1980; Polley & Van Dyne, 1994; Rose, 1988; Tjosvold, 1986). Rose (1988) has suggested that it is unlikely that an organization has a single culture. He has explained that the likelihood becomes less as the size of the organization becomes large and complex, new employees are brought in from outside the organization, and parts of the organization are dominated by differing professional and occupational affiliations.

Within the four organizations we studied (ranging in size from 70 to thousands of employees), we found that the cultures within which the SMWTs were operating were affecting the SMWTs' performance. For example, for one of the government SMWTs that we studied, the culture assumed that managers, not teams, were responsible for seeing that the work got done. This assumption was supported by the organization's history of managers evaluating the work of employees and by the performance evaluation and compensation systems being controlled by managers and based on individual, not team, performance. This culture was found to have negative effects on the performance of the two SMWTs studied within this organization. The teams struggled with managers for decision-making authority and with nonmanagement employees outside the teams, who chose to share information with managers rather than the teams.

On the other hand, the culture surrounding two SMWTs in a manufacturing organization was found to have positive effects on the performance of the SMWTs studied. This culture emphasized a cooperative interdependence among employees rather than competitiveness. The various environmental systems reflected a culture that supported teamwork. This included sharing information with teams, providing education and training to facilitate inter-personal processes and decision making within teams, and using perfor-mance evaluation and compensation systems that rewarded cooperation and teamwork rather than competition and individual performance. The culture, expressed through employee assumptions and norms, seemed to assume that teams were to be respected and helped whenever possible. We found that this culture appeared to have multiple positive effects on the SMWTs operating within it.

## Organizational Culture and SMWT Performance

As noted above, we found that an SMWT's performance was positively affected to the extent that the culture supported the SMWT. On the other hand, where the culture did not support SMWTs, the team's performance was reduced. The most common characteristics of a nonsupportive culture were when the culture assumed that managers should manage employees rather than employees managing themselves; assumed that financial, strategic, and other information should not be shared with nonmanagement employees; and assumed that performance evaluations should be based on how well an employee outperformed fellow employees, rather than on how a team of employees performed.

To the extent that the organizational cultures did not support the SMWT, the SMWT's work process was negatively affected. Team members appeared to be demotivated by an unsupportive culture and were found to spend less effort on the work, as team members took time to work out differences with those who were not cooperating with the team. Furthermore, obtaining all the resources needed by the team was difficult because those who had the resources were unwilling to provide them directly to the team. On the other hand, where the organizational culture supported the SMWT, it appeared to positively affect most team members' motivation and allowed them to put more effort directly on the work as less time was spent justifying requests and obtaining needed information and resources.

The SMWT's design characteristics were also affected. In an unsupportive organizational culture, the team sometimes had difficulty making decisions because it could not get all the relevant information it needed. Furthermore, managers often ignored the teams' decisions where management action or approval was needed. The opposite was found to exist where the organiza-tional culture supported the SMWT. These teams found it much easier to obtain all the information they needed, to obtain ancillary assistance when needed, to work overtime with pay if necessary, and to obtain additional employees to assist the team when the workload was beyond their abilities to meet deadlines.

In those organizations with an unsupportive culture, the SMWTs' interpersonal processes between the team and those outside the team were poor—those outside the team did not adhere to the authority given to the team. Within these teams, however, the interpersonal processes appeared to be somewhat positively affected, as the team members developed an "us versus them" perspective that drew the team members closer together. We qualify this with "somewhat" because we also found that, at times, when confronted by managers and others outside the SMWT, team members had difficulty agreeing on the appropriate action to take or chose to blame one another.

Finally, when the organizational culture did not support teams, it was found that support from various environmental systems was also difficult to obtain. This lack of environmental supports, such as information sharing, rewarding team performance, and providing training that supports team roles, negatively affected the team's ability to make the best decisions possible and to apply the most appropriate knowledge and skills to the work, and it encouraged team members to be concerned about their individual performance rather than the team's performance.

## THE MISSION OF THE SMWT

A *mission* is a statement of purpose and objectives. This is uniquely different from the more specific goals that are established by the SMWT to accomplish the mission. The mission provides boundaries—in terms of constraints on the team as well as areas of autonomy. A clear mission clarifies any constraints such as budget limitations, delivery schedules, quality standards, legal restrictions, or technical requirements (Myers, 1991; Shonk, 1992). It also clarifies the areas in which the team has autonomy, such as assigning tasks and determining training needs. Hackman and Walton (1986) as well as Orsburn et al. (1990) have found that a clear sense of what is expected, and why it is important, was a prerequisite condition for high team performance. Orsburn et al. (1990) have explained that establishing clear boundaries provides "an operational and psychological anchor" for teams as well as managers. We also found that without these clear boundaries, the SMWT had difficulty establishing realistic, measurable goals. This has also been reported by Myers (1991) and Katzenbach and Smith (1993a).

A variety of researchers and consultants have concluded that, whereas it is important that the organization specify the SMWT's mission, the details for achieving the mission should *not* be completely specified. This reserves authority for the team members to develop realistic, measurable goals.

Hackman and Walton (1986) have explained that this allows the team members to tailor the objectives to fit with the team members' own inclinations. Furthermore, some theorists have proposed that, when management gives the SMWT specific mission goals, this clearly risks lowering the motivation of team members because they will react negatively to being told what to do. Waterman (1987) as well as Manz and Sims (1989) have summarized these views well by highlighting the importance of simultaneously (1) providing direction to the team in the form of a team mission and (2) empowering the team by allowing it to establish measurable, engaging goals based on the mission.

Our case studies support this conclusion—those SMWTs with a clear mission were found to have higher performance than those with a less than clear mission. A manager of a high-performing SMWT explained the importance of the SMWT mission in a memorandum to a subordinate manager this way:

> I'm talking about the *mission* for the team, the very purposes for having the team. Knowing this mission isn't optional, it is essential. It seems intuitive that people would know the purposes for their team's existence, but unfortunately, it is often not clear. Could we really expect greatness from any group of people, if they don't clearly understand their purposes for existing? . . . The key is to engage the team in thinking through the mission, and making sure it comprehends the business objectives of the group, and that it is aligned with the mission of the project. (Meeker, 1993, p. 1)

### A Clear, Engaging Mission and Team Performance

One of the government SMWTs we studied lacked a clear, engaging mission. The regional director of the government agency had decided to give the SMWT concept a try because it was apparently being used successfully by many other organizations. Prior to establishing the SMWT, the agency developed a one-page description of the SMWT's mission and how it would fit within the broader organization. However, the mission statement did not establish boundaries for the SMWT, such as constraints and areas of autonomy. Consequently, the team found it difficult to establish specific goals and performance measures. As the team attempted to do so, it often became entangled in heated debates with first-line managers over the team's level of autonomy. These heated discussions resulted in the team never establishing clear goals and performance measures and, subsequently, resulted in team members often being unsure of how their time could be best spent.

The lack of a clear, engaging mission had a variety of negative effects on team design characteristics, such as the team's decision-making processes and the team's selection of appropriate work procedures. For example, team decisions did not always consider what impact the decision would have on the team's performance because there were no clear goals or performance measures. Likewise, the most appropriate procedures for doing the work could only be determined by having a clear understanding of specific team goals, and these were largely missing.

Similar findings have been reported by Orsburn et al. (1990), Becker-Reems (1994), Buchholz, Roth, and Hess (1987), and Zander (1994). Zander has concluded that

> if a group's objectives provide little guidance, members' ideas about the group's activities will probably not fit together well, as each person favors a kind of activity that satisfies his or her own personal interests. Members may settle such disagreements by bargaining, and the final choice is often weighted with activities that meet members' private purposes; the group's needs are given less weight. (p. 40)

Our data support these conclusions.

A lack of measurable goals had negative effects on the team's work process. Team members were found spending large amounts of time trying to determine what their goals were instead of focusing their efforts on the work itself. On the other hand, an engaging mission, highlighting the importance of the work, was found to be a motivator and, subsequently, a positive influence on effort. A clear, engaging mission helped team members to understand the reasons for their efforts and the effects they could have by applying their efforts to the work.

Lack of a clear, engaging mission was further found to have negative effects on interpersonal processes within the team. Interviews with team members of a government SMWT revealed that, because the team's mission was unclear, team members often had difficulty seeing the connection between the team's decisions and the team's goals. Consequently, when team members sought reasons for their team's decisions, they sometimes felt that the decisions made were for someone's personal gain or to take advantage of someone on the team. Again, these perceptions were found to exist more often when team members had difficulty seeing the connection between the team decision and the team's goals. And, it was particularly difficult for team members to see such a connection when the team's mission and subsequent goals were unclear.

# 13

■

# Performance Measurement
Appraisal and Assessment Systems

■

Organizations have a variety of systems for supporting SMWTs as they perform their work. Each system can take a variety of forms. Organizations practicing a high-involvement philosophy tend to use certain forms, whereas those practicing a more traditional organizational philosophy tend to use others. For example, an organization with a high-involvement philosophy is likely to have a performance measurement system that emphasizes the performance of the team rather than the individual. Likewise, such an organization can be expected to provide meaningful rewards for team performance rather than, or in addition to, individual performance. Performance appraisal and assessment systems, including a review of tools for assessing team performance, are discussed in this chapter. Team-based reward systems are reviewed in the following chapter.

## AN OVERVIEW OF PERFORMANCE
## APPRAISAL AND ASSESSMENT SYSTEMS

We need to differentiate some commonly used terms at the outset. Traditionally, *performance appraisals* are assessments of *individuals,* typically conducted by supervisory personnel on an infrequent basis, such as every 6 months or yearly. Some authors have retained the term and talked about how performance appraisals can or need to be adapted to fit team circumstances. Others, notably Deming (1982, 1986), have criticized the traditional individual appraisals so much that the term itself has acquired a negative connotation in the eyes of many. On the other hand, *performance assessment* is a term often used to refer to collections of various measures in domains such as quality, efficiency, or productivity that are taken more regularly for an SMWT or for a larger administrative unit such as an entire plant. We will subsume both of these types of measurement under the generic heading of *performance measurement.* Both kinds of measurement, in some form, are currently used by organizations to assess team and individual progress.

### The Traditional Performance Appraisal

Performance appraisal systems evolved when traditional hierarchical management structures were dominant. This meant that, typically, a supervisor or manager evaluated subordinates on an individual basis. Performance appraisals can serve many purposes. According to Scholtes (1987), traditional performance appraisals have been used to serve too many purposes. For example, they could be used to identify candidates for promotion and as a basis for salary increases or bonus pay. They could also provide feedback to the employees regarding their performance in the review period and give them some direction. If skill deficits were identified, areas for training could be suggested. The performance appraisal also provided the opportunity for recognition for outstanding performance. It also enabled corporations to meet various Equal Employment Opportunity Commission (EEOC) guidelines regarding the need for documentation in promotion and termination decisions. In some limited sense, although perhaps the only sense in some organizations, the appraisal was a channel for management–employee communication.

Performance appraisals typically include some standard or goal, a performance period during which a manager presumably monitors employee performance, and a performance review and rating of the employee on various dimensions thought to be critical to the standard or goal. However, beginning with Deming (1982, 1986), many authors (e.g., Hitchcock & Willard, 1995; Scholtes, 1987) have identified major problems with traditional performance appraisals, especially when used in organizations employing SMWTs. First, the focus on appraising the individual tends to view individuals apart from the systems and groups in which they work. This emphasis implicitly assumes that it is individual effort and skills that make up the keys to job success. Obviously, in SMWTs, successful performance is highly interdependent on a variety of factors and dimensions. Furthermore, Deming argued that the majority of variance in performance was due to systems, not to attributes of the individual. Many performance appraisals devolve into personality assessments instead of retaining their focus on job accomplishments. An appraisal of individual personality attributes tells little about how the system and job processes are functioning.

Second, appraisals conducted by managers assume that managers *can* competently review the performance of the many individuals who work under them. As Hitchcock and Willard (1995) pointed out, managers may lack the proper data to make such judgments, or they may lack the expertise because they don't know the details of what employees actually do in their jobs. Also, manager-based appraisals assume implicitly that managers are objective and fair in their data-gathering and interpreting activities. However, there are a number of problems with this assumption. Managers may be biased toward certain employees for a number of reasons. Like all people, when asked to recall relevant information about individuals in evaluating them, managers may suffer from the many problems associated with long-term recall (e.g., recency or primacy effects, halo effects, recalling only salient episodes rather than long-term patterns of employee performance). In addition, some studies have shown that people fail to take into account situational constraints (i.e., factors affecting performance beyond the control of the employee) when rating performance (Freeman, 1996). This means that managers may downgrade an individual's performance rating despite the fact that the individual was doing the best he or she could given certain constraints, such as poor equipment or a shortage of resources.

In our study, we interviewed several team members who had been appraised by a manager and described their appraisal as unfair. In these cases, they felt that their appraisal was lower than some others on their team simply because they had made less of an effort to be "visible" to the manager. When we mentioned this to other team members, they typically agreed. Even the manager admitted that it was probably true to some extent.

A third major problem with performance appraisals is that this kind of manager–employee review encourages the traditional view of the organization as a hierarchical structure, with the omnipotent manager in charge and responsible for all employee performance. In SMWTs, the nature of management–team interactions should support the new, less hierarchical, less paternalistic structure. Teams should be encouraged to hold themselves accountable for reviewing their own performance, therefore opening the possibility of very nontraditional measurements such as peer appraisals.

Given this mismatch of traditional performance appraisals with the new team environment, what kinds of performance measurement seem best suited for SMWTs? Many organizations establish systems to assess two areas of performance: team development and team performance.

## ASSESSING THE SMWT'S DEVELOPMENT

Functioning well as a team is not something people automatically know how to do after forming a work team. Team members have to learn many new behaviors and skills in order for them to develop into a high-performing team. Many organizations make the transition to SMWTs in stages, with teams expected to achieve certain levels of progress in interpersonal and work processes at each stage before moving on to the next. This progress commonly focuses on interpersonal processes such as cooperation, coordination, participation by team members in team meetings, and interpersonal skill development in areas such as listening and conflict resolution. Less often considered is the work process, for example, the amount of effort applied directly to the work, the knowledge and skill applied to the work, and the appropriateness of the procedures used.

Management needs to measure team development in some way for several reasons. First, managers have to know when a team is ready to take more responsibility for tasks formerly done by a supervisor or first-line manager. For example, management would want to know whether a team gets along well enough with each other and has a technical understanding of work flow in the whole organization to be able to schedule its own work for the next week or for an upcoming project. Second, management needs to have information about team development to help the team decide what kind of training it needs to move on to the next stage of team development. Third, team development measures can serve as goals and standards for new teams so that they know what kinds of social and technical skills they are expected to learn and employ in their new roles as team members.

Monitoring team development is critical in its initial phases. During this period, small trouble areas can quickly lead to major dysfunctions if they are not addressed early. We observed a number of problems caused by failure to monitor team development. For example, a low-performing government team was in serious trouble less than a year after it had begun. In a key area, leadership, the team had never been able to make the transition from the former supervisor-based leadership to more team-based leadership. This was due in part to upper management's bypassing of the elected team leader when management wished to communicate to the team. Because the team was not developing its own distinct team leadership, many team members felt that the whole team idea was not working well.

A variety of team development measures have been proposed and used. Some are rating instruments that team members fill out on their team as a whole or on themselves. Becker-Reems (1994) proposed a team assessment that helps teams identify areas for improvement by rating how often key behaviors occur or essential conditions exist in each of the following categories: goals (e.g., goal clarity, accomplishment), communication (e.g., effectiveness in identifying and handling problems, maintaining a focus on work), working together (e.g., good decision-making processes, valuing differences on the team), leadership (e.g., sharing of leadership, encouraging participation), and meetings (e.g., using an agenda, accomplishing the purpose of the meeting). Becker-Reems also proposed a version of the team assessment that individual team members could use to gauge their own contribution to these important team characteristics.

Other team development measures involve judgments of team progress by people from outside the team, or even by customers who have frequent contact with the team. One manufacturing organization in our SMWT network had team progress certified by review of the team's coach. The coach checked off items making up four stages, as teams exhibited them. Stage 1 focused on interpersonal processes such as listening and participating. Stage 2 focused on meeting performance goals and understanding work processes. Stage 3 checked for whether the team had defined and obtained its training needs. Stage 4 was attained when the team assumed its own administration over budgeting and work scheduling. Stage 5 required that teams do their own evaluations and hiring/firing and handle other discipline issues. The coach's review counted as 60% of the overall review, with the remaining 40% coming from the team's impression of its progress. However, this system was modified because the organization's human resources personnel felt that the SMWTs were striving too hard just to "get their ticket punched" for each stage. Consequently, teams are now required to hold at each stage for a minimum of 2 months to ensure reliable performance of that stage's activities. The certification has also become less of a formal process, and plans are under way to have more of the judgment of team progress made by the team itself instead of by the team coach.

In another manufacturing organization, measures of team development are tied to an award system. Teams can apply for an excellence award by filling out a self-assessment and requesting a review. The explicitly stated purpose of the award is to communicate what elements are necessary for high-performing teams and to recognize such teams when they exist so they can serve as role models for others. Importantly, the award application also states a "nonpurpose": The award should not foster inter-team competition, and teams should not devote so much time to the application that they do not meet customer needs. Any teams that meet the criteria win the award; therefore, the risk of destructive competition is minimized because one team's success does not prevent any other teams from also winning.

In this case, the 50-item self-assessment asks how often the team exhibits critical team behaviors with respect to a number of domains, including goal setting and achievement, improvement of work procedures, training, communication, and commitment. The team is also expected to supply evidence of customer satisfaction as part of the application. A review team composed of three to five people from other teams visits the applicant team during team meetings and in the work area to give an opinion of the team's development. If this external judgment concurs with the team's self-assessment, the team is eligible to win an award, depending on the points earned by the two reviews. Three levels of award are available, with different cash awards (to be spent on things for the team or work area, not on individual compensation), a tangible symbol of their achievement of their choosing such as a pin, and recognition in the site newspaper. The team's classification as an award winner in one of the three levels does play a role in later determinations of team bonus compensation along with other factors. This is discussed further in our section on reward systems. The fact that this organization tied team development to awards meant that teams then had strong incentives to measure their progress and continue to develop. Unlike the previous organization, which decided to make this less of a formal system, this latter organization made it formal, which required more overhead in time and resources to verify team progress and administer the award system. Nevertheless, this organization felt that the benefits of this formal team development system outweighed the costs associated with it.

## APPRAISING TEAM MEMBER PERFORMANCE

In addition to team development measures, some organizations desire some method of measuring the development or contribution of individual team members. Because this was what supervisors did with traditional performance appraisals in nonteam environments, it is worth examining the need for a formal system of individual appraisal in team environments. Are the benefits derived from individual appraisal and feedback worth the inevitable time and effort the team will have to devote to such a formal system?

The answer probably depends on a number of factors about team development, as well as organizational factors. Imagine the following scenario. Team members find their work interesting and challenging. They get feedback about their success automatically from obvious signs of accomplishment built into the work task, and their peers on the team provide recognition for their success in an informal manner on a regular basis. The team is mature, smooth-running, and experienced and efficient in completing the tasks that compose its mission. The team monitors its own performance with a rigorous measurement system. The organization provides decent base pay, with variable pay available for accomplishing team production goals. Its product line is stable, and turnover is fairly low. In this rather ideal circumstance, a formal system for individual appraisals probably would not be necessary. This suggests that organizations should examine the need for individual appraisals in their teams before they automatically install them.

Under what conditions would formal individual appraisals be worthwhile? The scenario above suggests several factors:

■ When team members do not provide regular informal feedback to each other on a regular basis. This might be likely when communication skills are low, or there are interpersonal problems causing people to avoid talking to each other. It can also occur when teams are composed of people who don't see each other often, as can occur when they work in different locations, on different shifts, or have very different responsibilities.

■ When teams are immature or there is high turnover. This makes it likely that team members have not had time to learn the interpersonal skills necessary to work together on a daily basis.

■ When the nature of the work changes dramatically. New products may require new ways of interacting or new work procedures. This means that new training needs may arise or that more variation will occur in the work (some of which may not be acceptable, and some of which should be recognized as outstanding).

These conditions change as teams mature or as the rest of the organization changes, so organizations should periodically reevaluate the need for implementing or discontinuing any formal system for team member appraisals.

### Peer Appraisals

When organizations use individual appraisals, the most popular form is a peer appraisal. Team members are in the best position to judge other individuals on the team because of their more frequent interactions in the work area and in team meetings. Other management or support personnel (team coaches) probably have fewer interactions with individual team members, and their judgments of effort or contribution to team accomplishments might therefore be biased by their limited sample of performance. Peer appraisals also help to empower teams because they are another management responsibility the team can assume with the aid of some guidelines and a good appraisal system (Yeatts, Hipskind, & Barnes, 1994).

Transitioning from a traditional employee performance appraisal conducted by a supervisor to a team-based peer appraisal is not simple. In many cases, pay raises and promotion opportunities were related to the traditional performance appraisals, so the relationship between the new peer appraisals and such issues will have to be addressed in the planning stages. Teams should be at a sufficient level of development that team members are knowledgeable of what the job requirements are that define being a successful team member, and they should be comfortable appraising each other. These latter requirements are often hard to achieve early in the team's development, so some organizations have continued to use manager-conducted individual appraisals until teams are ready to use a peer appraisal system (Yeatts et al., 1994).

Many methods have been proposed and used for conducting peer appraisals. Most focus on the individual's technical skills, such as performing their job tasks accurately and efficiently, administrative skills such as paperwork or area responsibilities on the team, essential interpersonal skills such as cooperation and communication, and decision-making and problem-solving skills.

Orsburn et al. (1990) have outlined a method for conducting peer appraisals in teams. In their method, each team member is evaluated by two team members, one of his or her choosing and one chosen by the rest of the team. However, the two reviewers solicit input from other team members in developing their judgments. Each team member negotiates with reviewers a personal performance plan that is compatible with the team's performance goals. At the annual review period, the employee's accomplishments are judged relative to the performance plan. The reviewers write their judgments, and the individual writes a self-assessment according to the same criteria. In each of the technical, administrative, and interpersonal skill areas, the individual and the reviewers identify strengths and weaknesses (areas for improvement). The reviewers meet with the individual, and they discuss the appraisal and make any modifications or suggestions as they agree. Plans for next year are also negotiated at this time.

An examination of our case studies showed that three SMWTs were using peer appraisals, and all were high-performing teams. In one organization, teams were permitted to devise their own methods for conducting peer appraisals. They used the same general criteria as advocated by Orsburn et al. (1990), but some teams had everyone on the team review each member in a round-robin, marathon meeting, whereas other teams had team members write their reviews outside of a team meeting so that they could be collated by one person and presented at the team meeting designated for peer appraisals. The second method appeared to be the preferred technique after some experience with the marathon meetings.

It was reported by many team members that the peer appraisal process was somewhat intimidating at first. Team members felt very uncomfortable focusing on each individual, although most team members felt it was an extremely useful activity, especially after they had reduced the effort involved with a more efficient review procedure. Team members reported that it helped build a sense of team cohesion. Even after several years of conducting peer appraisals, many team members said the one thing they disliked the most was having to give negative feedback to their peers as part of the process to identify weaknesses and opportunities for improvement. This had led them to focus more on giving positive feedback on strengths, which is actually a desirable focus. If a team member had such severe weaknesses that his or her performance threatened the team's success, team members felt that they could confront the person, but with less severe issues, the awkwardness of focusing on the negatives of a peer made them avoid this topic. Despite the effort involved and the occasional discomfort, most team members felt the peer appraisal system was a superior replacement for the traditional supervisor-conducted performance appraisal.

From our observations of the teams using peer appraisals, the relationship between peer appraisals and monetary compensation lingers as a point of controversy. Orsburn et al. (1990) have reported that in some organizations the peer appraisal is seen as a tool for "local" feedback and personal development. There is no tie to money because it is believed that the tie-in has the undesirable effect of inhibiting free discussions of individuals by peers. This view was supported by our data. Team members told us that they would find it more difficult to point out a teammate's shortcomings if this might mean a smaller pay increase for the teammate. On the other hand, our data also provided support for providing a link between peer appraisals and pay. Some team members told us that they saw little point in going through the peer appraisal process, or at least in taking it seriously, if it was not linked to compensation in some way. These team members were in the minority. However, when there are team members with this perspective, it suggests that the peer appraisals will be ineffective without a tie-in to pay.

Where organizations provide monetary bonuses to teams for team accomplishments, or as part of a larger gainsharing program, mature teams are often allowed to decide how they want to divide up the bonus money among themselves. In one organization we studied, some teams decided to give equal shares to all team members. However, at least one other team divided the money based on a majority view of the contributions toward team goals of individual team members. In this case, information from the peer appraisals was used as a criterion for dividing up the bonus money. In any environment in which teams conduct peer appraisals and can decide for themselves how to divide up team bonus money, it would seem unlikely that team members would avoid using peer appraisal data, either implicitly or explicitly, to help them decide how money is divided among team members. Therefore, in this circumstance, there is a link between peer appraisals and compensation, even though it might not be formalized. It is too early yet to tell whether this link to money has affected the peer appraisal process in a positive or negative way, but the interesting point is that such a link is inevitable in this circumstance, unless teams decide on a rule of sharing team bonus money equally.

## ASSESSING SMWT PERFORMANCE

Performance assessment focuses on those measures that provide data on how well the team is accomplishing its primary mission. The emphasis is on *value-added* results or processes and, in some circumstances, critical behaviors necessary to achieve those results. *Added value* refers to something the team has done that transforms the product or service in a meaningful way, one that the team's customers consider valuable. For example, deburring and painting a part may be essential to improve the fit and finish in a given manufacturing sequence, and thus it adds value; moving a box of parts from one aisle of a warehouse to another aisle may not add any value for a customer. *Results* are what is left behind when work is done; they are distinct from activities or behaviors (Daniels, 1989; Gilbert, 1978; Zigon, 1995). Examples of results might include parts produced by a manufacturing cell team or the answers given to customers calling a customer service unit of an organization.

*Process-based measures* are necessary to provide information about how efficiently a team is accomplishing its duties. For example, a common process measure in manufacturing is cycle time, which includes the time to perform the value-added step of processing the product, together with the time for non-value-added steps of transporting the product through the plant, waiting to process it, setting up the machines that will process the part, and storing the part before it reaches the next *downstream* internal customer (Maskell, 1991). Process measures are subject to overuse in situations where clear accomplishments have not been specified. Sometimes teams can focus on process measures, such as time spent in work-related activities (labor hours devoted to a task, or hours of training attended), while neglecting to measure the value-added results of that activity. Process measures blend well with results measures to give a comprehensive picture of performance; either results or process measures by themselves are incomplete.

Sometimes teams may need to measure important performance-related behaviors, such as how often members of a customer service team greet customers with a smile, because the behaviors are an important component of a service interaction. In other cases, key behaviors occur more often than the results of such activities, which may be too delayed or too infrequent to measure for practical effect. A good example is the area of safety. Behaving safely around dangerous equipment can be measured directly and frequently, allowing team members to correct dangerous habits before they lead to infrequent but serious accidents (McSween, 1995). In this case, results measures such as the number of lost-time accidents may be inadequate for gauging how often people are putting themselves at risk on the job.

Usually, performance assessments are defined with respect to a team's mission and its more specific goals. Tying the assessments to the mission and goals is designed to prevent irrelevant measures from being used, but performance measures need to be reevaluated periodically to maintain this relationship. Missions may emphasize different concerns over time. Furthermore, measurement practices may drift to the point where the SMWT uses measures that are easy to obtain, even though there are other measures much more accurate but harder to obtain.

A good example of this was found in a low-performing government SMWT that we studied. This SMWT used financial measures of success, which, although widely used in other offices of the organization, inflated their perception of success because of some biases built into the measures. More specifically, the team used sales metrics that measured dollar volume of sales. However, the team sold higher-priced items than other teams to which it compared itself. Consequently, a review of the team's actual dollar volumes gave a distorted picture of the team's performance when it was compared with these others.

A key characteristic of performance assessment measures is that they should reflect things the team can control to some extent; the team must be able to affect what is measured. Financial measures are especially likely to fail this criterion. The wrong financial measures, such as holding a team responsible for profitability in a circumstance where the price of raw materials is escalating and beyond their control, can induce frustration or feelings of helplessness on the part of team members unable to effect the metric in a positive manner.

It is important for SMWT performance to be measured from the team's very beginning. Having clear performance measures from the outset helps keep the team focused on what the team is supposed to facilitate—accomplishing its mission and specific goals as effectively and efficiently as possible. Without a clear set of measures for key results, teams have no basis for judging the effectiveness of suggestions they might propose, such as a change in the work process, or a change in the scheduling of projects or workload. Competitive conflict may develop around issues such as work assignments, and the bickering may continue if there is no bottom-line criterion for deciding how well certain people accomplish certain work duties. In our case studies, one of the major causes of competitive conflict as well as low cohesion, cooperation, and communication appeared to be the absence of valid performance measures to keep everyone focused on the team's goals. It appeared that, without performance data to look at in team meetings, people in these teams started looking at each other, and they often found something annoying or threatening about a team member that distracted them from generating effective team solutions and work processes.

In sum, it is important, from the team's very beginning, to clarify team performance measures, as well as team development measures. Although at start-up more of the measurement emphasis may be on team development measures to ensure that the interpersonal processes are maturing and that individuals are learning to function well within the team, team performance measures should increase in importance the longer teams have been in place. In some organizations, product line and employee turnover may be so stable that many team development measures eventually become unnecessary. At this point, the return on the heavy investment put into developing teams should be manifest in the team performance measures.

## Performance Assessment Categories and Tools

Team performance measurement systems always include multiple measures. These measures may be grouped into categories that include quality, quantity, timeliness, financial, and customer satisfaction measures. Several authors (Maskell, 1991; Zigon, 1995) have stressed the importance of avoiding sole reliance on financial measures, which are often difficult to understand and relate to one's own work. Kaplan and Norton (1996) have advocated what they call a "balanced scorecard" approach; one that includes efficiency, customer satisfaction, and employee development in addition to financial measures for a more thorough measurement system. The business knowledge of team members should be taken into account in deciding the degree to which financial measures are used. Many organizations provide training in the financial aspects of the organization, either because they hope to broaden the employee's understanding of the entire operation or because such knowledge is essential when certain compensation systems (e.g., gain-sharing, profit sharing) are used. Therefore, some team members may be quite sophisticated in understanding financial measures and what variables affect them, whereas others with less business knowledge may need such training before they can relate to financial measures readily.

### The Oregon Productivity Matrix

Various measurement tools have been proposed for tracking multiple performance goals. Sink and Tuttle (1989) and Meyer (1994) described tools similar in appearance to a dashboard, with clusters of related measures grouped together much like an instrument panel in a car or airplane. In two high-performing SMWTs that we studied, a tool known as the Oregon Productivity Matrix was being used for team assessment. We have seen this tool, originally developed by the Oregon Productivity Center (1986) at Oregon State University, used by other teams as well. It is referred to as an OPM, or as a performance matrix (Daniels, 1989). Currently, there are several different versions in use. However, all of the versions contain the following basic elements, which make the matrix a useful measurement tool:

1. Multiple measurement categories (e.g., productivity, absenteeism)
2. Baseline or current performance level for each category
3. A goal level for each category to be achieved over a specified period (e.g., 4 weeks) with incremental subgoals
4. Weights to indicate relative importance of individual categories
5. Performance subscores for individual categories over the specified period
6. An overall performance score for all categories after applying the weights

The matrix displays individual categories and their data over the specified period and also standardizes the various measures so that they yield comparable scores. This permits users to track progress and obtain feedback on overall performance, as well as providing the ability to check the details of particular categories. The OPM has a track record of successful use in manufacturing, but it can be adapted easily for measuring performance in a service setting or any environment in which teams wish to track multiple categories. In our two case studies using the OPM, each team had its own matrix, and the broader administrative unit they were within had a compat-

| For: July | Schedule | Schedule | Cost | Quality | Quality | Customer Satisfaction |
|---|---|---|---|---|---|---|
| Score | Days Cycle | Percentage On Time Shipments | Labor Cost | DPMO | Scrap $/Hour | Survey (Last 3 Months) |
| 10 GOAL | 7.5 | 90 | $35.75 | 100 | 0.50 | 95% |
| 9 | 7.75 | 89.7 | $35.80 | 106 | 0.55 | 94% |
| 8 | 8 | 89.4 | $35.85 | 113 | 0.60 | 93% |
| 7 | 8.25 | 89 | $35.90 | 120 | 0.65 | 91% |
| 6 | 8.75 | 88.6 | $36.00 | 127 | 0.70 | 89% |
| 5 | 9.5 | 88 | $36.15 | 134 | 0.75 | 87% |
| 4 | 11 | 86 | $36.30 | 140 | 0.80 | 85% |
| 3 BASE | 13 | 85 | $36.50 | 147 | 0.85 | 82% |
| 2 | 14 | 84 | $37.00 | 155 | 0.90 | 80% |
| 1 | 15 | 83 | $37.50 | 162 | 0.95 | 78% |
| 0 | 16 | 80 | $38.00 | 170 | 1.00 | 75% |
| **ACTUAL** | 8.1 | 87 | $35.84 | 125 | 0.88 | 89% |
| **WEIGHT** | 20% | 10 | 20% | 25% | 15% | 10% |
| **VALUE** (Score X Weight) | 140 | 40 | 160 | 150 | 30 | 60 |
| **Summary GOAL** | 200 | 100 | 200 | 250 | 150 | 100 |
| **ACTUAL** | 140 | 40 | 160 | 150 | 30 | 60 |
| | | | | | **TOTAL** | **580/1000** |

**Figure 13.1.** Oregon Productivity Matrix Example

ible matrix appropriate for measuring unitwide performance. Different teams may include different particular categories that fit their work, but they should be aligned with the measures that matter the most to the broader business unit.

A generic example, similar to those we have seen in use in team-based manufacturing organizations, is shown in Figure 13.1. The top two rows show the measurement categories and the measures picked by our hypothetical team to best assess its performance. Categories include schedule, cost, quality, and customer satisfaction. Each category has a specific measure or measures. For example, the category *schedule* is measured as the *days cycle* and *percentage of on-time shipments.* Customer satisfaction is measured by an index taken from a quarterly survey. Each measure is assigned a weight, a percentage, to indicate its importance relative to the other measures. Weights become multipliers of scores. The left-hand column shows scores ranging from 0 to 10, with 3 as baseline level (the team's performance level at the beginning of measurement) and 10 as goal-level performance in each of the six measures. The goal levels may reflect a long-term best-possible performance, or they may reflect attainable medium-range goals. Each number in a cell below the goal level indicates a subgoal, so that progress can be easily observed.

Actual performance on each measure for the review period (in this case, for the month of July) is shown in the row of the same name; those levels fall in the highlighted cells in the 0 to 10 range. For example, the actual percentage of on-time shipments for July was 87%, which falls in the cell marked 86% (because that cell is actually 86% to 87.9%). That level gets a score of 4, which is then multiplied by the weight of 10 for that measure to yield a value of 40 for this review period. Goal-level performance of 90% would have yielded a value of 100 points for that measure. When the points across all of the measures for July performance are summed, the matrix shows 580 out of 1,000 possible points.

Despite the fact that the matrix appears to be a mass of numbers at first glance, the use of highlighting to indicate current performance levels makes the matrix a source of visual feedback. Most users of the matrix prefer to graph point totals across successive review periods for tracking progress. The overall point totals may be graphed, as well as point levels for each of the individual measures, to track the details of performance. The matrix is flexible enough to permit reassignment of weights if priorities change. Customer feedback may indicate that on-time shipments are more important now than they were 6 months ago, so that measure might be assigned a larger relative weight. Graphs of point totals would have to indicate that weights were changed, so that jumps in point totals (downward or upward) due to the new multipliers could not be confused with actual performance changes.

## FEEDBACK AND PERFORMANCE MEASUREMENT

Regardless of the particular measurement tool chosen, any performance measurement system should supply feedback and aid problem-solving activities of teams. A regular stream of performance data is the foundation for all performance improvement activities. Without it, it is impossible to be precise in gauging the impact of any performance interventions (e.g., process improvements, bonus pay). The feedback provided by examining frequently updated performance data has been shown to be an effective performance improvement device itself, in decades of empirical studies that have directly measured performance with objective measures (Balcazar, Hopkins, & Suarez, 1986; Nordstrom, Lorenzi, & Hall, 1990; Prue & Fairbank, 1981). Our data are no exception. All but one of the high-performing teams had clear, objective measures, whereas the low-performing teams were less likely to have these. Timely feedback about performance relative to clear and acceptable goals is almost universally recommended by performance-oriented consultants and academics as a basic component of well-managed work environments (Daniels, 1989; Dean, 1994; Deterline, 1992; Tosti, 1986; Zigon, 1995).

In organizations without work teams, supervisory personnel usually shoulder the responsibility of providing feedback to employees regarding their performance. All too often, supervisors do a poor job of this, giving little feedback except when serious errors are committed. Many consultants have made a living training supervisors to deliver more frequent and more positive feedback to the employees under them, resulting in improved productivity and happier employees.

In organizations with SMWTs, the supervisors are gone, along with their potential as sources of performance feedback. This is an opportunity for the SMWTs to "cut out the middle man." The SMWT can seek out data on its own performance without relying on another level of management to supply it. And, given that the philosophy of SMWTs is to empower employees, the ability to monitor their own performance data seems to be inherent in that empowerment. Therefore, a valid and comprehensive performance measurement system is essential for SMWT success, and *access to the data* for purposes of feedback is a key aspect of team empowerment. As Zigon (1995) has pointed out, performance feedback facilitates self-management because it enables the team to solve many problems on its own before management hears about them and steps in to intervene.

## Local Feedback

In several of our case studies, the SMWTs helped redesign information systems so that they could download their performance data to their workstations whenever they wanted to look at it. This can be thought of as *local* feedback because it is received at the work site. Local feedback has the shortest route from where the data were generated back to the performer who produced the object or service the data measure. Aspects of the job itself automatically provide local feedback. These might include, for example, instances when customers comment on their satisfaction with service in a face-to-face service interaction or when manufacturing equipment breaks down because of an incorrect operator setup.

A review of our case studies has indicated that performance assessment systems should be designed to provide feedback that is as local as possible. More specifically, a review of our cases suggests the following:

1. *Feedback should be specific to the tasks of the SMWT.* The best feedback is relevant to what the SMWT is accomplishing, rather than merely providing an aggregate of many work teams. However, some SMWTs may desire access to internal customer data in cases where the SMWT's performance may directly affect that of the internal customer. For example, speeding up production by an SMWT might suddenly cause a bottleneck for its internal customer. Monitoring the internal customer might help the SMWT avoid this problem.

2. *Feedback should be comprehensive but easily understood.* The data should reflect the multiple measures tailored to that team's performance, but the measures should not be confusing. Maskell (1991) urged the use of nonfinancial measures where such measures are more direct (e.g., setup times for equipment instead of setup labor costs).

3. *Feedback should be updated as frequently as possible.* If the interval between updates of performance data is too large, the usefulness of the data as on-line corrective feedback will be lost.

4. *Feedback should be easily accessible by team members.* Performance data used to be the province of managers, and some managers or support personnel may still jealously guard data. Barriers need to be removed between the SMWT and its performance data.

5. *Feedback should be designed to emphasize improvement.* Objective measures should reveal when performance is worsening or improving, but measures can emphasize failure more than success or vice versa. If too many measures emphasize negative aspects of performance, people will naturally learn to avoid such information, and the potential of the data as feedback will be lost.

One of the characteristics of the most successful SMWTs we observed was that these teams focused their team meetings on discussions of performance data. In several of the high-performing SMWTs, members took turns presenting data in their area of responsibility in weekly team meetings. Not only did this keep team members posted on progress in various areas, it also provided an empirical basis for problem-solving activities. Discussions of why the data were low or high led to suggestions for improvement that were subsequently implemented, and the effects of the suggestions were reviewed during team meetings in the following weeks. The low-performing SMWTs that we observed were found to have weak performance assessment systems. During their team meetings, very little was accomplished. This appeared to be because they had only a vague idea of their accomplishments and little guidance on the effectiveness of their suggestions. To reiterate, a primary function of performance assessment is to supply timely data as feedback and to give an empirical foundation for problem-solving activities.

## GOAL SETTING, MANAGEMENT SUPPORT, AND PERFORMANCE ASSESSMENT

Meyer (1994) has argued that empowered teams should be involved in the design of their performance assessment system. Senior managers can assist the SMWTs in developing the measures and ensuring that the measures are aligned with organizational priorities. An important component of the assessment system is goal setting. Teams should have some input into determining goal levels, probably through a negotiation process with management. The standard advice regarding the setting of goals is that they should be challenging yet attainable (Daniels, 1989). Management usually has a good idea of what is challenging; teams usually have a good idea of what is attainable. This is discussed further in our chapter on team goals.

One thing to remember in setting goals is that performance improvement is rarely linear. SMWT performance may have periods of apparently constant rates of improvement, but these may be punctuated by big jumps (as when a new work process is implemented) or slower changes in the rate of improvement. Without substantial changes in work processes or equipment, improvement often takes the form of a negatively accelerating hyperbola, in which dramatic improvement in the measures occurs for a while, before the rate of improvement slows as it approaches the asymptote of maximum possible improvement. Applying this knowledge about continuous improvement results in the SMWT setting goals that fit this improvement curve rather than assuming a constant linear rate of improvement (which demands less than possible improvement at first and more than possible improvement later).

We observed some teams operating under a measurement system with goals (for such things as quality improvement) that assumed linear improvement rates. Many team members complained that the goals were unreasonable, and this was a source of resentment toward the assessment system and management in general. In fact, some team members admitted to us that they "managed" the rate of improvement to keep it linear because that was clearly what made management happy. If unrealistic goals are imposed on SMWTs, they will find such ways to cope with the system.

It is perhaps inevitable that management has to put some pressure on teams to maintain continuous improvement, but knowing when performance is truly "topping out" as opposed to "burning out" is a skill mastered by few. In one case, we found that the pressure to continuously improve led an SMWT to discover a breakthrough way to redesign the workspace so that twice as much work could be done by the same number of team members. Of course, the rate of improvement in productivity would be large at first and then slow down as the team learned to operate in the new workspace up to their capacity. One way management could take advantage of this improvement curve is to emphasize performance improvement early on while large gains are possible and shift toward stimulating team members to discover or devise process improvements later as large performance gains become less likely.

Management's support of team performance progress, or the lack of it, is critical to the long-term performance of the team. Measurement experts such as Daniels (1994) and Meyer (1994) have emphasized that assessment systems should not be used punitively by management. Some managers leave teams alone when they are making good progress but intervene when the assessment system indicates poor performance. Even when managers think their visit to the team is helpful, team members may see the visit as punitive in nature. If managers only react to the assessment system when there are problems, assessment itself can become associated primarily with punishment or scrutiny. In this atmosphere, teams may feel pressure to cover up problems or downplay them instead of feeling free to address them in a constructive manner.

In one team meeting we observed, the SMWT members were discussing a low-performance area. Unfortunately, more time was devoted to answering the central question—How are we going to explain this to the manager?—than was spent trying to find ways to improve performance.

Thus, team members should confront low performance from a problem-solving perspective rather than a focus on blaming the problem on someone. However, we have found that whether the team does so is strongly influenced by management's reaction to low performance. If management can assist in the problem-solving process, such assistance would be helpful. But if management approaches it as a situation in which the SMWT must explain its low performance, the integrity and usefulness of the performance assessment system may be threatened. And the team may engage in more excuse making than problem solving. Even when managers announce that they will visit the SMWT to assist in a constructive problem-solving activity, what really matters is how the SMWT perceives the visit.

Whether a manager's visit is perceived as constructive or punitive has a lot to do with the history of interactions between the SMWT and the manager. How often the manager has reacted positively to progress and goal attainment in the past is crucial. Managers who have provided a lot of recognition for positive performance are more likely to be viewed as helpful when they visit SMWTs than those who only visit or discuss performance when there is a problem.

In sum, an examination of performance assessment shows that an assessment system is affected as much by how it is used as by how it is constructed. Assessment systems are never simply about assessment. They reflect, remind, and even instruct team members about organizational priorities; they provide feedback that can improve performance or aid in problem solving; they can help to focus team meetings; they can inspire or demoralize; they affect interpersonal processes within the SMWT and between the SMWT and others; and they can serve as the basis for monetary and nonmonetary rewards. We will discuss the issues of team-based reward systems, compensation systems, and their relationship to performance measurement in the next chapter.

# 14

■

# The Reward System

■

When organizations make the transition from traditionally managed work environments to SMWTs, they often change many systems at the outset. Some of these changes, such as abandoning traditional supervisory roles, designing team structure, and devising team charters, virtually define the new team-based environment. These changes are usually prefaced by a kickoff meeting or meetings in which the new features of teaming are explained and the benefits extolled so that the workforce is excited about the transition. Changes to the organization's reward system often occur later in the transition phase; indeed, they are often the last systems to change, sometimes months or even years after teams have been implemented. To ensure the long-term success of SMWTs, organizations must realign rewards to promote teamwork and team accomplishments. Keeping traditional reward systems in place after the transition to teams sets the stage for trouble and possible failure of the team concept.

## PROBLEMS WITH TRADITIONAL REWARD SYSTEMS

Traditional reward systems evolved to suit the needs of management and employees in traditionally managed, hierarchical organizations. This meant that rewards were coupled with measurement and evaluation systems that focused almost exclusively on individuals. Many criticisms have been leveled against this approach because of inherent weaknesses or because of the poor fit when used in a team-based environment (Becker-Reems, 1994; Belcher, 1991; Hackman & Oldham, 1980; Kanin-Lovers & Cameron, 1993; Lawler, 1986; Ray & Bronstein, 1995). Problems that have been highlighted include:

- Individual appraisals promote individual competition, in which the few top performers "beat out" their peers and reap the rewards of large pay increments and promotions (we discussed some of their problems in the previous chapter).

- There is little emphasis in most compensation systems on creating strong links between individual compensation and organizational performance, at least at the level of hourly or nonexempt employees. Salary or wage increases roll over into subsequent years, permanently paying for the performance in the past.

- Where monetary rewards are used, they are designed to motivate more effort but not necessarily innovation, exceptional quality, or a customer focus.

- Little emphasis is placed on enhancing the natural rewards of work by changing how work gets done or by empowering employees.

- Employees often have little involvement in the design of the reward system.

Whatever else can be said about traditional individual-based reward systems, one has to acknowledge that traditionally managed organizations have used them with reasonable success for most of the 20th century. Reward system consultants, such as Daniels (1989, 1994), have helped organizations optimize the components of their various reward systems by overcoming procedural weaknesses, and many successes have been documented empirically in journals such as the *Journal of Organizational Behavior Management*. Beyond the procedural weaknesses, which can be adjusted, the major problem with traditional individual-based reward systems is simply that they encourage employee competition and so are not well suited to SMWTs, which involve large amounts of collaborative work.

## REWARD SYSTEM OBJECTIVES FOR TEAM-BASED ORGANIZATIONS

Our experiences, research, and review of the literature suggest that reward systems in the newer, team-based, high-performance organizations must be designed to accomplish several things:

- Motivate team members to work hard, but also to work *together* and to work *smarter.* Permanent teams that work on highly interdependent tasks require collaboration rather than interpersonal competition between team members.

SMWTs are also expected to be involved in the search for more effective work processes, so reward systems need to encourage, or at least permit, some risk taking and innovation.

■ Motivate the right kind of performance. Reward systems should recognize and encourage behavior that leads to value-added results, as well as rewarding the accomplishments themselves. This depends heavily on the proper identification of these behaviors and results in the organization's business strategy (Lawler, 1995).

■ Motivate performance for the long term. Motivation is often increased by all the changes and hoopla associated with the beginning of a new program, but after this "startup excitement" wears off, the reward system should sustain performance.

■ Evolve as teams become more mature and desire to make more decisions about the rewards or their allocation (Kanin-Lovers & Cameron, 1993).

■ Be open so there are no secrets or hidden agendas behind rewarding certain people or teams that could cause suspicion or loss of trust between management and the teams (Lawler, 1988a).

■ Include teams, not just top executives, in a compensation system that links pay to important business outcomes (Gross, 1995).

■ Find the proper balance between rewarding individuals for their efforts and accomplishments and providing rewards for the group performance of the team or the business unit.

■ Attract and retain the desired kind of employees (Lawler, 1995). Teams require people who can work closely with others and share in the rewards for doing so, and the reward systems should be attractive to people like that. In nonteam environments, heavy use of individual recognition and pay increases are especially attractive to "independent operators," people who prefer to work on their own and reap personal rewards. Traditional reward systems probably reinforce such behavior in everyone, which makes it difficult to change to a team-based environment.

According to articles in business periodicals (e.g., "Companies Shift (Slowly)," 1995; Geber, 1995; Shaw & Schneier, 1995), many organizations that use SMWTs have been slow to change either their performance measurement systems or their reward systems to match the needs of their new team environment. Some of this slowness may be due to lack of knowledge about what changes to make, and some may be due to a reluctance to tackle the complicated issue of changing multifaceted reward systems that have taken years to develop. Nevertheless, changes in the entire reward system are essential to maintain a proper motivational environment that will support new team practices. We will examine the issue of motivation and work teams in the next section.

## REWARDS AND EMPLOYEE MOTIVATION

Most organizations have developed a formal reward system to one degree or another. This system typically includes basic elements such as recognition programs for outstanding performance in various areas, as well as some part of the compensation system that delivers money related in some way to performance (even if it is just an occasional discretionary bonus). These programs are administered at various levels within the organization (e.g., some recognition programs may be team-based whereas others may be organization-wide), but they represent the organization's official views on what is valued work and how it should be rewarded.

The formal reward system is, however, only part of a larger motivation system, some of which is beyond the control of formal organizational policies and procedures. Other components of the motivation system include: (1) natural rewards from the job itself, (2) natural punishers from the job itself, (3) rewards outside of work, (4) informal reward and punishment practices of management, (5) formal punishment policies of the organization, and (6) informal daily peer reactions.

*Natural rewards from the job.* Most people find something to like among the various work tasks in their job. They find some tasks to be intrinsically interesting, challenging, or important enough that they are naturally motivated to work on that task. They may feel a tremendous sense of accomplishment when they finish certain tasks, or they may get positive reactions from customers. It would be an ideal world if everyone could find their jobs so naturally rewarding that no other reward systems were necessary, but our experience suggests that is not reality. It does appear, however, that the degree to which team members find their work naturally rewarding will affect their reaction to other components in the motivation system.

The nature of that interaction between natural, intrinsic work rewards and other rewards provided by management contingent on working has been a source of controversy and much debate since laboratory studies in the 1970s reported that some extrinsic rewards undermined intrinsic interest (e.g., Deci, 1971; Lepper, Greene, & Nisbett, 1973; see summaries by Deci & Ryan, 1985; Lepper & Greene, 1978). Although the nature and prevalence of detrimental effects have been shown to depend on many procedural variables (see meta-analyses and reviews by Cameron & Pierce, 1994; Carton, 1996; Dickinson, 1989), some writers have used the evidence of some detrimental effects as a basis for developing positions against the use of extrinsic rewards by organizations. The most extreme case was put forth by Kohn (1993), who appeared to be arguing for throwing the baby (extrinsic rewards) out with the bathwater (poor or inappropriate reward procedures). Such antiextrinsic reward arguments have been countered by academics, as well as compensation professionals (e.g., Carr, Mawhiney, Dickinson, & Pearlstein, 1995; McAdams, 1996), who see the need and value for extrinsic rewards to supplement intrinsic rewards, provided that the extrinsic reward programs use proper guidelines for effectiveness and appropriateness.

*Natural punishers from the job.* There are usually features of work and work environments that are naturally demotivating. Hard work may tire you out. The stresses associated with deadlines or customer demands can put you in a bad mood. Both of these events may make you enjoy work, as well as nonwork, activities less. Spitzer (1995) identified a number of what he called demotivators common in workplaces: Poorly designed work, unproductive meetings, interpersonal conflict, and office politics are some that fall in this category.

*Rewards outside of work.* Being motivated to work is a relative thing; it is often relative to your motivation to do other things outside of work. Our nonwork lives have reward systems just as complicated as our work lives, so it is no surprise that motivation to work is strongly affected by nonwork rewards over which the organization has little control. Common examples include reduced work motivation immediately prior to and, in some cases, after holidays or vacations with all of their associated enjoyable activities and distractions. Opposite effects can also occur, as when work motivation is increased due to diminishing rewards outside of work.

*Informal reward and punishment practices of management.* The extent and nature of informal reward and punishment practices, usually by a manager closest to the team, can affect team members' motivation on particular tasks as well as their feelings toward the entire organization. The manager with the most contact with the team is the interface between the team and top management, so he or she represents the organization to employees. Manager reactions to success or trouble, even when not part of a deliberate plan, can affect motivation. For example, if managers discourage efforts or accomplishments in certain areas, subtly or otherwise, this can send a signal that work in this area is not valued by management.

*Formal punishment policies.* The organization usually has formal policies regarding what kind of activities will be punished and the means of punishment (e.g., verbal warning, written reprimand). The characteristics of these punishment policies, in terms of the nature and proportion of punishable activities, can affect motivation. Too much emphasis on punishment can reduce the motivation of employees to engage in risky or innovative activities. In such circumstances, employees strive to find ways to perform their jobs that won't get them in trouble.

*Informal daily peer reactions.* Peer reactions to one's work and accomplishments are often very important to people. Peers recognizing others for their work, and valuing their input into decisions, plays a large part in motivating work simply because peers are the social community with which employees have the most frequent contact. The effects of peer reaction are probably amplified by SMWTs, which are to some degree formally designated friends with whom frequent contact is required.

Viewing both the formal reward practices and the more informal factors listed above, as a whole system, enables us to predict *system effects. System effects* refers to those effects that occur when the various motivational components interact to affect our total motivation to work. Furthermore, the study of system effects includes examining how changes in one motivational component affect the reaction to the other components. The design and periodic upgrading of the organization's formal reward system should take the other factors into account when analyzing the total motivational environment.

## The Effect of SMWTs on Motivation

The characteristics of SMWTs can, by themselves, affect motivation in a positive manner. Work teams are empowered through having greater *involvement* in organizational decisions, greater *authority* to make changes in how they perform their work, and greater *responsibility* for managing themselves so that they perform successfully. These are some of the factors that are especially likely to make work more enjoyable; in other words, they enhance the natural rewards from work (Manz, 1992; Manz & Sims, 1989).

Furthermore, during the transition to teams, people are often given training in the social skills of teaming, such as listening, resolving conflicts cooperatively, and delivering feedback. These new social skills, if deployed properly, can make the day-to-day social environment more pleasant and constructive, reducing some of the demotivating aspects of a job fraught with bad peer relations. The use of teams is, of course, no guarantee of instant improvements in interpersonal relations. During start-up, there is often increased conflict as people adjust to working as a team. One team member told us he missed the old supervisory system because he could go to the supervisor to complain about a coworker, but with work teams, he had to confront the coworker himself. With more training and experience, the awkwardness of dealing with problems like that should subside.

Under the right conditions, teams can develop social norms that motivate performance. As a small, cohesive group, teams can provide intense social pressure to meet deadlines or improve quality (Lawler, 1986). Lawler has reported cases in which teams actually advised poorly performing team members to quit their jobs. We have run across similar cases. These performance norms can affect team composition in other ways also. We have seen teams that have considerable input into whom they admit onto their teams (job candidates were typically from another part of the plant). Team members told us that they held job interviews, like any employer, and that the candidate team member's performance record was a critical factor in their vote. They wanted high performers on their teams. Of course, team norms that are antiperformance can also develop, but we believe this can be prevented by careful design of the entire team-performance management system.

Organizations with SMWTs often provide education or training to increase the business knowledge of team members so that they will understand the role their team plays in the overall picture of organizational functioning. The training may include descriptions of organization-wide processes as well as identification of customer needs. For some team members, this is the first time they will have seen the "big picture," and this can motivate them by boosting their perception of the importance of their job to the organization.

In some manufacturing organizations we have seen, teams communicated directly with their internal and external customers about production, scheduling, or quality issues. Some teams even visited their external customers with airfare and hotel at company expense—something not one of the team members we spoke to complained about. In a defense plant, military customers (Air Force pilots) visited some teams to thank them for making weapons systems that helped save pilot lives and secure victory in Operation Desert Storm. Such close ties to customers help motivate team members because they can see how customers actually use their products, so their efforts in producing them seem worthwhile.

The net result of these changes associated with teams is that organizations do not have to rely on the formal reward system to carry the total motivational weight. More parts of the motivation system are working together in the same direction. Under these conditions, the effects of extrinsic rewards should be *amplified* because they are not trying to override demotivating job aspects, such as having no input, no control, and no intellectual challenge.

Are extrinsic rewards still needed in team environments that have successfully boosted the naturally rewarding properties of work? The answer appears to be "yes." First, even people who can regularly engage in naturally rewarding work need to reconnect with socially mediated rewards at some point. Despite the fact that musicians could remain in an isolated room making beautiful, naturally rewarding music for the rest of their lives, most seem compelled to perform in front of adoring audiences at least intermittently. This is probably because the naturally rewarding properties (what defines *beautiful*) originated socially; that is, most natural rewards intrinsic to tasks were established by social definition. The exception would be those rewards that directly produce pleasurable sensations through some automatic physiological route. Nevertheless, socially established natural rewards may need periodic "booster shots" to maintain their effectiveness over an extended period of time.

Second, whereas natural rewards of work can keep us motivated to work at those tasks, extrinsic rewards can have additional desirable effects. For example, such rewards communicate what is important to the larger organization and can stimulate people to find ways of working that benefit other teams and the entire organization. Thus, extrinsic rewards can broaden our perspective on work and enhance our understanding of larger organizational goals. If work was stimulated solely by rewards intrinsic to the job, employees might have little reason to seek out others for advice or information.

Finally, compensation-based rewards particularly address personal economic issues for people in SMWTs. Tying team performance to pay provides them with the opportunity for a fair return for the increased demands usually placed on teams. Empowered teams take over what were management responsibilities; under the old system, these problems were someone else's to wrestle with, and those managers were well paid for dealing with them. Team members acquire more interesting jobs when they assume these duties, but they also experience the heavy demands of self-leadership, data monitoring, process improvement, personal accountability for production quality and schedules, cost reduction pressures, extra time devoted to meetings, pressure to acquire new skills, and so on. According to Block (1993), such empowerment deserves a more equitable distribution of wealth. Organizations need to look at compensating teams for their performance.

## REWARDS BASED ON BEHAVIOR VERSUS RESULTS

Should rewards be contingent on behavior or on results? For a number of reasons, the weight of the reward system should be focused on results. First, for practical reasons, most performance measures are results measures, so that means that the performance requirement can be specified objectively on the basis of the data stream from the performance measurement system, as discussed in the previous chapter. Second, there is a broader issue concerned with team and individual autonomy. If the reward system has a heavy emphasis on specifying exactly what behaviors will be rewarded, the organization runs the risk of overspecifying certain forms of behavior and thereby restricting behavioral variability and flexibility; that is, team members might be less inclined to try new ways of behaving that might be more successful in leading to important results (for reviews of laboratory research on this topic, see Hayes, 1989). Part of the empowerment philosophy of work teams is to make the team more responsible for its performance. That requires that teams be permitted to try performance improvement ideas, whether they are new office layouts or new methods of accomplishing work. Teams must have relatively more freedom to find the best ways of producing important results, so there should be fewer dictates or specifications of forms of behavior than there might be in a traditionally managed organization.

Nevertheless, there are some circumstances in which rewards should be contingent on behavior. Team development, as discussed in the previous chapter, often includes a focus on behaviors essential to teamwork in the start-up phase of teaming. Behaviors such as leading team meetings well, communicating clearly and resolving conflict cooperatively, or assisting other team members may be measured through observation or employee surveys. Because these kinds of behavior are deemed fundamental prerequisites for successful team functioning, there is a strong justification for rewarding them so that they will be likely to persist and so others will model them. We also mentioned safety as an area in which it is more important to focus on behaviors than on results. McSween (1995) has made a compelling argument that traditional results-based safety reward programs (focused on providing rewards for fewer recorded accidents) more often lead to covering up accidents than behaving safely. By arranging peer-delivered rewards when safe behaviors are observed, people learn to make them a habit, thereby reducing the probability of serious accidents.

It should be noted in the discussion of rewarding behaviors versus results that the issue is whether specific behaviors should be required and rewarded. When rewards are contingent on results, behaviors are necessarily involved—that's how the results were produced. The question is whether *certain forms* of behavior should be required in the production of the results for rewards to be delivered. We have cautioned against overspecification of behaviors, but that does not mean that reward system designers should ignore behaviors in setting up a reward program. Even when behaviors are not specified in a results-focused reward contingency, some thought should be put into asking what behaviors are likely to occur to fulfill the performance requirement. If the reward contingency is capable of producing illegal, inappropriate, or unethical behaviors to produce the results, the contingencies may need to be altered to prevent this possibility. For example, in rewarding increased sales volume, it is possible that salespeople might increase the use of "hard sell" techniques. Monitoring a customer satisfaction measure might reveal increasing dissatisfaction with such behavior. The customer satisfaction measure might then become a qualifier of the results measure in the reward contingency to ensure that destructive behaviors are not encouraged.

## INDIVIDUAL VERSUS TEAM-BASED REWARDS

A related question regarding contingencies concerns whether rewards should be contingent on individual or group performance. Some researchers have argued against using individual rewards in team environments (e.g., Hackman, 1992), whereas others have identified some conditions under which it is acceptable or recommended (e.g., Lawler, 1992). Hackman's concern has been that individual rewards in a team environment can generate competition between team members, something incompatible with the collaborative behavior necessary for smooth team functioning. Competition is likely when there are limits on the number of people who can be rewarded, as we discussed above.

In one of our low-performing case studies, it was reported that only individual reward mechanisms were allowed by the organization. As a result, the team nominated one member for a prestigious award. Afterward, resentment toward the awardee grew, as other team members felt she was now acting as if she were a little better than everyone else. Both competition and resentment of team members are things to avoid in SMWTs, so caution in using individual rewards seems warranted.

On the other hand, Lawler has pointed out that team structures involve varying degrees of interdependence among team members. Some teams, for example, might be composed of salaried employees from different specialty areas. They work as a team in communicating vital process information and planning new products, but each also performs duties in specialty areas that contribute to the team goals. Where interdependence is low, rewards for individual performance may be quite acceptable to team members.

Even in highly interdependent teams, some researchers and managers feel that there should be some mechanism for rewarding individual efforts and contributions. In an article by Geber (1995), managers who redesigned reward systems reported they sometimes neglected individual rewards in developing group-based rewards and that, in retrospect, this was a mistake. They felt that individuals were being valued less with only group-based rewards. Myers (1991) has noted that too much of an emphasis on group rewards at the expense of individual rewards was a characteristic of the brand of socialism that failed so miserably in Eastern Europe. Other scholars of the behavioral effects of socialist reward contingencies have made similar assessments of the role group-based rewards played in the economic collapse of the Soviet bloc countries (Lamal, 1991; Rakos, 1991). It would indeed be ironic if modern, performance-oriented capitalism repeated the mistakes of its failed communist rivals. The issue, then, is what types of rewards should be made contingent on individual performance in team-based environments and how they should be administered.

## "LINE OF SIGHT" AND COST-EFFECTIVENESS ISSUES

In choosing reward types for the composition of the reward system, the design team should be aware that there is a catch-22 of motivation in work teams. When rewards are based on group performance, there is more incentive to cooperate with others than to compete. However, the larger the group is, the less incentive there is for any one individual to work hard because the impact of his or her work will be diluted by the larger team size. This latter issue is called a "line of sight" problem (Lawler, 1986, 1992). *Line of sight* refers to the perceived ability to affect an outcome (McAdams, 1996). It reflects how much control people feel they have to influence some outcome measure. Making rewards contingent on the aggregate performance can promote team cooperation, but it does so at the expense of individual motivation. Support for this observation has been reported recently by Zenger and Marshall (1995), who conducted an empirical study of the effects of group-based rewards. They found that group rewards were effective in increasing performance but that the performance gains were greater in smaller groups than larger ones. This line of sight problem means that multiple reward programs are necessary to maintain individual motivation as well as encourage greater cooperation within teams and between teams in a business unit.

Finally, we would be remiss if we did not mention that an obvious and important consideration in the design of any reward system, for individuals in traditionally managed organizations or for SMWTs, is that it must be financially sound. If the dollars expended on rewards are not outweighed by the dollar value of performance gains at goal performance levels, the reward system will not be sustainable and will need to be modified (see Gross, 1995, or McAdams, 1996, for discussions of the funding of reward programs).

## FACTORS ENSURING REWARD EFFECTIVENESS

Many of the factors identified as important to effective reward systems have been discovered through decades of basic research into the process of *positive reinforcement* (Skinner, 1938, 1974) combined with knowledge gained from observing its application in the business world. Despite criticisms of particular conceptualizations of reinforcement by scholars from various theoretical orientations (see Catania & Harnad, 1988), including behaviorists themselves (Malott, 1989, 1992), principles of effective reinforcement still permeate advice about the design and functioning of reward systems. And for good reason: They are tried and true (see, e.g., Belcher, 1991; Boyett & Conn, 1995; Daniels, 1989; Hackman & Oldham, 1980; Lawler, 1995; McAdams, 1996; McCoy, 1992; Nelson, 1994). Factors found to be important to effective reward systems are discussed below.

*Rewards valued by the recipients.* Those who administer reward systems often assume that because they value something, the recipients will also. Because of the difficulty of guessing what people value, some reward systems offer choices of rewards. Value translates into amount when discussing monetary rewards, and compensation experts such as Gross (1995) have suggested that organizations often give monetary rewards that are not as large as they need to be to affect motivation substantially.

*Certainty.* If the performance requirement has been fulfilled by the performers, the reward system should be certain to deliver rewards. This is a must with any formal reward program, but it is less of a problem with informal rewards such as spontaneous peer recognition. Violations of certainty with any formal reward program destroy the system's credibility. If people do not trust that earned rewards will be received, the effect on motivation can be devastating.

*Timely delivery.* Rewards should be delivered when they are earned. That may be immediate, as in the case of rewarding an observed behavior, or after some delay until the results have accumulated enough to be measured. Despite the fact that such rewards sometimes follow long after the behaviors that led to them, the rewards can still be effective in strengthening those behaviors as long as the rewards are certain and the person understands the performance–reward link. However, untimely reward delivery can make it harder to see or believe in strong performance–reward links. Failure to provide timely reward delivery can send a signal that management is reluctant to reward or is sloppy in its administration and therefore not serious about rewarding performance. This can lead to resentment and consequent reductions in motivation.

*A credible measurement system.* The most credible measurement systems are usually the most objective systems. Subjective, judgment-based systems always leave room for suspicion of favoritism or prejudice.

*Clear line of sight.* Team members must feel that they can influence the measures used as criteria for the reward. If they feel they have no control over the outcomes, the rewards will have minimal motivational power. A perceived lack of control might exist, for example, where there are other teams that affect the measure or where variables beyond the team's control affect the team's outcomes.

*Understandable contingencies.* Unclear performance requirements or a lack of specification of reward magnitudes weaken reward effectiveness. In one case, where we were asking team members about the reward systems in place in their organization, we found that very few could articulate what exactly it was that caused them to get a recent bonus. Those who had not received a bonus check were particularly perturbed; naturally, some of them suspected favoritism was at work. This organization had a very objective measurement system in place, but the reward contingencies were not clear to everyone.

*Attainable goal levels.* Team members must feel that the performance levels specified in the performance requirement are attainable within a reasonable time frame. For this reason, organizations often establish subgoals that are attainable relatively quickly (compared with the long-term goals) and deliver some form of reward for reaching the subgoals. Doing so ensures that sustained effort and progress are rewarded to keep motivation high.

*Team member involvement.* SMWT members should be involved in the reward system design. This can be accomplished by having SMWT representatives on a reward system design team. Or it might be accomplished by a management team soliciting input from SMWT members prior to designing or overhauling the reward system. Team involvement solves two problems with reward system design. First, reward system designers need to know up front what team members value as rewards. Everyone might like to see monetary rewards, but team members may have strong feelings for or against some of the many possible options for recognition or tangible rewards. A reward not valued by the recipients simply won't reinforce their efforts. Second, involvement ensures that teams have some input regarding what kinds and levels of performance will fall under the reward system. If powerful rewards were arranged for aspects of performance that team members considered inappropriate or unreasonable, the system would lose its motivational properties. With input on these two issues, the likelihood of teams buying into the reward system is enhanced. Hackman and Oldham (1980) have noted that involvement can eliminate a lot of the resentment that is sometimes felt toward an imposed reward system. It can also reduce perceptions that the new system is a control tactic.

*No limits on the number of winners.* To preserve the collaborative nature of team-based work environments, reward systems need to move away from the traditional "one-winner" programs. Reward programs that limit the number of recipients, usually through some ranking-based measurement or judgment system, set the stage for individuals or teams to compete for the rewards. The problem with competition of this sort is that it is usually accompanied by a corresponding reluctance to assist other individuals or teams. Furthermore, one winner means many losers. Other individuals or teams that improved a great deal or accomplished a lot get nothing for their performance, even if they are a hair's width below the performance level of the winner. Reward programs that adopt more of a rating-type philosophy (performance is judged against a standard rather than ranked relative to what other people did) ensure that everyone who meets the performance criteria receives the reward. This eliminates the incentive for destructive intra-or inter-team competition, and it means that, in principle, everyone in the organization can win at the same time. Most organizations would prefer to have massive numbers of winners than massive numbers of losers as employees, so they should design their reward systems accordingly.

*Customized mix of reward types.* Organizations using SMWTs need a customized mix of reward types tailored to their culture and performance needs. Usually, organizations have more than one reward program in their reward system, even in traditionally managed organizations. However, reward design teams need to examine these various programs to make sure that they are integrated well enough that they don't conflict with each other. An example of conflict might be a program that rewards only quality improvement (possibly encouraging slower work) while another program rewards only reduced cycle time (possibly encouraging less concern for quality). Another reason for having a custom mix is so one reward type can address the weaknesses of another reward type. As discussed above, each reward type has its own strengths and weaknesses for SMWTs.

# 15

■

# Types of Rewards

■

This chapter reviews several of the major types of rewards offered to SMWTs, including recognition, tangible rewards, and monetary rewards (e.g., pay-for-skills programs, team performance pay, and gainsharing).

## RECOGNITION

Most organizations of medium to large size have some form of recognition program in place (Flynn, 1996). By *recognition,* we mean nonmonetary rewards involving acknowledgment from other people such as praise, celebrations, and public notice. Traditional recognition programs focused on individuals and were often of the "one winner" type that can inadvertently promote interindividual competition. In addition, the source of the recognition was often from upper management levels or simply identified as the organization itself. In team-based environments, recognition can come from the team as well as the organization. In fact, teams can take more control over the reward system by enhancing their use of recognition. Formal or informal recognition is something the team always has at its disposal.

Recognition can be provided for several aspects of team performance. The team can recognize individuals for either behaviors or accomplishments. As we described earlier, team development requires that individuals learn and practice new behaviors essential for teamwork, and these behaviors should be recognized for their continued development. Such recognition can be informal and as simple as a few words of praise at a team meeting. Teams can also provide their own recognition when the team reaches developmental milestones (such as assuming responsibility for their own work scheduling) or performance goals. In this case, the recognition is often some sort of celebration administered by the team or a public notice of the team accomplishment in a newsletter. One of the high-performing teams we studied produced its own newsletters for circulation around the business unit, giving the team an opportunity to do a little justified bragging.

Of course, for such important team accomplishments, recognition should *also* come from management. Some organizations have a "wall of fame" in a highly visible place (e.g., a plant entrance or a cafeteria) where they hang photos of teams and descriptions of their accomplishments. Company newsletters can also recognize the team. Personal visits by management to the team work site or to team meetings to thank the team for its accomplishments are also used.

The advantage that teams have over management as the source of recognition is that they can provide recognition to themselves much faster than can upper levels of the organization. The team also has more intimate knowledge of the performance of individual team members than management, so team members are in a much better position to spot and recognize individual efforts and accomplishments, something that is risky for management to do. Having individual team members selected and recognized by management can be viewed as interfering with the team's autonomy; teams we have seen prefer to have control over recognition for any individuals. In fact, teams sometimes will nominate an individual for a company-wide individual recognition award where they feel strongly about one of their team members.

Provided that it is sincere and justified, it is hard to overdo recognition for a job well done. The high-performing teams we studied typically made it a habit to recognize individual as well as team performance. Because the responsibility for recognizing outstanding performance has traditionally been a management responsibility, teams may not automatically assume this responsibility. But the advantages of team-administered recognition, both formal and informal, make it an important aspect of team empowerment. In addition, praise and acknowledgment from team members can fulfill the need for individual recognition, which everyone feels to some extent, and thus fill in that gap in a reward system that focuses more rewards on performance at the team level. In other words, in team-based work environments, most of the rewards for individual effort and accomplishments will have to be administered by the team itself, and a large portion of those rewards will probably be in the form of recognition.

Many organizations show an astonishing lack of creativity when designing recognition programs. We are all familiar with the "Employee of the Month" variety. Criticisms of this practice by Daniels (1989) and McAdams (1996) suggest that recognition programs of this type typically suffer from a number of problems: weak identification of outstanding performance, leading to rotating the award until every employee has received it; failure to establish or maintain the meaningfulness of the award, forcing the delivery of the award into an artificial periodic time basis instead of whenever worthy performance occurs; and, again, a "one winner–many losers" type of reward. It would be pointless for team-based organizations to simply adapt this poor system into a "Team of the Month" award administered by some management committee based on fuzzy criteria.

Recognition programs administered by management should be noncompetitive and flexible enough to reward team progress and accomplishment as soon as it is identified. As McAdams (1996) has pointed out, recognition can add fun and excitement to the work environment, so organizations should employ more spontaneity and creativity in recognizing team performance. Team-administered recognition is bound to be more spontaneous and certainly more tailored to team members' likes and dislikes than any system implemented organization-wide by management. Recognition works best when it is spontaneous and after the fact, not something promised as an incentive for future performance. Recognition can be and should be frequent; so frequent that it routinely accompanies every other reward type in the reward system.

One final note on recognition programs: Many performance improvement specialists working with traditionally managed organizations train managers to deliver praise to subordinates for good performance rather than spending their time punishing bad performance. Although it sounds strange, it is often the case that managers need explicit coaching and role playing to learn how to praise. In other words, managers in many organizations have learned ways of dealing with their subordinates that make it unnatural for them to praise. If team members have worked in such traditionally managed work environments for long prior to changing to SMWTs, team members will also need training in the important skill of delivering praise face-to-face with a peer.

## TANGIBLE REWARDS

Some organizations provide tangible items as rewards for team accomplishments. Examples include award plaques or pins, clothing items with the organization's logo, sports tickets, additional training opportunities, and other nonmonetary items valued by team members. Sometimes nonwage funds are given to the team as a reward, as when they are given money to buy some nonessential item that would spruce up the work site or make a meeting room more pleasant. Some of these rewards are durable and thus have "trophy value," meaning that they are present to remind recipients and others of the accomplishment. This is thought to add to the value of the item as a reward (for example, plaques have no real inherent value other than that established by their use as a reward) because it gives the recipients a chance to tell others what they did to receive it. In one organization we studied, top-performing teams received gold medals (actually a small pin) that members proudly wore. People from other teams recognized them when they were out and about the plant and could ask their advice on a team question.

Other rewards in this class are more consumable than durable. Tickets to sports or entertainment events are used, as are additional training opportunities. An example from our research will reveal some key characteristics of the use of this type of tangible reward. One high-performing team we studied had received more training hours as a reward for excellent performance. Management had administered the reward for meeting performance and development criteria specified in advance. The reward had been accompanied by recognition from management and public notice in the company newsletter. Management had given the team its choice of courses on which members wished to spend their training hours. The team decided to choose a training seminar that they could attend together and all found beneficial. As it turned out, the training was one of the personal development courses offered by the organization on money management. Team members we spoke with were quite pleased with this training opportunity.

The reward in this example was administered by management, and it was accompanied by recognition in several forms. Any tangible reward should always be accompanied by recognition; no item should ever be sent to a team as if it is a prize doled out by some anonymous management team for some unspecified accomplishment. The reward was for team performance, and all team members benefited, not just one or two individuals. The team was given a choice of what it wanted most from the available rewards. Finally, the frequency of this reward was lower than that of any of the recognition programs in place. It was based on a noncompetitive assessment of team performance and development. These are ideal features of the use of tangible rewards, valued by the recipients, for team performance. Teams should come to a consensus on how they will consume or spend the reward, but it is not clear whether the reward should require that all team members use their portion identically. Again, leaving this up to the team appears to be the most effective approach.

## MONETARY REWARDS

The pay systems for SMWTs should be designed to support team practices (Eccles & Pyburn, 1992; Gross, 1995; Hackman & Oldham, 1980). Changing traditional compensation systems focused on individual performance can be very complex, but we have found that doing so is important for high team performance. Furthermore, making such changes conveys to everyone just how serious management is about SMWTs (Becker-Reems, 1994; Gross, 1995). In the message-sending business, changes in pay speak loudly! Our data suggest that how compensation is redesigned affected how everyone felt about the team concept, coworkers, management, and the organization itself. Compensation can affect the motivation to perform as well as more subtle aspects of employees' behavior, such as their interest in understanding how the entire organization functions. Whole books are written on compensation programs (e.g., Belcher, 1991; Gross, 1995), but we will summarize some of the major applications of pay as rewards for team performance.

### Pay-for-Skills Programs

Team-based organizations have to rethink job design, and many want to encourage team members to learn new skills so they can do a variety of jobs that used to be the province of someone with a particular job title. Team members also have to learn some of the management skills that were the responsibility of front-line supervisors whose positions have been absorbed. *Pay-for-skills* (PFS) programs provide for increases in the base pay of individuals contingent on their learning and demonstrating new job-specific skills or interpersonal skills thought to be essential for improved performance or flexibility. Variants of this idea may have different names or a focus on more generalized skills than job-specific skills (such as in pay for knowledge or competency-based pay), although the particular applications in teams may render cut-and-dried distinctions impossible.

When organizations need to diversify the skills of their employees, they first identify the number of different skills they want to encourage people to learn, as well as the depth of each skill. For example, a team's members may need to develop computer skills in using several different software packages, each package having several possible levels of proficiency. Or the team may need to have a few people who have mediational skills to deal with conflicts that come up among team members. Management then decides what increments in base pay should be associated with learning particular blocks of skills. Teams can assess their own needs for skill improvement among their team members or perhaps devise their own modified version of the system tailored to their work requirements in consultation with management.

The motivation for learning more skills under such a system is more complex than it would appear at first. Without any other constraints, individuals would have an incentive to simply add more skills to their repertoire and increase their pay. This could lead to individuals acquiring skills that aren't really needed or are redundant because so many others have learned them also. Many team-based organizations have become flatter, with less hierarchy and consequently fewer opportunities to be promoted vertically. Broadening job skills and enhancing base pay then becomes an alternative to the vertical career ladders that used to be the only way to make significant increases in base pay.

Organizations usually impose some constraints to limit the individual's incentive to "pad" skills without adding real value to the organization. Lawler, Ledford, and Chang (1993) have pointed out that PFS programs are often found together with gainsharing programs (to be discussed below). Gainsharing, or other incentive pay programs that include cost as a factor, impose a penalty for padding: If labor costs go up without productivity improvements, there is a reduction in the payout to everyone. This would create some peer pressure to keep people from just racking up skills for their own benefit.

In some teams we studied that were developing PFS programs, the team assessed the "skill mix" necessary to meet its own performance requirements. When a team skill deficit was identified, team members decided among themselves who should get trained. This was surely a complicated decision because the team had to consider the expected benefits to team performance as well as individual inequities in base pay when choosing the member to be trained. In some cases, teams were given authority over their own budgets, or their labor costs were included as a factor in the team's performance measures. Because the performance measures contributed to the determination of team bonuses, the team had a strong incentive to be careful in choosing what kind of training was needed for each team member.

The advantages for team members of a PFS program as a part of the reward system include the ability of the program to pay some individuals more for important skills, thus adding to the rewards for individual efforts and abilities in a context of many other team-based rewards. This can help retain high-skill individuals who might otherwise feel undervalued in a system in which less skilled teammates receive rewards based on the performance of the team as a whole.

Lawler (1992) has noted that PFS programs also show that the organization values people as a resource. Unfortunately, this message may be lost when PFS is used, as it often is, when organizations need to have cross-trained employees because they have laid off so many others as part of a downsizing move. Increased flexibility in a leaner workforce is a benefit of PFS programs that organizations find very attractive in these days of cost-conscious global competition.

Lawler (1992) has described a number of disadvantages of PFS programs. First, to ensure a return on investment, organizations must ensure that employees use their new skills. Teams can help in this endeavor because team members are in a good position to observe whether the skills of team members are being used in a regular fashion. Consequently, the utilization problem may be less of a concern with teams than in traditionally managed work environments, provided that the team has an incentive to hold down its labor costs (as we described in an example above). PFS programs also require an expansion of training opportunities (and their associated costs), as well as some kind of evaluation system. Evaluation of skills can be through a test or some kind of certification program, but developing and maintaining a system can consume time, money, and resources. There is also an inevitable "topping out" problem when people have learned all the skills eligible for pay. Some organizations have dealt with this by including so many possible skills, including management skills, that it would take a very long time to top out. Of course, PFS programs are not really designed to be the primary motivators of sustained productivity, so topping out problems are less of a concern where there are additional monetary rewards for productivity.

Some other problems associated with PFS programs seem either diminished or enhanced in team environments. *Skill fade* is a problem that can occur when the people don't use the skills often enough after they have been trained. This is often the case where there is little job rotation. However, in several teams we studied, job rotation was fairly common, so skill fade appeared less likely to occur than in a nonteam environment in which rotating jobs is more difficult due to the barriers thrown up by traditional job title and classification systems.

One problem with PFS programs that may be enhanced in team environments is the resentment of base pay inequities. Many team members we spoke with were acutely aware of base pay differentials between team members who often shared the same team duties. There was some feeling that the inherent equality concept of being a team should mean equal pay or at least pay that is more equal than before. If PFS programs lead to substantial base pay inequities, resentment can begin to destroy the interpersonal processes needed for high team performance. Perhaps the practice of letting teams choose who gets trained in particular skills will lead to the team preventing serious inequities from developing.

## Team Performance Pay

Variously called pay-for-performance or incentive compensation plans, *team performance pay* provides a monetary bonus to the team for meeting performance goals or subgoals. Those goals may include a family of measures (such as the Oregon Productivity Matrix discussed in Chapter 13) focusing on operational or financial results. Gross (1995) and McAdams (1996) contend that operational measures, such as productivity, cycle time, or quality, have a shorter line of sight than financial measures and thus should make up most of the measures at the lower levels in an organization. If teams develop a better understanding of financial measures in the organization, as they often do in team education programs, financial measures will seem less intimidating to them and their line of sight will improve.

We have already described team performance measurement systems earlier, so we will reiterate here an essential point: A sound measurement system is the foundation for an effective reward system. Deciding to tie pay to that measurement system makes it clear to everyone that the measures are important and that what is important should be measured. In fact, if the measurement system has been in place for a while before money is tied to it, the prospect of a monetary link will probably occasion a long, hard look at the existing measures.

Team performance pay has a number of strengths. It has strong potential for motivating performance improvements, provided that the measures and goals are clear and controllable. Paying a bonus to teams is a group incentive; it reinforces teamwork rather than simply individual effort. Team members have a strong financial incentive to get involved in every aspect of team functioning that can affect whether they earn that bonus, so performance pay can encourage commitment and effort (Lawler, 1986). Team performance pay plans are often easier to understand than higher-level profit-sharing or gainsharing programs. Finally, some reward specialists (e.g., Boyett & Conn, 1995) believe that performance pay for teams is entirely compatible with the more egalitarian approach inherent in the use of teams. And Gross (1995) has suggested that it is elitist to reserve monetary incentives for only top executives.

To be a motivating part of the reward system, the payout amounts must be large enough to be worth the effort of improving performance. Compensation professionals such as Gross (1995) have concluded that incentive pay should be at least a month's pay. Does that mean that payout amounts for team performance pay should be that large? The answer would depend on whether the team performance pay, contingent on the performance of individual teams, is the only source of incentive pay. In the one organization we studied that used incentive pay, a portion of the total amount of incentive pay was contingent on team performance, but some was contingent on the performance of the business unit as a whole. In this case, the total incentive pay available to team members was divided between several different reward contingencies.

Team performance pay is typically bonus money paid out in lump sums, not merit raises to salary or wages. Therefore, performance pay needs to be re-earned from period to period, continually motivating performance, unlike the raises that continue to pay higher amounts forever after (Lawler, 1995). It is a good idea to indicate somehow, either through distinct checks or an explanation on the pay stub, how much performance pay was earned apart from base pay. This helps team members see clearly what their accomplishments have earned them and helps reduce confusion about the reward system. In our experience, confusion regarding performance pay is commonplace. Confusion is the enemy of motivation in delayed reward programs such as performance pay.

How teams divide up the bonus money is an interesting issue. The manufacturing teams we studied consisted of people who generally performed similar job tasks. Under these conditions, there is more of an egalitarian emphasis in dividing up bonus money. Several teams reported giving each team member an equal share. But even in this circumstance, at least one team reported that it gave a team member less for "not pulling his share," indicating that some informal weighting of individual contribution to team results was in effect. Management left it up to teams to decide the split, a good idea, but one wonders how long it will be before a disgruntled employee sues his or her team for unfair compensation practices. There are already some legal complications imposed by federal law that we will describe in the next section.

A low-performing government team we studied consisted of people from varying specialties and job ranks; thus, they had existing differences in their base pay. Should equal shares of the bonus money be given to everyone on the team for the team performance in this case? Gross (1995) has pointed out that equal shares would be fair if there is equal contribution, but if the differences in base pay reflect different skills and contribution to team results, then a more appropriate division of bonus money would be to base the share on some measure of relative contribution or as equal percentages of base pay.

If teams are using a peer appraisal system, that may supply some data for team members deciding how to divide up team performance pay. We observed this occurring in several high-performing manufacturing teams. Using peer appraisals for that purpose, rather than strictly as developmental feedback, seems to violate their original intent, but with a monetary performance contingency in effect, it is hard to imagine that teams can avoid using the information from the peer appraisals in that manner.

An important decision in the design of team performance pay is whether to make any pay "at risk." Compensation programs with an at-risk element reduce or hold base pay constant while enabling employees to earn back that pay (and much more) contingent on different levels of performance. As McAdams (1996) has pointed out, this practice is common in sales but less often found in non-sales environments. Obviously, transitioning from a traditional pay program that doesn't have variable elements to one that does is a scary proposition for most employees. To date, few organizations have tried this with teams, although General Motors's Saturn plant is a notable exception. One way to put pay at risk without actually cutting base pay is to suspend future merit raises or cost-of-living adjustments and allocating that money to the incentive pool. Doing so prevents the shock of an immediate reduction in base pay and the consequent disruption of personal finances that would inevitably follow. The alternative to at-risk incentive pay is to make performance pay an add-on to existing base pay. This is far more comfortable for everyone, but many compensation professionals feel that keeping base pay intact (with the typical annual raises) while adding on performance pay preserves the entitlement mentality of pay and fails to establish a strong enough link between pay and team performance.

A problem with team performance pay arises when the pay motivates performance too well. In such cases, there may be a risk of "bottlenecking" other teams, as when an upstream team's increased productivity swamps a downstream team's ability to handle the work. The split between rewarding an individual team's performance and providing monetary incentives for a collection of teams in a business unit that we described above appears to be an attempt to minimize the occurrence of such system-disrupting performance improvement. There should be some element of the performance contingencies in the reward system that gives teams an incentive to care about the performance of other teams and even the organization as a whole. We will turn next to some programs that can have this effect.

### Gainsharing

*Gainsharing* programs pay groups of people monetary amounts, based on a formula, for productivity gains in the organizational unit to which those groups belong. One of the original purposes of gainsharing programs was to encourage employee involvement in finding ways to improve productivity and reduce costs. The reward for such efforts was to be some portion of the resulting savings or gains with the rest going to the organization. Because SMWTs have already set the stage for employee involvement in process and productivity improvement, gainsharing is a good fit with team-based organizations. In fact, it is compatible with and can complement other team rewards.

Several differences exist between gainsharing in team-based organizations and team performance pay. First, gainsharing is based on the performance of a larger group than the individual team; that is, the performance is the aggregate of many teams. It may be for a group of teams in a department, cost center, or even all the teams in a plant. Therefore, whereas team performance pay can do an excellent job in motivating particular teams to be more productive, gainsharing can motivate those teams to be concerned about other teams' productivity as well. Second, gainsharing is explicitly designed to be self-funding. Bonuses are only paid when there are gains that translate directly or indirectly into financial improvements, as determined by the gainsharing formula and its assumptions. Team performance pay could pay bonuses to particular teams for doing well when the rest of the organizational unit has slumped, not necessarily a bad practice if you want to reward good team performance, but it incurs financial risk to the organization if the situation persists. Gainsharing programs are not *superior* to team performance pay; they simply operate at a different level and address some of the areas of motivation not covered by team performance pay.

According to Belcher (1991), gainsharing programs include many variations typically based on several basic components we will examine: group composition, the baseline performance level, the formula for measuring gain, the share, payout frequency, and the split. *Group composition* in the context of gainsharing refers to the population of employees covered by the program. Should everyone, salaried or hourly, in the business unit be included? Should senior managers be excluded because they already have their own incentive pay programs? Should the plan cover everyone at the entire site, or should groups of teams have separate gainsharing programs? Each of these options exists in various organizations. Group composition will affect many other factors in the design of the gainsharing program, so this issue must be dealt with first.

The *baseline* is the performance level that future performance will be compared against to see whether there has been a gain. Baselines may be based on obtained historical performance, or they may be higher performance levels. They can also be fixed for a relatively long time or steadily change over time by moving upward with improving performance trends. The baseline affects one of the factors of reward effectiveness we have discussed earlier: attainability of goals. Team members must feel that, with reasonable effort in a reasonable time frame, they can produce the gains that will pay out.

The *formula* driving the gainsharing program can take many forms. There is no best formula; organizations should devise a formula tailored to their needs (Belcher, 1991). Formulas can measure gains based on physical productivity (operational) measures, which exclude dollar measures. Improshare is a standardized example of a plan driven by this kind of formula. Productivity measures ultimately can be translated into financial improvements, but the measures relate more directly to aspects of performance controllable by daily work processes. Financial formulas (e.g., Scanlon Plan) often relate some dollar measure of production to a measure of the labor costs of production in a ratio. Their advantage is their weakness: Financial formulas require that employees understand more about organizational finance. Although our study suggests that such knowledge has positive effects on team performance, it appears that most SMWT members today lack this knowledge. A newer type of formula is a hybrid of both formulas: It includes some mix of operational and financial measures. Important factors such as quality or safety measures could be included in such a formula. SMWTs that have experience with complex performance measurement systems like the Oregon Productivity Matrix will be prepared to understand most gainsharing formulas.

Belcher (1991) has reported that the majority of gainsharing programs share 25% to 50% of the gains with employees—the rest is kept by the organization. Some programs fix this share, but some vary the share as a function of some third variable, such as profitability. *Payout frequencies* are typically monthly or quarterly, so payouts are closely related in time to performance. This enhances the effectiveness of the payout as a reward for the behaviors involved in producing the gains, provided that the frequent payout does not reduce the size of the payout to such a small amount that it has little value as a reward (Belcher, 1991; Boyett & Conn, 1995; Scontrino, 1995). Some organizations using gainsharing also hold back a portion of the employee share until the end of the year. Because the holdbacks are only paid if performance across the year was above some level, they encourage a longer-term focus on performance improvement.

The *split* refers to the method by which gains are paid to individual employees. Splits can be based on the employee's total pay or the number of hours worked; or the gains can simply be divided equally among all participating employees. The latter "equal shares" approach would seem ideally suited for teams except that, according to Belcher (1991) and Boyett and Conn (1995), equal shares violates the federal Fair Labor Standards Act. The violation is that everyone receives the same payout regardless of any differences in the amount of overtime worked. Despite this, some organizations have used equal shares for years. There are technical ways of making it legal to pay equal shares, but splits based on more complicated factors are being developed.

Gainsharing programs seem to have many advantages as reward programs for teams. Indeed, Lawler (1986) has concluded that "gainsharing programs may need to be a key component of almost all high-involvement management systems" (p. 168). They can encourage and reward interpersonal processes between teams as well as within teams, preventing some of the risks associated with the narrow scope of team performance pay programs. They can help to broaden the business knowledge of team members because they focus attention on larger productivity and financial measures. Increased business knowledge has the potential to lead team members to suggest improvements in team or organizational functioning that have very large effects.

A typical problem of gainsharing programs is their weak line of sight. This has been attributed to the team members' lack of understanding of how the team's performance affects the scores needed to receive the bonus. However, it appears that it is possible to design a gainsharing system that has a strong line of sight comparable to that of team performance pay. Providing teams with access to education and training in business knowledge, as well as team experience with existing performance measurement systems, clarifies their understanding of the gainsharing formula. If gainsharing is to take advantage of its potential as a reward, the system must be understood by all those participating. Otherwise, payouts will seem like manna from heaven, or worse, entitlements that are being inconsistently provided by management.

Mitchell, Lewin, and Lawler (1990) have noted that many successful implementations of gainsharing programs have been reported, although the reports often have many confounding factors whose presence make clean interpretations of the effectiveness of gainsharing alone impossible. Gainsharing is typically part of a "package" intervention with other elements, such as changes in management practices. This is certainly the case where gainsharing has been introduced in organizations using, or transitioning to, SMWTs. For that reason, analyzing the effectiveness of gainsharing becomes difficult.

In a manufacturing organization we studied, a gainsharing program was operating together with the team performance pay program. The organization used the Oregon Productivity Matrix (OPM) as the heart of its performance measurement system. Gains across the entire business unit, consisting of 10 to 15 teams, were measured by an OPM reflecting the combined performance of all the teams in the unit. The teams' understanding of the basic measurement system, the OPM, gave them a leg up on understanding the gainsharing program. A larger proportion of incentive pay was given for team performance, reflecting the fact that teams could control their own performance more than that of the other teams. However, the gainsharing amounts were large enough to motivate concern for performance at the broader level. Thus, this is a good example of creating a mix of reward programs to address multiple aspects of performance. Furthermore, in this business unit, the gainsharing program appeared to be having the desired effects. Interviews with team members found that the team members were not only focused on their team's ability to reach its OPM goals. They were also concerned about the whole business unit reaching its OPM goals. The possibility of receiving additional money through gainsharing was clearly motivating team members to focus on how their team could enhance the unit's OPM scores. Both of the SMWTs studied in this business unit were high-performing SMWTs.

### Profit Sharing

Profit-sharing programs have been used in organizations for years to increase employee commitment and encourage retention. Traditionally, profit-sharing plans have returned a share of organizational profits to employees on an annual basis, with some or all of the payout often being deferred into a retirement plan. Some of the more recent profit-sharing plans have more flexible systems, permitting employees to choose between annual or deferred payouts (McCoy, 1992). Kruse (1993) has provided data from a review of research showing that profit-sharing plans have been associated with small but significant increases in organizational productivity. On the other hand, McAdams (1996) has been more skeptical about such positive effects. As with other gainsharing programs, organizations that implement profit sharing are often innovative in other respects (such as management structure and practices), so inferring a causal connection from the correlation of profit sharing and productivity is risky.

There are many reasons why profit-sharing programs would be expected to be weak as performance rewards in organizations with or without teams. The line of sight is very long and unclear. Because these programs are typically organization-wide, the larger the organization, the more individual or team contribution toward profitability is diluted. Furthermore, so many factors beyond individual or team performance can influence profitability that the effect of performance improvement is often unclear to the performers and may be negated by those other factors. For example, general economic

sions or devise and apply their own solutions to work problems. Training in problem solving typically includes learning techniques for identifying the problem, investigating possible causes, proposing alternative solutions, and selecting the best one. It may focus on what data to consider, examination of work processes, and when to include customers and suppliers in the problem-solving effort (Becker-Reems, 1994; Lawler, 1986). Furthermore, it may include determining when a single team member has the authority to make a decision, when a decision should be determined by a majority of the team, and when team consensus should be sought in making a decision.

## AVAILABILITY AND TIMING OF TRAINING

High-performing teams were found to make education and training easily accessible to team members, *and* team members were found to routinely take advantage of these. In one high-performing SMWT, for example, the team was given a training budget, required to take at least 40 hours of training per year, and allowed to decide what training was most needed. Furthermore, formal education was supported by assistance with tuition payments. On the other hand, a low-performing team was found to have training accessible, but team members were so pressured to improve team performance that they did not feel they could afford to take the time away from the job to attend training. In this case, the appropriate training could have assisted the team in improving its performance, but team members were too concerned about performance to recognize this.

Similar findings have been reported by others. In particular, Hackman and Oldham (1980) have noted the importance of making available the types of education and training that are needed by SMWTs. As they have stated, "too often self-managing work groups are formed, given a large and complex task to perform, and then left to 'work things out' on their own" (p. 196). Becker-Reems (1994) has noted the importance of encouraging SMWT members to obtain the education and training being made available to them. She has pointed out that most SMWT members were conditioned in the traditional work environment where one does not ask questions, seek out assistance, or in any other way display a lack of knowledge. As a result, such traditional attitudes must be changed in order for SMWT members to obtain the education and training they need in their new, more demanding environments.

Our data show that it is equally important that the timing of the education and training occur just when it is needed, rather than months before or after.

Otherwise, SMWT members become frustrated because they are unable to apply their new knowledge and skills. Furthermore, as Shonk (1992) and others have noted, when the time comes for them to apply the new skills, if training occurred some months before, much of what was learned is lost because it was not immediately used. Wellins et al. (1991) have referred to this as a "just-in-time approach to training" where the training is provided as close in time as possible to actual use of the skills.

## A BRIEF REVIEW OF TRAINING
## AND EDUCATION TECHNIQUES

Education and training were found to be effective when provided in a formal setting as well as when provided on the job by other team members who were knowledgeable and skilled in the areas being taught. Formal training programs can be viewed as including five phases. As outlined by Becker-Reems (1994), the first identifies the knowledge and skills needed by the team to accomplish its goals. The second assesses each team member's strengths. The third identifies gaps in team skills and knowledge and determines who will receive what training. The fourth selects the training methodology. If the purpose is to gain general knowledge about a subject, the methods might include reading books, using self-study materials, and attending professional meetings. If the purpose is to gain skills, the team members may learn through practicing or by working with a skilled team member on the job. During the planning phase, a formal training plan is sometimes developed for each team member or for the team as a whole, and appropriate materials are then purchased or developed. During the final, fifth phase, the training is implemented.

On-the-job training has been reported to be effective for a variety of reasons (Johnson & Johnson, 1994). Team members, as teachers, can explain and demonstrate the skills to be learned at the work site, and this makes it easier to transfer what is learned to the job situation. Furthermore, team members can provide immediate feedback and encouragement to the co-worker.

Cross-training (or multiskilling) has also been reported to be effective, and our data support these conclusions. *Cross-training* is the provision of multiple skills to team members—skills that are needed to perform the team's work (Fisher et al., 1995; Klein, 1994). In traditional environments, each employee is responsible for performing one or a few skills. In an SMWT, the team members typically perform most if not all of the skills required of the team and, consequently, need increased training to obtain the skills. Cross-training has been reported to have a variety of positive effects on the team's performance including providing increased staffing flexibility, providing coworkers who can be turned to for assistance when problems occur or performance demands increase, relieving the boredom associated with re-peatedly performing the same task, and giving team members a better understanding of how different jobs fit with each other and how each member contributes to the overall team performance (Neuhaus, 1990; Thomas & Thomas, 1990; Wellins et al., 1994). Wellins et al. (1991), in their review of SMWT case studies, have provided a particularly clear example of this last effect of cross-training:

> In one complex chemical process operation, two employees performed their jobs for years without realizing that the actions of each directly affected the other's work. Although they worked physically close to each other and carried on long conversations, they never discussed the process. This resulted in an almost comical and never-ending chain of unnecessary adjustments. As one operator would increase the temperature, the other would correct for it, causing the first to make even greater adjustments, and so on. This continued until management and the union instituted cross-training, and the two opera-tors began to understand the larger process and the nature of their interde-pendency. (p. 177)

Other training techniques that were reported to be effective included benchmarking visits to other SMWTs and experiential training. *Benchmark-ing* is the process of comparing one's own team with other teams, typically by visiting and sharing information with teams in other organizations (Shonk, 1992). The information gained during these trips can often be used to help orient new team members to the SMWT concept, can help the team evaluate its own performance relative to others, can provide new ideas to the team on how it might function more effectively, and can provide new ideas on how the team can be helpful to its larger organization. A related approach is the examination of case studies through videos. This can likewise help SMWT members learn what other teams have done and are doing.

*Experiential training* provides an opportunity for team members to en-gage in team-building training that goes beyond the classroom setting (Michalak, Fischer, & Meeker, 1994). Team members typically engage in action-oriented teamwork and problem solving as a means of increasing their interpersonal skills. One example of an experiential training exercise is blindfolding one team member and having a second lead the person through a "minefield" of obstacles that have been laid indiscriminately across the floor. This exercise is designed to build trust between the two team members as one leads the other.

An additional training technique advocated by a variety of consultants but not found in use among our case studies is the development of *mental models* (Cannon-Bowers, Salas, & Converse, 1991; Guzzo, Salas, & Associates, 1995). Mental models provide team members with shared or compatible models of behavior for various work situations. Such models help team members to anticipate how one another will respond to various work situations and what each other's needs will be. They have been reported to assist team members in making quick decisions because team members can accurately anticipate how the team will respond in various situations.

## TRAINING MANAGERS

In a memorandum to a subordinate, a manager wrote, "Management must also be included in our educational plans. Their changing role is not intuitive. We cannot leave their education to chance" (Meeker, 1993). The roles of management change markedly when the organization moves from a traditional to an SMWT environment. The manager shifts from a paternalistic role that requires monitoring individuals and sometimes "punishing" employees to a role more reflective of a partnership, where the manager becomes a resource, consultant, and advocate for the team. The philosophy of the manager is similar to McGregor's (1960) Theory Y as described above, rather than his Theory X, which is more commonly found in a traditional work environment.

Education and training can at least be expected to provide managers with an understanding of their new roles and responsibilities and at the most help them to shift their philosophy, if necessary (Fisher et al., 1995; Shonk, 1992; Varney, 1989). An examination of our data indicates that education and training did help with the former but much less so for the latter; that is, it was clear that education and training helped managers obtain a clear understanding of their new roles and responsibilities and what the new management philosophy was. However, the education and training did not appear to influence greatly the personal philosophy and, in some cases, behaviors of the managers. For example, managers of a low-performing government SMWT reported to us correctly what their new roles and responsibilities had become and what their new philosophy was as managers of an SMWT. However, reports from the team members and other managers indicated that their behavior did not reflect the new philosophy. This had detrimental effects on the SMWT, such as reducing its ability to obtain sufficient information to make good decisions.

In another example, managers of a manufacturing SMWT had been provided education and training on their new roles and responsibilities. In this case, it was clear that some of these managers were unwilling to accept the new philosophy and the new roles and responsibilities for managers. As a result, these managers either quit, were placed in jobs where they no longer worked with nonmanagement employees directly, or were released from the organization.

In these examples, it is unclear why there was a lack of behavioral change. It may have been because managers did not receive enough education and training, because the education and training received were not effective, or because the managers were simply unwilling to change their philosophy and behaviors. Our guess is that the lack of change was due to the latter. This is based on our observations and conversations with managers but not a thorough assessment of the training programs.

Thus, the data indicate that the education and training of managers was able to help them understand their new roles and responsibilities. It was less able to influence their personal philosophy and beliefs regarding nonmanagement employees. It appeared that managers who had always held a Theory Y perspective of employees continued to do so, whereas those who had always held a Theory X perspective did not necessarily change their views, even after extensive training and education. This does not mean that education and training cannot change a manager's perspective toward nonmanagement employees. However, it does make it clear that such a change may not come easily for managers holding a Theory X perspective.

Interestingly, it appears that the opposite is true as well. We received several reports of managers who, prior to transitioning to SMWTs, had continually been reprimanded for not practicing traditional, paternalistic behaviors such as punishing employees. At the time, these managers had received the traditional education and training in manager roles, responsibilities, and philosophies but did not practice the behaviors learned. When the organization transitioned to an SMWT environment, these managers were no longer reprimanded and became role models for other managers.

## EDUCATION, TRAINING, AND SMWT PERFORMANCE

Perhaps the greatest effects of the education and training systems, as identified from interviews with managers and team members, were on the personal characteristics of the team members. Technical training on specific aspects of the work increased team member knowledge and skills, which, in turn, increased the team members' level of talent available to be applied during the work process. Education and training for team members that focused on management skills appeared to influence the team members' willingness to participate in decision making and their desire for a broader variety of responsibilities. Conversations with team members revealed that, prior to education and training, some team members lacked the confidence to participate in decision making and were apprehensive about trying to perform more than the one or few tasks they knew they could do. It was often reported that apprehensions were reduced and the added variety became a welcomed change once workers had received education and training *and* been coaxed or encouraged to participate in decision making and performing multiple tasks by management and team members.

Education and training on interpersonal skills were found to have impacts on the interpersonal processes, although the extent of these effects is unclear. For example, in one manufacturing SMWT, there was a team member who was reportedly not a "team player." He did not participate in many of the decisions that were made as a team and instead chose to keep to himself. When the SMWT members chose to attend an experiential training program, he chose not to participate and sat away from the rest of the team during the first day's sessions. However, on the second day of the training, he had a change of heart, openly apologized to the team for not participating, and proceeded to participate in the remainder of the experiential exercises. This experience appeared to subsequently increase his commitment to the team and his cooperation and to improve the team's other interpersonal processes that directly involved him. However, the extent to which the actual training affected his behavior is unclear.

It can also be expected that education and training had positive effects on specific interpersonal relationships, such as achieving conflict resolution and cooperative conflict. However, here again, such effects could not be clearly determined from our data. Although we did note some cases where such training had been provided, the effects of the training on behavior were not easily discernible and, in the case of management training, appeared to be nonexistent.

Education and training were clearly found to influence the SMWT design characteristics, particularly with regard to the various roles that the team was responsible for performing. For example, education and training on the SMWT's mission and responsibilities clearly influenced the team's ability to define specific measurable goals. Education and training on decision making and problem solving clearly assisted teams in the procedures that they chose to use to accomplish these. Teams that had received education and training on decision making appeared to follow a more structured decision-making approach. This typically included beginning the decision-making process by identifying a variety of possible alternatives, then assessing the strengths and weaknesses of each, and finally selecting the best decisions based on the assessments.

High-performing teams were found to have received extensive training in many aspects of team design and interpersonal processes, such as conducting performance appraisals and peer evaluations, performing team roles, and interacting with customers and suppliers. Low-performing teams, on the other hand, were less likely to have received extensive education and training in these areas. One common reason was unavailability, particularly of training with regard to SMWT design. A second reason low-performing teams lacked education and training was the team members' reluctance to make use of the training that was available. In these cases, team members did not want to leave their jobs long enough to receive the training because they perceived their team's performance to be questionable and feared that their absence would jeopardize it further.

Thus, it is clear that high-performing teams had used much more training than low-performing teams. However, without thorough assessments of the education and training programs, it is difficult to determine to what extent the use or nonuse of education and training programs affected various aspects of the SMWTs, particularly with regard to interpersonal processes and management philosophy and behavior.

# 17

■

# Information Systems

■

Information is valuable to anyone or to any group of people who must make decisions and choose between alternatives. An *information system* is a means or system for communicating information from one point to another (Holt, 1990). SMWTs need information systems that are effective at providing the team with all the information necessary to make the best decisions possible. Our study found that an organization's information system had direct effects on the decisions reached by SMWTs, including identification of goals, assignment of tasks, and the work procedures selected for doing the work. The information system was also found to affect the team's ability to provide information to management and was found to influence the SMWT's interpersonal processes within the team as well as between the team and those outside the team. This variety of effects was found to subsequently influence the team's work process and performance. Provided below is an examination of the kinds of information needed by SMWTs, followed by a review of the means by which SMWTs obtain and share information. Next is an examination of the obstacles to obtaining needed information. Finally, a review is provided of the effects we found information systems to have on the SMWTs.

## KINDS OF INFORMATION NEEDED BY SMWTs

SMWTs have a variety of decision-making and problem-solving responsibilities that are left to management in traditional work environments (Holt,

1990; Orsburn et al., 1990). These many new responsibilities require a variety of information in order to be successfully performed. For example, SMWTs are responsible for setting clear, challenging, measurable goals. This requires information on the team's broader mission, on its past performance, and on any anticipated changes in the technologies used, personnel, and so on. SMWTs are also responsible for planning and managing the work process, including, for example, scheduling what work is to be done each day, who will do what work, and who will take what training. Information needed might include current day-to-day demands for the team's product or service, available supplies, and knowledge and skill requirements for producing the team's products or services. Thus, the SMWT's many responsibilities require a variety of information and, in turn, an information system that can get the information to the team, as well as getting information from the team to others outside the team.

The optimal amount of information needed by the SMWT will vary, depending on the team's tasks and the responsibilities handed to the team by management (Streufert & Nogami, 1992). However, some teams have reported difficulty determining the optimal amount of information. Several researchers have pointed out that the team's ability to make good decisions is affected by its ability to determine as precisely as possible the exact information it needs and then request and receive this information—no more and no less (Barnes, 1996; Becker-Reems, 1994; Wetherbe, 1991).

Our data support these conclusions. In several SMWTs we studied, the information system provided a shortage of information that prevented the teams from considering all the facts prior to making a decision. In other SMWTs, it was reported that an excess of information prevented the teams from identifying the information that was most useful and relevant to the decisions being made. This has been referred to as *information overload.* More specifically, in one high-performing manufacturing SMWT, it was explained that when the team first took over many of the tactical and operational responsibilities, the team requested and was provided too much information. The result was too much time spent trying to identify, among all the information, that which was most relevant for the team's decisions. Gradually, the team streamlined its requests for information so that it would receive only what was needed.

Researchers have found that the information system must not only be able to provide the information requested by the SMWT—it must also be able to provide information that is easily accessible, accurate (or credible), understandable, verifiable, complete, and timely (Holt, 1990; Johnson & Johnson, 1994; Larson & LaFasto, 1989). Decisions will be made based on the information received. The quality of the decisions will likely be reduced if the information received is not accurate or team members have questions about the information but cannot trace the information to its source to get answers and verify its accuracy. Similarly, if team members have difficulty getting the information they request, do not get complete information, or receive information that is difficult to understand, the information will do little to help the team and could result in the team making poor decisions based on misunderstood information.

## TECHNIQUES FOR OBTAINING INFORMATION

Studies have found that SMWTs use a variety of techniques for obtaining information (Lawler, 1988b, 1989), and our study was no different in this regard. We found that in some cases, the SMWT chose to request information from appropriate managers or, where available, the organization's information specialists. This had the advantage of providing information fairly rapidly and with little time or effort spent by team members. On the other hand, sometimes the managers involved were unable to respond in a timely manner or chose not to provide the team with the information it requested. For example, in a high-performing manufacturing SMWT studied, we learned, while observing a team meeting, that the team had requested information and assistance from a manager who disagreed with what the team wanted to do and consequently was not responding to their requests. As a result, the team decided to turn for help to a higher-ranking manager who was more supportive of the team and could "force" the uncooperative manager to comply with the team's requests.

A generally more time-intensive approach was the direct collection of information by observation and interviewing. For example, in another manufacturing SMWT studied, the SMWT was considering sending a proposal to management that would request that the SMWT be allowed to assume responsibility for operating a machine that was currently being operated by a team that was overburdened. The SMWT had already received some information about the machine from management. To obtain additional information about the machine, several SMWT members observed it in operation and informally interviewed several people who had operated it in the past.

More general information was often obtained during regular, monthly state-of-the-business meetings that were held by management for all employees and from newsletters and the organization's bulletin boards. This type of information assisted some teams in planning, advising management, and understanding constraints and opportunities.

In some cases, people from other SMWTs or people from other parts of the organization with valuable information were invited to attend a team meeting to share information. Similarly, at times, senior managers and engineers were invited to share information about the future direction of the organization or about specific product changes anticipated for the team.

Some organizations used a *star point system,* which assisted the SMWTs in receiving as well as sharing information. In this arrangement, the various management responsibilities of the SMWT were grouped into star points, such as a safety point, productivity point, scheduling point, and so on. One team member had primary responsibility for measuring and keeping track of each point on the star. With this arrangement, a meeting of people from different SMWTs who all had responsibility for the same star point could be held. During such meetings, the participants would share information regarding the responsibility. For example, a meeting of safety star points might include a meeting of five people representing five different SMWTs, each responsible for safety issues on his or her respective team. Such a meeting would include a sharing of any safety problems that had been encountered, solutions discovered, and innovations tried.

Several of the organizations we studied had begun providing computer terminals and had developed a computer network for the SMWTs as a means for them to directly enter and maintain their own information about their work processes and performance, to obtain needed information from others within the organization, and to provide information to others. Productivity data, quality data, and personnel data, such as hours of work, overtime, and peer appraisals, were recorded. As a result, much of the record keeping was done by the individuals on the team by directly entering team data. Furthermore, this ability to easily obtain access to this information from others assisted the teams in planning, scheduling, and adjusting their own work to fit what others were doing and, subsequently, enhanced the coordination between the SMWTs.

## IMPORTANCE OF SHARING INFORMATION

Researchers have found that it is not only important for SMWTs to obtain the information they need to plan and make good decisions, but it is also important for the SMWT to keep management, suppliers, and customers apprised of its activities and performance (Ancona, 1990; Ancona & Caldwell, 1992; Lawler, 1988c). This allows management to recognize the team's successes and have an understanding of the situation when the team encounters problems. Information provided to management can be crucial in long-term strategic decisions at the organizational level, such as the establishment of new products and removal of unprofitable ones. Furthermore, information from the SMWTs can be used to evaluate the performance of managers, identify opportunities for the organization to improve, and assist the teams in better coordinating their efforts.

When considering suppliers and customers, our study found that providing and receiving feedback helped the SMWT to influence the supplier's performance so that appropriate supplies were more likely to be provided in a timely fashion. Furthermore, it allowed the SMWT to better understand the constraints of its suppliers. Similarly, keeping customers abreast of the team activities, successes, and problems allowed customers to better anticipate the team's output and make recommendations to the team that could allow the team to better serve the customers.

A variety of techniques were used to share information with those outside the SMWT. Most of the techniques noted above for obtaining information were also used for sharing information. In some organizations, computers were used to share information with managers and internal suppliers and customers. This allowed senior managers to access information on production and cost measures throughout the organization and allowed internal suppliers and customers to better coordinate their activities with the SMWT. Direct contact with suppliers and customers typically occurred via telephone conversations and in-person visits. Furthermore, in most organizations an employee attitude survey was regularly conducted to obtain employee attitudes toward management and the organization, as well as to get input on products and services.

## OBSTACLES TO INFORMATION EXCHANGE

A variety of obstacles to information exchange were identified from our case studies. If a team was not clear as to its mission and specific goals, it was unable to request the exact information it needed to achieve these. This problem also occurred when the team lacked a clear understanding of a specific problem it was attempting to address or a decision to be made—in these cases the team was unable to accurately request the information needed. A lack of clarity similarly affected the information exchange when the team was unclear what specific information was being requested. In these cases, too much, too little, or the wrong information was typically provided.

Information exchange was also affected by how thoroughly the organization collected information and how well the information was catalogued and categorized. The team was unable to receive or provide information if the information was not collected, or if the information was collected but not stored in a way that allowed the team to get access to it in a reasonable amount of time.

If the team clearly understood what it needed and the information was accessible, the SMWT still had difficulty getting the information if those who could provide access to the information chose to keep the information from the team. This was found to occur where managers disliked the team concept and chose not to assume their new management roles, or managers lacked confidence in the particular team's decisions and, consequently, were reluctant to encourage the team's decision-making activities by providing it with needed information.

In some cases, the SMWT was unable to readily obtain information it was requesting because the holder of the information had not been informed that the team had been given the authority to have access to the confidential information. This obstacle to information exchange could sometimes result in valuable time passing as the team went through the chain of command to get authorization.

Still another obstacle to information exchange was people on the team who held valuable information but chose not to share it with the remainder of the team and/or with others outside the team. In the cases observed, the information holder appeared to be using the information as a means of displaying "superiority" over teammates and causing teammates to feel inferior. Furthermore, withholding information could be used as a means of inhibiting the activities of an individual outside the team or inhibiting the activities of another team.

## THE INFORMATION SYSTEM
## AND SMWT PERFORMANCE

The information system had direct effects on the SMWT's work process, particularly with regard to the effort placed on doing the work, the procedures for doing the work, and the resources applied to the work. When team members clearly understood the challenges their organization faced, they appeared more motivated and committed to helping the organization by applying more effort and seeking improved procedures. For example, in a high-performing manufacturing SMWT, the team members were provided clear information on the organization's financial viability—the organization was not likely to continue as it currently was without identifying new customers and new products, and reducing the costs of the products it was producing. Subsequently, the SMWT members committed themselves to finding ways of reducing costs that led to the identification of major cost-saving procedures for the products that the team was producing. More specifically, in this case, the team recommended that several machines be reorganized on the plant floor so that a single team member could operate a second machine while waiting for the first machine to run its cycle. Prior to this rearrangement, the team member would idly stand by for 30 to 45 minutes at a time waiting for the first machine to complete a cycle. Rearranging the machines and their operation resulted in reducing the cost of the product by one third, allowing the organization to pass on this dramatic savings to its customer, and, subsequently, helping the organization keep the customer.

The information system was found to also influence the team's interpersonal processes, including cooperation, trust, and cohesion among team members, interpersonal relations with management, and communication and coordination between the team and other teams. In the example noted above, the information system clarified for the SMWT the urgency of the organization's financial situation, and this subsequently drew the SMWT closer together, increasing the cohesiveness and cooperation within the team as team members looked for ways to help. It was reported that this financial information was also shared with other SMWTs in the affected division, and the result was teams working more closely together and looking for ways to assist each other. Furthermore, it was reported that the teams were more responsive to suggestions by management and vice versa as everyone was seeking ways of salvaging the division's financial condition.

In a second example, the information system was not as open. A nursing home management team chose to withhold information from others in the organization. The particular information withheld showed that the nursing home was operating below financial expectations. Those within this management SMWT reasoned that if this information got out into the local community, it might be damaging to the nursing home. Consequently, the information was not shared at all—not with people in the local community or other employees and SMWTs within the nursing home. The result was a wave of rumors within the nursing home that appeared to reduce the level of trust between the management SMWT and those SMWTs and other employees outside the team.

As noted above, the information system was particularly important when an SMWT attempted to coordinate its activities with other SMWTs, as well as with its suppliers and customers. Where information was clearly and accurately provided and received by the SMWT, coordination was increased.

Furthermore, the information system affected the SMWT's team design characteristics, including the team's ability to set clear goals, identify best solutions, and make the best decisions possible. SMWTs had difficulty establishing measurable goals if the information system was unable to provide the team with the data it needed to best measure its performance. Similarly, if the team understood the problem to be solved or the decision that needed to be made but lacked all the information needed, it was less likely to choose the best solution or make the best decision.

Finally, as noted above, the environmental factors most important to the information system included management roles and support, supplier and customer support, education and training, and the establishment of a clear purpose and mission. These were found to be crucial to the SMWTs in requesting and getting the information they needed.

# 18

■

# Management Support, Encouragement, and Roles

■

We found that there are a variety of roles managers need to play in order for an SMWT to perform at a high level. We have organized these into four broad areas. Two include providing support and encouragement to the SMWT. A description of these and the other management roles is provided below. Also discussed are obstacles and enablers found to influence the manager's ability to perform these roles.

## SUPPORT FROM MANAGEMENT

A major role found to be performed by the managers of high-performing teams was the provision of emotional and other supports to the SMWTs. Perhaps the single most influential emotional support reported was the unspoken message that it was the team that held primary responsibility for monitoring the team's performance and that the manager could be counted on to help the team whenever possible. The managers' behaviors and what they said were the means of conveying this support. Of course, this did not mean that the managers never monitored the team's performance. On the contrary, the managers of high-performing teams constantly monitored the team's performance by reviewing the performance reports prepared and used by the SMWTs. When a high-performing team scored low on a particular performance measure, the manager was likely to question the team leader or the team's selected management liaison about the dip in performance. Typically, the manager asked what the team was planning to do to overcome the problem and what management could do to assist the team in overcoming the problem.

On the other hand, some of the managers of low-performing teams held negative attitudes about the SMWTs and implicitly expressed these to the team. These managers were more likely to provide an unspoken message that the team was not performing well, was not doing a good job at taking responsibility for its performance, and perhaps should not be allowed to continue working as an SMWT. This lack of support caused team members to doubt their own abilities, to spend many hours justifying their decisions and behaviors, and to feel high levels of stress. It is interesting to note that not all low-performing teams lacked management support. In two of the low-performing SMWTs that we studied, their managers were providing both technical and emotional supports. However, these SMWTs had other problems that were causing the low performance, such as a lack of trust and cooperation among team members.

The importance of emotional and other supports has been noted by a variety of researchers (Sims & Lorenzi, 1992). In their survey of 692 employees and 141 managers, Parker and Price (1994) found that employees were more likely to perceive themselves as having control over decision making where managers were perceived as supportive. Becker-Reems (1994) has noted, "Senior management behavior can be an inspiration to teams. . . . It can provide positive feedback and recognition that will be communicated throughout the organization" (p. 34). She has included as particularly valuable supports the recognition of team accomplishments over individual accomplishments and the support of team ideas and suggestions. Larson and LaFasto (1989) have reported in their review of case studies that important supports from management include trusting team members with meaningful levels of responsibility, providing team autonomy to achieve results, presenting challenging opportunities to the team, recognizing and rewarding superior performance, and standing behind the team. Orsburn et al. (1990) have listed as supports spending time with the team, not making decisions for the team, obtaining team input on management decisions, and providing the team credit when it deserves it. And Ephross and Vassil (1988) have emphasized the importance of providing support based on realistic assessments. As they have stated, "It is not supportive, but often the opposite, to accept as the best the group can produce a product that is really poor in quality" (p. 152).

The findings reported in these previous studies were supported by our own data. The members of high-performing teams reported receiving high levels of support from management, whereas the low-performing teams were less likely to report this. Furthermore, interviews with team members suggested that their perception of "high levels of support" was not so much the result of management telling the team it was doing a good job as it was management being patient with the team and allowing the team to make mistakes as it sought ways of overcoming the problems that it encountered.

Finally, it is important to note that, among most of the high-performing teams, it was all levels of management that provided emotional and other supports. This was not found to the same extent among the low-performing teams. For example, in one low-performing government SMWT, senior management supported the SMWTs, whereas junior management did not. This created a variety of problems, including the SMWT having to go to senior management to receive support and a rift between senior and junior management regarding how to view and work with the SMWTs. Such struggles appeared to demotivate the team, contribute to members' lack of focus on their goals, and reduce their effort placed on doing the work.

## ENCOURAGEMENT FROM MANAGEMENT

Manz and Sims (1987) have emphasized the important role of management in encouraging the SMWT to take and maintain responsibility for its own performance. They have explained that team members need to be encouraged to conduct self-management activities. They need to be encouraged to set their own measurable performance goals, to establish high expectations for themselves, and to double-check important decisions they have made before implementing them. SMWTs need to be encouraged to evaluate their own performance, to be self-critical when performance is low, and to be self-rewarding when it is high. Our data support these conclusions. High-performing teams were found to receive constant encouragement from their managers to self-manage, whereas low-performing teams were less likely to receive such encouragement.

## OTHER MANAGEMENT ROLES

Researchers have identified numerous other roles for those who are managing SMWTs. Fisher et al. (1995), for example, has noted the importance of motivating team members, instilling team values and goals, being a role model, providing appropriate training, identifying and correcting any problems created by the team's environment, removing barriers to innovation, and providing necessary resources, tools, and information. Harper and Harper (1989) have listed 21 roles. A few of these include the importance of empowering team members by turning over power, information, knowledge, skills, and decisions; being a teacher and counselor; being people-oriented and a facilitator rather than a decision maker; removing environmental barriers that hinder teams; being a motivator; and promoting teamwork. We found from our in-depth study of SMWTs that the many specific roles of managers can be organized into two additional broad roles: (1) assisting with the SMWT's dimensions, that is, team design, environment, member characteristics, and work and interpersonal processes, and (2) acting as a team resource and coach. The first includes looking for ways to help the SMWT improve its work process, interpersonal process, team design, environment, and team member characteristics. Each is reviewed below.

## Management Assistance With Improving SMWT Dimensions

Our study of SMWTs showed that all the high-performing teams had managers who routinely examined each of the SMWT dimensions and encouraged SMWTs to do the same in order to identify any ways that one or more dimensions could be revised to increase the SMWT's performance. When considering the dimension work processes, the managers of high-performing teams were found to look for ways to increase the team members' motivation and commitment and subsequently their effort on the tasks. Similarly, these managers provided any assistance that would help the SMWT better apply its talents, resources, and procedures directly to the work.

When considering the interpersonal processes, the managers of high-performing teams were found to be available to the teams to assist them with these. In one manufacturing SMWT, for example, the manager was asked by the team to help solve a dispute between team members. In this case, the manager did not step in and act as judge to determine who was "most correct." Instead, he provided the team with a conflict resolution technique for solving disputes that enabled the SMWT to overcome the impasse.

The managers of high-performing teams were found to spend their time helping to develop environmental systems that would enhance SMWT performance. This included creating information systems that allowed teams to obtain all the information they needed for decision making as quickly as possible and developing performance appraisal and reward systems that encouraged employees to seek ways of achieving high team performance as well as high individual performance. Other environmental characteristics addressed by managers included seeking out new education and training programs that the SMWTs wanted and informing the teams of any new education and training programs discovered that the teams might be interested in. Likewise, the manager assisted the teams in obtaining the resources needed and would provide the teams with any new information obtained regarding procedures for doing the work.

A team design factor that all managers gave a lot of attention to was the team's goals. Managers of high-performing teams were found to work with the SMWTs in a partnership atmosphere to help the SMWTs establish clear, challenging, measurable goals. In one case, for example, this was called the "catch-ball" process. The SMWT members initially identified what they perceived to be clear, challenging goals and then "passed" these on to management, who then reviewed them and would typically have recommendations on how the goals might be improved. These would then be passed back to the team for its consideration. The team would then either change its original goals to reflect management's recommendations or pass back to management a further rationale for their initial goals and a response to management's recommendations. This process would continue until the SMWT and management agreed on the goals for the SMWT.

Still another SMWT dimension important to team performance and addressed by managers of high-performing teams was the characteristics of the team members themselves. In all the cases studied, the managers had considerable influence on the selection of any new people who joined the SMWT. In some cases, management provided the SMWT with a short list of people the team could choose from. In others, management selected the new team member after receiving input from the team. In either case, the managers of high-performing teams allowed the SMWTs to consider only people who desired to work in a team environment. On the other hand, the managers of low-performing teams were less likely to consider "attitudes toward teamwork" as one of the criteria for selecting potential people to join the SMWT and, instead, focused on factors such as the technical skill of the individual and availability.

We found a similar situation when senior managers of low-performing teams were hiring junior managers. Attitudes toward teamwork were not typically considered when senior managers selected junior managers for positions that would include management of SMWTs. For example, in a government organization where a low-performing SMWT was studied, the senior manager—who had encouraged the establishment of several SMWTs—was found to hire a manager of the SMWTs' division without considering the manager's attitudes toward teams. In this case, this resulted in hiring a division manager who felt that SMWTs could not work in a government setting and, subsequently, chose to provide only token support for the SMWTs in his division.

## Management as a Resource and Coach

A second broad management role practiced by the managers of high-performing teams was that of a resource and coach for the team. Being a resource to the team included helping the team obtain whatever resources it needed to carry out its technical and management responsibilities. For example, as noted above, the SMWT needs a wide variety of information to carry out its roles. The quality, timeliness, and appropriate amount of information the team receives will affect the team's ability to perform its roles at a high level. Managers of high-performing teams made themselves available to SMWTs and attempted to provide the teams with any information the team requested or the manager felt was relevant.

On the other hand, we found that the managers of low-performing teams tended to hold back information from the SMWTs, and this reduced their ability to perform their technical and management roles. In one case, for example, the SMWT was asked by management to determine what to do with several aging company vehicles. After weeks of team discussion and consideration, the team provided management with its recommendation, only to learn that several important facts had not been shared with the team, and this made their recommendation look naive. Without all the information, the team was unable to make a good recommendation. This not only resulted in a poor decision by the team but also demotivated the team, as it concluded that placing large amounts of energy into making recommendations was a waste of time.

In addition to being a resource for the team, the managers of high-performing teams were also a coach to the teams, particularly with regard to technical and management responsibilities. Similar findings have been reported by others. For example, Lawler (1989) has noted that team members should not be expected to take over decision-making responsibilities about work methods without initial coaching from human resource personnel and managers. And Wellins et al. (1991) have expressed this point by stating, "Effective and empowering leaders . . . coach for success *before* the team member's action, not *after* the failure. Coaching for success increases the likelihood of success, which in turn builds confidence" (p. 175).

Hackman and Walton (1986) have noted the value of coaching regarding team decision making and working collaboratively. They have made this point by stating,

Too often a task is tossed to group members with the assumption that "they'll work it out among themselves." And, too often, members may not know how to do that. A leader or consultant can do much to promote team effectiveness by helping team members learn *how* to work interdependently—although this is probably a hopeless task if the group has an unsupportive organizational context [environment] or was poorly structured in the first place [team design]. (p. 85)

Our findings support these conclusions. The managers of high-performing teams were constantly seeking ways to coach the team in technical and management skills. This was found to provide the team members foremost with added skills. Furthermore, the manager as coach appeared to provide the team members with an added incentive to learn the new skills. Our general observation was that team members preferred to work without a coach but recognized that they could only be successful without a coach if they learned the technical and management skills being provided through the coach. Thus, the team members were motivated to learn the needed technical and management skills so that they would no longer need to rely on their manager for coaching.

The managers of low-performing teams were less likely to provide coaching as a means of assisting the team. For example, two low-performing government teams were found to be receiving no management assistance and were struggling with no solution in sight for how to overcome their problems. For one of these teams, team members and several managers reported that the team initially performed at a much higher level because it had a manager who constantly coached the team as well as acting as an advocate for the team. However, after her departure from the SMWT's division, she was not replaced and the team began to flounder, its mission became increasingly unclear, and no new manager coach/advocate stepped forward to assist the team.

## OBSTACLES TO PERFORMING
## EFFECTIVE MANAGEMENT ROLES

A variety of obstacles were found to prevent the managers of SMWTs from performing the management roles that helped SMWTs achieve high performance. These have been described in some detail by a number of researchers. Klein (1984), in her article, "Why Supervisors Resist Employee Involvement," has noted that in some cases, managers fear for their job security, believing that if they do a particularly good job, the SMWT will be able to perform completely on its own and the manager will no longer be needed or will be assigned to a position with lower compensation. These beliefs become stronger as the manager hears or reads of other managers in other organizations that were released once the SMWTs were set in place, or when senior management provides no reason to believe otherwise.

Another obstacle we found stems from the fact that the use of SMWTs requires a change in management philosophy, and some managers choose not to accept the new perspective. Interviews with these managers indicated that they felt they had spent many years getting to the stage in their careers where they could tell others what to do instead of always being told what to do. They had typically invested many years developing personal rationales for working in the traditional hierarchical environment and felt that they had "paid their dues" as required by the traditional management approach and were "entitled" to the payoffs, such as telling others what to do. To be told that the management approach was now changing and they would be a consultant or coach for the team was perceived by some to be a demotion and unacceptable.

Another obstacle stems from management fears that they will not be able to successfully perform their new participative management roles. It appeared that such fears led some to not try at all in order to avoid the failure that could come. These managers typically had become very secure in their traditional management roles based on their past successes working in a traditional environment. However, they had no basis for such confidence in an untried teamwork environment where their new roles typically required them to develop new expanded relationships with the employees who were now SMWT members.

Closely tied to this fear is the uncertainty of what is expected of them in a participative management environment. Typically, managers who did not receive adequate training regarding their new roles were more unsure of what was expected of them. A lack of training made it particularly difficult for them to successfully perform their new roles because they were unsure what all the new roles were.

Hitchcock and Willard (1995) have described a variety of similar obstacles preventing managers from performing their new roles. They have noted,

Their self-image as the people with the answers will be questioned. They may fear that they will lose control over the team but still be held accountable for the team's performance. Many secretly fear that they will not be able to perform in this new environment. With this new role comes a loss of competence and predictability. For some, a perceived loss of power and status is paramount. (p. 22)

Tjosvold (1986) has noted similar obstacles and pointed out further that management sometimes lacks understanding of and faith in the SMWT members. He has clarified this obstacle by stating,

> [Managers] dismiss employees' personal aspirations and difficulties as unimportant. They wrongly assume that it does not matter what employees think as long as they do what is expected. But employees who do not understand why a task is important and needs to be done are not very motivated or knowledgeable about how to complete the task well. (p. 151)

Closely tied to this obstacle is the manager's belief that SMWT members do not have the intelligence to make good decisions. In one organization where several managers held this view, it was found that the SMWT members had not received sufficient training to perform the management responsibilities turned over to them. Consequently, in a sense, the managers were justified in believing that the SMWT members could not do the work. However, the reason did not appear to be a lack of intelligence but instead a lack of education and training, which was eventually recognized as a major management oversight.

It is also important to note that the obstacles to performing effective management roles are not always easily detectable. For example, in the study of a low-performing government SMWT that had been established by the senior manager in the region, almost all the managers involved with the SMWTs expressed a general belief that the SMWT concept was a good one. However, interviews with team members and an examination of specific activities undertaken (and not undertaken) by managers suggested that they had not changed their roles to match the new participative management philosophy they said they supported. It became obvious, once going beyond the rhetoric of the managers, that they were professing the new philosophy but probably did not really believe it and definitely were not practicing it. The difficulty in recognizing this obstacle has been well expressed by Klein (1984):

> Supervisors rarely show open resistance to programs top management initiates. After all, they are part of management, too. More to the point, few have access to formal mechanisms for voicing disenchantment, and most perceive that their job security depends in no small measure on following upper management's instructions. Nonetheless, the negative attitudes are not far below the surface—negative not only toward proposed changes in management style but also toward the process of change itself. (p. 88)

In our example above, the nonsupportive government managers did have a formal mechanism for voicing disenchantment and were given the opportunity to do so prior to the establishment of the SMWTs. However, interviews suggested that these managers did not voice disenchantment with the self-management concept for two reasons: First, they knew that the regional director was in favor of SMWTs, and they didn't want to appear to be trouble-makers, and second, they did not understand very well the major philosophical differences between traditional and participative management until after the opportunities to express their disenchantment had passed. Consequently, they did not speak up against SMWTs when the formal opportunities to do so were available.

## ENABLERS FOR PERFORMING
## EFFECTIVE MANAGEMENT ROLES

Two important enablers that assist managers in overcoming the obstacles noted above are training and orientation activities. Our data showed that those managers who clearly understood what their roles and responsibilities were and could see that there was a place for them in the participative management environment experienced fewer obstacles to practicing the management roles important to SMWT performance. Managers who were provided new decision-making responsibilities to replace the ones they turned over to the SMWTs likewise experienced fewer obstacles.

Senior managers who acted as exemplary role models for other managers likewise had the effect of reducing obstacles. For example, we found in one organization that the senior managers of each division of the plant made up their own SMWT. Furthermore, each senior manager created a management SMWT made up of the managers in his or her own division. By working within SMWTs, the junior and senior managers became directly aware of the advantages of this management approach and of the skills needed to perform effectively.

Other effective means of reducing obstacles included management visits to other organizations successfully using SMWTs to learn what the managers of these organizations do and do not do, clarifying for management the advantages of using SMWTs, and providing training in the new management skills that are needed, such as coaching and providing support and encour-agement. Similar enablers have been identified from previous research (e.g., Hitchcock & Willard, 1995; Klein, 1984; Shonk, 1992; Tjosvold, 1986).

# 19

■

# Union, Customer, Supplier, and Ancillary Support Within the Organization

■

It was clear from our case studies that a supportive environment was essential to a team achieving high performance. As noted above, without support from management, SMWTs often became demotivated and had difficulty obtaining needed information. We also found that a lack of supplier, ancillary, and customer supports resulted in insufficient feedback, which affected the team's ability to meet the customer's preferences. Furthermore, without a supportive union, the organization had difficulty providing supportive systems. This chapter reviews each of these and the effects they were found to have on SMWT performance.

Our data confirmed the findings of previous research that high-performing teams do not typically work in isolation (e.g., Ancona, 1990; Fisher, Ury, & Patton, 1991; Orsburn et al., 1990). It was found that the high-performing SMWTs had made their internal customers, suppliers, and ancillaries (i.e., those internal to their organization) aware of their team's self-management status and had clarified for them whom they were to communicate with on the SMWT. Furthermore, the high-performing SMWTs had identified specific people among their internal customers, suppliers, and ancillaries whom they could contact when there was a need to communicate with these groups, coordinate activities, or share feedback.

## INTERNAL CUSTOMERS

*Internal customers* include individuals and groups within the SMWT's organization who receive a product or service from the SMWT. High-performing teams were found to be in constant contact with their customers and routinely reevaluating what the customer expected of the team. This included, for example, reviewing the customer's needs, when the product or service was needed, how it was used by the customer, and any other concerns or requirements expressed by the customer. Similar findings have been reported by others (e.g., Orsburn et al., 1990).

The initial development of relationships with internal customers was typically reported to have been achieved with the assistance and support of management. Initially, the manager of the SMWT encouraged the team members to contact the customers directly with questions. Simultaneously, the manager referred the customer's inquiries and feedback directly to specific team members.

Direct contacts between the SMWT and internal customers were found to have several major advantages. Direct contacts gave the SMWT members a clearer understanding of whom the customers were and what their needs were. Knowing who they were meant that the SMWT members received feedback from and responded to specific individuals instead of responding to an order form or the dictates of management. This appeared to increase the team members' feelings of responsibility for their products and services and appeared to increase their motivation to satisfy the customer. Similar results have been reported by Lawler (1988b, 1988c).

Obtaining firsthand information from the internal customer eliminated the information distortions that were reported to occur when receiving the information secondhand from a manager. Furthermore, for the high-performing teams, direct communication increased the wealth of information received and appeared to reduce conflicts between the SMWT and customer. Similar results have been reported by others (e.g., Brett & Rognes, 1986). Lawler (1992) has emphasized this advantage by noting that

> all too often, individuals performing work or offering a service get information about their customers through their supervisor or through others who are removed from the work group. The feedback then tends to be diluted and important customer demands may seem arbitrary and capricious. (p. 258)

Thus, receiving direct communications from the customer, such as "the product is needed tomorrow" or "the service can be improved in these ways," appeared to carry more weight and be more motivating than when the same information was conveyed through the manager with no direct customer contact.

As a result, the team's *work processes* were positively affected. An increase in motivation resulted in more effort being placed directly on the work. As the team became more informed on exactly what the customer desired, the team's work strategies were better focused. Also, the team's *interpersonal processes* were found to be improved with those outside the team. Receiving firsthand information left less room for misunderstandings than when the information was received second- or thirdhand.

In our examination of SMWTs, we found that several of the low-performing teams had relatively little contact with customers. In a low-performing government SMWT, most customer contact was found to occur through one team member. This contact occurred not because this person was selected by the team to be the team liaison with customers but, instead, because this person had at one time been a supervisor and had, over the years, built personal relationships with the customers. Consequently, customers contacted this team member rather than the team member selected by the team to be the customer liaison. Furthermore, this team member/past supervisor who was routinely contacted typically chose to work with the customer alone and commit the SMWT to specific time schedules without consulting other SMWT members. This resulted in SMWT members resisting the established schedules even though they actually reflected the preferences of the customers.

## INTERNAL SUPPLIERS

*Internal suppliers* include those individuals and groups of individuals within the SMWT's organization who provide materials and/or services to the SMWT that are used by the SMWT in producing a product or service. High-performing SMWTs appeared to have strong, well-defined relationships with their suppliers. The suppliers recognized that the team was self-managed and knew who on the team was to be contacted, instead of contacting a manager. The SMWT was found to have regular communications with suppliers to clarify for them the team's needs and expectations. This required that the SMWT have a clear understanding of what its customers required because without this knowledge, the SMWT would not know what it needed from its suppliers.

Furthermore, high-performing SMWTs were found to monitor the performance of the suppliers and to provide them with continual feedback on opportunities for improvement. For example, in one high-performing manufacturing SMWT, the team was in regular communication with its suppliers. So when the team received a batch of bolts that were not adequately deburred, the team immediately informed the supplier of the problem and helped the supplier identify a solution. On the other hand, a low-performing manufacturing SMWT was not in regular contact with its internal suppliers. Consequently, when the supplier began oversupplying the SMWT, the team did not immediately inform the supplier, and an expensive oversupply began to accumulate in the team's inventories.

## ANCILLARY SUPPORT

*Ancillary support* includes those individuals and groups that provide assistance and support to the SMWT. These might include engineers who assist the team in moving and realigning machinery, accountants who assist the team in recordkeeping, and purchasing agents who order supplies and equipment requested by the team.

As with customers and suppliers, the initial development of direct relationships with ancillary support was reported to have been achieved by the direct assistance and support of management. Furthermore, in some of the organizations we examined, the ancillary personnel received training and education about SMWTs and how they were to interact with SMWTs, and this subsequently enhanced their direct interactions with SMWTs. Wellins et al. (1991) have reported similar findings and have noted that ancillary support must realize that they are not to take responsibility from the SMWTs or make decisions for them. They have noted that "such a role change can be difficult for support people because it sometimes calls for a drastic readjustment of the self-image these professionals hold" (p. 176).

We found that high-performing SMWTs made a practice of rewarding ancillary support people who were particularly helpful to the SMWT. This was accomplished by entering an ancillary's name for rewards offered by the organization or, in one case, sharing with an ancillary a portion of a team bonus that the team had received for outstanding performance. In this case, the team recognized the significant contribution made by the ancillary and concluded that in fairness the bonus should be shared.

Direct contacts between the SMWT and ancillary support were found to have several major advantages. As with customers and suppliers, interpersonal processes and environmental factors were positively affected. In particular, communication and information exchange were much more accurate. The ancillary personnel knew more precisely what the team needed and whom on the team to ask if there were any questions. The SMWT members were able to get more in-depth explanations when dealing directly with the ancillary personnel and to ask questions directly instead of through a manager.

A primary result of ancillary support was an improved work process. More effort could be placed directly on doing the work and less time was devoted to sending and receiving information through a manager. The SMWT's resources were more likely to be applied to the work, where the ancillary personnel were involved in making these available and were receiving requests directly from the SMWT rather than from a manager. Likewise, the needed talent for the work process was more likely to be available, particularly when the SMWT requested ancillary assistance directly.

## UNION SUPPORT

A review of the literature addressing unions and the use of SMWTs finds overwhelming agreement that when management and unions are working cooperatively and the union is willing to allow for substantial changes to the traditional way of doing things, the probability that SMWTs can be successfully implemented and perform at a high level will be increased (Lawler, 1992; Orsburn et al., 1990; Ray & Bronstein, 1995; Shonk, 1992). Wellins et al. (1991) have noted, for example, that in Japan, the Japanese Union of Scientists and Engineers not only endorses the concept of work teams but has helped to install them in private companies. And, in Sweden, the Swedish Employee's Federation has served as a consultant to companies that are interested in increasing employee involvement.

Our data support this proposition emphasizing the positive effects of union support. Two of the four organizations from which our case studies were drawn were unionized. In each case, the unions had endorsed the new roles and responsibilities of the team members prior to the teams being created. However, in these cases, the unions had not provided any specific substantial supports that assisted the SMWTs, and this appeared to inhibit the development of some of the teams.

For example, in one of the government organizations we studied, the employees were unionized. Although interviews with union representatives indicated that the union supported the concept of teams, the union was doing nothing to assist or encourage the teams or the team concept. Perhaps the single biggest issues that had not been adequately addressed by management and the union were the performance evaluation and compensation systems—the traditional systems were still being used; that is, employees were still being evaluated and compensated for individual performance. As noted

above, individual-based performance evaluation and compensation can un-
dermine the team because they do not encourage teamwork and do encourage
employees to be most concerned about their personal evaluations, even at the
expense of the team and the larger organization.

This can be clearly seen in one instance. A government SMWT wanted to
apply for an award that had always been given to an individual in the past.
The team was told that the union-sanctioned compensation system did not
allow for a team of employees to receive awards, and therefore the award
would have to be presented to one individual on the team. This resulted in
damaging the cohesiveness and cooperation within the team, as several team
members began competing for the award.

Thus, support from the union was found to be important. It was needed
not only to allow for the establishment of the SMWTs but also to allow for
major changes in the traditional work environment.

Similar conclusions were reached after examining the SMWTs in the
second unionized organization. In this nursing home organization, two of the
three SMWTs we studied were made up of hourly workers who were
unionized. Here again, the union was not opposed to teams but had not agreed
to any major workplace changes that would support the teams, such as
changes to the traditional performance evaluation and compensation systems. This appeared to contribute to a lack of development of one of the
teams. In this case, the team members placed more importance on their own
individual performance than that of the team. The second team appeared to
overcome this by providing its team members with nonmonetary rewards
when high levels of team-oriented behavior were displayed. Nonmonetary
rewards included pats on the back, displays of respect, and positive comments. These appeared to be particularly valuable to the team members
because of their longtime friendships (in some cases established prior to
joining the organization), high team-oriented commitment, and desire for
positive feedback.

In the third nursing home SMWT, made up of managers, the team
members were not unionized. However, the traditional practice was still
being used by the organization's parent company of giving managers an
annual percentage increase based on the increase given to hourly workers
that had been negotiated with the union. Consequently, here again, the
compensation system did not reward team performance. On the other hand,
the performance evaluation system had been revised. On this management
SMWT, each individual on the team was rated by the team's manager (the
chief executive officer of the facility) on his or her contribution to the team
and ability to work cooperatively. Furthermore, similar to the team described
above, the members of the management team provided each other with a

variety of nonmonetary rewards for high team-oriented behavior, such as showing high levels of respect. These rewards were reported to be highly valued, which was not surprising given the high level of team-oriented commitment found among the team members.

In one of the two organizations studied where there was not a union, it appeared that this lack made the transition to SMWTs easier. Management, the employees, and several consultants from outside the organization worked together to design the SMWTs. It appeared that both management and the employees perceived that SMWTs could be beneficial to the organization's well-being, and the majority of managers and employees were willing to make substantial workplace changes. The performance evaluation and compensation systems in this organization were modified significantly to reward team performance, although the rewarding of individual performance had not been discarded. It was in this organization that the highest levels of team performance were found, and it was the ability to make substantial changes to the organization's systems that appeared to contribute greatly to this high performance.

Thus, our data suggest that, where a union exists, it is important that the organization receive the union's support not only to establish teams but also to make substantial changes to the traditional work environment. There have been many cases where the union prevented or made it extremely difficult for the organization to make the kinds of environmental and team design changes that were needed to implement high-performing SMWTs. In our study, it was clear that the lack of a union allowed the organization to more easily implement changes, for example, to the performance evaluation and compensation systems. Such changes are crucial to the SMWT's performance.

# 20

![black square decoration]

# The Environment Outside the Organization

![black square decoration]

Open systems theorists have pointed to the importance of studying factors outside or external to the organization when attempting to understanding organizational performance (see Part I for a discussion of systems theory). They have noted the importance to organizations of being aware of environmental demands, anticipating environmental changes, protecting themselves from undesirable environmental influences, and manipulating the environment when possible and advantageous to do so. Most important here is that open systems theorists have recognized that the external environment has important and extensive effects on the organization's performance (Pasmore, 1988). Our research, along with that of others, has found that the same can be concluded with regard to SMWTs—the external environment has large multiple effects on the SMWT's performance.

Most research on organizational and SMWT performance has taken a closed systems approach by focusing on factors within the organization. This choice has not been because of a belief that the external environment is unimportant, but, rather, because of the difficulty of conducting rigorous methodological studies that are able to quantify (measure statistically) the effects of the important external environmental factors. Unfortunately, whenever statistical analyses leave out important factors, such as variables external to the organization, specification error is the result. Specification error is a statistical problem that can produce extremely inaccurate statistics and result in inaccurate conclusions being drawn. An advantage of our case study approach is that it has not been limited by these statistical difficulties. However, the case study approach has been limited somewhat because of questions of generalizability (please see Appendix A for a thorough discussion of the case study approach and procedures for increasing confidence in generalizability).

A review of the literature has shown that the external environment is treated as consisting of two major components: the specific and the general environments. The *specific environment* (also referred to as the micro- and task environment) consists of individuals, groups, and organizations in the environment who directly affect the SMWT's ability to achieve its mission and goals. These include, for example, suppliers, customers, competitors, and government regulators specific to the SMWT's mission. The *general environment* (also referred to as the macroenvironment) consists of social institutions and forces that shape the specific environment and affect the ability of all of a society's organizations to achieve their missions and goals. This includes, for example, the economy, technology, demographics, education, and societal culture (Jones, 1995).

## THE SPECIFIC ENVIRONMENT

One of the high-performing, manufacturing SMWTs we studied was constantly interacting with a supplier of machine tools so that the team could obtain a machine tool that was strong enough to do the work but not any stronger than needed, because the cost of the tool was based on its degree of hardness. Another high-performing SMWT was constantly interacting with its customers (nursing home residents and their families) to be sure that the customer was getting what was most desired and the team was not spending time doing things the customer really did not care about. In a third team, the four members routinely visited their primary customer—firefighters—at least once a year to discuss their equipment and supply needs and whether their needs were being met. In each of these examples, the SMWT was interacting with its specific environment, and we found the result to ultimately have positive effects on the SMWT's performance.

### Customer Interaction

Interaction with the specific environment was found to have a variety of effects on the SMWT's work process. Communication with and feedback from customers appeared to have positive effects on the team members' motivation and effort placed directly on doing the work. As has been found by a variety of researchers (Deming, 1986; Juran, 1989; Lawler, 1992), we found workers to be more motivated and subsequently place more effort on the work, when they could see what impacts their work was having and who benefited from the work.

This was particularly evident in the case of a four-person government SMWT. These four were responsible for supplying firefighters with the equipment and supplies they needed. The four team members flew out to the northwest region of the United States annually to get firsthand feedback from the fire fighters (their customers) to be sure their needs were being met. Furthermore, these contacts clarified for the team members the importance of their work, as they learned how the supplies they had provided to the fire-fighters in the past had been used to save lives, property, and thousands of acres of forests. Not surprisingly, these four team members were found to be much more motivated and placed much more effort directly on their work than did a second government work team we studied. This team was providing office supplies—perceived to be much less important than fire equipment—to a warehouse that they would resupply as the warehouse became low on particular items (e.g., pens, staplers). These team members had no opportunity to interact with those who were using the supplies, that is, those government employees who obtained the supplies from the warehouse. It appeared from a comparison of these two teams that this latter team's lack of communication and feedback from those actually using the supplies was resulting in less motivation and effort on the work.

Communication and feedback from customers was also found to affect the work process by influencing the procedures being used to do the work. Direct contact with and feedback from customers helped the SMWT members determine whether they were using the best procedures possible and how the procedures could be changed to better meet customer preferences.

Furthermore, by being able to interact directly with customers, ask questions, and receive information from them, the team members spent less time trying to understand their customer's needs than when this information was received secondhand from a supervisor. Thus, direct communication and feedback resulted in more time available that could be used for doing the work and less effort spent on procedures that were not the best for meeting the customer's preferences.

## Supplier Interaction

When considering suppliers in the specific environment, similar effects on the work process were found. Direct contacts with suppliers allowed the team to specify exactly what the supplier needed to provide to the team. This resulted in the team receiving more precise resources that could be applied to the work. Communication and feedback also allowed the SMWT to learn from the supplier what supplies were available. This information allowed the team to better plan which tasks to perform and which procedures would best use the available supplies.

### Government Regulators

Continuous contact with government regulators was found to allow the SMWT to keep abreast of existing and anticipated regulations. This allowed the teams to revise their work processes when needed to reflect the changing regulations. For example, in a government SMWT we studied, we found that the SMWT was continually contacting federal housing regulators to keep abreast of any new or anticipated regulations. Keeping in regular contact allowed the team to learn about new regulations before they were to be implemented. This provided the team with the time needed to develop new procedures and revise old ones before they had to be implemented.

### Other Effects of the Specific Environment

Direct contacts with those outside the organization affected positively the environment within the organization. It was found that the information system was improved as information was obtained firsthand by the SMWT. Training and education needs were identified quicker and more precisely than when received secondhand through a supervisor. Likewise, it was reported that the resources needed by the team were determined more precisely and quickly and consequently ordered and received sooner.

The SMWT's design characteristics were also found to be affected positively by direct contacts with customers and suppliers. It was found that specific production and quality goals could be set best when they were based on both the customer needs and preferences and the supplier's constraints. Firsthand knowledge of these through contacts with the customers and suppliers provided this information most accurately and timely. Likewise, knowledge of customer needs and preferences and of supplier constraints were found to directly affect the size of the team, the need for overtime, and decisions on who should do what.

When considering the decision-making process, the decisions made were best when the SMWT obtained information that was firsthand, complete, and understandable. As noted above, contacts with customers, suppliers, and regulators allowed the team members to ask for all the information they needed and to ask questions when facts were unclear. Similar findings have been reported by others such as Ancona (1990), Orsburn et al. (1990), Fisher et al. (1995), and Holder (1995).

## THE GENERAL ENVIRONMENT

The effects of the *general environment* on SMWT performance have received relatively little attention among work team theorists and researchers. However, it was clear from our case studies that factors in the general environment were vital to SMWT performance. Considered here are the economy, technology, demographic conditions, education, political–legal conditions, and societal culture.

### Economic Conditions

Economic conditions have had a variety of important effects on SMWTs. In fact, the emergence of SMWTs in the United States can be attributed to economic conditions internationally that have led U.S. organizations to seek new ways of competing. Most U.S. organizations did not consider implementing teams until economic pressures forced them to look for more effective ways of producing high-quality products and services at less cost.

As SMWTs have emerged, economic conditions have affected the extent to which organizations have been able to adequately invest in SMWT development—when economic conditions are poor, the organization may lack adequate financial resources to invest in SMWTs. This includes providing SMWT members with adequate training in interpersonal skills, decision making, and conflict resolution and managers with adequate training in their new roles. There are high costs in time and human resources related to overhauling the organization's other major systems as well, including the performance evaluation system, reward system, and information system. On the other hand, where economic conditions are positive, the organization is more able to invest in the revision of their systems.

Poor economic conditions can result in the organization sometimes supplying the SMWT with inadequate equipment and materials to do the work. Although we did not see this in the two cases where poor economic conditions were affecting the SMWT's organization, it is reasonable to expect that it does occur in some cases. Of course, inadequate materials and equipment can impede the work process and reduce performance. Thus, economic conditions can have a variety of effects on the SMWT's environment within the organization, such as its systems and resources. These effects, in turn, affect other dimensions of the SMWT (Polley & Van Dyne, 1994, have also provided a discussion of these effects).

Economic conditions can affect the SMWT's design characteristics in a variety of ways. As economic conditions change, the size of the SMWT may be reduced or increased. The team's goals may change to reflect new customer demands, and even the mission of the team can change as economic conditions influence the broader organization. In some cases, where economic conditions are poor, a lack of support from the organizational systems (e.g., training, information exchange) can result in management reverting back to more traditional ways of doing things. This can result in the SMWT losing some of its management responsibilities.

On the other hand, poor economic conditions have resulted in some organizations providing additional responsibilities to the SMWTs, as the organization chooses to reduce costs by streamlining its management ranks (Lawler, 1986; Peters & Waterman, 1982). Unfortunately, in these latter cases, we have observed where the organization did not accompany such changes with revisions to its internal systems, such as the performance evaluation, information, and education and training systems. Consequently, the SMWT's likelihood for high performance was low because the environment surrounding the SMWT was unsupportive.

When considering the effects of economic conditions on the specific SMWTs that we studied, we observed one SMWT that had been negatively affected. This government SMWT had dropped from eight to five team members as a result of retirement and attrition. However, poor economic conditions, fostered by a high federal deficit, were forcing the larger agency to withhold replacing the three team members. This, in turn, was having a variety of negative effects on the SMWT. For example, when considering the *work process,* the team was using inappropriate procedures to compensate for the lack of personnel and was applying insufficient knowledge and skill to the work because the remaining team members lacked the experience of those who had left.

## Technological Conditions

Technological conditions in the external environment likewise affect the SMWT in a variety of ways. (A discussion of the effects of technology on organizational performance has been provided in Part I in the discussion of contingency theory.) The environment within the organization, and more specifically, the information, reward, performance evaluation, and training systems, can all be affected by new technologies in the external environment. For example, new information-processing technologies such as computers have had large effects on the information systems of organizations. This has made it easier and quicker for SMWTs to obtain needed information and provide information to others, such as suppliers and managers. New technologies have affected education and training systems by requiring them to provide SMWT members with new knowledge and skills to use the technologies. Furthermore, new techniques in how to train employees have affected the organization's training system as new techniques are adopted to train SMWT members.

New technologies have also directly affected the SMWT's work process. In some cases, this has meant improving work procedures so that boring and tedious work is done by machines. Furthermore, this has had the added benefit of increasing motivation, in cases where team members have begun spending more of their time doing interesting and challenging work.

New technologies can also affect the SMWT's design characteristics in a variety of ways. New technologies can result in the size of the SMWT changing. In some cases, fewer members are needed to produce the same product or service. In others, additional team members are needed to operate the new technology. New technologies can result in the SMWT developing new job tasks to use the technology and eliminating old job tasks no longer needed. New technologies can drastically alter the SMWT's goals as the new technology allows for higher production or perhaps higher quality goals.

## Demographic Conditions

Demographic conditions in the general environment appear to have their largest impacts on the characteristics of the team members and, through these, other dimensions of the SMWT and subsequently its performance. An examination of birth rates suggests that, as we enter the 21st century, we will continue to see an increasingly diverse workforce with fewer white males and higher percentages of females, minorities, and older workers (Johnston & Packer, 1987; U.S. Bureau of the Census, 1994). More women are entering the workforce than ever before, while fewer are choosing to forgo employment and stay at home with their children (U.S. Department of Labor, 1989). Simultaneously, the number of white males entering working age has dropped over the last quarter of the 20th century, while the number of minorities has increased. And the number of older workers has been increasing and will continue to do so well into the 21st century (Johnston & Packer, 1987; U.S. Department of Labor, 1989).

These demographic trends are affecting who is available to work for organizations and, more specifically, as team members of SMWTs. Furthermore, the demographic profile of the workforce brings with it unique values, interests, needs, and prejudices. For example, women (and to a growing extent men) tend to value flextime work schedules that allow them to maintain family responsibilities while working full-time jobs (Seward, Yeatts, Seward, & Stanley-Stevens, 1993). And many older workers prefer part-time and flextime employment so they can ease into retirement (American Association of Retired Persons, 1988; Fyock, 1990). Demographic conditions also affect the SMWT's design characteristics. The design characteristic *composition of the team* is affected by who is available in the broader society to work. In turn, the composition of the team can affect other SMWT design characteristics. For example, in one SMWT we studied, one of the team members requested, during a team meeting, that flextime be implemented so that she would have time to take her son to school before work. In this particular case, the team chose not to allow flextime, concluding that it was essential that all team members be at work at the same time because they depended on each other's presence to get the work done. In this particular case, the SMWT chose not to alter its work schedule to accommodate the special needs of a team member. In other cases, such accommodations are allowed, and the design of the work is altered.

Demographic conditions that affect the characteristics of team members and subsequently the composition of the team also subsequently affect interpersonal processes within the team and between the team and others outside the team. Research findings on the effects of heterogeneous groups (Clement & Schiereck, 1973; Kent & McGrath, 1969; Tannen, 1990) suggest that, as the composition of the team becomes more diversified with regard to gender, race, and age, trust and clear communications can be expected to decrease somewhat and, in turn, negatively affect interpersonal processes. Although our data provide some support for this proposition, the data suggest that these effects may be less important than others in affecting interpersonal processes. For example, a team that we perceived to have one of the lowest levels of interpersonal processes was almost completely homogeneous with regard to gender, age, and race. A second team with poor interpersonal processes was heterogeneous with regard to these factors, but it was not apparent that these factors were contributing to the poor interpersonal processes. Instead, we found factors such as wide differences between team members in pay scale and work experience to be more important to interpersonal processes.

Examples of these latter effects include a government SMWT that had very poor interpersonal processes. The employees on this team ranged in rank from a GS-5 to a GS-13 (i.e., high school level to postgraduate level), and this appeared to contribute greatly to low trust and communication. Furthermore, a manufacturing SMWT that demonstrated very poor interpersonal processes had team members ranging in tenure from a few months to over 5 years. Thus, diversity in pay ranges and experience appeared to be more important than diversity in gender, race, or age.

## Education of the Society

The quality of education in the United States has received mixed reviews, with some stating that there is a "rising tide of mediocrity in our education system" (McEnery & Lifter, 1987, p. 70). Apparent evidence for this is the growing establishment of basic skills programs by U.S. corporations, designed to teach reading, writing, math, problem solving, and the like (Carnevale, Gainer, & Meltzer, 1990; Craig, 1987). However, a review of Americans' level of education throughout the 20th century shows that education of Americans has steadily increased. In fact, it is reasonable to propose that an extensive use of SMWTs was not practical in the early 1900s because the workforce did not have enough education. It has only been since the large majority of the general population has been educated in reading, writing, math, and problem solving that nonmanagement employees have had the basic skills to manage themselves. This suggests that education of the general population plays a key role in the performance of SMWTs; that is, education of the general population has a direct effect on the characteristics of the SMWT members. It determines the basic level of knowledge that team members in general will have.

Education of the general population also affects the environment within the SMWT's organization. The organization's education and training systems are affected because the level of education of the workforce, coming from the general population, determines what the education and training systems will teach. More specifically, steps in determining what to teach employees typically include identifying the education needs of the jobs and the education levels of the organization's workforce, determining the gaps between the education needs and the existing education levels, and then developing education and training programs to close the gap between the two. The education level of the general population, along with the education demands of the jobs, affects the training and education needs and subsequently the training and education programs offered.

Similarly, the kinds of education provided in business schools within a society can be expected to affect the kinds of management training that an organization finds it needs to provide to its managers. More specifically, to the extent that business schools do not teach students the importance of supporting and encouraging SMWTs and carrying out other roles related to SMWTs, the organizations' education and training systems will need to provide this. Similar conclusions have been drawn by Evans (1993), who has noted the impacts that business schools have had on management's ability to understand and have confidence in employee involvement initiatives and to effectively manage SMWTs. He has noted that Channon (1973) has attributed Great Britain's slow movement away from the traditional management paradigm to a lack of any management education at all up to the 1970s—it was pointed out that many managers in Great Britain prior to the 1970s had received no special training in management skills.

Still another dimension of the SMWT that is affected by the education of the society at large is the team design characteristics. The level of team members' general education can be expected to have positive effects on the SMWT's ability to identify best work procedures and follow effective decision-making processes. Unfortunately, no studies were identified that have examined these relationships, and our own data are not specific enough to allow for conclusions in this regard.

### Political–Legal Conditions

The political–legal conditions of the society have had large impacts on the initiation of SMWTs, on how the SMWTs operate, and on the SMWT's customers and suppliers. The political–legal conditions in some societies have encouraged the establishment of employee involvement programs, whereas the conditions in other societies have not. For example, in the 1960s, the political–legal conditions in Sweden and Japan supported the development of employee involvement programs. On the other hand, the political–legal conditions in the United States have traditionally supported union policies that have conflicted with the use of SMWTs. These include, for example, union demands that corporations limit the number of different tasks an employee can be required to perform. Such policy has inhibited the use of SMWTs because part of their advantage stems from team members' sharing responsibilities and rotating tasks.

More recently, in the 1990s, U.S. political–legal conditions have allowed unions to challenge the legality of SMWTs altogether. Some unions have claimed that SMWTs are a method used by management to circumvent the unions. However, the most recent court cases suggest that the political–legal system will uphold the use of SMWTs (Wellins et al., 1991).

Another example of the U.S. political–legal condition beginning to favor SMWTs is the establishment by the U.S. Congress of the Malcolm Baldrige National Quality Award. This award for high quality includes as a quality indicator the use of "self-directed" or "self-managed" work teams.

At a more general level, the political–legal conditions can be found to have a variety of effects on workers, including those in SMWTs, through a myriad of laws. These include, for example, safety regulations that influence how employees function and laws that affect the transportation of goods and services and, subsequently, the transactions that occur between organizations. These specific laws, supported by the political–legal establishment, directly affect what employees can and cannot do.

Finally, political–legal conditions can influence who does business with whom. For example, laws can prohibit certain employees from working with others, such as U.S. regulations that prohibit collaboration in price controls or developing a monopoly. At a broader level, political–legal conditions can result in the government becoming a customer or being eliminated as a customer, and this can have large effects on the organizations and employees involved. For example, the U.S. bombing of Libya reduced the U.S. supply of bombs and subsequently required the transferring of government funds to organizations that make bombs for the United States (including one of our case studies). This affected organizations in the defense industry and, more specifically, SMWTs connected in some way with weapons production— whether it was directly through building bombs or indirectly through the purification of metals. Similarly, other employees in other industries had expected to do work for the government but learned that the government funds had been transferred away from their line of business in order to pay for the weapons replenishment. Thus, the political–legal system affects who does business with whom, not only through the laws that are established but also by allowing the government to become a buyer of goods and services.

## Societal Culture

*Culture* can be simply defined as "the values, beliefs, behavior, and material objects that constitute a people's way of life" (Macionis, 1993, p. 62). A more encompassing definition has been provided by Hofstede (1985): "The collective programming of the mind which distinguishes the members of one category of people from those of others" (p. 389). Perhaps the most complex definition has been provided by Kroeber and Parsons (1958): "The transmitted and created content and patterns of values, ideas, and other symbolic meaningful systems as factors in the shaping of human behavior and in the artifacts produced through behavior" (cited in Evans, 1993, p. 300).

Researchers examining the relationship between culture and organizational performance have identified at least four dimensions of culture that are important (Ferdman, 1992; Hofstede, 1980; Hofstede & Bond, 1984, provides a review of numerous studies). And it becomes clear from these examinations that societal culture is likely to have hindered or enhanced the emergence of SMWTs. One cultural dimension is *power distribution* or "the extent to which the members of a society accept that power in institutions and organizations is distributed unequally" (Evans, 1993, p. 298). It is reasonable to expect that a culture will be more likely to favor SMWTs if it prefers an equal power distribution—in SMWTs, team members are typically considered equals, and the relationship between team members and management is more of a partnership than in more traditional management approaches. On the other hand, if the culture accepts power inequality, it is less likely to question and more likely to accept the traditional hierarchical management approach. The Swedish culture has been used as an example of the first and the U.S. culture as an example of the second (Evans, 1993; Hofstede, 1985). Sweden was among the first countries where SMWTs were used, whereas the use of SMWTs in the United States came much later, as economic conditions forced U.S. organizations to look for new ways of doing things.

A second cultural dimension is *uncertainty avoidance* or "the degree to which the members of a society feel uncomfortable with uncertainty and ambiguity, which leads them to support beliefs promising certainty and to maintain institutions protecting conformity" (Evans, 1993, p. 298). We found that the employees of SMWTs typically began experiencing much more uncertainty once working within an SMWT. Prior to this, the employee was told what to do, and most uncertainties were addressed by management. Consequently, to the extent that the culture practices uncertainty avoidance, employees will find their new responsibilities in SMWTs uncomfortable. Where the culture does not associate uncertainty with discomfort, it is reasonable to expect the employees will be more comfortable with their responsibilities in SMWTs.

A third cultural dimension is individualism versus collectivism. *Individualism* is "a preference for a loosely knit social framework in society in which individuals are supposed to take care of themselves and their immediate families only" (Evans, 1993, p. 298). *Collectivism* is "a preference for a tightly knit social framework in which individuals can expect their relatives, clan, or other in-group to look after them, in exchange for unquestioning loyalty" (Evans, 1993, p.298). It is reasonable to expect that employees living in a culture practicing collectivism will be more accepting of SMWTs because SMWTs require that the team members work together, support one another, and make decisions that consider the social circumstances of the specific team members as well as the technical requirements of the work.

A fourth dimension of societal culture is closely linked to the third, self versus other orientation. A *self-oriented* culture has a preference for material success, assertiveness, achievement, and heroism. An *other-oriented* culture prefers modesty, caring for the weak, relationships with others, and the quality of life (Evans, 1993). Competition between employees is more accepted and expected in a self-oriented culture, whereas cooperation is the preference in an other-oriented culture. SMWTs require a high level of cooperation among team members to be successful. Cooperative conflict is valued rather than competition. Consequently, it is reasonable to expect that the employees of an other-oriented culture may find it easier to carry out their roles as team members.

There has been relatively little research examining specifically the relationship between societal culture and SMWT performance. However, it is reasonable to expect that societal culture does have important effects. If the societal culture practices individualism, self-orientation, and competition, it is reasonable to expect that the employees of the society will be less interested in using a team approach to work. Furthermore, they will be less prepared to perform the interpersonal processes needed for a high-performing SMWT.

There have been several notable studies that have examined the attitudinal differences between workers of differing cultures (Evans, 1993). Hofstede (1985) has studied a matched sample of employees of a single, multinational corporation in 40 countries. When examining attitudes toward collaboration, he found wide variation between cultures. For example, he reported that in 1974, six American automobile workers visited the Saab-Scania plant in Sweden, where a new system of group assembly had been installed. Five of them rejected the system. This was attributed, in part, to American workers preferring to work on their own, whereas Swedish workers preferred collaborating with others (Evans, 1993).

Another study by Kelly and Reeser (1973) has examined the differences between American managers of Japanese ancestry and those of Caucasian ancestry. And, similarly, a study by Pizam and Reichel (1977) has examined the differences between Israeli managers of Oriental ancestry and those of Western ancestry. In both studies, cultural differences were observed in areas such as respect for formal authority, commitment to long-term employment, paternalism with respect to subordinates, and interest in teamwork. It is reasonable to expect that such cultural differences will influence the managers' and employees' desire and ability to support and encourage SMWTs and carry out other important roles that affect the SMWT's performance.

A consideration of the effects of societal culture on SMWT dimensions suggests that culture has a variety of effects. Unfortunately, our study was unable to test these relationships because we had no variation in societal culture—all the SMWTs we studied were located in the United States. However, based on previous studies examining the effects of culture on organizations and on our understanding of the factors that enhance SMWT performance, we can propose a number of likely relationships.

It is reasonable to expect that societal culture affects the SMWT's environment within the organization in a variety of ways. The level of management support, encouragement, and practice of appropriate roles is likely to be greater where the culture has a positive attitude toward cooperative work and work teams. The education and training systems are likely to be affected because cultures vary in their levels of education. Where education and training receive high value, the workforce is likely to be more educated and consequently need less education and training. Furthermore, the need for education programs will be influenced by the culture's emphasis on interpersonal relationships. Where the culture does not strongly endorse cooperation, the organization's education programs will need to address this in order to enhance the SMWT's interpersonal processes. Still another environmental factor likely to be affected is the reward system. The culture is likely to influence the types of rewards that the team members value. Consequently, the organization's reward system will need to be designed to offer such rewards valued by the broader culture. McEnery and Lifter (1987) have drawn similar conclusions in their discussion of social values and job satisfaction.

Societal culture can also be expected to influence the SMWT's interpersonal processes. Societal cultures that are more other oriented and collectivist in nature can be expected to positively influence the SMWT's level of cooperation, cohesion, communication, and trust, and, subsequently, the SMWT's performance. On the other hand, such a culture may cause SMWT members to experience a higher incidence of groupthink, where there is a lack of consideration of differing ideas because the team members do not want to appear uncooperative. This has been negatively related to SMWT performance.

Finally, team member characteristics represent another SMWT dimension likely to be influenced by the societal culture. These characteristics include team member values, interests, needs, and prejudices. These are likely to come from the broader societal culture and have been found to have varying effects on the SMWT's performance through their effects on the other SMWT dimensions.

# PART V

## Team Member Characteristics

We were attending the annual International Conference on Self-Managed Work Teams (Bullock, Friday, & Belcher, 1996) as part of our study to identify those factors most important to SMWT performance. We were wondering why the importance of team member characteristics had not been given more attention by the participants at the conference, particularly because our case studies of SMWTs were making it clear that team member characteristics were extremely important. We noted that most theoretical frameworks explaining SMWT performance have incorporated discussions of team member characteristics within a broader discussion on the composition of the team. Happily, our conversation was overheard and interrupted by a high-level manager of a large corporation. He proceeded to tell us about his experiences with SMWTs.

At his organization, management decided to establish a pilot SMWT. One of the first steps was to ask for volunteers to join the team. As the team had an opportunity to work together and learn to work as a team, its performance began to increase to very impressive levels. The performance of this team has subsequently been extremely high. Consequently, management decided to establish more SMWTs. The new teams were created by drawing together those employees who were already working together on the same product or service. These employees were required to be a part of the team. It was a surprise to management when these new teams never reached the same high level of performance reached by the pilot team.

The manager we were speaking with attributed this to the characteristics of the team members. The volunteers on the pilot SMWT were some of the organization's most knowledgeable employees and had demonstrated high levels of skill and ability. It was explained that their personal values and needs were a close match for what the SMWT offered—more responsibility, interpersonal interaction, and decision making—and that is why they wanted to work on an SMWT in the first place. Furthermore, it was explained that even their personalities appeared to be more conducive to a team or collaborative environment because they appeared to be highly people-oriented and more outgoing or extroverted.

The manager continued by explaining that the new teams had members with lower levels of knowledge, skill, and ability. Some of these team members clearly did not want to be on a team, did not value the team concept, and were more individualistic in nature. Other conditions that might have contributed to the differences between the pilot and later teams, for the most part, appeared to be equal.

Certainly this example does not represent a rigorous scientific study. However, our rigorous case studies made it clear that team member characteristics are crucial to an SMWT's high performance, and the example provides a good summary of what we found.

Rentsch and Hall (1994) have provided a good rationale for the importance of team member characteristics in the context of the *person–environment fit*. High team performance requires that the team members have the specific knowledge, skills, and abilities that fit or match those needed to do the team's work. Likewise, team performance can be expected to increase if the type of work being performed fits or matches

the values of the team members (Greenhouse & Parasuraman, 1986; Holland, 1985). And the evidence suggests
that a team member's personality can be more or less conducive to working on a team and that this can also affect the
level of team performance. These team member characteristics are reviewed in the following chapters.

# 21

■

# Talents, Values, Needs, Interests, and Prejudices

■

## TALENTS

Knowledge, skill, and ability are talents of team members that were found to have large impacts on other dimensions of the SMWT and in turn the team's performance. Our data support the findings of Larson and LaFasto (1989), who have stated, "Not much can be accomplished if team members do not possess the skills, abilities, and knowledge that are relevant to the team's objectives" (p. 69).

These are unique characteristics. *Knowledge* refers to one's awareness and familiarity with general facts and principles that are typically obtained through experience. *Ability* refers to one's potential or capacity to achieve. Ability is often defined in terms of objective measures, such as intelligence test scores, academic course grades, or peer ratings of intelligence and competence (Morgan & Lassiter, 1992). *Skill* refers to one's ability to do a specific thing well and is typically obtained through training and practice. Team member skills include interpersonal skills and problem-solving skills, as well as technical skills.

### Knowledge

Some of the knowledge "areas" we found to be particularly important to the team's performance include team member knowledge of the work, of other team members, and of management expectations. Knowledge of the work allowed the team members to be aware of the skills and abilities required and to identify varying possible ways of accomplishing the work. Knowledge of the team members allowed the SMWT to identify team member task preferences, as well as current skills and abilities. This allowed the team to be sensitive to both technical and social needs and to match the work to the team members (Cannon-Bowers et al., 1991). Knowledge of management expectations helped the team to develop goals that were acceptable to management or that, at least, addressed management's expectations. This subsequently increased management's confidence and support of the SMWT.

We found that the high-performing teams had team members who were very knowledgeable about the team's work and that these teams allowed this knowledge to have a large influence on team decisions. Low-performing teams, on the other hand, were less likely to have highly knowledgeable team members and were less likely to allow the knowledge that was available to highly influence team decisions.

In one low-performing government SMWT, for example, one of the six team members had been a supervisor prior to the SMWT's establishment. It was clear that this particular team member/past supervisor was extremely knowledgeable in all aspects of the work, as indicated by interviews with this person, the team members, and managers. Furthermore, there was a second team member who also appeared to be very knowledgeable about the work, and this was reflected by the fact that this person held the second-highest civil service ranking, being lower only than that of the past supervisor. Thus, it appeared that there was ample knowledge from these two team members to allow the team to make the most appropriate decisions possible. However, many of the team's decisions ignored the advice of these two. In the case of the past supervisor, the team members were having a continual feud with this person and would not heed her advice. In the case of the second highest-ranking team member, the remaining members felt he was conceited and so chose to ignore much of his advice. Our examination of the procedures that were being used by the team clearly revealed that in some important situations the most appropriate procedures were not being used and that this was because the knowledge of the two high-ranking team members was not being used.

## Ability

The ability of team members affects what the SMWT can and cannot do. Most SMWTs are periodically given new tasks to be carried out. The team must decide the most appropriate procedures for performing the tasks, and this will be dependent on the abilities of the team members. In some cases, the team may not be able to select the most appropriate procedure if no one on the team has the unique abilities required of the procedure. Ideally, the team members are selected for the team based on their existing abilities as well as current skills, so that when a new task is assigned to the team that requires new skills, there will be team members who have the ability to learn the new skills quickly. Katzenbach and Smith (1993b) have described the importance of ability or what they term *skill potential*:

> In all the successful teams we've encountered, not one had all the needed skills at the outset. The Burlington Northern team, for example, initially had no members who were skilled marketers despite the fact that their performance challenge was a marketing one. In fact, we discovered that teams are powerful vehicles for developing the skills needed to meet the team's performance challenge. Accordingly, team member selection ought to ride as much on skill potential as on skills already proven.

## Skills

Team member skills are often treated as synonymous with technical skills. However, in SMWTs, team members need a variety of skills to be successful, including technical skills, interpersonal skills, problem-solving skills, management skills, and decision-making skills. These have been defined and discussed in Chapter 16. Without such skills, the SMWT will be unable to perform the technical work, to choose the most appropriate work procedures, or to make effective decisions related to the team and its work.

In our case studies, we found that the level and types of skills of the team members directly affected all dimensions of the SMWT, including the team's interpersonal processes, decision-making abilities, training needs, and talent applied to the work. For example, in the government team noted above, an inability to use the existing knowledge on the team was not its only shortcoming. The team members lacked the interpersonal skills needed to work together, to select the most appropriate procedures for the team, and to assign tasks according to who had the skill and ability to accomplish the tasks. The team lacked decision-making skills that would assist the team in choosing the best decisions without allowing personal prejudices to influence decisions. The team lacked problem-solving skills, which resulted in decisions that created additional problems rather than solving the ones already existing. The team lacked management skills, which resulted in inefficiently scheduling the work so that what could have been done in 2 days sometimes took 3. It was clear that the SMWT needed training and coaching in these many areas. Unfortunately, for a variety of reasons, none was forthcoming. The result was a work process where effort was low and the appropriate talent and procedures were lacking. This, in conjunction with other shortcomings, resulted in team performance that was not as high as it could have been.

## VALUES HELD BY TEAM MEMBERS

The kinds of values held by team members are crucial to the success of SMWTs. An underlying assumption of SMWTs is that all employees value using a variety of skills, being autonomous, working cooperatively with others, and being personally responsible for the work (Hulin, 1971). As Lawler (1988d) has noted, "For any form of involvement to work, most employees have to want to learn, grow, develop, contribute, and take on new responsibilities" (p. 203). Our in-depth interviews with team members revealed that there were employees who did not value these things or want to work in an environment where they must practice them. Furthermore, as might be expected, the performance of the SMWT was sometimes reduced where employee values did not fit the SMWT environment. This was found to occur through negative effects on the team's interpersonal processes, decision-making processes, and effort applied to the work.

For example, in a government SMWT, one of the team members did not value an "enriched" environment and had not wanted to work within an SMWT when it was established. Team members and management reported that he continually undermined team trust and cooperation, practiced what was described as competitive conflict rather than cooperative conflict during the decision-making processes, and caused team members to reduce effort on the work as they were distracted by him. From this case, it became clear that just one team member with a poor "value-SMWT" match could cause large negative effects on the team's performance.

Surprisingly, in one high-performing manufacturing SMWT we studied, we found several people on the SMWT's third shift who did not have a good value-SMWT match. These team members had discovered that the third shift (working from 11 p.m. to 7 a.m.) allowed them to avoid several aspects of the SMWT that they did not value. Because of their late-night work, there were not enough other personnel on-site for major team decisions to be made, and when such decisions were made—during the day shift—these third-shift employees were typically not at work. This allowed them to spend almost all their time operating their machines, an activity that they highly valued, and relatively little time in team meetings, which they did not value.

Our assessment was that these employees would have left the organization when SMWTs were implemented except that they found they could avoid those aspects of the SMWT they did not value by working on the third shift. These employees expressed to us their dislike of cooperative decision making and their preference for managers to make the decisions. It appeared that part of their dislike for employee involvement stemmed from their lack of trust in the decisions being made by their teammates. Interestingly, these people were described by several others on the team as being exceptionally skillful at performing the technical work. As a result, the division of labor among SMWT members had informally and unconsciously developed such that the first-shift members spent much more of their time on decision-making responsibilities and necessary interactions with people outside the team, whereas the third-shift members spent much more of their time on the work itself. This arrangement had obvious positive effects on the team's performance.

Thus, we found that the SMWT's performance can be negatively affected where one or more team members does not value SMWTs. The negative effects were found to occur through interpersonal processes, decision-making processes, and effort applied to the work. However, the SMWT can avoid some or all of these negative effects, and in the case we studied, this was accomplished through work shift assignments.

## GROWTH NEEDS AND SOCIAL NEEDS

Two sets of needs have been closely linked to SMWT performance—growth needs and social needs. The *need for growth* refers to a personal requirement or need for achievement and personal development. Hackman and Lawler (1971), in their study of 208 telephone employees, found that those with a need for growth in their job preferred work that provided variety, autonomy, and feedback. Other work characteristics associated with growth need include a need for self-direction, learning, personal accomplishment, and development beyond where one is now—all characteristics believed to be provided by SMWTs (Cummings, 1981; Peters & Champoux, 1979; Steers & Spencer, 1977).

On the other hand, some employees have very little or no need for growth and prefer that they simply "do their time" at work and avoid the stress of added responsibilities. For those not expressing a need to grow in their job, the SMWT is sometimes viewed as an obstacle to be endured until it goes away. Thus, as Hackman and Walton (1986) have noted,

> Individuals with strong needs for growth should respond eagerly and positively to the opportunities provided by enriched work. Individuals with low needs for growth, on the other hand, may not recognize the existence of such opportunities, or may not value them, or may even find them threatening and balk at being "pushed" or stretched too far by their work. (p. 85)

*Social needs* refer to an employee's desire or need to work in interactive groups or teams rather than working alone. Empirical studies have indicated that employees who have social needs exhibit higher motivation when working within teamwork settings (Cummings, 1981; Lorsch & Morse, 1974; Morse & Wagner, 1978). This can, subsequently, be expected to have positive effects on a team's performance. On the other hand, employees who have little or no need for social involvement can be expected to be more motivated when working individually. Plunkett and Fournier (1991) have provided what they perceive to be the characteristics of employees with an individualistic rather than social orientation. Such people are described as preferring privacy and liking one-on-one competition, are considered to be experts in their line of work, and are people who sincerely believe they can accomplish more on their own than by collaborating with others who know less than they do. This description appears to fit well with those team members we interviewed who expressed no need for social involvement.

Hackman and Walton (1986) have concluded that it is important that high social *and* growth need exist simultaneously among the SMWT members:

> It would, however, be risky to form work teams if most members were high in social need strength but *low* in growth need strength. In this case, members might use the group experience to obtain desired social satisfactions, but at the expense of work on the task. Similarly, if the prospective group members are high in growth need strength but low in social need strength, then designing enriched work for *individuals* would seem to be the more appropriate alternative. It would be difficult for team members to maintain the considerable energy required to develop an effective group in such circumstances because of individual apathy to working in social situations. (p. 183)

## INTERESTS AND PREJUDICES

The interests and prejudices of the team members can likewise be expected to affect the level of SMWT performance. The more interest employees have in their work, the greater their level of motivation and commitment to the work. An employee who considers himself a pacifist would likely lack motivation and commitment to work within an SMWT that assembles bombs for the U.S. government. Likewise, an employee who considers herself a conservationist would likely be highly motivated and committed to working within an SMWT that was responsible for maintaining a wildlife refuge or national park.

In our case studies, the high-performing teams generally had team members who were highly interested in their work. A high-performing nursing home SMWT had team members who had a high regard for older people and expressed an interest in the older population. All members of a high-performing manufacturing SMWT were found to be highly interested in the product they made, so much so that they insisted on showing us all the details of the production process as well as the successful effects their product had displayed.

On the other hand, the low-performing teams were more likely to produce a product or service that did not evoke a person's interest. Ordering office supplies to replenish a warehouse full of office supplies was not found to stimulate a lot of interest among the team members. The result appeared to be less motivation and commitment to the team's goals and subsequently less effort and team performance.

*Prejudice* can be thought of as a favorable or unfavorable opinion that is not based on fact or reason. Prejudices, particularly with regard to other people, can be expected to affect the interpersonal processes within the SMWT. Team members who hold unfavorable prejudices toward others, such as older workers, people of a different race, or people of a different gender, can be expected to have a lower quality of interpersonal interactions with these people. For example, age discrimination in the workplace has been described by Rosen and Jerdee (1985). They have noted that some young employees believe that an older worker has little to offer and does not belong in a team environment. In these cases, interpersonal processes are found to be low, and negative effects occur in the work process and subsequently team performance.

The effects of prejudice have also been examined in terms of influences on those who are the recipients of prejudice. Sanchez and Brock (1996) have found that those who perceive themselves to be discriminated against experience stress that can be directly linked to perceptions of discrimination. To the extent that this stress draws the employees away from applying their efforts on the work, the SMWT's work process and, subsequently, performance will be negatively affected.

In our case studies, we were unable to detect any prejudices among the team members. However, a comparison of the high- and low-performing teams shows that the high-performing teams more explicitly demonstrated equality and a lack of prejudice. For example, on one high-performing team consisting of 15 men and 2 women, one of the women had been elected to be the team leader. On another high-performing team, consisting of 1 black and 5 white men, the interactions during team meetings clearly demonstrated the mutual respect between the people of differing races. On the other hand, on the low-performing teams, it was obvious that in some cases, men and women were having poor interpersonal interactions. However, in these cases, it was not clear that this was a gender prejudice. Instead, it appeared to be due to differences in civil service rank, with the higher-ranking team members showing little regard for the lower-ranking people and the lower-ranking people being intimidated by the higher-ranking team members.

# 22

■

# Personality and Demographic Characteristics

■

This chapter reviews personality characteristics that have been reported to affect SMWT performance. Although we did not administer personality tests, we were able to identify team members displaying various personality characteristics, such as conscientiousness and extroversion. The chapter also reviews diversity and demography research and considers the effects of several demographic characteristics, including gender, race, and age.

## PERSONALITY AND SMWT PERFORMANCE

*Personality* can be thought of as an individual's relatively consistent way of thinking, feeling, and acting, which is the result of the individual's combined physical, mental, emotional, and social characteristics and experiences (Macionis, 1997). Personality has been treated as expressing itself through a variety of ways or traits that include, for example, a collaborative versus egocentric orientation, an introverted versus extroverted orientation, and an authoritarian versus nonauthoritarian orientation.

In our case studies, we did *not* administer personality tests to the team members. However, for some team members, personality traits became apparent during in-person interviews and observations of them during their team meetings. For example, team members who were highly extroverted or

**TABLE 22.1.** Personality Traits Examined as Factors Affecting Work Team Performance

| Mann (1959) | Driskell et al. (1987) | Kichuk & Wiesner (1996) |
|---|---|---|
| Extroversion | Ambition | Extroversion |
| Interpersonal sensitivity | Likability | Agreeability/likability |
| | Sociability | Conscientiousness |
| Adjustment | Adjustment | Neuroticism |
| Intelligence | Intelligence | Openness to experience |
| | Prudence | |
| Dominance | | |
| Masculinity-femininity | | |
| Conservatism | | |

highly introverted were identified from in-person interviews that questioned them about their interactions with others and from observations of their interactions with others during team meetings. Although this allowed us to draw some suppositions regarding the effects of personality on team performance, we believe it is inappropriate to draw any firm conclusions without more precise measures of personality.

There has been relatively little research on the relationship between personality and SMWT performance. The research findings that do exist have been mixed (Morgan & Lassiter, 1992). Researchers who have found no significant relationships have generally concluded that personality traits are too broad to be of much use in predicting team performance (Bouchard, 1969; Butler & Burr, 1980; Haythorn, 1953; Kahan, Webb, Shavelson, & Stolzenberg, 1985). Researchers who have found significant effects have typically found them after examining a large array of personality traits (Driskell, Hogan, & Salas, 1987; Spence & Helmreich, 1978; Spence, Helmreich, & Pred, 1987). For example, Mann (1959) examined seven personality traits, and Driskell et al. (1987) presented a taxonomy of six.

Most recently, a group of researchers concluded that there are five broad personality traits, or sets of traits, particularly important to work team performance (Kichuk & Wiesner, 1996, Table 1). Kichuk and Wiesner (1996) have provided an overview of this work, which is partially summarized here. Kichuk and Wiesner have concluded that the earlier studies, which did not find significant effects, were hampered by making sweeping generalizations about personality traits and attempting to apply these to a wide array of work situations. They have explained that more recent studies have overcome these problems by using more sophisticated analysis techniques, a consistent taxonomy of five broad personality traits (Table 22.1), and specific performance criteria that have allowed for a clearer understanding of the effects of personality on work team performance (Barrick & Mount, 1991; Digman, 1990; Digman & Inouye, 1986; Goldberg, 1990; McCrae & Costa, 1987; Norman, 1963).

These more recent studies have concluded that specific personality traits are related to specific types of teamwork. When the relevant personality traits are present for a specific type of task, the team's performance will be enhanced; that is, the team's performance will be enhanced if there is a good match between the personality traits and the specific tasks of the team. Furthermore, the mix of personality traits among the members of the work team can enhance team performance (Driskell et al., 1987; Klimoski & Jones, 1994). In this case, when the *personality profile* of the team—the combination of team member personality traits—matches the requirements of the task, the team's performance will be enhanced.

Among the five personality traits, *conscientiousness* is exemplified by dependability, carefulness, responsibility, organization, hard work, perseverance, and an achievement orientation (Barrick & Mount, 1991; Kichuk & Wiesner, 1996; Tett, Jackson, Rothstein, & Reddon, 1994). Conscientiousness has been described as influencing work team performance through its positive effect on the work process and, in particular, on the effort applied to the work in the form of hard work, perseverance, and an achievement orientation.

A second personality trait, *extroversion,* is exemplified by such traits as sociability, gregariousness, assertiveness, talkativeness, and activeness (Barrick & Mount, 1991; Digman, 1990). Kichuk and Wiesner (1996) have reported that extroversion has been shown to have positive effects on individual job performance for those occupations that have large social components (Barrick & Mount, 1991; Tett et al., 1994). Given the nature of SMWTs, it is reasonable to expect that extroversion may also have positive effects on the SMWT's performance, particularly through its stimulation of coworker interactions. Of course, more interactions do not necessarily mean more effective interpersonal processes. However, without interactions, there is no possibility of achieving effective interpersonal processes. Our own observations suggest that the extroverted personality increases the chances for an effective interpersonal process by encouraging team member interaction. Furthermore, the extroverted personality may enhance a team's decision-making process, for example, by offering more different ideas during brainstorming sessions. Less clear is the optimal mix of extroverted and introverted personalities for enhancing interpersonal and decision-making processes and subsequently SMWT performance. No research was identified that has examined this relationship.

*Neuroticism* is a third personality trait identified as important to work team performance and is characterized by emotional instability (nervous tendencies) and an inability to adjust. This includes anxiety, depression, anger, embarrassment, emotionality, and insecurity (Barrick & Mount, 1991; Digman, 1990; Kichuk & Wiesner, 1996). Studies have reported work adjustment and emotional stability to be related to team performance (Haythorn, 1953; Heslin, 1964; Mann, 1959; Shaw, 1971). It is reasonable to expect that team members, who routinely receive new tasks, who must identify new procedures, and who must adjust to these, will have difficulty if they are unable to adjust well to these constant work changes. Such difficulties might result in a variety of negative effects. For example, difficulty in adjusting may result in negative effects on the SMWT's work process and, in particular, may reduce the level of effort and talent applied to the work as the team member takes time away from the work in an attempt to adjust. Similarly, it is reasonable to expect that emotional instability will have negative effects on the SMWT's interpersonal and decision-making processes to the extent that such instability corrupts communication, coordination, and dependability.

A fourth personality trait, *agreeableness (likability)* is characterized by being courteous, flexible, trusting, good-natured, cooperative, forgiving, soft-hearted, and tolerant. Kichuk and Wiesner (1996) have reported that the studies examining likability have been inconclusive. Some studies have found negative effects on team performance (Berkowitz, 1959; McGrath, 1962; Terborg, Castore, & DeNinno, 1976; Weick & Penner, 1969), whereas others have found positive effects in cases where the team tasks require high levels of social interaction (Driskell et al., 1987; Kichuk & Wiesner, 1996). One reasonable explanation for these mixed findings is that agreeableness/likability has negative effects in some situations and positive effects in others. Research studies of *groupthink* (described in Chapter 9 on cooperation) suggest that too much agreeableness among the team members will produce negative effects on the SMWT's decision-making process. Too much agreeableness reduces the pool of differing ideas because no one wants to disagree with the first idea presented. On the other hand, agreeableness is needed to allow for cooperation, trust, and group cohesion to develop.

The fifth personality trait that has been identified is *openness to experience.* This has been characterized as intelligence, imagination, curiosity, originality, broad-mindedness, and artisticness (Barrick & Mount, 1991; Kichuk & Wiesner, 1996). Several researchers have suggested that this personality trait is directly linked to a team member's training proficiency and subsequently the team's performance (Barrick & Mount, 1991; Kichuk & Wiesner, 1996). Furthermore, it is reasonable to expect that if team members are high on this trait and the team can benefit from imaginative ideas—such as how to perform the work, then this trait will have positive effects. Likewise, where high levels of ability and intellect are beneficial to the team, such as when the team is consistently obtaining new work tasks that require new skills, this personality trait can be expected to have positive effects.

A sixth broad personality trait has been described as *individualism* (Wagner, 1995; Wagner & Moch, 1986). Wagner (1995) has defined individualism as the condition in which personal interests are accorded greater importance than are the team's interests if they conflict with personal desires. At the opposite extreme of individualism is collectivism. This occurs when the demands and interests of the team take precedence over the desires and needs of the individual. Collectivists look out for the well-being of the groups to which they belong, even at the expense of personal interests (Wagner, 1995). In a study of 492 college students, Wagner (1995) concluded that this personality trait affects an individual's level of cooperation within a team: "Individualists who feel independent and self-reliant are less apt to engage in cooperative behavior, and collectivists who feel interdependent and reliant on groups are more likely to behave cooperatively" (p. 167). It is reasonable to expect that this personality trait will have effects on the interpersonal processes of the SMWT and subsequently its performance.

Furthermore, Comer (1995) as well as Earley (1989, 1993) have found that individualism is associated with social loafing and, subsequently, has a negative effect on effort. It was reasoned that collectivists within SMWTs are less likely to loaf because they feel responsible to the group and feel their team members will likewise "pull their weight" by not loafing. Individualists, on the other hand, do not share this commitment to the group and are less inclined to work hard unless an individual reward is offered.

In sum, researchers have identified a variety of personality traits that appear to have positive effects on an SMWT's performance through their effects on the various dimensions of the SMWT. The work process factors *effort* and *talent applied to the work* appear to be tied to the personality traits *conscientiousness* and *openness to experience*. Interpersonal processes within the team appear to be closely linked to the personality traits *extroversion, neuroticism, agreeableness,* and *collectivism*. The team design characteristic *the decision-making process* appears to be affected by all six of the personality traits discussed above. Finally, another team member characteristic, *talent,* appears to be influenced by the personality trait *openness to experience.* Additional research on the relationship between personality and SMWT performance is needed to clarify these relationships and determine the degree of influence personality has.

## DEMOGRAPHIC CHARACTERISTICS

Each team member brings to the team a set of characteristics that can affect the team's performance. We have already discussed several, including knowledge, skill, ability, values, needs, interests, and prejudices. Less clear are the effects of demographic factors such as age, race, and gender. Most research on these has focused on comparisons between homogeneous teams that are composed almost exclusively of one characteristic (e.g., all women or all Hispanics) versus a heterogeneous team made up of a variety of characteristics (e.g., an even mix of men and women or an even mix of races). Tsui, Egan, and Xin (1995) have referred to this line of research as *diversity research,* the study of the effects of heterogeneity and homogeneity of a variety of demographic characteristics. This research asks, for example, how is team performance affected when the composition of the team is all males versus a mixture of males and females, or how is team performance affected when the composition of the team is all older workers versus a mixture of older and younger workers. Diversity research is primarily concerned with the composition of the team, not the individual effects of specific demographic factors.

A second line of research has been referred to by Tsui et al. (1995) as *demography research.* This includes the study of the effects of specific demographic characteristics on work team performance. The focus is more on the independent effects of demographic characteristics and less on the demographic composition of the team. Perhaps the most frequently studied demographic characteristics are age, race, and gender. Two other characteristics that have received more attention than most are education and length of tenure (Pfeffer, 1983; Tsui et al., 1995). We have examined education above in the context of knowledge, skill, and ability, and length of tenure is discussed later in a chapter on team design and composition.

Provided below is a review of age, race, and gender. Our study was unable to detect any independent effects of these. However, some researchers have found these to be important to employee performance, and others have a keen interest in them.

## Age of Team Members

Research on the effects of age suggests that it can have both positive and negative effects on an SMWT's performance. Laboratory research has found that older workers typically are somewhat slower than younger workers when performing technical, high-paced work. They have scored lower on sensory/ perceptual sensitivity, speed of responding, and fine motor responding (Morgan & Lassiter, 1992). On the other hand, older workers have been found to be as effective or more effective than younger workers when the work is related to sales and customer relations and when there is an emphasis on the quality of the work performed rather than the quantity (American Association of Retired Persons, 1989; The Commonwealth Fund, 1990). Older workers have also been found to bring more knowledge and experience to the work, although these characteristics have been shown to be more a result of length of tenure on the job than chronological age (Dennis, 1988; Fyock, 1990; Hale, 1990; Rosen & Jerdee, 1985). Such findings suggest that age may have positive or negative effects on the SMWT's work process depending on the type of work that the SMWT is performing.

Studies of older workers have also examined the effects of age on absenteeism and accident rates. These have found that older workers are generally absent less often than younger workers and have fewer accidents (American Association of Retired Persons, 1989; The Commonwealth Fund, 1990; Tindale, 1991). This can be expected to have positive effects on the SMWT's work process because older workers are at work more often and so have more opportunity to apply their effort and talents to the work.

An examination of the older workers in our case studies was unable to uncover any clear differences between younger and older workers that could be attributed to age. In the teams we studied, there were very few older team members. In a manufacturing SMWT, where technical work was being performed, there were several older workers, but no difference in individual performance could be detected between them and younger workers. It did appear that one of these older workers may have been somewhat distracted from the work by thoughts of her future retirement. However, several younger workers also appeared to be somewhat distracted from the work, although the reasons were different, for example, thoughts about an anticipated baby arriving or how to take care of an aging parent.

## Race of Team Members

Our review of the literature did not reveal any studies that have reported independent effects of race on SMWT performance. On the other hand, there are numerous studies that have examined the relationship between various racial compositions of an SMWT and its performance. These studies are reviewed in our chapter on team design and composition of the team.

Ferdman (1992) has provided a review of the literature on the related concept of *ethnic groups*—people perceived to be of a similar group and typically with a common ancestral heritage. He found that researchers have focused on two areas related to organizations: intergroup prejudice and discrimination and intergroup differences in cultural features. With regard to the first, the literature suggests that when team members focus on social categories, a mental representation or stereotype of the group is typically triggered. When this happens, biases may result, because information is then processed primarily in terms of the mental category (Braddock & McPartland, 1987; Fiske & Pavelchak, 1986). With regard to the focus on ethnic cultures, Ferdman (1992) found much literature documenting ways that ethnic cultures vary in terms of behaviors, values, and beliefs (Kagitcibasi & Berry, 1989; Triandis & Brislin, 1980) but much less on how these affect an organization's performance. However, it is pointed out that unless people take great care, misunderstandings and negative views of others can develop as a result of differing cultures.

This literature suggests that racial differences may produce miscommunications and misunderstandings between people of differing races to the extent that the people hold stereotypes and have differing behaviors, values, and beliefs. Within an SMWT, such miscommunications and misunderstandings can be expected to have negative impacts on interpersonal processes, the information system, and decision making.

An examination of our case studies did not reveal any effects of race. In one six-member manufacturing SMWT, there was one black team member, and in another 12-member SMWT, there were two. In both teams, no effects on SMWT performance could be attributed to race. Nor was race observed to affect technical skill, knowledge, ability, or interpersonal processes. In a seven-member government SMWT, the majority of team members were black or Hispanic. This team was found to perform at a moderately high level. We were unable to identify any effects on team performance that could be attributed to race.

### Gender of Team Members

There are some widely held stereotypes regarding gender and work (de Vaus & McAllister, 1991). Women are often thought to have lower job commitment and satisfaction than men. Men are thought to be more concerned with intrinsic rewards of work (e.g., meaningfulness of work). Such factors could affect the person's level of effort applied to the work (see Hare, Blumberg, Davies, & Kent, 1996, for a review of differences).

A review of the literature indicates a lack of consistent findings. Some studies support the stereotype that men are more interested in intrinsic rewards (Herzberg, Mausner, Peterson, & Capwell, 1957), some have found the opposite (Neil & Snizek, 1987), and others have found no differences between men and women (Brief, Rose, & Aldag, 1977; Centers & Bugental, 1966). Similar inconsistent findings have been reported with regard to job satisfaction (Crowley, Letvin, & Quinn, 1973; Mannheim, 1983; Stanley-Stevens, 1994).

De Vaus and McAllister (1991) have attributed existing inconsistencies in research findings to differing samples, measures, cultures, and methodologies of the various studies. They have noted that some studies are limited to a single social class or organization; some to a particular demographic group, such as married workers or urban dwellers; and all to a single country. De Vaus and McAllister (1991) have addressed this shortcoming by conducting a cross-national study of gender differences in nine Western European countries. They found gender differences to be small, varying by country, once factors such as job characteristics, religion, and education are taken into account. For example, when considering job satisfaction, a gender difference was initially found, but it largely disappeared once the characteristics of the job and family, and social characteristics were taken into account. Similarly, in terms of intrinsic values, the predominant influence was found to be religion rather than gender.

More recently, similar conclusions have been reached by Lefkowitz (1994) in an analysis of questionnaire data from 371 men and 361 women regarding job attitudes. He reported that "analyses revealed 18 significant differences reflecting traditional gender stereotypes. However, almost all the differences disappeared when sex-related differences in perceived job characteristics, age and tenure, level of education, income, and occupational level were controlled" (p. 323). Lefkowitz concluded that men and women react similarly in the workplace but that this can only be seen by comparing men and women with similar jobs and rewards, particularly income levels.

Studies that have focused more specifically on gender and work teams have examined the effects of the team's gender composition, suggesting that more or fewer women or men on the team affects other dimensions of the team, such as the interpersonal processes. This is discussed in detail in our chapter on team design and composition.

When considering our case studies, the men and women in most of the SMWTs were doing similar work and receiving similar pay. Our review of the data shows no effects of gender on team performance. Some of the high-performing teams we studied were composed primarily of women, whereas others were made up primarily of men. In some cases, we saw differences between men and women that were affecting the team's performance, but these differences were not attributed to gender. It appeared that other factors, such as interest in working on an SMWT, interest in the work itself, and personality were negatively affecting effort of the team members and subsequently SMWT performance. Gender itself did not appear to be having an effect.

# PART VI

■                                                    ■

## Team Design Characteristics

■                                                    ■

Team design characteristics range from very visible factors, such as the number of people on the team, to less discernable factors, such as how the team makes decisions. The design of the team was found to have large effects on the SMWT's performance. For example, unclear goals prevented the team from developing and using the most appropriate work procedures because it was unclear what should be done. The size of the team sometimes contributed to interpersonal process problems, whereas the right combination of employees allowed for an effective decision-making process. The team leader was found to be crucial to the SMWT's success, and the roles and responsibilities handed over to the SMWT greatly affected other dimensions of the team, such as its environment and work process. These and other factors are discussed in the following chapters.

# 23

■

# Team Goals and Job Design

■

This chapter reviews two important team design characteristics: team goals and the design of the jobs carried out by team members. Clear, challenging, and measurable goals were found to be essential to high team performance, as was a job design that provided an "enriched" environment.

## TEAM GOALS: CLEAR, CHALLENGING, AND MEASURABLE

SMWT *goals* are specific, measurable levels of performance that the SMWT is trying to accomplish in a given amount of time. Researchers and consultants have found that clear goals can direct the team member's attention and action (Ilgen & Klein, 1988; Landy & Becker, 1987; Locke, 1968; Locke, Shaw, Saari, & Latham, 1981; Sims & Lorenzi, 1992). Challenging goals, if accepted, have been found to result in higher levels of effort than easy ones, because the team members will work to obtain the goals until the goals are achieved or a decision is reached to lower or abandon the goal (for a meta-analysis see Mento, Steel, & Karren, 1987). And it has also been found that clear, measurable goals lead to greater outputs than vague goals such as "do your best" (Fisher et al., 1995; Ilgen & Klein, 1988; Locke, 1968; Manz & Sims, 1989). Clear goals are distinct, unique, specific, and perhaps most important, measurable.

As a result of these findings, *goal theory* has emerged as an explanation for team member motivation and effort and subsequently SMWT performance (Ilgen & Klein, 1988; Locke, 1968; Locke & Latham, 1990). Proponents of goal theory have explained that in order for goals to affect performance, there must be commitment to the goals; that is, individuals or groups must be truly trying to attain them (Erez & Zidon, 1984; Locke & Latham, 1990). It is explained that goal commitment is generally highest when people think they can attain the goals and when there are things of value associated with goal attainment (Locke, Latham, & Erez, 1988). For example, Locke and Latham (1990) have reported that monetary incentives can strengthen goal commitment if money is a motivator for the team members.

Furthermore, many researchers have concluded that goal commitment is highest when the team is allowed to establish its own goals based on management's mission for the team (Hackman & Walton, 1986; Katzenbach & Smith, 1993a; Myers, 1991). It is reasoned that commitment will be higher where employees can tailor the goals to their own values and interests.

Perhaps the greatest advantage to allowing the team to clarify the specific goals is the expertise that the team members bring to the decision making. Team members have firsthand knowledge of the work, and this knowledge is essential when developing goals that are realistic. If the goals are unrealistic, they will be perceived by the team as unreachable, with the result being a reduction in effort because the team members will conclude that no matter how much effort is applied, the goals cannot be reached.

On the other hand, some researchers have questioned the importance of team member involvement in establishing the team's goals. The work of Locke and Latham (1990) and Latham and Lee (1986) has suggested that goal commitment can be just as high or higher where management dictates the team's goals. They have found that with the proper management-employee relationship, team members become committed because the goals come from people with legitimate authority (as compared to team members), because the goals are a challenge from management, and because the assigned goals provide clear standards.

Our own research suggests that the team goals were clearest and most challenging when developed jointly by the team and management. We found a need for management to provide the SMWT with a clear mission that provided the team with the direction it needed to develop initial goals. Once the team applied its firsthand knowledge in establishing goals, management reviewed the goals and, in some cases, questioned whether they were challenging enough. The team would then reconsider these particular goals, make them more challenging, or provide the rationale for not making them more challenging. This back-and-forth negotiating between the team and management continued until both sides were comfortable with the specified goals.

Such a give-and-take process has been referred to as a *catch-ball* technique by a high-performing manufacturing SMWT. In one instance, the team was given a mission by management to assemble a particular product. The team set specific goals as to how many would be produced each week, the weekly error rate, the safety standard, absenteeism rate, and so on. Management then reviewed these goals and challenged the team to increase one or more if it seemed reasonable to management. The team would receive this challenge and then accept it or explain why it was unreasonable. This process continued until the team developed clear, challenging goals acceptable to the team and to management.

## Team Goals and SMWT Performance

As noted above, clear, challenging, measurable goals directly affect the SMWT's work process through their positive effects on the amount of effort applied to the work and subsequently the team's performance. Clear, challenging goals direct the team members' efforts to what needs to be done and require a high level of motivation and commitment in order for them to be accomplished. Vague, unchallenging goals leave the team members unsure of the best way to spend their time and require relatively little effort to be accomplished. Clear, challenging, measurable goals leave little question as to what talents must be applied to the work and what resources will be needed. On the other hand, vague goals leave team members wondering what talent and resources are needed.

Clear, challenging, measurable goals also affect the team's design characteristics. They provide the team with the direction needed to determine the most appropriate procedures for doing the work and to determine who should do what. Unclear, unchallenging goals leave the team unsure of what procedures to adopt and who should be assigned to what.

Also affected are the interpersonal processes. Vague goals leave team members discussing among themselves what should be done. This can result in decisions that are heavily influenced by personal initiatives and preferences. For example, in a low-performing government SMWT, the team needed to make a decision regarding flextime. Should team members be allowed to have flexibility in terms of what time they arrived to work in the morning? The team was unable to consider this question in light of clear, challenging goals because it did not have any; that is, it was not clear whether flextime would affect the team's goals because the goals were not clear. Consequently, it appeared that the decision about flextime was based on personal preferences of team members and, in the view of one team member, was specifically designed to "get even" by making a decision that was contrary to her needs.

### Factors Affecting Team Goals

The primary factors that have been reported to affect the clarity and challenge of the team's goals include the clarity of the team's mission, feedback, political agendas, and personal goals of team members and managers (Johnson & Johnson, 1994; Larson & LaFasto, 1989). As noted above, a number of researchers have found that a clear team mission enhances the SMWT's opportunity to establish clear, challenging goals (Johnson & Johnson, 1994; Larson & LaFasto, 1989). Similarly, feedback from management and customers provides the team with information that can help the team to establish its goals and determine how well its goals have been accomplished. For example, if a customer needs a product within a given time frame, this may become the team's goal. The team may then begin establishing procedures that require working overtime and on weekends to achieve the goal. Or feedback from management may indicate that the team's quality goals need to be heightened or reduced to meet customer demands.

Personal agendas and goals can affect the team's goals by infiltrating the team's decision-making process. In these cases, certain team members may have influence over others that results in the team accepting goals that focus, in part, on the team members' personal preferences. In one of our case studies, for example, a new team member was convinced by a long-tenured team member that the team's productivity goal should not be substantially increased from that of the past, even though it was clear that it could be increased dramatically, given the new team member's skills. It was explained to the new team member that a smaller gradual increase in the team's productivity goal would fit better with management's push for continuous improvement. This decision had the added benefit of protecting certain team members because, otherwise, management would have wanted an explanation as to why the team had not been producing at this higher level in the past. Thus, the productivity goal was based, at least in part, on a team member's fear that setting it too high would result in personal demerits from management.

### Goal Priorities and SMWT Performance

Establishing *goal priorities* refers to assessing the relative importance or value of the team's goals and then ranking them by importance (Becker-

Reems, 1994). It is reasonable to suspect that high-performing teams give high priority to those goals most closely linked to customer requirements and preferences because customer satisfaction is a measure of team performance. An examination of our case studies shows that all the high-performing teams had goals that were closely linked to customer preferences and requirements. On the other hand, several of the low-performing teams had given high priority to one or more goals that were not closely linked to customer preferences and had allowed these to take precedence over other goals more closely tied to the customer.

For example, in a low-performing government SMWT, one of the team members continually pushed for the team to adopt new computer technologies. This was certainly a goal of the team, but it was not nearly as important as their top priority of completing monthly government records required by law. Nevertheless, this particular team member gave computer use a top priority and continually encouraged the team to do so as well. This resulted in insufficient effort placed on maintaining records. Thus, to the extent that the goal of learning new computer technologies kept the team from achieving its more important goal of maintaining current, accurate records, the performance of the team was negatively affected.

## JOB DESIGN

The goals of an SMWT are achieved through the specific jobs performed by the team members. The design of an employee's job has been reported to have various effects on the individual's performance, as noted in Chapter 2. Job designs that enrich the work environment by providing variety in the work, responsibility, autonomy, and the ability to complete a whole piece of work have been reported to have positive effects on the worker's motivation, satisfaction, and performance. At a broader level, the job designs of SMWTs that spread across work shifts and/or geographical areas have also been reported to affect various dimensions of the work team and subsequently team performance.

### An Enriched Job Design

Hundreds of studies have examined the effects of an enriched job design on employee satisfaction and performance. The findings have been impressively consistent with regard to satisfaction—an enriched environment has positive effects on employee satisfaction, particularly for those employees who desire to experience growth in their job; that is, people who desire growth will be more satisfied with an enriched job design because it offers job characteristics such as skill variety, responsibility, and autonomy.

The research examining the effects of job design on performance has been equally remarkable. The effects are still unclear even after dozens of empirical studies have been conducted to determine the effects. For example, Kelly (1992) conducted a review of such studies, making sure to consider only the most empirically rigorous, and concluded that "the evidence from these cases shows only limited support for the Job Characteristics Model. Links between perceived job content, intrinsic motivation, and job performance were found in only three out of nine cases" (p. 767).

On the other hand, Berlinger, Glick, and Rodgers (1988) reviewed past research, conducted a meta-analysis, and concluded that

> consistent with previous qualitative and quantitative reviews, these results indicate that, on average, job characteristics are correlated with performance ($r = .21$). . . . Our findings suggest that job enrichment in actual work situations can yield significant improvements in performance. (p. 239)

They attributed the inconsistent findings in part to the need to carefully consider the employee's preference for experiencing growth on the job.

Studies that have reported a positive effect of job enrichment on performance generally draw on need theory and/or expectancy theory to explain the positive relationship. The *need theory* rationale explains that people who are given meaningful tasks perform better because they believe that doing a meaningful task will subsequently satisfy their needs for growth and development. These theorists have explained that enriched jobs make the tasks more meaningful. The *expectancy theory* rationale is that people will be motivated to perform well when they (1) expect that working hard will lead to good performance (expectancy), (2) expect that good performance will lead to having higher-order needs fulfilled, and (3) desire satisfaction of higher-order needs. Researchers using this rationale explain that employees generally believe that performing enriched jobs well leads to the fulfillment of higher-order needs.

Rationales for a lack of effect of an enriched job on performance generally provide reasons for discounting need theory and expectancy theory. Salancik and Pfeffer (1978) have noted that the rationale behind need theory is that employees are motivated because they anticipate satisfying their higher-order needs. The authors have further explained that, if this is true, it can be expected that the satiation of needs will reduce subsequent motivation and performance—the enriched job will be progressively less motivating as the higher-order needs are met. Satisfaction of needs through job enrichment therefore could not sustain high levels of performance. Berlinger et al. (1988) have noted that this critique of need theory is in contrast to the view of others, such as Hackman and Lawler (1971), who have stated that "a person may experience higher order need satisfaction without the strength of desire for additional satisfaction of these needs diminishing" (p. 262).

A third rationale that has been offered to explain the relationship between an enriched job environment and performance appears to rely on a contingency perspective. As Berlinger et al. (1988) have explained, "The job characteristics-performance relationship is likely to be weaker or nonexistent in some situations and stronger in others" (p. 222). For example, employees who lack the technical skills or variety of skills to adequately do the work in an enriched environment will view the tasks as unreachable and subsequently perform poorly. Similarly, employees who suspect that management is taking advantage of them by requiring them to take on added job responsibilities that accompany an enriched job will not likely be highly motivated—instead, the employees may conclude that job enrichment efforts are exploitative (Berlinger et al., 1988; Fein, 1974). On the other hand, other employees will view the enriched job as an opportunity to satisfy higher-order needs and subsequently be motivated by such jobs.

An examination of our case studies was unable to clearly confirm or dispute previous rationales. Our methodology did not include examining the employees before and after their jobs were enriched through the creation of self-managed teams. However, we did obtain some insights through our interviews with team members. These interviews provided support for the third rationale, which relies on a contingency perspective—some employees were highly motivated in an enriched environment, whereas others were not.

Some of those we interviewed clearly preferred the "old way" of doing things. For example, one team member told us that he much preferred it when he simply came to work, operated his machine, and left the administrative "stuff" to management. He felt he was one of the best at operating his machine, and that's what he should be spending his time doing. Participating in "teaming" activities increased his anxiety level and reduced the amount of effort he placed directly on the work. Working just on "his" machine, on the other hand, increased his motivation to obtain and maintain a high level of admiration from his coworkers. Furthermore, it was clear that it enhanced his self-esteem.

In a second case, a team member expressed her high satisfaction with SMWTs. She explained that prior to joining the team she had not been given the opportunity to use her brains. Consequently, work had been more of a drudgery, and she had been much less motivated to place her efforts on the work. It appeared that within the SMWT, she was more motivated and placed more effort on the work because the work allowed her to satisfy her need for self-actualization and self-esteem.

In sum, our data suggest that the effects of job enrichment on performance are contingent upon the particular characteristics of the employee. Our study has not clarified what these characteristics are, but it appears clear that they include more than an individual's growth need. It is interesting to note that on one of the high-performing manufacturing teams, the members appeared to have recognized these differences in attitude toward their enriched jobs. Their solution was to allow those team members who disliked "teaming" activities to spend almost all of their time and effort directly on the work itself. Likewise, other team members, who found that teaming activities satisfied their higher-order needs, were allowed to spend a larger portion of their time on these. This appeared to satisfy the desires of all involved and result in higher motivation among the team members.

### Job Designs Across Work Shifts

Relatively few researchers have focused on the effects of multiple work shifts on SMWT performance. However, several of our case studies showed that multiple work shifts can have large impacts on team performance. Becker-Reems (1994) is one of the few researchers who has described some of the effects that can occur. In her study of health care teams, she found that the day-shift members often felt they had the most work to do, the evening-shift employees believed they inherited the day shift's unwanted work, and the night-shift members believed that they never got the attention or resources they needed to function effectively. The review of our data found remarkable similarities in attitude among the three work shifts. It is reasonable to suspect that such attitudes can negatively affect the team's interpersonal processes by reducing the level of cohesion and trust within the team.

Wellins et al. (1991) have described the effects that a team's multiple shifts can have on the environmental factor, information exchange, and the interpersonal processes of communication and coordination. Because team members are not working at the same time, they are unable to share information as it is received. Consequently, the information is often communicated through notes or a third party. This can result in misunderstandings and misinformation, which, in turn, can negatively affect coordination of work activities and cohesion and trust among the team members.

Wellins et al. (1991) have explained that these negative effects can be largely avoided by assigning the role of *shift communicator* to one of the team members. The shift communicator is responsible for seeing that information is accurately passed from one shift to the next. A second method suggested for reducing these negative effects is for team members of one shift to meet with the members of the next shift during the shift transfer to report any activities and information of importance. Wellins et al. have explained that this face-to-face interaction can enhance information exchange, communication, coordination, cohesion, and trust.

Becker-Reems (1994) has found that team members typically stick rigidly to their shift assignments, and this has negative effects on the team's work process. When team members of one shift find their workload temporarily light, they are not likely to fill up their spare time by voluntarily doing the work of another shift. The team members' rationale is that otherwise, the other shift might come to expect them to perform the work routinely. This rationale results in negative effects on the work process, as opportunities are lost to increase the amount of effort placed on the work.

An examination of our case studies supports these findings. One of the manufacturing teams we examined was spread across three shifts, and two nursing home teams needed to work closely with other teams that took over their work following their shift. As noted above, interviews with the members of the manufacturing team found that their attitudes mirrored those described by Becker-Reems (1994)—the day-shift members felt they were doing the bulk of the work, those on the second shift felt they were doing what the first shift didn't want to do (e.g., cleaning a machine), and the third-shift workers felt they were neglected and overlooked by management.

In spite of these attitudes, this team was high-performing. Members had found methods for overcoming potential communication and coordination problems. In particular, the team had elected a team leader who worked on the second shift. She routinely arrived at the worksite a little early, met with members of the first shift, obtained any new information important to the second and third shifts, and then shared this information with the second shift as they arrived to work. She also left work a little later than others on the second shift when there was information to be passed on to the third-shift members. In addition, the first and second shifts met together for their weekly team meeting. Similarly, the second and third shifts met together for their weekly team meeting. This meant that the members of the second shift attended two team meetings weekly, both of which covered much of the same information. However, this was found to be valuable, because it allowed the first and third shifts to learn what each other was thinking via the second shift. This helped to reduce miscommunications and enhanced cohesion. Furthermore, the team leader facilitated both of these weekly meetings and acted as a voice for those members of the shift not present.

The nursing home work teams demonstrated several problems that can arise when such methods are not implemented to improve communication between shifts. When the teams were first implemented, there were three work teams serving the same residents, with each work team covering a different shift. The first-shift team met with the second-shift team for about 15 minutes during their shift change to provide any important information about the residents whom they jointly cared for. However, during this 15-minute period, the residents would go largely unattended. This resulted in several mishaps, including a resident falling out of bed. The result was to scrap the shift-change meetings. This greatly reduced the performance of the work teams because they no longer received updates on what had happened during the previous shift. For example, in some cases, residents did not receive proper care because the new shift was unaware of changes in the residents' requirements and preferences. Thus, in this work environment, where the existence of shifts was necessary, the sharing of information and communication was more difficult than for teams that did not have to contend with shift work.

### Job Designs Across Geographical Areas

There are some work teams whose members are geographically dispersed; that is, the members are not all located together within the same work area but are instead dispersed geographically. In these cases, the team's primary responsibilities or jobs typically require that they be dispersed. This might mean being located in different parts of a building, in different buildings, in different cities, or in different states or countries. Geographical dispersion has been reported to have similar effects as those of multiple work shifts, including effects on the team's information system and interpersonal processes. However, research on geographically dispersed teams is relatively small.

Fisher et al. (1995) have described some of the communication problems that can arise with this team design. These include difficulty in getting information to others on the team and misunderstandings of received messages that result in misguided effort placed on the work, mistrust, and negative effects on cohesion. Fisher et al. have suggested that such negative effects on the environment's information system and interpersonal processes can be overcome through intense face-to-face interactions when the team is initially formed. This includes a focused effort to develop thorough operating procedures, including how the team members will communicate and delegate work assignments and make decisions. Fisher et al. have also suggested that negative effects can be reduced through periodic face-to-face interactions among team members, once the team is in operation; by conducting brief, routine teleconference meetings; and by establishing an office location to serve as a home base for the team. He has suggested that the home office might be something as simple as a common electronic bulletin board or mailbox location, or something as substantive as a centrally located team room or team office with desks and chairs. It is pointed out that such office space, even when used only occasionally, can be valuable by providing a psychological base for the SMWT members.

Armstrong and Cole (1995) have noted that the geographical dispersion of a team has large impacts on the team's need for electronic communications, with the team's information system becoming critical to the team's ability to perform at a high level. They also stress as equally important the need for face-to-face team meetings. And De Meyer (1991, 1993) found in his study of research and development teams that regular face-to-face contact was essential to increase team member confidence in their understanding of each other's work, particularly if it involved innovative ideas. Similarly, it has been reported by Nohria and Eccles (1992) that electronic links are not substitutes for face-to-face communication, particularly when communications involve high levels of complexity and ambiguity. And Armstrong and Cole (1995) have reviewed studies showing that people prefer face-to-face contact where subtle and complex exchanges are needed (Allen & Hauptman, 1990; Davenport, 1994; Trevino, Lengel, & Daft, 1987).

An examination of our case studies was unable to uncover any additional information about the effects of geographically dispersed team members because none of the teams we examined were designed in this way. However, our other experiences with SMWTs suggest that information exchange and communication problems are inherent in such teams. And unless the team members are clearly dependent on one another for their work to be completed, the team members may drift apart and the team may dissolve.

# 24

■

# Team Size and Composition

■

The SMWT's size can range from a handful of people to dozens. Its composition can range from very homogeneous to extremely heterogeneous with regard to a variety of demographic factors. The effects of these differences are reviewed in this chapter.

## TEAM SIZE

The size of the SMWT affects the team's performance through its effects on the various dimensions of the SMWT, including the work process, the environment, and the team's design characteristics. The size of the team is most directly affected by the team's environment and, more specifically, by the team's mission.

### Factors Affecting Team Size

Research indicates that the size of the team is most likely to be optimal when it is determined by the talent and resource needs of the team's mission (Cohen, 1994; Hackman & Oldham, 1980; Steiner, 1972). The team's mission can be used to determine the amount and kinds of talent needed as well as resources (e.g., machinery, tools, work stations) These, in turn, will influence how many people will be needed on the team to supply the various talents required and to use the various resources. Thus, there is no specific number of individuals that produces the most optimal team size. Instead, the optimal size depends in large part on the mission of the team (Cohen, 1994; Hackman & Oldham, 1980; Steiner, 1972).

## Team Size and SMWT Performance

The largest impacts of team size may be on the interpersonal and work processes. Researchers have reported that the optimal team size for an effective work process is roughly four to seven team members (Brightman, 1988; Ray & Bronstein, 1995). It is explained that this size is conducive to high cohesion and motivation and subsequently effort and performance. This size is small enough so that team members get to know one another, have input into the decisions that are made, and so feel a responsibility for the outcomes and a responsibility to their fellow teammates. Of course, if the team's size is not large enough to successfully accomplish the team's mission, no levels of commitment and responsibility will be high enough to offset the lack of size.

As the size of the team increases, it is more likely that a few team members will begin to dominate the decision-making process and that there will not be enough time for all the team members to have input into the decisions. This, in turn, reduces the team members' feelings of responsibility and commitment to the decisions and subsequently their effort applied to the work.

As the size of the team increases, studies have found that *social loafing* is more likely (Johnson & Johnson, 1994). Employees are less likely to see that their own personal contribution to the team is important to the team's performance. Furthermore, the team members' individual accountability is less. All these factors have been reported to be associated with large teams and to result in reduced team member effort.

An examination of our case studies found a large team that was low-performing and also a large team that was high-performing. We found a small team that was high-performing but also one that was low-performing. The large low-performing SMWT appeared to support the conclusions of the research noted above. However, the high-performing large team did not. We found that this high-performing 17-member team had developed means of overcoming some of the problems that have been described as inherent in large teams. Team member responsibility, accountability, and commitment appeared to be maintained in this large manufacturing team through the assignment of tasks. About five of the team members across three shifts were elected or emerged to be responsible for all the "teaming" activities or roles, including scheduling meetings and interacting with management on a daily basis. The remaining 12 team members were responsible for running one of about six machines (roughly two team members per machine). On a weekly basis, the team reviewed the performance for each machine. Consequently, these 12 team members were held accountable for the output of these machines, and they could see how their efforts directly affected the team's performance. Thus, although the team was relatively large, it was designed so that the team members felt a great deal of responsibility for their work and were held accountable.

The small high-performing SMWT again supported the conclusions that have been drawn from previous research. However, the small low-performing team did not. In this case, there were other factors that prevented the team members from feeling motivated, responsible, and accountable. These largely centered around interpersonal process problems that caused team members to feel there was nothing they could do that would improve the team's performance and that the opinions of the other team members were to be discounted as vengeful rather than constructive.

Size of the team has also been reported to affect the resources applied to the work and the procedures used (Ray & Bronstein, 1995; Steiner, 1972). Obviously, as the size of the team decreases, there will be fewer people available to operate or otherwise use any resources that must be used to achieve the tasks. If the size is too small, there will not be enough people to use the resources, and performance will suffer. The most optimal procedures for doing the work can likewise be affected by the number of people available. If not enough are available, the most optimal procedures cannot be used, and if too many employees are available, this can result in people getting into each other's way.

Team size has been reported to have a negative effect on interpersonal processes (Becker-Reems, 1994; Johnson & Johnson, 1994; Katzenbach & Smith, 1993). As the size of the team increases, team members find it more difficult to get to know everyone well. If time is taken to do this, effort applied to the work is reduced. If time isn't taken to do this, communications and cohesion between team members is reduced, and factions can develop within the team. The factions become, in a sense, small teams within a large team. These can negatively affect interpersonal processes to the extent that the factions feud with one another. On the other hand, small teams allow for the intense sharing of views and the opportunity to understand the rationales of others without large amounts of time being taken away from effort on the work itself. Steiner (1972) has explained it this way:

If a group is repeatedly enlarged, a size will eventually be reached beyond which direct, face-to-face interaction among all members is prohibitively cumbersome. In order to maintain such a pattern of interaction, each participant in a group containing $n$ members must monitor $n - 1$ communication channels and transmit messages along many of them. Unless messages are exceedingly simple and deal with matters that are familiar to all, coping with more than a few channels will constitute an intolerable burden. (p. 100)

Team size has been reported to affect the decision-making process of the team and team norms (Brightman, 1988; Johnson & Johnson, 1994; Katzenbach & Smith, 1993). In large teams, team members generally have less time to share their views and, even with a reduction in input from the members, the decision-making process is likely to take longer than when the team is small. This leaves less time to actually do the work. Similarly, coordinating activities and determining who should do what and when are more time-consuming. Tjosvold (1986) has reported that large teams require more administrative skill than smaller teams.

In the high-performing large SMWT we studied, we found similar conditions. The large team spent more time in meetings than the smaller teams. Furthermore, it was divided into three shifts. As a result, the first and second shifts met together for a team meeting once a week, the second and third shifts also met together for a team meeting once a week, and the whole team met together rarely. When they did all meet together, it was typically due to special circumstances, such as when an unusual decision had to be made that affected the whole team. The team leader, elected by the whole team, attended both weekly team meetings (as did all people on the second shift) and provided continuity.

This arrangement reduced the amount of interpersonal interaction among team members and resulted in factions within the team. However, all team members wanted to see the team do well and, consequently, practiced cooperative conflict rather than competitive conflict. The motivation to do well appeared to stem, at least in part, from the organization's reward system, which rewarded individuals largely on how well their team performed. Furthermore, the team was highly respected by managers and other teams alike, and the team members were proud of this and wanted to maintain their high status.

We also found that the high-performing large team required more administrative skill and time to coordinate activities among the many team members and across shifts. Several team members had emerged who wanted the administrative responsibilities and appeared to already have some experience in this area. Furthermore, a number of the other team members preferred to stay out of the teaming activities and focus their efforts on the work itself. Several of these team members appeared to be particularly talented with regard to the technical work. Consequently, although the coordination activities took more time for some team members, resulting in them placing less effort on the work itself, other team members appeared to make up for this loss by spending almost all their time and effort directly on the work.

## TEAM COMPOSITION

*Team composition* refers to how a team is composed—that is, who is on the team (Hackman & Oldham, 1980). The team's composition can vary on a wide range of team member characteristics. These have been organized by Maznevski (1994) into two groups of characteristics—role-related characteristics and personal characteristics. *Role-related characteristics* include those related to the job such as occupation, organizational position, and specialized knowledge and skills. Team members may be very homogeneous with regard to one or more of these, or they may be very diverse or heterogeneous. In our case studies, one of the manufacturing SMWTs was made up of all machinists—people skilled in operating a variety of machines. There was little diversity on the team with regard to the role-related characteristics. On the other hand, a nursing home SMWT included a social worker, mental health specialist, director of nursing, and nursing home administrator. This team's composition was very diverse with regard to role-related characteristics.

*Personal characteristics* have been defined by Maznevski (1994) as those personal attributes that cannot be changed in most cases, including age, gender, nationality, cultural values, race, and personality. The SMWTs we studied were remarkably homogeneous with regard to several personal characteristics. Of the four manufacturing teams, two were over 90% male and two were over 90% female. Of the three nursing home teams, one was over 90% female, and the remaining two were 100% female. Only the government teams displayed diversity with regard to gender. Similar findings were found with regard to age, with only the government teams displaying diversity. Of the 10 SMWTs we studied, 9 were at least 80% Caucasian, while the 10th was 90% non-Caucasian. On the other hand, although we did not measure personality, it appeared that all the teams had a wide diversity of personalities, based on in-person interviews and multiple observations of interpersonal interactions during team meetings.

A third aspect of team composition is the *stability* of the team, or the length of time each team member has been a part of the team. Team stability has received much less attention among researchers, but our findings indicate that it is important to SMWT performance.

## Role-Related Diversity

Role-related diversity has been found to have positive effects on several dimensions of the team (Hackman & Oldham, 1980; Jones, 1995). Heterogeneity of talent can have positive effects on the team's work process in cases where the tasks of the SMWT require many different skills and abilities. A lack of heterogeneity, on the other hand, would result in the team lacking the talents needed to perform the work. Similarly, heterogeneity of role-related characteristics can have positive effects on the team's ability to be innovative in the procedures it uses as well as in the decisions it makes (Ancona & Caldwell, 1992; Wiersema & Bantel, 1992). More different ideas are likely to be offered when there are people from a variety of professional backgrounds (Jones, 1995). And, as Maznevski (1994) has explained, people in different roles notice different information and perceive the same information differently, which can help the team consider multiple viewpoints and can contribute to better decisions being made.

Brightman (1988) has provided a good overview of what many researchers and consultants have concluded and recommended:

> Critical thinking is more important than team tranquility. And the quest for critical thinking begins with having the right mix of team members. Avoid selecting team members who are clones of one another. Remember, similar members think alike. They reinforce each other's opinions and mistake unanimity of opinion for a thorough analysis. . . . The lack of controversy may be desired in social clubs; in problem-solving teams, however, it is the kiss of death. When members are alike, they may find it difficult to submit their ideas to rigorous analysis or scrutiny. (p. 94)

In the SMWTs we studied, only the team members in the four manufacturing teams held the same job titles and similar skills and training. The remaining six teams were at least somewhat heterogeneous in role-related characteristics. Of the four manufacturing teams, two were high-performing and two were low-performing. In the two high-performing SMWTs, it did not appear that role-related homogeneity resulted in less than the best procedures being selected. In fact, one of these teams had developed procedures for doing the work that were saving the company hundreds of thousands of dollars. However, when considering the low-performing teams, the homogeneity of role-related characteristics may have been contributing to their low performance. We found that management was concerned about the procedures being used by these teams and was meeting with the teams for an hour each day to reevaluate their existing work procedures. Perhaps greater role-related diversity would have enhanced the variety of possible procedures considered by these two teams and resulted in more appropriate procedures being used.

Pearce and Ravlin (1987) have suggested that role-related diversity can have positive effects on the SMWT's interpersonal processes within the team. They have suggested that role-related heterogeneity reduces the amount of competition among team members to do the same tasks because each team member has her or his own special skills on the team. A lack of heterogeneity, on the other hand, can result in team members competing to do the same tasks because they have been trained to do them or find them most enjoyable or because they are attempting to avoid tasks for which they have not been trained or that they dislike doing.

On the other hand, Bettenhausen (1991) has noted circumstances where the heterogeneity of role-related characteristics can produce negative effects on the SMWT's interpersonal processes. In these cases, diversity can result in team members using different professional vocabularies. Furthermore, team members may not understand what others do on the team. These conditions can reduce effective communication and coordination. In addition, heterogeneity of role-related characteristics may make it more difficult for team members to "cross-train" (i.e., train one another) and rotate tasks (Beyerlein & Johnson, 1994).

Much less research has focused on role-related heterogeneity with regard to other role-related characteristics such as job occupation or ranks on the team. In one case, *diversity in rank* had negative effects on interpersonal processes and work processes. Higher-ranked team members lacked respect for lower-ranked team members, and lower-ranked team members were intimidated by the higher-ranked team members. This inhibited communication, coordination, and trust and reduced the amount of effort applied directly to the work. In a second SMWT, where there was a diversity in job occupation but not rank, none of these negative effects were found. Instead, we found positive effects of heterogeneity. In this case, team members did not have the knowledge to do what other team members were doing and vice versa. This appeared to contribute to the team members' feelings of respect for one another and enhanced cooperation and cohesion.

When considering the team's interpersonal relationships with those outside the team, Brightman (1988) has noted that heterogeneity of role-related characteristics can have positive effects on such relationships. It is explained that a heterogeneous team is more aware of the concerns of others outside the team, including internal suppliers to the team, auxiliary people assisting the team, and internal customers. This is due to the variety of knowledge that a heterogeneous team can draw upon from its members' experiences with others. Because the team is more likely to have one or more team members sensitive to the concerns of people outside the team, the team is more aware of the concerns and can incorporate them into the team's decisions. Our case studies support these conclusions.

In sum, the relationship between diversity of role-related characteristics and team performance is a complex one. We found that homogeneity of skills and training did not result in competition for the best or most enjoyable tasks because the team members rotated tasks. Heterogeneity of *rank* was found to have negative effects on interpersonal processes and effort, and heterogeneity of *job occupations* was found to have positive effects on interpersonal processes through cooperation and cohesion and on decision-making processes through the variety of ideas contributed by the team members.

### Personal Diversity

Like role-related heterogeneity, several researchers have proposed a positive effect of personal heterogeneity on the quality of decisions made by teams, particularly where a wide variety of viewpoints is advantageous to the types of decisions that are made or where the tasks require creativity (Buller, 1986; Chemers, Oskamp, & Costanzo, 1995; Janis, 1982; Kowitz & Knutson, 1980; Tsui et al., 1995). In a study of homogeneous and heterogeneous student groups, Watson, Kumar, and Michaelsen (1993) found that over time the heterogeneous groups generated a higher range of perspectives and alternatives. They concluded from their results that heterogeneity is likely to have positive effects for those teams where considering a variety of viewpoints is beneficial (Watson et al., 1993).

A review of our data provided support for this view. For example, our observations of a nursing home SMWT suggested that additional personal diversity would have been beneficial. This team was made up of four women, all about the same age. Some of the decisions made by this SMWT directly affected their customers—residents of the nursing home. Our observation was that better decisions might have been made if the SMWT had had a better understanding of the diverse viewpoints of the residents. This might have been better achieved if the personal diversity within the SMWT had been broader and more reflective of its customers. For example, within this particular SMWT, there were no male team members. It appeared that the team would have benefited from having a team member with this characteristic. This would have increased the chances that someone on the team better understood the viewpoints of the male residents and could have passed this information on to the team prior to the team making decisions that affected these residents.

Brightman (1988) has noted the advantages of heterogeneity of *personalities* within a team. He has explained that having a variety of personality types on the team will increase the probability that the team will bring up pertinent facts during diagnosis, see the possibilities in the alternatives generated, analyze the problem, organize the decision-making effort, and persuade others to participate and look for common ground between different viewpoints.

Our case studies appeared to support this view—although we are only able to speculate because we did not administer personality tests. For example, a high-performing 17-member manufacturing team appeared to have both introverts and extroverts—some people who preferred not to get involved in discussions and others who preferred lengthy conversations with whomever would listen. The team also had several people who appeared to have a natural ability or personality conducive to helping introverts contribute to decision making and helping extroverts avoid dominating discussions. The combination of personality types that appeared to exist within the team allowed for multiple views to be considered during the team's decision-making process.

When considering interpersonal processes, heterogeneity in personal characteristics has been reported to have negative effects (Adler, 1991; Bettenhausen, 1991; Nemeth, 1986; Watson et al., 1993). It has been explained that team members composed of a mix of personal characteristics have more difficulty working together. Furthermore, Watson et al. (1993) have reported that racial and national differences appear to have larger negative effects than age or gender differences.

On the other hand, Watson et al. (1993) have also pointed out that the existing empirical studies are cross-sectional (one point in time) rather than longitudinal. In their longitudinal study of 36 student work groups, they found that initially the homogeneous groups displayed more effective interpersonal processes than the heterogeneous groups, with heterogeneity based on culture and ethnicity. However, by Week 17 of the study, no differences were found between the homogeneous and heterogeneous groups. This suggests that these negative effects of heterogeneity may be reduced or disappear over time.

An examination of our case studies suggests that this relationship to time was true for members of some teams but not for members of other teams. For example, in one low-performing team, it appeared that time only magnified the negative effects of heterogeneity and eventually resulted in one of the team members leaving the team. In a second high-performing team, where heterogeneity in personality was apparent, the team members had learned how to work together over time, resulting in positive effects or at least no negative effects.

### Stability of the SMWT

The composition of the team can also be viewed in terms of the length of time each team member has worked on the team. The smaller the disruption of the team through additions or losses of team members, the greater the team's *stability*. Stability has been reported to have positive effects on the SMWT's work process, development of norms, interpersonal processes, and decision making. Cohen (1994) has noted that

> the greater the turnover of team members, the more time will be spent to orient new members to technical requirements and to the way the team works together. If team members turn over constantly, performance will suffer. The team will not be able to develop the performance norms it requires to succeed. (p. 82)

Our data support this view. The highest-performing SMWT we studied consisted of six team members who had been working together for more than 5 years. These team members had learned the strengths and weaknesses that each brought to the team and appeared to consider these in their decision-making process. Norms and mental models (i.e., mental pictures of how to respond in given situations and how others will respond) were well developed so that team members knew how others on the team would react in given situations (Beyerlein & Johnson, 1994). Consequently, when quick decisions had to be made, team members could consider the preferences of others, even though the others were not present when the decision was made. Time was saved doing the work because team members could anticipate what others on the team would do—few questions had to be asked of teammates. Thus, we found that the work processes were positively affected in terms of the effort applied directly to the work, the procedures used, and the talent applied to the work. The interpersonal processes were positively affected as communication, coordination, cohesion, and trust developed over the years.

Cohen (1994) has noted that stability can have a negative effect on various dimensions of the SMWT if it produces stagnation and groupthink (i.e., desire to agree with others on the team). In these cases, the positive effects of developing norms and mental models may be neutralized by the lack of innovation and consideration of multiple alternatives during the decision-making process.

A review of our case studies did reveal one stable team that also displayed a noticeable level of groupthink. In this team, it appeared that the stability did contribute to a reduction in the number of alternatives considered during the decision-making process. Team members appeared willing to put forth alternatives at the initial search for a solution but, once a solution appeared acceptable to several team members, the presentation of additional alternatives was rare.

### Factors Affecting Team Composition

The team's composition has been found to be affected by the environment outside the organization, by the characteristics of the employees working within the organization, and by the philosophy of management. As noted above in Chapter 20 on the environment outside the organization, the characteristics of potential employees will be influenced by the demographic characteristics of the larger society (Jackson & Ruderman, 1995; Morrison & Van Glinow, 1990). For example, in the United States, there will be in the 21st century a large number of older people available to work as the "baby boom" generation ages. And as more and more of these women chose to seek careers rather than fill the roll of housewife, there will be more women available. At the same time, the numbers of white Anglo-Saxon males entering the workforce has dropped in the latter 20th century, making people with these characteristics less available to hire.

Similarly, the education system of the broader environment influences the amount of knowledge obtained by potential employees in the broader environment. This, in turn, will influence the education level of those who are ultimately hired and placed on an SMWT. Furthermore, the economic conditions in the broader environment will influence the ease with which team members can obtain employment outside the organization. This is likely to influence the stability of the team.

Another factor affecting the composition of the SMWT is the philosophy of management. It has been reported that some managers choose to purposely build an SMWT that is homogeneous in order to obtain all the advantages of this composition. Similarly, other managers choose to build an SMWT that is heterogeneous to gain its advantages (Brightman, 1988; Tjosvold, 1986). The philosophy held by those constructing the team will influence the characteristics of those who ultimately become team members.

The characteristics of the employees working within the organization will likewise influence those who are available to work within the SMWT. As management assembles employees to work on an SMWT, employees already working for the organization are usually the first people considered. To the extent that this policy is practiced, the characteristics of the employees placed on the team will be limited to those currently existing among the organization's workforce. This was the case in all the SMWTs we studied. The employees of each team were initially assembled from among those employees already working for the organization. As new team members were needed, they were sought first from among those already working for the organization and, where positions were not or could not be filled from among the existing employees, people were solicited from the environment outside the organization.

## Summary: Team Composition and SMWT Performance

Becker-Reems (1994) has provided a good overview of much of what has been found with regard to team composition:

> Teams whose members share characteristics that are too similar will have difficulty achieving high levels of creativity or reaching the best alternative solutions to complex problems. However, team member differences frequently can lead to conflict that will prevent a team from moving forward. The teams that are most effective have learned how to value, work with, and balance member differences so that the team and organization benefit from the energy they create. (p. 223)

Similar conclusions have been drawn by Maznevski (1994), who has noted that those studies finding positive effects of diversity typically have reported that the team members had found a way of understanding each other and building on each other's ideas.

A closer examination of past research and our own findings indicates that the various effects of role-related and personal characteristics are complex. The effects of any one characteristic can typically be enhanced by other characteristics of the SMWT or neutralized. For example, past studies have reported that heterogeneity of job professions negatively affects interpersonal processes due to differences in professional vocabularies and lack of understanding of each other's profession. An examination of our case studies indicates that these negative effects can be neutralized and even reversed by other factors. In one SMWT studied, high heterogeneity of job professions appeared to have positive rather than negative effects on interpersonal processes. This was at least partially due to the team's high stability, which had allowed team members time to appreciate the value that other professions brought to the team and to learn how to effectively communicate with each other.

Thus, the effects of team composition on other dimensions of the team and subsequently team performance are complex and depend on the particular role-related and personal characteristics and combinations of characteristics being considered. Tsui et al. (1995) have made clear this complexity in the effects of personal and role-related heterogeneity by asking,

Are their effects cumulative or interactive in nature? Are there nonlinear patterns or configurations of attributes that may be associated with different process and performance outcomes? We would encourage explorations on various configurations of demographic attributes and their consequences for individuals and groups. (p. 204)

# 25

■

# Roles of Self-Managed Teams

■

Self-managed work teams can carry out a variety of roles, ranging from goal setting and managing the work to monitoring performance and providing peer appraisals. These responsibilities have a variety of effects on the SMWT and its performance. Likewise, the team's ability to carry them out is affected by various dimensions of the SMWT and its environment. Provided below is a review of major roles of SMWTs and some of their effects and factors affecting them.

## ESTABLISHING A TEAM CHARTER

The purpose of a *team charter* is to clarify for the team members their mission and the management responsibilities that are being turned over to the team (Brightman, 1988; Pasmore, 1988). It may also be used to clarify who the team is authorized to work with and clarify the team's operating rules, such as the procedures to be followed in making decisions and whether the decisions will require team member consensus or majority agreement. Fisher et al. (1995), in their study of team charters, have recommended that the charter include (1) the team's mission or overall purpose; (2) identification of key customers; (3) clarification of what the team is expected to accomplish; (4) guiding principles, including basic beliefs, values, and parameters by which the team will operate; and (5) time commitments, including major deadlines and time needed to accomplish team objectives.

269

We found that clarifying the team's mission, customers, and commitments assisted the team in clarifying specific tasks, setting its goals, determining procedures and training needs, and subsequently focusing more effort and skill directly on the work. As one manager of several high-performing teams pointed out to us, without such clarity, team members are likely to be unsure of the team's functions. And, as he noted in a communication to a subordinate, "It seems intuitive that people would know the purposes for their team's existence, but unfortunately, it is often not clear" (Meeker, 1993).

When the charter clarifies the specific management responsibilities to be carried out by the team, this also can reduce confusion and avoid wasting team-member time trying to determine their decision-making boundaries. In a low-performing government SMWT, for example, the team members spent many hours arguing over whether they had the authority to make a variety of decisions. This had negative effects on the team's interpersonal processes as team members sometimes disagreed vehemently. And the large amounts of time spent arguing subsequently reduced the amount of effort devoted to actually doing the work. Furthermore, without clarity of management responsibilities, interpersonal processes with others outside the team became more difficult because those outside the team were unsure whether the team actually had the authority to carry out the responsibilities it had assumed. A team charter can help to clear up such uncertainties and ambiguities.

Several researchers have reported that the development of the team charter should include substantial input from all team members as well as management. In this way, when the charter is complete, the team members will be clearer on what is included in the charter and will be more committed to carrying it out (Brightman, 1988; Orsburn et al., 1990).

Furthermore, it has also been reported that the development of the team's charter can benefit from the involvement of employees from outside the team's department. Such involvement has been reported to result in achieving a more realistic, focused team mission and in helping the team clarify with whom members should work within the organization. In addition, for those outside the team, it can clarify the SMWT's authority and management responsibilities. This can result in positive effects on the team's interpersonal processes within the team as well as with those outside the team and can help team members to better focus their efforts, talents, and resources.

## SETTING TEAM GOALS AND ESTABLISHING PRIORITIES

The substantial involvement of team members in establishing the goals for the team has been found to have a variety of positive effects (Ilgen & Klein, 1988; Mento, Steel, & Karren, 1987). Team members are closest to the actual work and many times most knowledgeable about what can and cannot be accomplished within a given time frame. Consequently, the team is often in the best position to determine goals that are challenging but not unrealistic. And team members are best able to specify goals that are clear to everyone on the team and that are measurable.

As noted in Chapter 23, we found that goal setting was most effective when a catch-ball approach was used—the team set the initial goals, management then reviewed them and questioned those that did not seem challenging enough, the team then either changed the goals or provided an explanation for the goals being questioned, management then considered this response from the team and responded back to the team, and so on. This back-and-forth catch-ball process continued until the team and management agreed on the goals for the team. As a result, clear, realistic goals were set that were perceived by team members as challenging but not impossible.

Setting clear, challenging, measurable team goals has been found to be crucial to the SMWT (for a meta-analysis, see O'Leary-Kelly, Martocchio, & Frink, 1994). Clear, specific, measurable goals can direct the team members' attention and effort (Ilgen & Klein, 1988; Landy & Becker, 1987). Challenging goals can stretch the team members' efforts beyond what they would have otherwise provided (Manz & Sims, 1989; Mento et al., 1987).

Goal theory proposes that clear, measurable, challenging goals will have these positive effects if the team members are committed to the goals. Researchers have reported that team members become committed to goals when they are able to establish their own goals or at least have substantial influence on them. This is also discussed in Chapter 23.

The team members' ability to establish clear, challenging, measurable goals is affected by a variety of factors. These include training, the clarity of the team's mission, feedback from customers and management, and the political agendas and personal goals of team members (Johnson & Johnson, 1994; Larson & LaFasto, 1989). Again, these are discussed in Chapter 23. Also discussed is the importance of establishing goal priorities. Without clear priorities, the team can place too much effort on tangential goals and not enough on those goals that are most crucial to the team's performance. The mission of the team has been found to provide team members with guidance in establishing goal priorities.

## CLARIFYING TEAM-MEMBER RESPONSIBILITIES AND NEEDED TRAINING

One of the advantages attributed to SMWTs is their ability to match the talents and preferences of team members to the tasks to be performed (Beyerlein & Johnson, 1994; Manz & Sims, 1987). Team members are responsible for assigning each other to those tasks for which they are best suited. This results in the team applying the highest level of talent available in the team to the team's tasks. It also has positive effects on effort because the team member's interests are considered during the matching process. These positive effects on the work process (i.e., talent and effort), in turn, have positive effects on the team's performance. Typical steps that team members might use in matching team member talents and interests to the team's tasks include:

1. Identifying the tasks of the team
2. Identifying talent requirements and other characteristics of each task (e.g., skill requirements, amount of social contact required)
3. Assessing team members' existing talents, values, interests, needs, and prejudices
4. Matching team members to task components

Larson and LaFasto (1989) have also noted that such matching has the important effect of clarifying the specific responsibilities of each team member and that this, in turn, allows for accountability. Individual responsibility and accountability have been associated with reductions in social loafing within the team and, in turn, more effort applied to the work. As Larson and LaFasto (1989) have pointed out, "Each member of any successful team must understand at the outset what he or she will be held accountable for and measured against in terms of performance. . . . Without clear roles and accountabilities, all efforts become random and haphazard" (pp. 55-56). Our case studies suggested that unless each team member is clear as to his or her roles and responsibilities, team member efforts become guesswork as to what should be done.

A clear understanding of the team's mission, goals, and roles directly affects the team's ability to identify its training needs. In the process of matching team member talents and preferences to task requirements, the team can identify any talents and preferences that are missing or are in short supply among the team's members. This, in turn, can help in determining the training most needed. Well-focused training can result in a higher level of talent applied to the work and subsequently higher team performance.

## SELECTING TEAM MEMBERS

In traditional organizations, management selects employees. The selection process typically focuses on work experience, educational level, and references. In organizations that use SMWTs, the team is often involved in the hiring process. The employee characteristics sought include not only whether the individual can do the work involved in a particular job but also a host of others that are conducive to working on a self-managed team. These include the applicant's preferences for a job that includes responsibility, challenge, and creativity. And they include the applicant's ability to contribute to and support the culture and management style of the organization and to grow and develop as a member of an SMWT (Becker-Reems, 1994; Lawler, 1992).

### Environmental and Interpersonal Factors Affect the Selection of Team Members

Researchers have reported that the ability of the team to successfully hire team members is largely affected by the environmental factor *training* (Hitchcock & Willard, 1995; Ray & Bronstein, 1995). Team members need to be taught the laws and regulations associated with hiring new employees. Furthermore, team members typically need to be taught to hire employees who provide a complementary fit rather than a supplementary fit to the team. A *supplementary fit* occurs when the applicant's characteristics are similar to those of others on the team. A *complementary fit* occurs when the individual brings unique characteristics to the environment that complement the team's existing characteristics (Rentsch & Hall, 1994). As Hitchcock and Willard (1995) have noted, "Each team needs to learn to strike a balance between creating a team on which everyone is in sync and creating a team that has enough different views, ideas, and styles to keep it creative and stimulating" (p. 144).

Hitchcock and Willard (1995) have suggested walking the team members through the hiring process in conjunction with their training on hiring practices. They suggest that team members first be given the opportunity to observe, but not participate in, the hiring process. The next time someone is to be hired, the team members would share in the process by contributing interview questions and perhaps having a vote in the final decision. The third time someone is to be hired, the team would be given the authority to do the hiring, but only after a manager reviews the process to be used by the team and critiques the selection criteria and interview questions. Finally, the manager would hand over full responsibility to the team.

The success in selecting a team member is also influenced by the extent and appropriateness of information obtained by the team and clarity of the team's mission and tasks. Information needed includes feedback from customers and management that can help identify technical areas where the team could use additional expertise. Similarly, it is important that the team be cognizant of its mission and tasks and of the team-member characteristics needed to achieve them.

### Selecting Their Own Team Members Has a Variety of Effects

The role of selecting its own team members can have a variety of positive and negative effects on the team's performance. Selecting members who supplement rather than complement the team can positively affect interpersonal processes. On the other hand, selecting members who complement the team can have the positive effects of meeting all talent requirements and can result in more innovative ideas being applied to decision making.

It has been reported that team member participation in hiring teammates has positive effects on cross-training and interpersonal processes (Becker-Reems, 1994; Lawler, 1992; Ray & Bronstein, 1995). Cross-training occurs more freely because team members take more responsibility for the performance of those they have hired. And team members are more committed to seeing that the new member successfully adapts to the team. Consequently, team members are more willing to take the time needed to train the new member. The team's interpersonal processes are likewise positively affected. Team members tend to select people who fit in well with others on the team. An examination of our case studies shows that four of the teams, two high-performing and two low-performing, were involved in selecting new team members. These teams were all in manufacturing settings and selected members from among people already working for the organization because of the downsizing of the organization and subsequent availability of employees. The selection procedures used by all four teams were the same and appeared to work well. They were a joint effort by management and the team. Typically, management conducted the initial screening of potential candidates and presented the names of three to five people to the team. The SMWT then conducted a review of the team's needs and of each applicant's talents. Each applicant was interviewed by the team prior to the team making the final selection.

These procedures appeared to have a variety of positive effects. The talents of the selected team members appeared to complement the team. Once the applicant was hired, team members demonstrated a sincere effort to help the new employee adjust to the team through cross-training where needed. And interpersonal processes within the team appeared to be positively influenced. Interviews with team members indicated that the SMWT's hiring practices might have been improved by involving employees from other teams and departments within the organization with whom the team interacts (Lawler, 1992). This would have allowed for a more thorough review of the team's talent needs and allowed the team to observe how the applicant responded to people outside the team.

In one of the low-performing government SMWTs we studied, we found that the team members were unhappy with the lack of authority to select or have input in the selection of their new team members. They reported that several recent new members selected by management had chosen to leave the team. These people had not gotten along with others on the team and had been unwilling to share in team responsibilities. This appeared to have resulted in lower levels of effort placed on the work as team members spent time complaining about and arguing with the new team members. Furthermore, it appeared to result in an inability of the team to use the most appropriate procedures for doing the work because some team members refused to work with others.

## SELECTING THE TEAM LEADER

Organizations that have not fully implemented self-managed teams typically appoint a team leader to each of their teams (Wellins et al., 1991). This is often to prevent a loss of control or reduce turmoil within the teams. In more advanced self-managed environments, the team members determine who will be the team's leader. The length of the appointment to team leader varies from team to team. Some SMWTs are designed so that the team leader must step down after a few terms (e.g., two 6-month periods), whereas others allow more permanent arrangements. Some teams have a policy requiring all team members to rotate into the team leader position, whereas others have an election that includes only those who have an interest in the position.

Authority to select its own team leader can have a variety of effects on the team's performance (Orsburn et al., 1990). The team selection of someone who is effective at performing the team leader roles will result in positive effects on interpersonal processes within the team as the team leader helps team members to understand and respect one another and facilitates cooperative conflict. Similarly, the effective team leader will positively influence the interpersonal processes with those outside the team, including the team's customers and management. An effective team leader will encourage a variety of ideas to be considered during the decision-making process, which can improve the decisions made, such as the work procedures to be followed and the appropriate talents and resources to be applied to the work. These are discussed in more detail in Chapter 27.

On the other hand, the team's selection of an ineffective team leader can result in all the opposite effects. These include hampering interpersonal processes within the team as well as with those outside the team, allowing a few team members to dominate discussions while most team members listen passively, and allowing decisions to be made that are inferior for reasons such as not obtaining everyone's input and not considering the feelings of all involved. Thus, the team's role of selecting a team leader is clearly a crucial one that has large impacts on SMWT performance.

Perhaps the most important factor affecting the team's selection of a team leader is again the environmental factor *training*. Training that teaches the team members what to look for in an effective team leader can result in the team selecting a person who has these desirable characteristics. These include, for example, the ability to facilitate team meetings and discussions by obtaining input from all members, effectively organizing and leading team problem-solving sessions, maintaining good relationships with teammates and managers, and accurately passing information between the team and management.

There are a variety of other factors that can affect the team's selection, including the team's interpersonal processes, the organization's information system, and management input. A lack of good interpersonal processes, such as when there is a lack of trust and cohesion, can cause team members to vote for the person they believe is most supportive of them personally rather than objectively considering the personal characteristics important to team leadership. A lack of reliable information can result in team members not getting all the facts about the potential team leaders. And management can subtly influence team members to vote for its favorite candidate. Or, on the other hand, the team may respond negatively to management's subtle pressures and not vote for someone management prefers—even when this person might be an excellent choice.

## HOLDING REGULAR, EFFECTIVE TEAM MEETINGS

The members of an SMWT need to meet periodically for a variety of reasons, such as reviewing new team assignments and team member responsibilities, obtaining information from management, reviewing team performance and the performance of team members, and problem solving. Regular meetings might occur, for example, once a week, with brief 10-minute meetings occurring daily. There are dozens of books describing the characteristics of an effective team meeting. Such characteristics include, for example, providing participants an agenda that clarifies the purposes of the meeting, starting on time, keeping on track, encouraging participation, allowing some time for socializing, and finishing on time (Plunkett & Fournier, 1991; Ray & Bronstein, 1995; Rees, 1991). Furthermore, our observations of meetings held by high-performing teams suggest that there are specific topics that should be covered routinely. These typically include the regular review of team assignments, team member responsibilities, customer and management feedback, team performance, team member performance, sharing of information, problem solving, and the review of new opportunities. When these were part of the self-managed team meeting on a regular basis, the meetings appeared to have a variety of positive effects on the team's performance.

### Team Meetings, the Environment, and Interpersonal Processes

Holding regular, effective meetings was found to have positive effects on the organization's information and performance evaluation systems. Regular, effective meetings provided management and the team members a means of routinely sharing information. The routineness avoided lapses in information sharing. Such lapses were found to have a variety of negative effects, such as overlooking problems with customers, reducing coordination, or not taking advantage of existing opportunities. Similarly, regular, effective meetings allowed for regular reviews of performance. This allowed teams to identify performance problems at their initial stages, when they were typically the easiest to address and solve.

A typical example of the negative effects that can occur when routine reviews were not done was reported by a team that did assembly work. In this team, a series of components were typically assembled in a specific order. Problems arose when one of the first components in the series was not received on time. When this occurred, the team needed either to have the supplier send the missing components immediately or to stop receiving other components and take on different work until the missing components could be obtained. Otherwise, the team would have a whole lot of parts and people to assemble them but lack a crucial first component that prevented the assembly work from proceeding. In this case, a lack of effective team meetings resulted in the shortage of a component going undetected for a period long enough to result in an expensive correction that could have been avoided with routine reviews of inventory and future work.

Holding regular, effective meetings has a variety of positive effects on the team's interpersonal processes with those *outside* the team. Such meetings allow the team to review information received by those outside the team, including customers, suppliers, and ancillary employees, and respond as a team to them. For example, in a government SMWT we studied, federal regulations changed routinely. This, in turn, affected how the team carried out its work. Routine meetings allowed the team members to learn of the new regulations before they became official, discuss them, and send questions and comments back to the federal agency.

Interpersonal processes occurring *within* the team are affected as well. Regular team meetings provide team members the opportunity to work out differences, understand one another, clarify miscommunications, and build trust and commitment (Fisher et al., 1995; Johnson & Johnson, 1994). As Becker-Reems (1994) has noted, "Team rapport evolves as members meet with each other and work together on assignments. Employees who rarely see each other often become distanced, which can lead to a lack of trust and eventually to unsuccessful team performance" (p. 213). And Johnson and Johnson (1994) have noted that frequent team meetings can result in *promotive interaction,* or "individuals encouraging and facilitating each other's efforts to achieve, complete tasks, and produce in order to reach the group's goals" (p. 247).

In sum, the positive effects of regular team meetings on the environmental characteristics (e.g., information system, performance reviews) and interpersonal processes, both within and outside the team, in turn, positively influence the team's work process and performance. More effort is placed directly on the work as commitment to the team increases and less time is spent in interpersonal conflicts and trying to decipher misunderstandings. The most appropriate talent and resources are applied to the work as the team shares information and reviews work assignments on a regular basis. And the team is able to identify the most appropriate procedures for doing the work because alternatives can be considered in a trusting environment that allows for cooperative conflict.

### Factors Influencing Team Meetings

Factors affecting the team's ability to hold regular, effective team meetings include environmental characteristics such as training and management, team design characteristics such as team leader skills and team norms, and interpersonal processes. Team members can be taught the characteristics that should be included in a team meeting (e.g., provide an agenda, start on time, respect the opinions of others) and the topics that should be covered (e.g., review of new information, team performance update). The team can also be provided a facilitator who can work with the team leader, attend team meetings, and help the team to observe effective procedures until they become routine. As routines develop, so do *norms,* or the expected or anticipated ways of behaving within a group (Allen, 1987). Such norms influence whether the team holds regular meetings and follows effective procedures.

Holding regular meetings is also determined by management, who must allow the team members to take time away from their work for these. In some organizations, the team members must account for their time at work by charging their time to either specific customer projects or to the organization's internal "overhead" account. In these cases, management must set aside enough funds in the organization's overhead account to accommodate regular team meetings.

The skills of the team leader or other person who organizes and facilitates the team meeting will influence the effectiveness of the meeting (Rees, 1991). This person is responsible for seeing that effective procedures and important topics are covered, including starting and finishing meetings on time, covering the most crucial topics, and encouraging people to participate.

Interpersonal processes also influence the team's ability to hold regular, effective team meetings. And, as noted above, regular, effective team meetings also affect the interpersonal processes. It appeared that regular, effective meetings enhanced interpersonal processes such as communication, cohesion, and trust, as noted above. Simultaneously, it appeared that positive interpersonal processes (e.g., high levels of trust, clear communication) enhanced the effectiveness of the meetings.

## IDENTIFYING WORK PROCEDURES AND SOLVING PROBLEMS

An important role of team members is to identify the most appropriate procedures for doing the team's work and to solve work-related problems. When team members identify the most appropriate procedures and find effective solutions to work-related problems, the team's performance is positively influenced through the positive effects on the team's work process. More specifically, the identification of the most appropriate procedures and solutions can be applied directly to the work so that the most appropriate procedures, talents, and resources are used. Furthermore, the amount of effort applied to the work is more likely to be relatively high because the most appropriate procedures typically have fewer unnecessary steps in the work process.

A primary factor affecting the identification of work procedures and solutions to work-related problems is training. Training can introduce team members to the importance of identifying effective work procedures and to specific techniques for doing so, including, for example, brainstorming and flowcharting techniques (these and other techniques are reviewed in Chapter 26). Furthermore, facilitation of these techniques—for example, assisting team members in using them in the workplace—can help the team learn how to use them.

Other factors affecting the selection of work procedures and solutions include the team members' characteristics, the information and reward systems, decision-making procedures, and interpersonal processes. The team members' characteristics, in the form of existing talents and interests, can contribute a wealth of knowledge and experience that assists the team in identifying best work procedures and solving problems. The information system provides all the relevant information needed to make good choices. The reward system can provide specific rewards to teams that develop best procedures and solutions. The team's decision-making procedures can determine the extent to which team members participate in and contribute to the work procedures and solutions selected. Finally, interpersonal processes can enhance the team members' ability to work together, make good decisions, and successfully use techniques for identifying best procedures.

In a low-performing, government SMWT that we studied, members informed us that the most appropriate procedures for doing the work were not always being used. It was reported that team members had received no special training for identifying good work procedures, often lacked relevant information or received it too late, often lacked the involvement of some of the team members when decisions were made, and had very low cohesion and trust within the team. These all appeared to contribute to an inability to identify the most appropriate work procedures and to solve work-related problems.

On the other hand, a high-performing manufacturing team appeared to be using the most appropriate procedures and successfully solving work-related problems. For example, management reported that the team had identified procedures for saving time in the production of several products, allowing the company to save hundreds of thousands of dollars in production costs. This SMWT typically received all the information it requested prior to making decisions, appeared to receive input from all team members who held knowledge on the product being considered, and demonstrated high levels of coordination, communication, and cohesion.

Furthermore, the team members believed that their ability to continue working as a team and perhaps maintaining their employment hinged greatly on their ability to identify the most appropriate procedures. Thus, in this case, having the job itself became a reward and motivated the team members to seek out best procedures. On the other hand, the members of the government SMWT saw a much smaller, if any, connection between the security of their jobs and their team's ability to identify effective procedures.

## MANAGING THE WORK AND MONITORING PERFORMANCE

SMWTs are typically responsible for managing the day-to-day operations of the work. This includes receiving new jobs or work orders and determining the job's task requirements, when the tasks need to be completed, and who on the team will do what and when. The teams we observed that effectively managed their work were found to be high-performing, whereas those that did not were among the low-performing SMWTs we examined. Effective management resulted in a high level of coordination and good use of team members' time and talents. Poor management resulted in team members spending more time than needed to perform tasks because they found themselves waiting on others prior to beginning their tasks or waiting on others to complete their tasks. Furthermore, some team members performed their tasks out of turn and needed to go back and redo work at a later time.

Monitoring measures of team performance was also found to be extremely important to the team's performance. We found that the high-performing teams established performance goals through measurable criteria and monitored their success at achieving their performance goals during weekly team meetings. Monitoring performance allowed the team to recognize when a problem in performance was occurring and subsequently examine and correct the problem. By monitoring their own performance, team members appeared to take ownership of any performance problems and to take on responsibility for improving areas that were not up to performance goals. This appeared to result in better focusing of team efforts, talents, resources, and procedures because the team was routinely evaluating whether its current work processes were resulting in high performance and, when they were not, revising the work processes to enhance performance.

For example, one high-performing manufacturing team discovered that its performance of a particular job was below its performance goals. As a result, the job was examined more closely, whereby it was determined that a particular tool being used was slowing down production. Subsequently, the team began using a more effective tool, and its performance increased substantially. On the other hand, one low-performing government team lacked clear, measurable performance goals. Consequently, the team was typically unable to identify areas for improvement because team members were uncertain as to what constituted "high" performance.

The ability of the SMWT to manage its own work effectively and monitor its own performance was found to be affected by a variety of factors, including interpersonal processes, other team design characteristics such as goal clarity, and environmental characteristics such as the information and education system, management and supplier support, and team mission. Managing and monitoring the work was found to be most effective in those teams where a high level of trust, communication, cohesiveness, and coordination existed. Where team members were willing to admit when a performance problem had developed and trusted their teammates not to place blame, the problem was quickly addressed and a solution found. On the other hand, where blame and a lack of trust were the norm, performance problems were not identified as quickly and were found to cause noticeable performance setbacks before they were found and corrected.

The education and information systems were particularly important to the team's use of effective management procedures and monitoring strategies. Team members who had received training in managing the work appeared to be much more effective at establishing effective work schedules for the team in a timely manner. Training in how to monitor performance provided the team with effective procedures to follow that improved its ability to establish measurable goals and monitor performance. Up-to-date information, such as that related to suppliers, customer needs, and availability of ancillary assistance, was crucial to the team's ability to establish effective work schedules for members and to accurately measure the team's performance. Furthermore, a clear team mission and measurable goals were necessary to establish measurable performance criteria. And the team relied on management support to provide the information it needed, advise the team when it set priorities for doing the work, and assist the team when scheduling problems developed.

## OBTAINING FEEDBACK FROM CUSTOMERS, SUPPLIERS, AND MANAGEMENT

An essential role of SMWTs is to provide and receive feedback from customers, suppliers, and management. Feedback to customers was found to take the form of information regarding the team's abilities and limitations. Such feedback helped customers maintain realistic expectations of the SMWT and understand the difficulties that had to be overcome in providing what the customer wanted. In turn, the customer was able to provide feedback to the SMWT in the form of orders that were realistic requests. Similarly, the SMWT received feedback from its suppliers as to what could realistically be provided to the SMWT. The SMWT responded to this information by making realistic requests of the suppliers. This subsequently resulted in the SMWT improving its ability to predict what supplies it would have available during the work process. Thus, the feedback between the SMWT and its customers and suppliers greatly enhanced the SMWT's ability to meet the customer's expectations—the SMWT knew what supplies it could reasonably expect to have available to it, and what it could reasonably be able to provide to the customer in a given period of time, and this information was shared freely with the customer. The result was requests from the team's customers that enabled the team to effectively focus its effort, talent, resources, and procedures.

Receiving feedback from customers is also extremely important to the team's ability to identify problems with work it has already done and to improve existing work processes in order to overcome any previous shortcomings in the work. Customers can provide feedback that lets the team know what needs to be changed to better satisfy the customer. Similarly, the SMWT can provide feedback to suppliers that can help the suppliers provide more precisely what the SMWT wants. Such feedback to suppliers was sometimes found to be the direct result of feedback from the SMWT's customers. Once learning from the customer how to better meet the customer's needs, the SMWT sometimes needed to make new requests of suppliers to meet these needs.

Feedback from and to management helps the team to interact more effectively with its environment. For example, a high-performing manufacturing SMWT provided regular feedback to its immediate manager on resources that it needed and on its ability to identify best procedures for doing the work. The manager then attempted to assist the team with these in whatever way was available to him. In some cases, this meant approaching another manager to request that certain machines or other resources be made available to the team or in having the training or industrial engineering department assist the team in developing appropriate procedures. Feedback from management typically provided the SMWT with information about what resources could be made available to the team and when. This in turn helped the team to assess what it would be able to produce and how to best schedule its work.

Feedback from management also takes the form of formal and informal evaluations of the team's performance. We found that in some cases, the manager received information from the SMWT's customer, which was then shared with the team. In others, management shared information with the SMWT that let it know how it was performing relative to other teams that were performing similar work. Such feedback was found to help the team identify areas for improvement as well as work processes that were effective. On the other hand, we found that the comparisons between teams sometimes caused problems if the team's performance was not considered in context with its customers and suppliers. For example, in one case, measures of quantity were used to measure performance, and subsequently an SMWT was informed by management that its quantity was lower than other SMWTs doing similar work. In response, the team began producing a higher quantity of the product. However, the team's customer, another SMWT within the organization, did not need so many in such a short time. This resulted in large stockpiles of the product, which was undesirable. Thus, this and other observations suggest that comparisons between teams can have positive results or, perhaps more often the case, a variety of negative results.

The most important factors affecting feedback appeared to be the information system and interpersonal processes with those outside the team. The information system was crucial in supplying the SMWT with the information it needed to provide good estimates to customers of what could be reasonably expected of the SMWT in a given period of time. Similarly, the information system was important to the managers working with the SMWTs and to the team's suppliers. An effective information system allowed managers and suppliers to provide accurate feedback to the SMWT, which, in turn, was used by the team to estimate what it would be able to do and when.

Good interpersonal processes with those outside the team were essential to ensure that the feedback given and received was accurate and included information that was most important to the team. Trust was an essential ingredient here. For example, a low-performing government SMWT was cautious of what information it shared with management. Because the team did not always reveal areas where it needed help, management was not as helpful to the team as it could have been.

Furthermore, we found that, even among the high-performing teams, some were less than willing to share weaknesses of the team. However, it appeared that those SMWTs with the highest performance expressed the highest levels of trust. The members of these SMWTs were most likely to believe that management would do whatever it could to help the team and was not looking for reasons to degrade the team or any particular team member. At the opposite extreme, the lowest-performing SMWTs suspected that the managers were looking for excuses to abandon the team concept altogether. Consequently, these teams were much more reluctant to provide management with any feedback that might make the team appear ineffective.

## CONDUCTING PEER APPRAISALS

*Peer appraisals* are evaluations of each team member by the remaining team members (Brief, 1980; Kane & Lawler, 1978, 1980). These typically highlight a team member's strengths and identify opportunities for improvement. The use of peer appraisals has been reported to be on the increase (Wellins et al., 1991). Management's use of its results ranges from an additional piece of information during the employee evaluation process to the primary source of information used in evaluating employees. It appears that peer appraisals have taken on a higher level of importance with the growing use of SMWTs. In the SMWT environment, the supervisor, who has traditionally evaluated the employee, is no longer present or is overseeing such a large number of employees (multiple teams) that a valid evaluation of each employee is not possible (Lawler, 1992).

The process of the peer appraisal has been found to take a variety of forms. Some teams choose or are instructed to simply provide a written statement about each team member. The statements are then aggregated by a team-appointed member, and each team member reviews all the comments about himself or herself. The team's manager may or may not review these as well. More elaborate processes have well-developed appraisal forms that are filled out by each team member for every other team member. Each team member reviews the forms filled out on him- or herself and then has an opportunity to respond to the comments during a team meeting. A discussion ensues wherever there is a point of confusion or disagreement. The appraisal form is subsequently revised if the team agrees. It may or may not be submitted to the team's manager.

The use of peer appraisals by an SMWT has been reported to have a variety of positive and negative effects. The peer appraisal may be the best means available for an employee to identify opportunities for improvement, particularly where supervisors are rarely present to observe team member performance. Identifying opportunities for improvement can, for example, result in employees increasing their talents, with subsequent positive effects on the team's work process and team performance. Or it can result in the team member taking the team's advice and working toward improving interpersonal skills, and this, in turn, can improve the team's work process. On the other hand, the peer appraisal has been found to have negative effects on interpersonal processes when team members disagree (DeNisi, Randolph, & Blencoe, 1983). A team member may choose to retaliate for being given a lower peer appraisal than he or she felt was warranted, and this, in turn, can negatively affect interpersonal processes, the work process, and ultimately the team's performance.

A variety of environmental, interpersonal, and team member characteristics have been found to affect the degree to which the peer appraisal
process has positive or negative effects on the team's performance. Training
is essential to help the team learn what should be included in the peer
appraisal, how to structure the peer appraisal process, and particularly how
to be sensitive to others during the process. The information system is
important to peer appraisals by providing relevant data about the work that
has been done. Teams experiencing a high level of cohesion and trust are
more likely to have team members who respond constructively to the peer
appraisal process by taking the team's suggestions to heart and attempting
to improve in the recommended areas. On the other hand, where cohesion
and trust are low, team members are less likely to accept the suggestions for
improvement, concluding that the "criticisms" were a personal attack. Team
member characteristics may also play a role in how well the peer appraisals
are accepted. Some personalities may be more open to suggestions for
improvement than others (Kichuk & Wiesner, 1996)

## DISCIPLINE AND REWARDING RESULTS

Perhaps the least preferred role of SMWT members is providing *team
member discipline*—action taken to address unacceptable behavior by a team
member. As reported to us by numerous team members, "I'm not paid enough
to do that" and "That's the manager's job." For some teams, disciplining
becomes a moot point because union-management agreements specifically
designate discipline as a role of management—in these cases, the SMWTs
cannot legally discipline other employees (Hitchcock & Willard, 1995).
Otherwise, however, a team can perform this role if it is delegated to them
by management.

Team member discipline can have positive effects by identifying firsthand
unwanted behavior, taking actions to stop it, and, where necessary, removing
ineffective members from the team. A good example was reported to us by
a manager of an SMWT at Boeing, a member of our SMWT network. In this
case, one of the team members was sleeping on the job. This was, in turn,
hurting the team's performance. Consequently, the team members met informally without the problem member present and, subsequently, confronted
the employee during a formal team meeting. The team member explained
that he was holding down two jobs and not getting enough sleep but that he
would quit his second job and stop sleeping on the job. Unfortunately, he did
not quit sleeping on the job, and the team leader subsequently approached
the organization's personnel department about what to do. Eventually, after

several official warnings by the team, the team member was asked to meet with the personnel director, who then asked the employee what he felt should be done to solve this problem. The employee responded that he should quit, and he subsequently left the team and organization.

Rewarding the team's results provides the team an opportunity to celebrate its successes and recognize team members' contributions to the team's success. This can occur either by monetary rewards or by some other type of recognition or award for outstanding performance (Johnson & Johnson, 1994). When such a reward is given to the whole team, it can have positive effects on the team's interpersonal processes within as well as outside the team, on personal motivation, and, subsequently, on the team's work process and performance. Our data show that, when a monetary reward was given to the whole team, it appeared to result in team members taking pride in their work and their team, increased cohesion, and team members working hard to maintain the distinction that the reward symbolized.

On the other hand, the potential for negative effects was found where individual rewards were distributed to team members. In these cases, the process used for rewarding team member contributions was not perceived to be fair by some team members and resulted in some team members feeling slighted. This had negative effects on the team's interpersonal processes and, subsequently, performance. In the case, for example, where a low-performing government SMWT was told that only one person, not the whole team, could be given an award, the team subsequently chose to vote by secret ballot for the person on the team who should receive the award. The result was that one team member received one more vote than a second team member and so received the award. The second team member was extremely upset because, as she put it, "I know that she voted for herself, and that's why she had the one extra vote." As a result, interpersonal processes were negatively affected and, subsequently, so also were the work process and team performance.

Our data also show that individual rewards, handed out by the team, can have positive effects. For example, in a high-performing manufacturing SMWT, the team received a team bonus and was instructed to divide it among the team members in whatever way the team chose. The team subsequently reviewed peer evaluations and determined that one of the team members should receive less than the rest of the team members, who should receive equal amounts. It was reported that all were in agreement, including the unfortunate member getting the lower amount. It was also reported that the unfortunate member was making successful efforts to improve, which was having positive impacts on the team's work process and performance.

The SMWT's ability to successfully discipline team members and distribute rewards within the team was found to be dependent on training and good interpersonal processes. Disciplining team members required training regarding the appropriate steps to follow in providing warnings to the problem team member and being sensitive to the problem employee's possible reactions to what could be perceived as negative treatment. It also appeared that it would have been helpful to have received some sensitivity training in the area of employee personal problems that can cause an employee to temporarily perform at a lower than expected level. Good interpersonal processes were important in helping the team reach a consensus on how to handle a disciplinary problem or distribute a reward. Still another important factor affecting successful discipline was management support of the team's decisions. This was needed to successfully follow through with the disciplinary action.

# 26

■

# Decision-Making
# Methods and Processes

■

A *decision-making method* refers to the sequence of steps (or lack of steps) that a team follows prior to making a decision. For example, the *rational choice* method for decision making requires that clear, sequential steps be followed prior to making a decision, including generating alternative choices and weighing the pros and cons of each. On the other hand, the *unstructured, emergent* method of decision making is unique in that there are no or few steps that are followed prior to making a decision. Each has its advantages and disadvantages and is described in detail below.

The *decision-making process* refers to the means by which the team selects a choice, once the decision-making method has been completed. There are two primary decision-making processes: consensus and majority vote. The *consensus* process refers to making a team decision that all team members are willing to support and no team member opposes. The decision is not necessarily a unanimous choice, but it must be acceptable to all team members. The *majority-rule* process refers to taking a vote of team members to determine which of several decisions will be selected by the team. The decision receiving a majority of the votes is the one selected (Fisher et al., 1995; Johnson & Johnson, 1994). These two decision-making processes are also discussed below.

## DECISION-MAKING METHODS
## FOR SELECTING WORK PROCEDURES
## AND SOLVING PROBLEMS

Several team members of a low-performing government SMWT we studied reported that team members sometimes had to spend extra days working off-site because poor decisions had been made regarding the work procedures used. The result was a work process that was less effective than it could have been. This subsequently had negative impacts on the team's performance. On the other hand, a high-performing SMWT was found to use a decision-making method that appeared to contribute to the team identifying extremely effective work procedures and resulted in extremely high team performance.

As noted in Chapter 25, the team's role of identifying best work procedures and solving problems is crucial to an SMWT's work process and, subsequently, performance. SMWTs have been reported to use a variety of decision-making methods for identifying work procedures and solving problems. Two of the most prominent are the rational choice method and the unstructured, emergent method. A third, less studied method is the *incremental* model. Our own observations and interviews found examples of several of these being used by both high- and low-performing teams.

### The Rational Choice Method

The rational choice method for identifying best work procedures and solving problems is a premeditated, planned approach with formal, explicit decision-making steps (Weldon, 1993). To find the best solution or to identify the most appropriate work procedures, prescribed steps are followed in a sequential process. Decision makers scan the environment for best work procedures or solutions to problems, develop action plans to pursue them, and then implement those plans. These steps to the rational choice method were originally identified by researchers during studies of management problem solving. However, we found this method for solving problems and identifying work procedures to be highly effective for SMWTs under certain conditions that are discussed below.

Zey (1992, p. 12) has noted that there are a variety of perspectives on the rational choice method that are closely linked to varying academic disciplines. As a result, the rational choice model has been labeled by political scientists as *public choice,* by economists as *neoclassicism* and *rational choice theory,* by psychologists as *expected utility theory,* and by sociologists as *rational choice theory.* Nevertheless, it is generally agreed that this method includes at least five steps (Neuhaus, 1990; Rees, 1991; Zey, 1992):

1. Identifying the problem to be solved or goal to be achieved
2. Generating a wide range of alternative courses of action
3. Carefully weighing the negative and positive consequences of each alternative
4. Deciding on the alternative that provides the most appropriate solution for solving the problem or achieving the goal
5. Implementing the alternative chosen

These five steps are descriptive of how work procedures and solutions to problems are obtained using rational choices based on alternative options. However, the actual implementation of these steps has been reported to be somewhat more complex than each step might indicate (Nutt, 1984). For example, Step 1, identifying the problem or goal, might be largely determined by the values and interests of the people involved, with little consideration for the goals of the team or larger organization. Cyert and March (1963) have shown how managers can impose their personal views at this stage, and our data have shown that SMWT members can do the same. Similarly, Step 2, generating alternatives, might be influenced by personal interests and values so that certain alternatives receive little if any consideration, whereas others receive intense consideration. Here again, Cyert and March (1963) found that the alternatives selected for consideration were sometimes determined more by their conspicuousness and the clout of those supporting them, and less by their expected effects on the problem or work process.

Nutt (1984) has found that Steps 2 and 3, generating and weighing alternatives, can be accomplished by a variety of methods that have been used by decision makers. For example, the historical method generates alternatives by examining the practices of others who are viewed as successful. This includes visiting other organizations and interviewing people who have addressed the problem in the past to extract the most promising alternatives. Pfiffner (1960) has described this method in noting that imitation and tradition have often dictated what solutions could be considered. Nutt (1984) has also described an "off-the-shelf" or "ready-made" method for identifying alternatives (Mintzberg, Raisinghani, & Theoret, 1976). This sometimes relies on vendors to provide ready-made alternatives that can be tailored to the needs of the situation.

Additional steps to those listed above for the rational choice method have been suggested by Ephross and Vassil (1988) and include:

6. Reexamining the positive and negative consequences of all known alternatives, including those originally regarded as unacceptable, before making a final choice

7. Making detailed provisions for implementing or executing the chosen course of action, with special attention to required contingency plans if various known risks were to appear

8. Making choices within the time frame that is required for those decisions to have impact upon the subject

9. Making choices that consider the impacts of the organization's structure

Our data indicate that the rational choice approach was used by both high- and low-performing SMWTs but much less so by low-performing teams. Low-performing teams appeared more willing to do things as they had always been done or to be unaware that things could be done more effectively. Consequently, they were less likely to see an opportunity for using the rational choice approach.

When low-performing teams did use this approach, they were observed to sometimes have difficulty getting beyond the first step, because they sometimes did not have clear, measurable goals. Identifying alternative procedures for doing the work was difficult for teams that were not clear on what the selected procedures were suppose to achieve. Other factors found to affect the usefulness of the rational choice method included the time available for decision making, the organization's information system, management support, and the team's decision-making process.

### Factors Affecting the Use of the Rational Choice Method

The rational choice method worked best when the team had time to make a decision. A thorough review of the positive and negative consequences of varying alternatives takes time. If a decision had to be made quickly, a thorough review was not possible. Sometimes the availability of time was determined by the characteristics of the tasks, as with a government SMWT we studied. In this case, team members routinely traveled to the customer's location, which could be thousands of miles away. The team members then proceeded to carry out their agreed-upon services. Any procedural questions or problems that arose had to be addressed immediately while at the customer's location. There was no time to generate alternative procedures or solutions and weigh the strengths and weaknesses of each.

Sometimes the availability of time is determined by other environmental factors, such as the influences of management. If the team was informed of a decision to be made far enough in advance so that varying alternatives could be weighed, then the rational choice method was more likely to be used. However, in some cases, management informed the team that a decision was needed and that it had to be made within a few days or even hours. For example, in a manufacturing organization, a manager told a high-performing team that it would be given the authority to decide how the team's bonus money would be distributed among the team's members. The team was asked to make a decision by the next morning. This allowed the team little time to consider alternatives and the potential consequences of each. As a result, the team chose what they described as the "safe" route and simply distributed the bonus money evenly among all the team members. This has been referred to as *satisficing* (March & Simon, 1958) or selecting an alternative that meets a minimal set of requirements. Satisficing allows for quick decisions but is not focused on choosing the best decision possible.

It is interesting to note that a second high-performing team was given the same decision-making opportunity several months later. In this case, the SMWT was given much more time to make the decision. Consequently, the team considered a variety of alternatives and subsequently chose to consider their annual peer evaluations in determining how the team's bonus money would be distributed among the team members. Thus, management can influence the team's ability to use the rational choice method by controlling the amount of time the team has to consider alternatives. Management support of team decisions was also found to affect the team's use of the rational choice method. A lack of management support was typically expressed by management disregarding the alternative selected by the team, if it was not what management perceived to be the best alternative. In these cases, the team members were less motivated to place a high degree of effort in identifying alternatives and weighing strengths and weaknesses because the alternative they selected might be rejected by management.

A third environmental factor affecting the team's use of the rational choice method was the availability of relevant information to the team. The rational choice method may require that a large variety of information be available so that the team can evaluate the positive and negative consequences of varying alternatives (Dean & Sharfman, 1993; Mintzberg, 1987). If adequate information is not available, the rational choice method cannot be used. The ability of the organization's information system to get information to the team is crucial, and management support was found to be an essential component of the organization's information system. One of the most frustrating circumstances, as described by team members, was to be asked by management to make a decision but not to be given all the relevant information (Johnson & Johnson, 1994; Jones, 1995).

In one such case reported to us, the team spent weeks and many hours poring over alternative choices before finally reporting back to management what the team concluded was the best choice. The manager then proceeded to show the team that this was not the best alternative available by presenting information that had never been shared with the team. This resulted in the team members concluding that management "was going to do what they wanted to anyway." Furthermore, they concluded that in the future, they would not take such requests from management seriously.

Another environmental factor affecting the use of the rational choice method is training (Rees, 1991). Team members need to understand all the steps of the method and how to apply them. This includes clarifying the problem or procedure that needs to be addressed; knowing where relevant information can be obtained; generating, organizing, and evaluating alternatives; and selecting and implementing the most appropriate alternative. A variety of techniques can be learned to assist the team in carrying out these steps, including questioning, brainstorming, and clustering (Rees, 1991). Ephross and Vassil (1988) have explained that the use of facilitators during the team's decision-making process can assist the team in maintaining its focus, applying cooperative conflict, and weighing alternatives. Furthermore, increasing the team's knowledge of the organization's information system and where relevant information can be obtained will assist the team.

Closely linked to training are team member characteristics (Jones, 1995; Zey, 1992). Team members must have the knowledge and ability to not only generate and evaluate a wide array of possible alternative choices but also to select the best solution. To the extent that the team members have limited abilities to process information, the rational choice method will be unsuccessful. Other characteristics of importance include team member values, interests, needs, and prejudices. These can influence the alternatives selected for consideration and play an important role in the final selection of an alternative.

Interpersonal processes are still another set of factors that influence the team's ability to successfully use this method. It is important that alternatives be evaluated objectively. To the extent that objectivity is lacking, the team risks the possibility of not choosing the most appropriate alternative. Objectivity can be compromised when there are one or more team members who are highly respected by others and use this unofficial authority to have undue influence over the team's decision-making process. Ephross and Vassil (1988) have found that a member who dominates discussions or simply talks more is more likely to have his or her suggested solutions accepted by the team than is one who talks very little, regardless of which solution is more appropriate.

There is also a tendency for highly cohesive teams to fall into a pattern of groupthink. As noted above, in this situation, the team members do not want to disagree with others, and so the first suggestion offered is the one accepted by the team, even when evaluations of other alternatives would show it to be clearly inferior to other choices.

### The Unstructured, Emergent Method

Sometimes teams have to make quick decisions regarding a procedure to be used or a problem to be solved. At other times, team members make decisions unconsciously without realizing that they are making a decision that will affect how things are done or what solution will be applied to a problem. In these cases, the team members may be simply reacting quickly in order to take advantage of an opportunity that has presented itself, to respond to an unexpected event that has occurred, or to respond to task demands that have become known and require immediate action. This unstructured, emergent method of decision making is unlike the rational choice method because large amounts of time are not devoted to generating alternatives, evaluating the strengths and weaknesses of each, and selecting the best one. Instead, procedures and solutions to problems are typically chosen quickly to take advantage of the immediate situation or to eliminate a problem quickly.

Weldon (1993) has explained that the unstructured, emergent method has typically been used when a team member needs to respond immediately to a customer's demand for a product modification, a potential customer inquires how the team can perform particular jobs, or the team needs to respond immediately to task-related problems. In these cases, the unstructured, emergent method allows the team members to respond in a timely fashion to avoid producing an unhappy customer, to increase the chances of obtaining a new customer, or to complete a task on time. Furthermore, the unstructured, emergent method allows for creativity and innovation as new ideas are tried before more rational and typically traditional solutions and work procedures can be selected. This can result in effective solutions and work procedures that would not have been seriously considered with the rational choice method (Scott & Bruce, 1994).

A major weakness of the unstructured, emergent method is that a solution or work procedure selected may be found to be less effective than what would have been selected if a variety of possible alternatives had been reviewed.

This weakness is magnified when a poor selection becomes the routine choice by the team without the team realizing it (Mintzberg, 1987; Weldon, 1993). For example, in the case described above, team members were forced to make a quick decision regarding how they would divide the team's bonus money among team members and as a result chose to divide it evenly among all members. If in the following year management again allows the team to make this decision, team members may simply recall how it was done in the previous year and choose to use the same procedure, even though a more effective procedure may be available. This weakness is diminished when the SMWT chooses to revisit the problem or work procedure at a later time to determine whether there is a more appropriate procedure.

A review of our data shows that several teams relied heavily on the unstructured, emergent method. For example, the low-performing government team that routinely sent team members out to customer locations had team members who often faced unique situations that required quick solutions while at the customer's facility. These team members had no time to apply the rational choice model. They had no time to weigh all the reasonable alternatives, collect the data needed to determine their strengths and weaknesses, and then choose the best one. Instead, they had to rely primarily on their personal knowledge and on their intuition or best guess when selecting a solution or procedure.

### Factors Affecting the Use of the Unstructured, Emergent Method

Clarity of team mission and purpose are environmental factors that are essential to the success of any decision-making method, as noted above (Dean & Sharfman, 1993). Without a clear understanding of what is to be accomplished, there is no decision-making method that will consistently allow the team to identify the most appropriate solution or work procedure.

The characteristics of the tasks assigned to the team were additional environmental factors important to the usefulness of the unstructured, emergent method (Dean & Sharfman, 1993). The strength of this method is its ability to generate solutions or work procedures quickly. When the team's task and/or environment are constantly changing, this decision-making method is an asset. For example, in a high-performing nursing home SMWT studied, the team members needed to constantly react quickly to resident demands and concerns. There was often no time to generate an array of possible alternatives and weigh the effects of each. In these cases, there was a problem that had to be immediately addressed. The team members relied on their existing knowledge and intuition to find a quick solution or appropriate work procedure.

Characteristics of the team members were also found to have large effects on the success of the unstructured, emergent method. Quick, reasonable solutions and procedures were most likely to be identified when team members had a great deal of knowledge, skill, and ability to draw upon. Furthermore, the personal values and prejudices of the team members were found to influence the solutions and work procedures selected. When decisions had to be made quickly or were made unconsciously, the team members had no time to identify an array of alternatives to choose from. Instead, the alternatives generated came from existing knowledge and personal values and prejudices.

## The Incremental Method

The incremental method of decision making relies on the existence of already established work procedures and solutions to problems. When a new solution or work procedure is needed, the incremental method requires that the alternative procedures or solutions considered include only those that are similar to existing procedures or previously selected solutions. These alternatives are then considered in terms of their strengths and weaknesses. As a result, the work procedures and solutions selected are only slightly, or incrementally, different from those of the past (Jones, 1995). The team does not make a decision that is radically different from decisions they have made before (Lindblom, 1959). Large mistakes are avoided through a succession of incremental changes, which eventually may lead to a completely new course of action.

The advantage to this method is that there is less chance of making a large error when selecting a procedure or solution. Because change is small, any error in selection can be easily corrected. The incremental method also has the advantage of requiring less information than the rational choice method, with the latter requiring that all reasonable alternatives be considered regardless of their likeness to existing procedures and solutions.

The disadvantage of the incremental method of decision making is that it results in change that is relatively slow. If the circumstances surrounding a team warrant major changes in a short amount of time, the incremental method will be unable to respond adequately. Furthermore, the team will be unable to take advantage of any innovations that require substantial change from the status quo. Consequently, when new, highly effective innovations are available, those teams using an incremental method will be unable to incorporate these in a timely manner and risk the possibility of their work processes becoming obsolete.

## DECISION-MAKING PROCESSES

In a high-performing nursing home SMWT studied, we found that the decision-making process most often used to make decisions was to seek a consensus among the team members before a decision was chosen. This slowed down the decision-making process because decisions were often put off and delayed until a mutually agreed upon decision could be reached. Using consensus appeared to heighten team member commitment to the decisions reached, but it also frustrated team members because decisions were not made in a "timely fashion." Similar findings were identified in two high-performing manufacturing teams. However, rather than delaying decision making, these teams held intense, sometimes lengthy debates until a decision could be reached that all were willing to accept.

A second decision-making process, majority rule, was found to be most typically used by a low-performing government SMWT we studied. Majority rule was found to create factions within the team as members jostled among themselves to create voting blocs. As a result, the minority bloc was typically unhappy with and uncommitted to the team's decisions and more likely to express a desire to leave the team. Not surprising, the turnover rate on the team was found to be high.

Consensus and majority rule are two primary processes used by SMWTs for making decisions. The examples above might lead one to conclude that the decision-making process of consensus is best and that majority rule should be avoided. However, a closer examination of the case studies found that consensus was most appropriate for some decisions, whereas majority rule was best for others. Some of the factors that were considered when determining which process to use included the need for a quick decision, the need for a high-quality decision, the importance of the decision to the team members, and the importance that all team members be committed to the decision.

### Majority Rule as a Decision-Making Process

The process of majority rule refers to taking a vote of team members to determine which of several decisions will be selected by the team. The decision receiving a majority of the votes is the one selected (Fisher et al., 1995; Johnson & Johnson, 1994). Typically, the process is to discuss an issue until at least 51% of the members agree on the decision to be selected. This process appeared to be used most often by teams that had received no formal training in team decision making. Without training, the team members appeared less likely to be aware of any other process for making a decision.

The use of majority rule is particularly advantageous for teams when sufficient time is lacking for decision by consensus or when the decision is not so important that the time-consuming consensus process needs to be used. As Plunkett and Fournier (1991) have observed, "It is quite clear that many decisions do not warrant the time, effort, and energy that consensus requires" (p. 163). Majority rule also becomes an advantage when a decision cannot be reached by consensus and may be the best process in cases where commitment by all team members is not necessary for implementing the decision (Fisher et al., 1995; Johnson & Johnson, 1994).

When majority rule is used, it is important that all team members feel that they have had an opportunity to express their view, that their view was seriously considered, and that the decision made is not for an individual's personal gain or advantage. Majority rule appeared to work best when team members trusted one another and believed that those with opposing views were supporting their particular view because they thought it was best for the team—not for one or a few individuals.

The use of majority rule appeared to be particularly detrimental when commitment to the decision was needed by all team members in order for it to be implemented. Majority rule tended to result in some team members feeling like they were winners, while others felt like they were losers. In these cases, the losers showed little commitment to carrying out the majority decision. The use of majority rule was also detrimental when the decision was personally important to the team members—such as establishing the daily working hours. In one case when majority rule was the process used, a team member in the minority took the vote personally and felt that others on the team were either "getting back at her" for some earlier disagreements or did not care enough to take seriously her personal situation.

These problems, stemming from the majority-rule process, were found to result in difficulty implementing the decision at best, and to resentment, distrust, competitive conflict, and dissolution of the team at worst. Furthermore, the majority-rule process appeared to sometimes result in lower-quality decisions. In these cases, inadequate time was devoted to reviewing the pros and cons of alternative choices before a vote was taken. This was not a problem if the decision had no effect on the team's performance. However, it became a serious problem to the extent that the decision affected team performance.

Thus, majority rule appeared to be a good decision-making process for decisions that had to be made quickly, could not be reached by consensus, did not require commitment from all the team members, or were not particularly important to the team members. The majority-rule process was much less effective if the decision selected needed high commitment from all the team members, was personally important to the team members, or had large effects on team performance and so required a thorough review of all the alternatives and their pros and cons.

### Consensus as a Decision-Making Process

The process of consensus refers to selecting a decision that all team members are willing to support and no team member opposes. The decision is not necessarily a unanimous choice, but it must be acceptable to all team members. All team members must have the opportunity to actively participate in the consideration and selection of the decision. A report by the U.S. Department of Defense (1994) has suggested that the "rule of thumb" procedure be followed. They have explained,

> Team members use their thumbs to create three signals to show how they feel about an issue. A "thumbs up" signal indicates that a team member favors a proposal. The "thumbs down" sign means that the member is opposed to the idea and in no way can support it. If a team member is not wild about a proposal, but can support it, he/she will turn the thumb sideways. If any member is "thumbs down" on a proposition, it may have to be modified or reworded in a way that the resistor can buy in. (p. 49)

Thus, this rule of thumb procedure clarifies what needs to occur when using the consensus process. Only when there are no team members showing a "thumbs down" for a particular decision is consensus reached. In these cases, all team members either support or can live with the decision.

Numerous advantages have been attributed to the consensus process. It has been described as enhancing the opportunity for innovation, creativity, and high-quality decisions because team members may spend many hours looking for an alternative that is acceptable to all. The process has been described as creating a win-win situation and enhancing trust because discussions tend to clarify and account for individual team members' reasons for their choices. Furthermore, consensus has been reported to create commitment for the decision because it is acceptable to everyone and not considered to be a bad decision by anyone (Johnson & Johnson, 1994; Plunkett & Fournier, 1991; U.S. Department of Defense, 1994). Our own study supports these conclusions.

Using the process of consensus has been found to be detrimental when a decision must be made quickly such as in a crisis situation. In these cases, there is typically not enough time to come to a consensus. If the team insists on obtaining a consensus, the advantages of making a quick decision may be lost or the crisis may overwhelm the team before it has time to react.

In sum, consensus, as a decision-making process, is advantageous to the extent that the decision is important to the team's performance, there is time available to reach a consensus, and it is important that team members be committed to the decision reached. It becomes detrimental in situations that require that a quick decision be made, such as in a crisis or when an opportunity presents itself that requires a quick decision.

# 27

■

# Team Leader Roles
# and Responsibilities

■

Our review of the organizational literature discussing the team leader found that the discussion, more often than not, defined the team leader as a manager responsible for a group of work teams. In the case of *self-managed* work teams, we refer to the team leader as a team member who has typically been selected by the team members with the approval of management to carry out a variety of the team's leadership functions in addition to performing her or his share of the team's technical work (Ray & Bronstein, 1995; Wellins et al., 1991). These leadership functions include administrating and facilitating team meetings, serving as spokesperson for the team, helping the team decide how various leadership responsibilities will be divided among team members, and facilitating coordination between team members and between the team and those outside the team. Wellins et al. (1991) have recognized the important functions of the SMWT leader:

> Usually the team leader is not a member of management but is, in fact, a team member who is willing and able to take on some of the coordination functions for the team. Typically, a team leader still spends time actually performing various production or service tasks but also helps the team accomplish its leadership responsibilities. (p. 35)

This chapter reviews how team leaders are typically selected, their major roles and responsibilities, and how the successful accomplishment of these are related to the team's performance.

## SELECTING THE TEAM LEADER

In some cases, teams elect their own leader with no input from management, whereas in others, management may require that it approve the team's selection or that it simply select the leader for the team. In still other cases, the team may not have a designated leader at all. In these cases, the team leader responsibilities are equally shared among the team members (Becker-Reems, 1994). Ray and Bronstein (1995) have noted that when teams are given the opportunity to select their own team leader, it contributes to team member feelings of ownership and responsibility for the team. On the other hand, when management selects the team leader, the assigned leader is generally viewed as another form of manager, and the team's ability to "self-manage" suffers. In this case, management is still maintaining control and sends a message to the team that, while management may be "preaching" empowerment, it will not be providing meaningful support for empowerment or self-management.

Among our case studies, six SMWTs had team leaders who were elected, whereas four had team leaders appointed by management. In teams where appointments occurred, the empowerment of the team members was less. The team leaders were less likely to seek consensus on team decisions, and their viewpoint was likely to carry more weight than that of other team members. In some teams, the appointment of a team leader appeared to reduce the team members' feelings of ownership and responsibility for the decisions made, whereas in other teams, no such effect was detected. The difference appeared to be related to the decision-making process. In teams where the appointed leader made most decisions for the team after obtaining advice from team members, team member ownership and responsibility appeared to be relatively low. On the other hand, where the team leader sought consensus among the team members for decisions related to the team's work, feelings of ownership and responsibility appeared to be high.

Our experiences with SMWTs beyond our case studies have suggested that newly developed SMWTs might benefit from management's initial appointment of a team leader, with the understanding that the team would select its own team leader at the end of the team leader's term. This arrangement allows time for the SMWT members to gain experience working together within an SMWT before taking on the team leader role. Ray and Bronstein (1995) have come to a similar conclusion:

> The election of leadership can create unnecessary turmoil and interpersonal conflict, especially at a time when skills for dealing with these challenges are limited. The election system is best used after the teams have had a couple of years experience in the team process. (p. 145)

Our departure from Ray and Bronstein's view concerns the optimal amount of time that should elapse before the team selects its own leader. Elections appear to work best in a mature team that has demonstrated consistency in practicing management skills. The time a team needs to reach this point may be only a few months or, as they suggest, a couple of years. However, in either case, if selection of the team leader is not turned over to the SMWT when it is ready, the advantages associated with feelings of responsibility and ownership for the work may not be completely realized.

## ROTATING TEAM LEADERSHIP

The selection of a team leader can be permanent with periodic performance reviews, or it can be made with the understanding that the position is temporary and must be rotated with others on the team. Typically, teams establish a length of time that a team member serves as a team leader (e.g., 6 months). Once this term is served, a new team leader is selected. In some SMWTs, a team leader is allowed to continue as team leader for multiple terms. In others, at least one term must go by before the person can once again be elected as team leader. In still other teams, the team leader position is rotated among all team members so that everyone on the team eventually takes a turn as team leader.

Advantages that have been attributed to rotating the team leader position include the encouragement of leadership development among less dominant team members. As Ray and Bronstein (1995) have noted, "Most people have tremendous leadership capabilities, but many do not believe this. Lack of opportunity has left many unaware of their own ability to lead . . . leadership sharing will encourage development of these raw skills in everyone" (p. 144). Although rotating the leadership may slow the development of any one person, it facilitates the development of the whole team. Furthermore, with the experience of being a team leader, team members will experience first-hand the problems and challenges that must be addressed to perform the leadership role. They will have an opportunity to learn firsthand the concerns of management and to gain more understanding of financial matters, organizational constraints, and the complexities involved in leading others.

Becker-Reems (1994, p. 65) has attributed other advantages to rotating team leadership. She has noted that it encourages the team leader to moderate his or her behavior and serve the interests of the other employees on the team, particularly when the team leader knows that he or she will be holding the position for only a few months. In these cases, the team leader recognizes that the next team leader can retaliate if there has been a perceived injustice. Becker-Reems has also noted the disadvantage of a learning curve that must be tolerated as the shift is made from one team leader to the next. This can ultimately result in reduced productivity.

## ROLES AND RESPONSIBILITIES
## OF THE TEAM LEADER

A review of the literature has found that there is little consensus regarding the specific roles and responsibilities that should be turned over to the team leader. Some researchers and consultants believe that the team leader should hold a great deal of decision-making authority, including scheduling the work, making work assignments, scheduling vacations and time off, serving as liaison to the rest of the organization, monitoring performance, conducting meetings, and maintaining team records (Becker-Reems, 1994; Larson & LaFasto, 1989). Our case studies included team leaders who held many of these responsibilities, as well as team leaders who held only a handful of these, with most being distributed among the others on the team.

One of the most important roles we found among the team leaders of high-performing teams was the facilitation of interpersonal processes and, in particular, the team's ability to reach decisions and solve problems (Harper & Harper, 1990; Wellins et al., 1991). Rather than dictating to the team the right decision or solution, these team leaders encouraged discussion of the issues and the pros and cons of various alternatives. They sought to obtain a consensus rather than a simple majority in favor of their view.

By facilitating the interpersonal processes, these team leaders were encouraging the team to let everyone have a say, to give everyone respect, and to stay on the issues at hand. Other team leader roles that have been associated with the interpersonal processes include seeing that diversity is valued, that cooperative conflict is the norm rather than competitive conflict, that a climate of trust and open communication is encouraged, and that achievement is recognized and rewarded (Buchholz et al., 1987; Harper & Harper, 1989; Larson & LaFasto, 1989). Furthermore, all these roles were found to be fulfilled best when each team member saw these as shared responsibilities among all team members and not as belonging only to team leaders.

A second major role found among team leaders was responsibility for the logistics of the team meetings (Buchholz et al., 1987). This included being sure that team members were informed of the meeting time and place, that the time and place had been scheduled to allow for all team members to attend, that the room was prepared and equipped for the meeting (e.g., flip chart, overhead projector, chalkboard), that the equipment was working, and that any needed supplies were available (e.g., markers, paper, pencils). Closely linked to this was the team leader's responsibility for making sure all the team members knew the purpose of the meeting, what the meeting was intended to achieve, and what significance it had for the team.

A third set of team leader roles that was identified is the maintenance of open, positive communications and good working relationships with those who are outside the team. This includes management, other teams, customers, suppliers, and others whom the team must interact with to be successful. In all but one of the high-performing teams we studied, the team leader had a good working relationship with the managers overseeing the team. Typically, these team leaders informed the managers of the team's successes, progress, and problems and made requests of the managers when the team was in need of something a manager could provide. The team leader acted as an advocate for the team, was constantly highlighting the team's virtues, and was constantly looking for ways to gain management's confidence and favor.

On the other hand, the low-performing teams were more likely to have team leaders who were constantly on the defensive, trying to provide management with explanations for what appeared to be inadequate team performance. These team leaders appeared to be most successful at interacting with management when they were able to convince management that team inadequacies were due primarily to circumstances beyond the control of the team. Less successful team leaders left management believing that the team was unable or uninterested in taking on its self-management responsibilities.

The team leader's roles also extended to interactions with others outside the team. The team leader was often responsible for obtaining information needed by the team for undertaking various technical responsibilities or for decision making. Information from customers might include their preferred product specifications or preferences in how a service was to be delivered. Suppliers might be asked by the team leader to provide information about materials or equipment provided to the team. Technical experts such as industrial engineers might be asked whether certain machines could be placed in a particular arrangement. Or human resource personnel might be asked the proper procedures for officially reprimanding a team member. Thus, the team leader was typically found to be a "gofer"—he or she would often "go for" whatever information was important to the team's work process and performance.

A low-performing government team we studied provided a good example of a team leader who had difficulty maintaining open, positive communications and good working relationships with others outside the team. This team leader was typically not given information that was important to her team's work process and high performance. Managers tended to ignore her leadership position within the team. When managers had important information to share with the team, they would typically provide it to another person on the team, who had at one time been a supervisor but since then had been reassigned to the SMWT as a team member. Furthermore, customers, suppliers, and others outside the team were typically unaware that an SMWT had been created. Consequently, they also gave any important information they had to the team member whom they had dealt with in the past, the same team member who had previously been a supervisor. As a result, the team leader was not getting important information the team needed. Furthermore, the team member who was getting the information was not sharing it freely with the team. Thus, the team was not getting all the information it needed, and this was having a negative effect on the team's work process and performance.

## TEAM LEADERSHIP AND TEAM PERFORMANCE

Our data indicate that the team leader has a number of large effects on the SMWT, some of which have been noted above. The team leader was found to have large impacts on the interpersonal processes both within the team and between the team and important others outside the team. These include communication, coordination, level of cooperation, cohesion, and trust. An effective team leader was able to enhance these. Less effective team leaders were unable to do so, and in some cases, these team leaders contributed to poor interpersonal processes. The most noteworthy case is described above—the team leader was not accepted by management, was unknown to other important people outside the team, and was competing with another team member for leadership of the team. This team leader was unable to focus the team members on a common goal or to facilitate trust and cohesion.

A second major influence of the team leader is on the SMWT's design characteristics. The team leader typically has a large influence on the team's specific goals. This occurs from the team leader's input during team discussions, as well as the team leader's unique position, which allows some control over the directions that team discussions take. In a similar way, the team leader often has more influence than others with regard to the design of the work and the methods for identifying solutions to problems and new work procedures.

The team leader has large effects on the SMWT's environment, both within and outside the organization. The team leader influences how management, customers, suppliers, and other important people view the SMWT. Gaining the confidence of these people can affect the level of support from them and, subsequently, influence the SMWT's availability of resources, supplies, training, and other team needs. The team leader's influence on the environment, as well as on the team's design and interpersonal processes, results in effects on the SMWT's work process. The design of the work and the interpersonal processes influence the team members' level of effort. The amount and types of training affect the talent applied to the work. Management and supplier support influence the resources applied to the team's tasks. And the methods used to make decisions and identify new work procedures affect the specific procedures used for doing the work.

# Appendix A
## Research Methods

Data for this book come from three sources, as described in the preface. One source is a 3-year study (1990-1993) of SMWTs and employee attitudes, funded by the Texas Advanced Research Program. A second is the Network on Self-Managed Work Teams, a network of organizations that use SMWTs and share experiences with each other regarding their successes and problems. The third and primary source of data is 10 case studies of SMWTs, funded by a 3-year grant (1994-1997) from the National Science Foundation. The purpose of the study was to identify those factors most important to SMWT performance. The specific methodology used to collect these primary data is described below.

## A MULTICASE, MULTIMETHOD REPLICATION DESIGN

A multicase, multimethod replication design (Yin, 1989) was used to assess the accuracy of existing theoretical models explaining SMWT and work team performance. Such a research design requires multiple case studies (e.g., SMWTs) and uses multiple methods to collect data on each case. With a replication design, the multiple cases are viewed as one would view multiple experiments—that is, a *replication* logic is used. As described by Yin (1989), this is quite different from the multiple respondent survey research design, where a *sampling* logic is used. The multiple-case replication design uses a theory or theories to predict what should be found for each experiment (or case). The experiments (or cases) either support or refute the theory. The replication logic is particularly effective when the theoretical framework clarifies the conditions under which a particular phenomenon (such as high team performance) is expected to be found, as well as the conditions where the opposite is expected to occur (e.g., low team performance). The cases can then be carefully selected so that one is known to have produced the phenomenon (high team performance), whereas the other has produced the opposite effect (low team performance). If the existing conditions/characteristics of both cases exist as the theoretical framework proposes, the case studies, in the aggregate, would provide strong support for the initial set of theoretical propositions. If the cases are in some way contradictory, the initial propositions must be revised and retested with another set of cases. This logic is similar to the way scientists deal with contradictory experimental findings. It is quite different from the sampling logic commonly used in surveys (Yin, 1989, provides a thorough discussion of the distinctions; see also Lee, 1992).

The decision to use the multicase, multimethod replication design was not taken lightly. A sampling logic and the accompanying survey data were seriously considered as the primary rationale and source of information because these would allow for statistical analyses, including structural equation modeling (use of LISREL). However, to adequately test a theoretical model by using a survey research design, one would need to survey hundreds of teams so that the many independent variables included within each model could be considered. This would likely equate to surveying over 1,000 employees. Furthermore, the use of survey data alone would produce the problem of *common method variance*. To overcome this problem would require the use of a multimethod approach, such as employing observation, for each of the many teams in the analysis, in addition to surveying the employees. Due to these methodological shortcomings of the sampling logic and the strengths of the replication logic, it was concluded that the survey research design was *not* the most practical method available.

The initial step in the multicase, multimethod replication design is the development or identification of an appropriate theory(ies). This is followed by selecting cases, developing the data collection protocol, doing a pilot study, conducting the case studies, analyzing the data, writing case reports, and drawing cross-case conclusions. A discussion of how each of these steps was carried out for the study is provided below. First, however, is a discussion of the procedures and techniques used to address the validity and reliability of the case studies.

## Criteria for Judging the Quality of the Research Design

Yin (1989) has identified a variety of case study tactics that can be used to increase a case study's construct validity, internal validity, external validity, and reliability.

*Construct validity* refers to establishing correct operational measures for the concepts being studied (Yin, 1989). Case studies have often been criticized for failing to develop a sufficiently operational set of measures and for using "subjective" judgments to collect the data. To increase construct validity requires that the investigator first clarify the propositions to be examined and then justify why particular measures do indeed reflect the concepts in the propositions. Our study has clarified the propositions by presenting and discussing in some depth a variety of theoretical models that led to a synthesis of the models. To increase the construct validity of the study, we attempted to use at least two sources of evidence to measure each concept, in a manner encouraging convergent lines of inquiry.

*Internal validity* refers to establishing a causal relationship, whereby certain conditions are shown to lead to other conditions, as distinguished from spurious relationships (Campbell & Stanley, 1966; Yin, 1989). If the investigator incorrectly concludes that there is a causal relationship between *x* and *y* without knowing that some third factor *z* may actually have caused *y*, the research design has failed to deal with some threat to internal validity. Furthermore, when an investigator of a case study infers that a particular event resulted from some earlier occurrence, the internal validity of the inferences comes into question. Questions that should be asked include: Have all the rival explanations and possibilities been considered? Is the evidence convergent? Does it appear to be airtight? (Yin, 1989). Tactics for obtaining the answers to these questions, and more pointedly for addressing the studies' internal validity, included pattern matching and chronology analysis.

*Pattern matching* requires examining the case to determine whether the causal relationships proposed by the theory(ies) match the experiences of the case. The use of rival theories, such as those presented in Part I, is helpful here by providing alternative causal relationships and, subsequently, a consideration of rival explanations.

The *analysis of chronological events* is a special form of time-series analysis (Yin, 1989) that traces events over time. The arraying of events into a chronology permits the investigator to compare the chronology with that predicted by the explanatory theory(ies).

*External validity* refers to whether a study's findings are generalizable beyond the immediate case study. This has been a major barrier in doing case studies. Critics typically state that single cases offer a poor basis for generalizing. However, as Yin (1989) has pointed out,

Such critics are implicitly contrasting the situation to survey research, where a "sample" (if selected correctly) readily generalizes to a larger universe. *This analogy to samples and universes is incorrect when dealing with case studies.* This is because survey research relies on *statistical* generalization, whereas case studies (as with experiments) rely on *analytical* generalization. (p. 43)

In analytical generalization, the investigator generalizes a particular set of results to some broader theory. As Yin has noted, however, the generalization is not automatic. A theory must be tested through replications of the findings in a second, third, and so on study. This replication logic is the same that underlies the use of experiments (and allows scientists to generalize from one experiment to another). The tactic of using a replication logic in multiple case studies was used with the case studies conducted in four different organizations.

*Reliability* exists when an investigator follows exactly the same procedures as described by an earlier investigator, conducts the same case study all over again, and arrives at the same findings and conclusions. Yin (1989) has pointed out that the emphasis is on doing the *same* case study over again, not on replicating the results of one case study by doing another case study. The goal of reliability is to minimize the errors and biases in the study. The tactics for increasing reliability involve obtaining accurate documentation of the procedures followed. This was accomplished through the use of a case study protocol and a case study database. The protocol contains the data collection instruments used as well as the procedures and general rules followed in employing the instruments. Having a case study protocol is desirable under all circumstances but is essential when using a multiple-case design and is discussed further below. The case study database includes all the data collected for the case studies. It is independent of the case study report, which presents and draws conclusions from the data. Included in the database are all responses from those interviewed, notes from observations, other case notes, records, and miscellaneous materials.

## Identification of Appropriate Theories

Theory development, prior to the collection of case study data, is an essential step in doing case studies. The nine theoretical frameworks and theoretical synthesis discussed in Part I provided study propositions that were used as a blueprint for the research design. The propositions provided guidance in determining what data were collected and the strategies for analyzing the data, as well as providing a vehicle for generalizing the results of the case studies.

## Case Selection

Primary questions to be addressed here are the types and numbers of cases selected. Ideally, we would have conducted two case studies at a time, with one SMWT having high team performance and the second low team performance. However, our choice was largely determined by those managers and teams that agreed to participate in the study. Consequently, we initially studied two low- performing SMWTs, both from the same federal agency. After completing the two case studies and data analysis, modifications to our synthesized theory were made. We then conducted two more case studies of high-performing SMWTs coming from a private corporation. After data analysis and further modification of our theory, we selected two more low-performing SMWTs from this same organization and repeated the procedure, with our total number of cases studied at six. We subsequently selected three SMWTs from a nursing home and again undertook data analysis and made some additional modifications to our theory, although few modifications were found necessary. A final SMWT was selected from a fourth organization, a local housing authority, and the same procedure was followed with no major modifications to our theory found necessary. Yin (1989) suggests that up to five or six replications may be necessary before the theoretical framework(s) are adequately modified to reflect what exists in practice. In our study, we found 10 case studies to be sufficient. The first four cases (two low-performing and two high-performing) provided the most insights and modifications to ou theory. The later cases provided progressively fewer.

It is also important to note that we studied SMWTs from three different types of industries: production within a private corporation, public service at the federal and local levels, and health care within a nursing home. This allowed for variation in work technology and provided a check for external validity.

## Data Collection Protocol

The data collection protocol is used as a guide in carrying out each case study and includes the field procedures and schedule, specific methods used, study questions, and respondent questions.

### Field Procedures and Schedule

Managers from four different organizations volunteered their SMWTs for the study. Manager interviews and, where possible, customer interviews were conducted to determine the performance level of the teams. Once we identified a high- or low-performing team, the team members were asked whether they wanted to participate in the study. Once we identified a team interested in participating, interviews were conducted with a manager or team leader to obtain information on the team's tasks and context within the organization. Next, a manager provided a name and telephone number of a team member within the SMWT. In most cases, this was followed by interviews of, first, the team leader and SMWT members, and second, the team's manager(s), including those at all levels within the team's facility. Observations of the SMWT's meetings occurred over the same period of time and in some cases continued after the interviews were completed.

The specific schedule followed for carrying out the interviews and observations was determined with the assistance of the team contact person and other relevant people (e.g., team member, manager). The length of time to complete a case study varied greatly and depended on the number of team members and managers involved, as well as the team members' level of interest in participating (less interested team members were often more difficult to schedule for an interview).

### Specific Methods Used and
### the Procedures for Each

At least two research methods were used to measure each concept, to increase construct validity (Yin, 1989). The research methods that were employed included (1) in-person interviews with the teams' members (Appendix B) and managers (Appendix C), (2) observations of team meetings and team members performing their work (Appendix D), (3) self-administered surveys of team members (Appendix E), and (4) where accessible, organizational records.

There were four survey instruments developed—one self-administered (team members), two in-person (team members and managers), and one for the observers of team meetings.

The *self-administered questionnaire* was developed for team members. Questionnaires were distributed by one of the principal investigators at the team's location; it was completed by team members and then collected by the principal investigator. Team members were provided verbal and written assurances of confidentiality.

*In-person interviews* were conducted with each team member and the team's managers at all levels within the team's facility. Present at all but a few interviews were both of the principal investigators. One asked the questions while the second said nothing and wrote down the respondent's answers as close to verbatim as possible. The principal investigators rotated these two roles.

Up to four team meetings were *observed* for each team. The number of team visits per team was determined by our judgment of the amount of additional information that could be obtained by observing an additional meeting. Our judgment was largely based on the amount of additional information that was obtained from the previous observation. In some cases, the number of visits was determined by the team's willingness to allow us to attend multiple meetings. Both principal investigators were present, and each completed an instrument for observers for each case study (Lofland, 1971; Patton, 1990; Selltiz, Jahoda, Deutsch, & Cook, 1959; Swezey & Salas, 1992). A limitation of this approach is the potential for the team members to alter their behavior when the observers are present. This heightens the need for a multiple method approach (Aldag & Stearns, 1988; Simon, 1969; Webb, Campbell, Schwartz, Sechrest, & Grove, 1981).

### Development of Questionnaires

Where possible, we used existing survey questions that had already been modified to fit a similar environment and had been tested for reliability and validity (e.g., questions from Hackman and Oldham's, 1980, Job Diagnostic Survey). The instrument for in-person interviews included open-ended questions related to causal relationships and followed a line of questioning that obtained the chronology of the team's performance of primary task(s). As data analysis occurred and the theoretical model was modified, the in-person and observation instruments were also modified to allow for additional focus on those variables proving to be particularly important.

## The Pilot Case Study

A final preparation prior to conducting the case studies was to undertake a pilot study. The pilot study was used to refine the data collection plans and the procedures to be followed. It was used to assess the wording of the questions developed for the instruments discussed above and helped to develop better clarification where necessary. With regard to logistics, the pilot case study was helpful in identifying the best order in which to complete the various data collection methods. Data from the pilot study were found to be valuable and were used to represent our first of 10 case studies.

## Conducting the Case Studies

As the case studies were conducted, a case study database was created. The case study database is a formal, retrievable database, so that other investigators can review the evidence directly and not be limited to the written reports. The database includes case study notes (from interviews and observations) and case study documents (including any organizational records collected).

## Analysis of Data

The theoretical propositions were used to guide the data analysis. The propositions were used to focus attention on certain data and contributed to the organization of the entire case study. The specific modes of analysis included pattern matching (using rival explanations) and chronologies. With regard to pattern matching, Yin (1989) has stated that

> for case-study analysis, one of the most desirable strategies is the use of a pattern-matching logic. Such a logic compares an empirically based pattern with a predicted one (or with several alternative predictions). If the patterns coincide, the results can help a case study to strengthen its *internal validity*. (p. 109)

The value of pattern matching was enhanced by the examination of cases that allowed for the opposite to be predicted (e.g., propositions relating to high-performing versus low-performing teams). When the results from a particular case study did not coincide as predicted by the synthesized theoretical model, the proposition in question was reexamined and modified to reflect the empirical evidence. An advantage of using rival explanations, as provided by varying theoretical models, was that alternative variables and causal relationships were readily available for consideration.

The analysis of chronological events is a special form of time-series analysis. The chronological sequence focuses directly on the major strength of case studies over other methods—the case studies allow for the tracing of events over time. For each of the SMWT'S primary tasks, the causal events leading to the team's performance of the task were documented. The analytic goal was to compare the chronology with that predicted by the theoretical model we were developing. If the actual events of a case study supported a proposition(s) of one theory over the other, or suggested a new proposition(s), then the case study provided the initial basis for causal inferences.

## Writing Case Reports and Drawing Cross-Case Conclusions

For each case study, a single narrative was written to describe and analyze the case. The narrative referred back to the case study database. Also, for each case study, a report listing all the study questions and answers for each was prepared. This allows a reader to examine the answers to the same question(s) within each case study and, subsequently, to begin making cross-case comparisons. Because each reader may be interested in different questions, the question-answer format facilitates the development of a cross-case analysis tailored to the specific interest of its readers.

# Appendix B
## In-Person Survey Instrument
## for All Team Members

DATE: _____

ORGANIZATION: _____

TEAM: _____

TEAM MEMBER: _____

NOTE TAKER: _____

## HISTORY/BACKGROUND

[Note: Questions 1 to 3 were only asked of the first few team members interviewed until we were confident that all available facts had been obtained.]

1. Could you please give us a background of your team? When was it first *formed,* how was it *put together,* and how were team members *prepared* for working on the team?

---

AUTHORS' NOTE: This survey instrument was continually revised throughout most of the research project. Some questions were deleted if they were found to have little relationship to team performance, whereas others were added as facts were discovered that identified new variables important to team performance.

## CHARACTERISTICS OF THE WORK/TASKS

2. What is your team's primary task or tasks?

3. Who do you see as your team's customers and suppliers?

4. What types of training do you receive?

   **PROBE:** Technical? Teamwork training?

## PERFORMANCE:
## QUANTITY, QUALITY, TIMELINESS

5. How do you know when your team is performing at a high level with regard to the *quantity, quality, and timeliness of the work* completed?

   **PROBE:** What measures are used for each?

6. How would you rate your team's overall performance on a scale from 1 to 10 with 1 being the best?

## PERFORMANCE:
## CAPABILITY TO CONTINUE

7. When thinking about your team's ability to continue in the future, are there conditions within your team that could eventually cause the team to break down or perform poorly, unless something is changed?
   Yes, No, or Possibly?

## TEAM SATISFACTION

8. Do you like working on a team, or would you prefer going back to having a supervisor?

## GROUP SYNERGY

9. How efficiently would you say your team carries out its work, on a scale of 1 to 10, with 1 being completely efficient. For example, is there highly effective coordination among the team members, and are the members willing to do whatever it takes for the work to be done efficiently?

   **[If some employees _un_willing]** Why are some unwilling to do what it takes to be highly efficient?

10. Has your team done anything specifically to improve efficiency?
    [If yes, what?]

11. If you could discuss one issue in an open way, involving the whole team in the discussion, what would that issue be?

## PROCEDURES FOLLOWED

12. When thinking about your team's primary task or one of them, what procedures are generally followed to accomplish the task?

13. Are these procedures exactly the same as those your team originally followed when it first took on this task?

   a. **[If procedures same]** How did your team originally decide on following these particular procedures?

   b. **[If procedures somewhat different]** How are they different now?

   c. **[If procedures somewhat different]** How did these new procedures come about? Was it gradual over time, or did they occur at specific points in time, such as every quarter they were reviewed and modified as needed?

14. What factors *help your team* to produce the best possible *procedures* for doing the work?

15. What factors *can prevent your team* from producing the best possible procedures?

Now I'm going to ask you a few questions about decision making.

16. I am going to read a list of responsibilities a team might have. Please tell me which ones your team has [check the ones they do]:

   a. _____ holds regular team meetings

   b. _____ selects its own team coordinator or leader

   c. _____ assigns work to team members

   d. _____ determines what work will be done each day

Maintains data on:

   e. _____ productivity

   f. _____ quality such as defects per week

   g. _____ safety

   h. _____ absenteeism

   i. _____ makes decisions regarding training

   j. _____ makes decisions regarding overtime, with management approval

   k _____ does peer appraisals

   l. _____ selects persons who are to be new team members

   m. _____ determines how bonuses are to be divided up among team members

17. Do one or a few team members *dominate* team decision making, or does everyone have a say in the decisions made by the team?

    a. **[If dominate]** What effect does this have on the team's performance?

18. When making a team decision, do the team members with the most knowledge about the issue have the most influence on the decision made?

19. Do team members tend to avoid making suggestions that might *conflict* with those already made by another team member?

    a. **[If yes]** Does this seem to have positive or negative consequences for the team's performance?

20. How important is it that everyone agree before making a team decision?

    **PROBE:** Could you give us an example where *striving for everyone to agree* had positive or negative consequences?

21. What generally happens when team members *disagree* during the decision-making process?

    **PROBE:** Do hard feelings generally result?

22. Do you feel that your team can make better decisions about its work than management?

    **PROBE:** Can you think of any examples to illustrate this?

    **PROBE:** What factors allow the team to make better decisions?

## RESPONSIBILITIES OF MANAGERS

23. What are the responsibilities of first-line management with regard to your team?

    **PROBE:** Have these responsibilities been clearly stated by management?

24. What are the responsibilities of middle- and upper-level management with regard to your team?

    **PROBE:** Have these roles been clearly stated by management?

The next questions are about management.

25. What kinds of things does management do that *help* your team in decision making and getting the job done?

    **PROBE:** Are there differences between first-line and upper-level management?

26. What kinds of things does management do that *hinder* your team in decision making and getting the job done?

    **PROBE:** Are there differences between first-line and upper-level management?

27. How often does management step in and make decisions for the team that were supposed to be made by the team?

28. Does management generally *support* your team's decisions, once made?

    **PROBE:** How is your team's performance affected when the team *lacks support* from management?

The next questions are related to performance evaluations and compensation.

## PERFORMANCE EVALUATION

29. How is your personal performance formally evaluated and how often?

30. Is your performance evaluation linked to *how well your team does*?

31. Is your performance evaluation linked to how well you *work with others* on your team?

32. Is your performance evaluation linked to your *pay increases and promotions*?

33. Would you say your current performance evaluation system has a positive, negative, or no influence on your *team's* performance? Please explain.

34. Are you happy with the current way that performance is evaluated and, if not, how would you like to see it changed?

## COMPENSATION

35. Is there anyone on your team who feels he or she is *not* fairly compensated for work?

    a. **[If yes]** Why do they feel they are unfairly compensated?

    b. **[If yes]** What have they done, if anything, to overcome this problem?

    c. **[If yes]** Has this affected their performance and, if so, how?

36. Finally, if you could change one thing in order to help your team reach its productivity, quality, and/or scheduling goals, what would it be?

The next few questions deal with feedback.

37. Do you receive feedback from *management?*

    **PROBE:** What is the nature of the feedback and how is it useful?

38. Do you receive feedback from *internal or outside customers?*

    **PROBE:** What is the nature of the feedback and how is it useful?

39. Do you receive feedback from your *teammates?*

    **PROBE:** What is the nature of the feedback and how is it useful?

40. Research has found that in some jobs, when one team member is working a lot harder than others on the team, he or she receives pressure from team members to work less hard. Have you ever felt something like this was happening in your team?

The last questions ask about persons outside your team [Boundary Management].

## RELATION TO OTHERS OUTSIDE TEAM

41. Are there persons outside your team who *assist* your team or are otherwise *important* to your team in getting the work done (other than management)?

    **PROBE:** Who are these persons? How are they related to the team?

    **PROBE:** What about customers? Internal customers? External customers?

42. [If there are important persons] What happens when your team lacks support from these persons?

43. [If there are important persons] What kinds of things does your team do to gain and maintain support from these persons?

    **PROBE:** Are any of the persons on your team assigned the specific task of developing and maintaining good relationships with these persons? [Who are they?]

## RELATION TO COMPETITORS, MARKET, NEW TECHNOLOGIES

44. How important is it to your team's performance that team members collect information about competitors, the market, or new technologies?

    **PROBE:** Please explain.

45. [If this is important] What happens when your team lacks this kind of information?

46. [If this is important] What kinds of things does your team do to gain this kind of information?

    **PROBE:** Are any of the persons on your team assigned the specific task of collecting information on competitors, the market, or new technologies? [Who are they?]

## RELATION TO MANAGEMENT

47. What kinds of things does your team do to *gain and maintain support* from management?

    **PROBE:** Who on your team does this?

## NEED TO KEEP INFO
## FROM OUTSIDE PERSONS

48. How important is it to your team's performance that your team keep certain *information to itself.* This might include, for example, facts that could hurt the team's image or product.

49. **[If information kept within team)** What kinds of things does your team do to keep this kind of information from going outside the team?

    **PROBE:** Are any of the persons on your team assigned the specific task of making sure that such information is kept within the team? [Who are they?]

■

# Appendix C

In-Person Survey Instrument
for All Relevant Managers

■


DATE: _____

ORGANIZATION: _____

TEAM: _____

TEAM MEMBER: _____

NOTE TAKER: _____

## HISTORY/BACKGROUND

1. When did you start working with the team?
2. How long have you been with [name of organization]?

---

AUTHORS' NOTE: Each survey instrument for managers was designed for the specific person and organization being studied. For example, first-line managers were asked more specific questions about the team than higher-level managers. Or, if the particular organization used the Oregon Productivity Matrix, then questions were asked about this. All instruments were kept brief due to the time constraints of the managers. This instrument includes questions from several different organizations in order to display a broader set of questions than any one of our management survey instruments.

3. Could you please give me a background of the team? When was it first formed, how was it put together, and how were team members prepared for working on the team?

4. What is the team's primary task or tasks?

5. What do you see as the major advantages and disadvantages to using self-managed work teams?

## PERFORMANCE

6. Who are the team's customers?

7. How do you know when the team is performing at a high level?

8. What do you see as the strengths and weaknesses of the team?

9. How would you rate the team's overall performance?

### Oregon Productivity Matrix (OPM)

10. How are the OPM goals established?

11. What problems, if any, have you had with the OPM?

### Capability to Continue

12. When thinking about the team's ability to continue as a team in the future, are there conditions within the team that could eventually cause the team to break down or perform poorly, unless something is changed? (Yes, No, or Possibly?)

## INTERMEDIATE FACTORS

### Work Process

13. Do you feel the team's work procedures are the best possible, or do you think there might be a better way for the team to accomplish its tasks?

### Teaming Process—Internal

14. Is there highly effective coordination among the team members?

15. What have you found to work best when trying to deal with persons who are resistant to participating in teams?

### Team Process—External (Boundary Management)

#### Persons Outside Team

16. Who outside the team assists the team in getting the team's tasks accomplished?

Relation to Competitors, Market, New Technologies

17. How important is it to the team's performance that team members collect information about competitors, the market, or new technologies?

## ENVIRONMENT

Organizational Factors—Within Organization

Information

18. What information is crucial to the team's success?

Training/Education

19. When considering training and education, what do they receive?

Reward System—Performance Evaluation

20. How is their personal performance formally evaluated and how often?
21. Is their performance evaluation linked to how well their team does?
22. Is their performance evaluation linked to how well they work with others on their team?
23. Is their performance evaluation linked to their pay increases and promotions?
24. Are you happy with the current way that performance is evaluated and, if not, how would you like to see it changed?
25. With regard to bonuses, who determines who will get a bonus and who won't?
26. What criteria are used in determining who will receive a bonus?

Management Support

27. What are the responsibilities of [first-line] management with regard to the team?
28. What are the responsibilities of middle- and upper-level management with regard to the team?
29. Have you ever had a problem with one or more team members trying to take a supervisory role within one of the teams?
30. How often do you have to step in and make decisions for the team that were supposed to be made by the team?
31. How do you provide feedback to the teams?
32. What kinds of things can teams do to gain and maintain your support?

[The last few questions are related to you and upper-level management]

33. How is your personal performance formally evaluated and how often?

34. Is your performance evaluation linked to how well your teams do?

35. How important is it that you receive support from your boss with regard to teaming?

36. How has this affected your ability to make teaming effective?

### Organizational Factors—Outside Organization

37. How important is the economic climate to the team's success?

38. How are new technologies affecting the team?

## TEAM DESIGN

### Decision Making

39. I am going to read a list of responsibilities a team might have. Please tell me which ones the team has:

    a. _____ holds regular team meetings

    b. _____ selects its own team leader

    c. _____ assigns work to team members

    d. _____ determines what work will be done each day

    Maintains data on:

    e. _____ productivity

    f. _____ quality such as defects per week

    g. _____ safety

    h. _____ absenteeism

    i. _____ makes decisions regarding training

    j. _____ makes decisions regarding overtime, with management approval

    k. _____ does peer appraisals

    l. _____ selects persons who are to be new team members

    m. _____ determines how bonuses are to be divided up among team members

40. How important is it that everyone agree before the team makes a decision?

### Composition of the Team

41. How important do you feel the composition of the team is to the success of the team (that is, the makeup of the team in terms of types of professionals and types of people)?

## Peer Evaluations

42. What are the advantages and disadvantages of the peer evaluation?

43. What procedures do you feel work best for doing the peer evaluation?

44. What are the advantages and disadvantages to linking the peer evaluation to bonuses?

## Other Team Design Issues

45. Is there a best size for an effective team?

46. Have you run into any major problems having three shifts on one team?

    **PROBE:** Has the third shift had difficulty participating in teaming activities?

47. How do you handle team overhead and have you found that some star points require more overhead time than others?

48. Should all team members be equally involved in teaming activities such as scheduling, productivity, and quality star points, *or,* should those less interested in teaming activities be allowed to spend more time on the technical work while those more interested in teaming activities be allowed to do more of this?

    **PROBE:** How does all this relate to bonuses?

## FEEDBACK

49. Do you provide the team feedback?

50. Does the team receive feedback from internal or outside customers?

■

# Appendix D
## Survey Instrument Completed by Observer/Interviewer After Multiple Observations of the Team and In-Person Interviews

■

DATE: _____

NAME OF TEAM: _____

OBSERVER NAME: _____

## HISTORY/BACKGROUND

1. Which best describes the team's level of development:

   a. just getting started

---

AUTHORS' NOTE: This survey instrument was continually revised throughout most of the research project. Some questions were deleted if they were found to have little relationship to team performance, whereas others were added as facts were discovered that identified new variables important to team performance.

    b. currently struggling with how it can best get its tasks accomplished

    c. effective working procedures have been developed, and team members are becoming clear on what their responsibilities are

    d. team members are clear on their responsibilities, and most of their time is spent on performing the team's tasks

    **PROBE:** Please explain.

2. Briefly, provide your perception of the "background" of the team. When was it first formed, how was it put together, who is on the team, and how were team members prepared for working on the team?

3. How has the team's background affected its performance in terms of how it was put together and how it was prepared for working as a team?

## Characteristics of the Work/Tasks

4. What is the team's primary task or tasks?

5. Who are the team's customers and suppliers?

6. Did team members rotate through all existing tasks of the team, only through certain tasks, or did not rotate at all? Please explain.

## PERFORMANCE

### Quantity, Quality, Timeliness

7. How does the team determine its level of performance with regard to the quantity, quality, and timeliness of the work completed? What measures are used for each?

8. Are all the team members regularly informed on how their team is performing?

9. Would you rate the team's performance as exceptional, above average, average, below average, or extremely poor? Why would you rate them this way? Who are you comparing them to when making this judgment?

10. Which three factors (ranked if possible) would you say had the most positive impact on the team's performance? Please explain each.

### Capability to Continue

11. When thinking about the team's ability to continue in the future, were there conditions within the team that could eventually cause the team to break down or perform poorly, unless something is changed? If yes or possibly, what were these conditions? What caused them?

## Satisfaction

12. On a scale of 1 to 5, with 1 being very satisfied and 5 very *dis*satisfied, how satisfied would you say the team members were overall? Please explain.

## INTERMEDIATE CRITERIA

### Motivation and Effort

13. How would you rate the motivation level of the team overall: exceptional, above average, average, below average, exceptionally poor? Please explain.
14. Is the level of team motivation affecting the team's performance?
15. What factors appear to be affecting the team's motivation?
16. How would you rate the team members' effort placed directly on doing the work: exceptional, above average, average, below average, exceptionally poor? Please explain. The idea of *effort* here is how much of the team members' time is actually spent doing the work versus doing other things?
17. Is the level of team effort affecting the team's performance?
18. What factors appear to be affecting the team's effort?

### Knowledge and Skill

19. What knowledge (know things) and what skill (do things) are needed by the team to perform at a high level?
20. Did all team members have the same knowledge or were some responsible for some types of knowledge while others were responsible for other types of knowledge?
21. Where were the places and who were the people from which the team members got the knowledge they needed?
22. How would you rate the team's level of work knowledge: has all the knowledge needed to perform at the highest levels, lacks some knowledge, or lacks a lot of knowledge needed. Please explain.
23. What factors are affecting the team's level of knowledge? Please explain.
24. Did all team members have the same skill (doing things), or were some responsible for having certain skills while others were responsible for having other skills?
25. Where were the places and who were the people from which the team got the skill it needed?

26. How would you rate the team's level of work skill: has all the skill needed to perform at the highest levels, lacks some skill, or lacks a lot of skill needed. Please explain.

## Available Materials and Equipment

27. What materials and equipment were most crucial to the team performing at a high level?

28. Where were the places and who were the people from which the team got the materials and equipment it needed?

29. Which persons on the team were responsible for getting materials and equipment for the team?

30. How would you rate the team's level of materials and equipment available: has all the materials and equipment needed to perform at the highest levels, lacks some materials and/or equipment, or lacks a lot of materials and/or equipment needed. Please explain.

31. Who or what was responsible for the lack of (or sufficiency of) materials and equipment? What factors were affecting the team's level of these? Please explain.

32. How did the amount of material and equipment available affect the team's performance?

## Appropriate Strategies

### Strategies Used

33. When thinking about the team's primary task or tasks, does the team seem to be using: (1) the very best strategy(ies) possible for accomplishing the task(s), (2) good strategies but perhaps not the best, (3) adequate strategies, or (4) somewhat inappropriate strategies? Please explain—use as an example one of the team's primary tasks in your explanation.

34. How did the team develop this (these) strategy(ies)? Were they well thought out, or did they occur gradually over time? If it was well thought out, what procedures were used?

35. If it was more evolutionary, please provide whatever you know about how this evolution occurred; for example, did the strategy develop at specific points in time such as every quarter they looked at what they were doing and documented any changes in procedures?

36. Are any specific procedures used to develop work strategies?

37. Which factors most help and which most hinder the team's ability to develop the best possible strategies for doing the work?

38. How do the work strategies affect the team's performance. Please explain.

## Boundary Management

### Relation to Others Outside Team but Within Same Organization

39. Are there persons outside the team but within the same organization who assist the team or are otherwise important to the team in getting the work done (other than management, including internal customers)?

40. Are there persons outside the organization who assist the team or are otherwise important to the team in getting the work done (including external customers)?

41. **[If there are important others]** Who are these (e.g., individuals? teams? departments?), how are they related to the team, and what happens when the team lacks support from these persons? How is the team's performance affected?

42. **[If there are important others]** What kinds of things does the team do to gain and maintain support from them?

43. **[If there are important others]** Which factors have the largest effect on the team's ability to develop and maintain a good relationship with them?

44. Are any of the persons on the team assigned the specific task of developing and maintaining good relationships with them? Who are they?

### Relation to Competitors, Suppliers, Market, New Technologies

45. How important is it to the team's performance that team members collect information about competitors, suppliers, the market, or new technologies? Please explain.

46. **[If this is important]** What happens when the team lacks this kind of information? How does it affect the team's performance?

47. What factors affect the team's ability to collect information about competitors, suppliers, the market, or new technologies? Please explain.

48. **[If this is important]** What kinds of things does the team do to gain this kind of information? Are any of the persons on the team assigned the specific task of collecting information on competitors, the market, or new technologies? Who are they?

### Relation to Management

49. What kinds of things does the team do to gain and maintain support from management?

50. Who on the team does this?

51. How important is management to the team ability to perform at a high level?

52. What are the major factors that have positive and negative effects on the team's relationship with management?

### Need to Keep Info from Outside Persons

53. How important is it to the team that it keep certain information to itself? This might include, for example, facts that could hurt the team's image or product. Please explain.

54. **[If information kept within team]** How important is this to the team's high performance?

55. **[If information kept within team]** What kinds of things does the team do to keep this kind of information from going outside the team? Are any of the persons on the team assigned the specific task of making sure that such information is kept within the team? Who are they?

56. **[If information kept within team]** What factors aid and what factors prevent the team from successfully keeping this kind of information from going outside the team?

## GROUP SYNERGY

57. How efficiently would you say the team has carried out its work? For example, is there highly effective coordination among the team members and are the members willing to do whatever it takes for the work to be done efficiently? Please explain.

58. **[If some employees *un*willing]** Why are some unwilling to do what it takes to be highly efficient?

59. Has the team done anything specifically to improve efficiency/coordination? **[If yes, what?]**

60. What are the major factors that affect the team's efficiency/coordination?

61. How would you rate each of the following: commitment, communication, trust among team members, creativity, interpersonal skills. Please provide a brief statement about your evaluation of each—what has caused each to be at the level you perceive, and what effect has each had on each of the intermediate factors (motivation, effort, knowledge, skill, use of appropriate strategies)?

62. Overall, what effect has the combined influence of these factors had on the team's performance? Please explain. On the intermediate factors? Please explain.

## GROUP DESIGN

### Decision-Making Process

63. How much authority does the team have over its tasks? That is, how much decision making is the team authorized to do?

64. What kinds of decisions does the team make?

65. When making a decision, does the team consider foremost its performance goals? Does it consider how its decision will affect its goals?

66. Do one or a few team members dominate team decision making, or does everyone have a say in the decisions made by the team?

67. [If dominate] What effect does this have on the team's effort and motivation? Knowledge and skill? Appropriate strategies? Overall performance?

68. When making a team decision, do the team members with the most knowledge about the issue have the most influence on the decision made? Please explain.

69. Do team members tend to avoid making suggestions that might conflict with those already made by another team member?

70. [If yes] Does this seem to have positive or negative consequences for the team's motivation and effort? Knowledge and skill? Appropriate strategies? Overall performance?

71. How important is it that a consensus be reached at any cost during decision making?

72. [If important] Does this seem to have positive or negative consequences for the team's motivation and effort? Knowledge and skill? Appropriate strategies? Overall performance?

73. Give an example where striving for consensus had positive or negative consequences.

74. What generally happens when team members disagree during the decision-making process?

75. Does this seem to have positive or negative consequences for the team's motivation and effort? Knowledge and skill? Appropriate strategies? Overall performance?

76. Does it appear that the team can make better decisions about its work than management? Please explain. What factors allow the team/management to make better decisions?

77. Can you think of any examples to illustrate this?

## Homogeneity Versus Heterogeneity of Group

78. What was the gender makeup of the team, and did it seem to affect the team's performance? What about effort? Motivation? Knowledge and skill? Appropriate strategies used? Boundary management (working with persons outside the team)?

79. What was the racial makeup of the team, and did it seem to affect the team's performance? What about effort? Motivation? Knowledge and skill? Appropriate strategies used?

## Normative Procedures for Decision-Making Process

80. When thinking about the team's primary task or one of them, what procedures are generally followed to accomplish the task?

81. Are these procedures exactly the same as those the team originally followed when it first took on this task?

82. **[If procedures same]** How did the team originally decide on following these particular procedures?

83. **[If procedures somewhat different]** How are they different now?

84. **[If procedures somewhat different]** How did these new procedures come about? Was it gradual over time, or did they occur at specific points in time, such as every quarter they were reviewed and modified as needed?

85. What factors helped the team to produce the best possible procedures for doing the work?

86. What factors prevented the team from producing the best possible procedures?

## Job Characteristics

87. How would you describe the job characteristics with regard to skill variety? Task identity (can see how her/his work fits into big picture)? Task significance? Meaningfulness? Responsibility in hands of team members? Autonomy?

## ORGANIZATIONAL CHARACTERISTICS

### Available Information

88. What information was most crucial to the team performing at a high level?

89. Where were the places and who were the people from which the team got the information it needed? Please briefly consider each of the following: management, customers, suppliers, others outside the organization (e.g., technicians), persons/teams inside the organization.

90. Which persons on the team were responsible for getting information for the team?

91. How would you rate the team's level of information available: (1) has all the information needed to perform at the highest levels, (2) lacks some information, or (3) lacks a lot of information needed. Please explain. Who or what was responsible for the lack of (or sufficiency of) information?

92. How did the amount of information available affect the team's performance? Motivation? Effort? Use of appropriate strategies? Knowledge and skill? Boundary management? Please address each briefly.

## Available Training

93. What training was needed in order for the team to perform at a high level?

94. Did team members receive training on how to work together as a team? If so, was it adequate?

95. Did team members receive adequate technical training?

96. Where were the places and who were the people from which the team got the training it needed?

97. How was it determined who would receive what training among the team members?

98. How would you rate the team's "available" training? [The organization has the particular training available for employees. This is different from accessibility, which asks whether employees are able to access the available training]: (1) has all the training available to perform at the highest levels, (2) some training was unavailable, or (3) a lot of needed training was unavailable. Please explain. Who or what was responsible for the lack of (or sufficiency of) available training?

99. How would you rate the team's ability to access training [as opposed to availability]: (1) can access all the training needed to perform at the highest levels, (2) could not access some of the training needed, or (3) a lot of needed training could not be accessed. Please explain. Who or what was responsible for the lack of (or sufficiency of) accessible training?

100. How did the level of availability and accessibility of training affect the team's performance? Motivation? Effort? Use of appropriate strategies? Knowledge and skill? Boundary management? Please address each briefly.

## Performance Evaluation

101. How is individual performance formally evaluated and how often?
102. Are individual performance evaluations linked to how well the team does?
103. Are individual performance evaluations linked to how well the individual works with others on his/her team?
104. Are individual performance evaluations linked to individual pay increases and promotions?
105. Would you say the current performance evaluation system has a positive, negative, or no influence on the team's performance [don't confuse this with compensation]? Please explain. What about motivation? Effort? Knowledge? Skill? Use of appropriate strategies? Boundary management? Please briefly consider each.
106. Are team members happy with the current way that performance is evaluated and, if not, how would they like to see it changed?

## Compensation

107. Is there anyone on the team who feels he or she is not fairly compensated for work?
108. **[If yes]** Why do they feel they are unfairly compensated? Are they comparing their salary to others?
109. **[If yes]** What have they done, if anything, to overcome this problem?
110. **[If yes]** Has this affected their performance and if so, how? What about motivation? Effort? Knowledge? Skill? Use of appropriate strategies? Boundary management? Please briefly consider each.
111. Do team members feel they are adequately recognized for good work?
112. **[If no]** How has this affected their performance? What about motivation? Effort? Knowledge? Skill? Use of appropriate strategies? Boundary management? Please briefly consider each.
113. Do team members feel that they receive valuable rewards for doing good work?
114. **[If no]** How has this affected their performance? What about motivation? Effort? Knowledge? Skill? Use of appropriate strategies? Boundary management? Please briefly consider each.

## Goals

115. What is the team's primary goal(s)?

116. Are the team members clear on what the goals are for the team? Please explain.

117. Is each team member clear on what the goals are for her/him within the team? Has goal clarity affected the team's performance and, if so, how? What about motivation? Effort? Knowledge? Skill? Use of appropriate strategies? Boundary management? Please briefly consider each.

118. Are the team members challenged by the goals for the team? Has this challenge or lack of challenge affected the team's performance and, if so, how? What about motivation? Effort? Knowledge? Skill? Use of appropriate strategies? Boundary management? Please briefly consider each.

## Feedback

119. Does the team receive feedback from management? What is the nature of the feedback and how is it useful?

120. Does the team receive feedback from internal or outside customers? What is the nature of the feedback and how is it useful?

121. Do team members receive feedback from each other? What is the nature of the feedback and how is it useful?

122. Research has found that in some jobs, when one team member is working a lot harder than others on the team, he or she receives pressure from team members to work less hard. Was anything like this evident? Were some working harder than others, and if so, how did this affect these persons' relationships with others on the team?

## Management Support

123. What kinds of things does management do that help the team? Please be sure to consider whether management provides help with regard to decision making and getting the job done, but don't limit yourself to these. Please explain. Are there differences between first-line and upper-level management? If yes, please explain.

124. What kinds of things does management do that hinder the team? Again, please be sure to consider team decision making and getting the job done, but don't limit yourself to these. Are there differences between first-line and upper-level management? If yes, please explain.

125. How often does management step in and make decisions for the team that were supposed to be made by the team?

126. Does management generally support the team's decisions once made?

127. What other responsibilities, if any, does management have with regard to the teams? Again, how are these different for first-line and upper-level management?

128. How does management's support and/or lack of support affect the team's performance? How are the team's motivation, effort, knowledge, skill, use of appropriate strategies, and boundary management (relations with others outside the team) affected? Please address each at least briefly.

# Appendix E
## Self-Administered Survey Instrument Completed by All Team Members

Date

Dear Work Team Member:

We have recently received a three-year federal grant to study self-managed work teams. In particular, we are interested in what enables or helps teams to work well and what hinders or keeps them from working well.

We are seeking input from work teams in a variety of organizations. We would appreciate very much your input to this study. This would include answering the attached questions and also meeting with Drs. Yeatts and Hyten personally to answer questions we have about teams. In return for your help, we will provide your team with a report showing how your team, as a whole, responded to our questions. This information may be helpful to your team as you look for opportunities to improve. Further, if you'd like, we would be happy to provide you with information showing how your team scored in comparison to other teams in the study.

All your responses will be kept strictly confidential. You will in no way be penalized, if you choose not to participate in the study. If you have any questions, please feel free to give us a call (940-565-2238).

Sincerely,

Dale E. Yeatts, Ph.D.
Associate Professor

Cloyd Hyten, Ph.D
Associate Professor

Please use the following scale:

| 1 | 2 | 3 | 4 | 5 |
|---|---|---|---|---|
| Strongly Disagree | Disagree | Neutral | Agree | Strongly Agree |

_____ 1. There is a good mix of knowledge and skill among those on my team.

_____ 2. Management helps my team obtain *training*.

_____ 3. This job is one where a lot of other people can be affected by how well the work gets done.

_____ 4. My team does *NOT* have the opportunity to use its own initiative or judgment in carrying out its work.

_____ 5. Managers often let me know how well they think I am performing.

_____ 6. First-line management gives my team a lot of freedom to make decisions about how the work gets done.

_____ 7. The job requires me to use a variety of skills.

_____ 8. I am able to see how my work contributes to a completed product or service.

_____ 9. My team members are creative in their job.

_____ 10. I feel a very high degree of *RESPONSIBILITY* for the work I do.

_____ 11. The people in my team efficiently *COORDINATE* their efforts.

_____ 12. I receive personal recognition at work for high performance.

_____ 13. My specific goals at work are *NOT* well defined.

_____ 14. I feel I am fairly paid, when comparing my pay to other employees.

_____ 15. People in my team get all the *information* they need to make good decisions.

_____ 16. My job is fairly simple and very repetitive.

_____ 17. I know I can *rely on* my team members when things get tough.

_____ 18. My team members have all the *KNOWLEDGE* needed to perform at a high level.

_____ 19. The persons on my team have good interpersonal skills.

_____ 20. One or two people generally dominate during team decision making, even when *others might be more knowledgeable.*

_____ 21. Upper-level management encourages my team to make its own decisions.

Please use the following scale for the next group of questions:

| 1 | 2 | 3 | 4 | 5 |
|---|---|---|---|---|
| Never | Seldom | Occasionally | Very Often | Always |

_____ 1. How often is your team permitted to decide *on its own* how to go about doing the work?

_____ 2. How often must team members rely on the grapevine or rumors for information?

_____ 3. How often are the results of your work likely to significantly affect the lives of others?

_____ 4. How often does *first-line* management step in and make decisions for the team that were supposed to be made by the team?

_____ 5. How often does *upper-level* management step in and make decisions for the team that were supposed to be made by the team?

_____ 6. How often is your work *CHALLENGING?*

_____ 7. How often is the equipment needed by your team working and easily available?

_____ 8. When considering a particular decision to be made, how often do the most knowledgeable team members have the most influence on the team's final decision?

_____ 9. How often are team members *tactful and sensitive* to one another during decision making?

_____ 10. How often does your organization make *training* available?

_____ 11. How often does your team use the best possible *PROCEDURES* for getting the work done?

_____ 12. Almost all my time and effort is spent directly on doing my job and *NOT* on other things like employee complaining or things unrelated to work.

_____ 13. When comparing my pay to others, I feel I am paid fairly.

_____ 14. I find no *challenge* in my work.

_____ 15. I have easy *ACCESS* to my organization's *training* resources.

_____ 16. My organization has a variety of *training* programs *AVAILABLE*.

_____ 17. The work I do on this job is very *MEANINGFUL* to me.

Please use the following scale for the next group of questions:

| 1 | 2 | 3 | 4 | 5 |
|---|---|---|---|---|
| Strongly Disagree | Disagree | Neutral | Agree | Strongly Agree |

_____ 1. My team uses the best *procedures* possible for getting the work done.

_____ 2. I can see how my tasks contribute to a whole product or service.

_____ 3. My opinion of myself goes up when I do this job well.

_____ 4. I am very clear on what my specific *GOALS* are at work.

_____ 5. A lot of *TRUST* exists between my team members.

_____ 6. Most of the things I have to do on this job seem useless or trivial.

_____ 7. I feel a great sense of personal satisfaction when I do this job well.

_____ 8. I frequently think of quitting/changing my job.

_____ 9. People in my team *COORDINATE* their efforts efficiently without getting in each other's way.

_____ 10. I often have trouble figuring out whether I'm doing well or poorly on this job.

_____ 11. My team comes up with *new ideas* regularly.

_____ 12. My own feelings generally are *NOT* affected by how well I do on this job.

_____ 13. I have *easy access* to the *training* resources that I need.

_____ 14. I feel a strong sense of *COMMITMENT* to the team concept.

_____ 15. I receive valuable rewards when I perform my work at a high level.

_____ 16. The persons on my team have the skills needed to perform at a high level.

_____ 17. The *procedures* used by my team have evolved over time rather than being specifically designed.

_____ 18. The *MATERIALS* needed by my team are always easily available.

_____ 19. At work, I find that I focus at least a quarter of my time on things other than the work itself.

_____ 20. I feel a great deal of personal *responsibility* for the work I do.

_____ 21. I have a pretty good idea of how well I am performing my work.

_____ 22. I feel bad or unhappy when I have performed my work poorly.

Please use the following scale for the next group of questions:

| 1 | 2 | 3 | 4 | 5 |
|---|---|---|---|---|
| Strongly Disagree | Disagree | Neutral | Agree | Strongly Agree |

_____ 1. I am highly *committed* to working on a team.

_____ 2. I feel a great sense of personal satisfaction when I do the job well.

_____ 3. Coworkers almost *NEVER* give me any feedback.

_____ 4. I have received enough training on *how to work together* as a team.

_____ 5. I have received enough *technical skills* training.

_____ 6. My performance evaluation is linked to *how well my team does*.

_____ 7. My performance evaluation is linked to *how well I work with others* on my team.

_____ 8. My performance evaluation is linked to my *pay increases and promotions*.

_____ 9. A lot of my pay is tied to my team's performance.

_____ 10. The way we get paid encourages our team to perform at a high level.

_____ 11. I *trust management* to consider the interests of employees when making decisions.

_____ 12. When compared to similar teams, my team's performance is second to none.

_____ 13. When considering the *mix of persons* on my team, I would say people are:

    a. too different (always disagreeing)

    b. too similar (always agreeing without considering alternative ideas)

    c. the mix is about right

_____ 14. The best description of my team's *level of development is*:

    a. just getting started

    b. currently struggling with how we can best get our tasks accomplished

    c. effective working procedures have been developed, and team members are becoming clear on what their responsibilities are

    d. team members are clear on their responsibilities, and most of their time is spent on performing the team's tasks

_____ 15. When considering the number of persons on your team, would you say it is:

   a. too large

   b. about right

   c. too small

Finally, we would like to get some biographical information:

16. Sex:_____

17. Age:   _____

18. Race:  _____

19. Education: What is the highest grade level you have completed?
    If beyond high school, please list degree _____

Name:_____

(We are asking for your name so we can combine this survey information with the information we collect from you in person. All information will be kept strictly confidential.)

# References

Adler, N. J. (1991). *International dimensions of organizational behavior.* Boston: PWS-Kent.

Aldag, R. J., & Brief, A. P. (1979). Examination of a measure of higher-order need strength. *Human Relations, 32*(8), 705-718.

Aldag, R. J., & Stearns, T. M. (1988). Issues in research methodology. *Journal of Management, 14*(2), 253-276.

Allen, R. F. (1987). Group norms: Their influence on training. In R. L. Craig (Ed.), *Training and development handbook: A guide to human resource development* (pp. 180-194). New York: McGraw-Hill.

Allen, T. J., & Hauptman, O. (1990). The substitution of communication technologies for organizational structure in research and development. In J. Fulk & C. Steinfield (Eds.), *Organizations and communication technology* (pp. 275-294). Newbury Park, CA: Sage.

Amason, A. C. (1996). Distinguishing the effects of functional and dysfunctional conflict on strategic decision making: Resolving a paradox for top management teams. *Academy of Management Journal, 39*(1), 123-148.

American Association of Retired Persons. (1988). *How to manage older workers.* Washington, DC: Public Policy Institute.

American Association of Retired Persons. (1989). *Business and older workers.* Washington, DC: Author.

Ancona, D. G. (1990). Outward bound: Strategies for team survival in an organization. *Academy of Management Journal, 33*(2), 234-365.

Ancona, D. G., & Caldwell, D. F. (1992). Bridging the boundary: External activity and performance in organizational teams. *Administrative Science Quarterly, 37,* 634-665.

Anthony, W. P. (1978). *Participative management.* Reading, MA: Addison-Wesley.

Argote, L. (1982). Input uncertainty and organizational coordination in hospital emergency units. *Administrative Science Quarterly, 27,* 420-434.

Argyris, C. (1990). *Overcoming organizational defenses.* Boston: Allyn & Bacon.

Armstrong, D. J., & Cole, P. (1995). Managing distances and differences in geographically distributed work groups. In S. E. Jackson & M. Ruderman (Eds.), *Diversity in work teams: Research paradigms for a changing workplace* (pp. 187-218). Washington, DC: American Psychological Association.

Balcazar, F. E., Hopkins, B. L., & Suarez, Y. (1986). A critical objective review of performance feedback. *Journal of Organizational Behavior Management, 7*(3/4), 65-89.

Banner, D. K., & Gagné, T. E. (1995). *Designing effective organizations: Tradition and transformational views.* Thousand Oaks, CA: Sage.

Barnard, C. I. (1938). *The functions of the executive.* Cambridge, MA: Harvard University Press.

Barnes, D. M. (1996). *Information use environment of self-managed teams: A case study.* Ph.D. dissertation, University of North Texas, Denton.

Barrick, M. R., & Mount, M. K. (1991). The big five personality dimensions and job performance: A meta-analysis. *Personnel Psychology, 44,* 1-26.

Becker-Reems, E. D. (1994). *Self-managed work teams in health care organizations.* Chicago: American Hospital Publications.

Belcher, J. G. (1991). *Gainsharing.* Houston: Gulf.

Berkowitz, L. (1959). Personality and group position. *Sociometry, 19,* 210-221.

Berlinger, L. R., Glick, W. H., & Rodgers, R. C. (1988). Job enrichment and performance improvements. In J. P. Campbell & R. J. Campbell (Eds.), *Productivity in organizations.* San Francisco: Jossey-Bass.

Bettenhausen, K. L. (1991). Five years of groups research: What we have learned and what needs to be addressed. *Journal of Management, 17*(2), 345-381.

Beyerlein, M., Flax, S., & Saiter, R. (1991). *Proceedings of the 1991 International Conference on Self-Managed Work Teams.* Denton: University of North Texas Press.

Beyerlein, M., & Johnson, D. (1994). *Advances in interdisciplinary studies of work teams: Vol. 1. Theories of self-managing teams.* Greenwich, CT: JAI Press.

Block, P. (1993). Empowerment means reform. *Executive Excellence, 10*(3), 11-12.

Blumberg, M., & Pringle, C. D. (1982). The missing opportunity in organizational research: Some implications for a theory of work performance. *Academy of Management Review, 7*(4), 560-569.

Bouchard, T. J. (1969). Personality, problem-solving procedure, and performance in small groups. *Journal of Applied Psychology Monograph, 53*(1), 1-29.

Boyer, C. E., & Pond, P. (1987). Employee participation and involvement. In R. Craig (Ed.), *Training and development handbook.* New York: McGraw-Hill.

Boyett, J. H., & Conn, H. P. (1995). *Maximum performance management: How to manage and compensate people to meet world competition.* Lakewood, CO: Glenbridge.

Braddock, J. H., & McPartland, J. M. (1987). How minorities continue to be excluded from equal employment opportunities: Research on labor market and institutional barriers. *Journal of Social Issues, 43,* 5-39.

Brett, J. M., & Rognes, J. K. (1986). Intergroup relations in organizations. In P. S. Goodman (Ed.), *Designing effective work groups.* San Francisco: Jossey-Bass.

Brief, A. P. (1980). Peer assessment revisited: A brief comment on Kane and Lawler. *Psychological Bulletin, 88,* 78-79.

Brief, A. P., Rose, G., & Aldag, R. J. (1977). Sex differences in preferences for job attributes revisited. *Journal of Applied Psychology, 62,* 645-646.

Brightman, H. J. (1988). *Group problem solving: An improved managerial approach.* Atlanta: Georgia State University, Business Publishing Division.

Buchholz, S., Roth, T., & Hess, K. (1987). *Creating the high-performance team.* New York: John Wiley.

Buller, P. F. (1986). The team-building, task performance relation: Some conceptual and methodological refinements. *Group and Organization Studies, 10,* 147-168.

Bullock, M., Friday, C., & Belcher, K. (1996). *The International Conference on Work Teams proceedings: Anniversary collection: The best of 1990-1994.* Denton, TX: The Interdisciplinary Center for the Study of Work Teams.

Burgelman, R. A. (1983). A process model of internal corporate venturing in the diversified major firm. *Administrative Science, 28,* 223-244.

Burns, T., & Stalker, G. M. (1961). *The management of innovation.* New York: Barnes & Noble.

Butler, J. K., & Cantrell, R. S. (1984). A behavioral decision theory approach to modeling dyadic trust in superiors and subordinates. *Psychological Reports, 55,* 19-28.

Butler, M. C., & Burr, R. G. (1980). Utility of a multidimensional locus of control scale in predicting health and job-related outcomes in military environments. *Psychological Reports, 47,* 719-728.

Cameron, J., & Pierce, D. (1994). Reinforcement, reward, and intrinsic motivation: A meta-analysis. *Review of Educational Research, 64,* 363-423.

Campbell, D. T., & Stanley, J. (1966). *Experimental designs and quasi-experimental designs for research.* Chicago: Rand McNally.

Campion, M. A., Medsker, G. J., & Higgs, A. C. (1993). Relations between work group characteristics and effectiveness: Implications for designing effective work groups. *Personnel Psychology, 46,* 823-850.

Cannon-Bowers, J. A., Salas, E., & Converse, S. A. (1991). Cognitive psychology and team training: Shared mental models of complex systems. *Human Factors Society Bulletin,* pp. 1-4.

Carnevale, A. P., Gainer, L. J., & Meltzer, A. S. (1990). *Workplace basics: The essential skills employers want.* San Francisco: Jossey-Bass.

Carr, C., Mawhiney, T., Dickinson, A., & Pearlstein, R. (1995). Punished by rewards? A behavioral perspective. *Performance Improvement Quarterly, 8*(2), 125-140.

Carton, J. S. (1996). The differential effects of tangible rewards and praise on intrinsic motivation: A comparison of cognitive evaluation theory and operant theory. *The Behavior Analyst, 19,* 237-255.

Catania, A. C., & Harnad, S. (1988). *The selection of behavior: The operant behaviorism of B. F. Skinner: Comments and consequences.* New York: Cambridge University Press.

Centers, R., & Bugental, D. (1966). Intrinsic and extrinsic job motivations among different segments of the working population. *Journal of Applied Psychology, 62,* 645-646.

Channon, D. F. (1973). *The strategy and structure of British enterprise.* Boston: Division of Research, Graduate School of Business Administration, Harvard University.

Chemers, M. M., Oskamp, S., & Costanzo, M. A. (1995). *Diversity in organizations: New perspectives for a changing workplace.* Thousand Oaks, CA: Sage.

Clement, D. E., & Schiereck, J. J., Jr. (1973). Sex composition and group performance in a visual signal detection task. *Memory and Cognition, 1,* 251-255.

Cohen, S. G. (1994). Designing effective self-managing work teams. In M. M. Beyerlein & D. A. Johnson (Eds.), *Advances in interdisciplinary studies of work teams: Theories of self-managed work teams* (pp. 67-102). London: JAI Press.

Comer, D. R. (1995). A model of social loafing in real work groups. *Human Relations, 48*(6), 647-667.

The Commonwealth Fund. (1990). *Americans over 55 at work* (Program Research Reports 1 & 2). New York: Author.

Companies shift (slowly) to team-based pay. (1995). *HR Focus, 72*(7), 11.

Cotton, J. L., Vollrath, D. A., Froggatt, K. L., Lengnick-Hall, M. L., & Jennings, K. R. (1988). Employee participation: Diverse forms and different outcomes. *Academy of Management Review, 13*(1), 8-22.

Craig, R. L. (Ed.). (1987). *Training and development handbook.* New York: McGraw-Hill.

Crowley, J., Letvin, T., & Quinn, R. (1973, March). Seven deadly half-truths about the American working woman. *Psychology Today,* p. 94.

Cummings, T. G. (1978). Self-regulating work groups: A socio-technical synthesis. *Academy of Management Review, 3*(3), 625-634.

Cummings, T. G. (1981). Designing effective work groups. In P. C. Nystrom & W. H. Starbrach (Eds.), *Handbook of organizational design* (pp. 250-271). New York: Oxford University Press.

Cummings, T. G., & Srivastva, S. (1977). *Management of work: A socio-technical systems approach.* Kent, OH: The Comparative Administration Research Institute of Kent State University.

Cyert, R. M., & March, J. G. (1963). *A behavioral theory of the firm.* Englewood Cliffs, NJ: Prentice Hall.

Daniels, A. C. (1989). *Performance management: Improving quality and productivity through positive reinforcement.* Tucker, GA: Performance Management.

Daniels, A. C. (1994). *Bringing out the best in people: How to apply the astonishing power of positive reinforcement.* New York: McGraw-Hill.

Davenport, T. (1994). Saving its soul: Human-centered information management. *Harvard Business Review, 72,* 119-131.

Davis, J. H. (1973). Group decision and social interaction: A theory of social decision schemes. *Psychological Review, 80,* 97-125.

Dean, J. W., Jr. (1987). *Deciding to innovate decision processes in the adoption of advanced technology.* Cambridge, MA: Ballinger.

Dean, J. W., Jr., & Sharfman, M. P. (1993). Procedural rationality in the strategic decision-making process. *Journal of Management Studies, 30*(4), 587-610.

Dean, P. J. (1994). Performance engineering. In P. J. Dean (Ed.), *Performance engineering at work* (pp. 3-28). Batavia, IL: International Board of Standards for Training Performance and Instruction.

Deci, E. L. (1971). Effects of externally-mediated reward on intrinsic motivations. *Journal of Personality and Social Psychology, 18,* 105-115.

Deci, E. L., & Ryan, R. M. (1985). *Intrinsic motivation and self-determination in human behavior.* New York: Plenum.

DeCotiis, T. A., & Summers, T. P. (1987). A path analysis of a model of the antecedents and consequences of organizational commitment. *Human Relations, 40*(7), 445-470.

De Meyer, A. (1991). Tech talk: How managers are stimulating global R&D communication. *Sloan Management Review, 32,* 49-58.

De Meyer, A. (1993). Management of an international network of industrial R&D laboratories. *R&D Management, 23,* 109-120.

Deming, W. E. (1982). *Out of the crises.* Cambridge: Center for Advanced Engineering Study, MIT.

Deming, W. E. (1986). *Quality, productivity, and competitve position.* Cambridge: Center for Advanced Engineering Study, MIT.

DeNisi, A. S., Randolph, W. A., & Blencoe, A. G. (1983). Potential problems with peer ratings. *Academy of Management Journal, 26*(3), 457-464.

Dennis, H. (1988). *Fourteen steps in managing an aging work force.* Lexington, MA: Lexington Books.

Deterline, W. A. (1992). Feedback systems. In H. D. Stolovich & E. J. Keeps (Eds.), *Handbook of human performance technology* (pp. 294-311). San Francisco: Jossey-Bass.

Deutsch, M. (1962). Cooperation and trust: Some theoretical notes. In M. R. Jones (Ed.), *Nebraska symposium on motivation* (pp. 275-320). Lincoln: University of Nebraska Press.

de Vaus, D., & McAllister, I. (1991). Gender and work orientation: Values and satisfaction in Western Europe. *Work and Occupations, 18*(1), 72-93.

Dickinson, A. M. (1989). The detrimental effects of extrinsic reinforcement on "intrinsic motivation. *The Behavior Analyst, 12,* 1-15.

Digman, J. M. (1990). Personality structure: Emergence of the five-factor model. *Annual Review of Psychology, 41,* 417-440.

Digman, J. M., & Inouye, J. (1986). Further specification of the five robust factors of personality. *Journal of Personality and Social Psychology, 50,* 116-123.

Driskell, J. E., Hogan, R., & Salas, E. (1987). Personality and group performance. *Review of Personality and Social Psychology, 9,* 91-112.

Dutton, J. E., & Ashford, S. J. (1992). *Selling issues to top management.* Ann Arbor: University of Michigan, School of Business.

Earley, P. C. (1989). Social loafing and collectivism: A comparison of the United States and the People's Republic of China. *Administrative Science Quarterly, 34,* 565-581.

Earley, P. C. (1993). East meets West meets Mideast: Further explorations of collectivistic and individualistic work groups. *Academy of Management Journal, 36,* 319-348.

Eccles, R. G., & Pyburn, P. J. (1992). Creating a comprehensive system to measure performance. *Management Accounting, 74*(4), 41-44.

Emery, F. E. (1959). *Characteristics of sociotechnical systems.* London: Tavistock Institute of Human Relations.

Emery, F. E., & Trist, E. L. (1965). The causal texture of organizational environments. *Human Relations, 18,* 21-31.

Ephross, P. H., & Vassil, T. V. (1988). *Groups that work: Structure & process.* New York: Columbia University Press.

Erez, M., & Zidon, I. (1984). Effect of goal acceptance on the relationship of goal difficulty to performance. *Journal of Applied Psychology, 69,* 69-78.

Evans, M. G. (1993). *Organizational theory research and design.* New York: Macmillan.

Evans, M. G., Kiggundu, M. N., & House, R. J. (1979). A partial test and extension of the job characteristics model of motivation. *Organizational Behavior and Human Performance, 24,* 354-381.

Fayol, H. (1949). *General and industrial management.* London: Pitman.

Fein, M. (1974, Winter). Job enrichment: A reevaluation. *Sloan Management Review, 15,* 68-88.

Ferdman, B. M. (1992). The dynamics of ethnic diversity in organizations: Toward integrative models. In K. Kelley (Ed.), *Issues, theory, and research in industrial organizational psychology* (pp. 339-384). New York: Elsevier Science.

Fiedler, F. E. (1967). *A theory of leadership effectiveness.* New York: McGraw-Hill.

Fisher, K. (1986). Management roles in the implementation of participation management systems: A ready reference for solving common team problems. *Human Resource Management, 25*(3), 459-479.

Fisher, K., Rayner, S., & Belgard, W. (1995). *Tips for teams.* New York: McGraw-Hill.

Fisher, R., Ury, W., & Patton, B. (1991). *Getting to yes: Negotiating agreement without giving in* (2nd ed.). New York: Penguin.

Fiske, S. T., & Pavelchak, M. A. (1986). Category-based versus piecemeal-based affective responses: Developments in schema-triggered affect. In R. M. Sorrention & E. T. Higgins (Eds.), *Handbook of motivation and cognition: Foundations of social behavior* (pp. 167-203). New York: Guilford.

Flynn, G. (1996). Teams won't push for more pay. *Personnel Journal, 75*(1), 26.

Freeman, K. A. (1996). An examination of the effects of situational constraints on appraised performance. *Performance Improvement Quarterly, 9*(3), 65-79.

Fyock, C. D. (1990). *America's work force is coming of age.* New York: Lexington Books.

Galbraith, J. (1973). *Designing complex organizations.* Reading, MA: Addison-Wesley.

Geber, B. (1995). The bugaboo of team pay. *Training, 32*(8), 25-34.

Gerth, H. H., & Mills, C. W. (1958). *From Max Weber: Essays in sociology.* New York: Oxford University Press.

Gilbert, T. F. (1978). *Human competence.* New York: McGraw-Hill.

Gladstein, D. L. (1984). Groups in context: A model of task group effectiveness. *Administrative Science Quarterly, 29*(4), 499-517.

Goldberg, L. R. (1990). An alternative "description of personality": The big-five factor structure. *Journal of Personality and Social Psychology, 59,* 1216-1229.

Goodman, P. S., Devadas, R., & Griffith Hughson, T. L. (1988). Groups and productivity: Analyzing the effectiveness of teams. In J. P. Campbell & R. J. Campbell (Eds.), *Productivity in organizations* (pp. 295-327). San Francisco: Jossey-Bass.

Greenhaus, J. H., & Parasuraman, S. (1986). Vocational and organizational behavior, 1985: A review. *Journal of Vocational Behavior, 29,* 115-176.

Gross, S. E. (1995). *Compensation for teams: How to design and implement team-based reward programs.* New York: Amacom.

Guetzkow, H., & Gyr, J. (1954). An analysis of conflict in decision-making groups. *Human Relations, 7,* 367-381.

Guzzo, R. A., Salas, E., & Associates. (1995). *Team effectiveness and decision making in organizations.* San Francisco: Jossey-Bass.

Hackman, J. R. (1978). The design of self-managing work groups. In S. Biking, S. Streufert, & F. E. Fiedler (Eds.), *Managerial control and organizational democracy* (pp. 61-91). New York: John Wiley.

Hackman, J. R. (1988). The design of work teams. In J. W. Lorsch (Ed.), *Handbook of organizational behavior* (pp. 315-342). Englewood Cliffs, NJ: Prentice Hall.

Hackman, J. R. (1990). *Groups that work (and those that don't).* San Francisco: Jossey-Bass.

Hackman, J. R. (1992). The psychology of self-management in organizations. In R. Glaser (Ed.), *Classic readings on self-managing teamwork* (pp. 141-193). King of Prussia, PA: Organization Design and Development.

Hackman, J. R., & Lawler, E. E., III. (1971). Employee reactions to job characteristics. *Journal of Applied Psychology Monograph, 55*(3), 259-286.

Hackman, J. R., & Morris, C. G. (1975). Group tasks, group interaction process, and group performance effectiveness: A review and proposed integration. In L. Berkowitz (Ed.), *Advances in experimental social psychology* (pp. 45-99). New York: Academic Press.

Hackman, J. R., & Oldham, G. R. (1975). Development of the job diagnostic survey. *Journal of Applied Psychology, 60*(2), 159-170.

Hackman, J. R., & Oldham, G. R. (1976). Motivation through the design of work: Test of a theory. *Organizational Behavior and Human Performance, 16,* 250-279.

Hackman, J. R., & Oldham, G. R. (1980). *Work redesign.* Reading, MA: Addison-Wesley.

Hackman, J. R., & Walton, R. E. (1986). Leading groups in organizations. In P. S. Goodman (Ed.), *Designing effective work groups* (pp. 72-119). San Francisco: Jossey-Bass.

Halaby, C. N., & Weakliem, D. L. (1989). Worker control and attachment to the firm. *American Journal of Sociology, 95*(3), 549-591.

Hale, N. (1990). *The older worker: Effective strategies for management and human resource development.* San Francisco: Jossey-Bass.

Hare, A. P., Blumberg, H. H., Davies, M. F., & Kent, M. V. (1996). *Small groups: An introduction.* Westport, CT: Praeger.

Harper, B., & Harper, A. (1989). *Succeeding as a self-directed work team.* Croton-on-Hudson, NY: MW Corp.

Hayes, S. C. (1989). *Rule-governed behavior: Cognition, contingencies, and instructional control.* New York: Plenum.

Haythorn, W. (1953). The influence of individual members on the characteristics of small groups. *Journal of Abnormal and Social Psychology, 48,* 276-284.

Hersey, P., & Blanchard, K. H. (1982). *Management of organizational behavior* (4th ed.). Englewood Cliffs, NJ: Prentice Hall.

Hersey, P., & Blanchard, K. H. (1988). *Management of organizational behavior* (5th ed.). Englewood Cliffs, NJ: Prentice Hall.

Herzberg, F., Mausner, B., Peterson, R. O., & Capwell, D. F. (1957). *Job attitudes: Review of research and opinion.* Pittsburgh: Psychological Services of Pittsburgh.

Heslin, R. (1964). Predicting group task effectiveness from member characteristics. *Psychological Bulletin, 62,* 248-256.

Hitchcock, D., & Willard, M. (1995). *Why teams can fail and what to do about it: Essential tools for anyone implementing self-directed work teams.* Chicago: Irwin.

Hofstede, G. (1980). *Culture's consequences: International differences in work-related values.* Beverly Hills, CA: Sage.

Hofstede, G. (1985). The interaction between national and organizational value systems. *Journal of Management Studies, 22*(4), 347-357.

Hofstede, G., & Bond, M. H. (1984). Hofstede's culture dimensions: An independent validation using Rokeach819,92's value survey. *Journal of Cross-Cultural Psychology, 15*(4), 417-433.

Hogan, E. A., & Martell, D. A. (1987). A confirmatory structural equations analysis of the job characteristics model. *Organizational Behavior and Human Decision Processes, 39,* 242-263.

Holder, B. (1995, January/February). Creating new games through scouting. *Journal for Quality and Participation,* pp. 30-36.

Holland, J. L. (1985). *Making vocational choices: A theory of vocational personalities and work environments* (2nd ed.). Englewood Cliffs, NJ: Prentice Hall.

Holt, D. H. (1990). *Management: Principles and practices.* Englewood Cliffs, NJ: Prentice Hall.

Homans, G. (1950). *The human group.* New York: Harcourt, Brace, Jovanovich.

Honeycutt, A. (1989). Creating a productive work environment. *Supervisory Management, 34*(11), 12-16.

Hulin, C. L. (1971). Individual differences and job enrichment: The case against general treatments. In J. R. Maher (Ed.), *New perspectives in job enrichment* (pp. 159-191). New York: Van Nostrand Reinhold.

Iaffaldano, M. T., & Muchinsky, P. M. (1985). Job satisfaction and job performance: A meta-analysis. *American Psychological Association, 97*(2), 251-273.

Ilgen, D. R., & Klein, H. J. (1988). Individual motivation and performance: Cognitive influences on effort and choice. In *Productivity in organizations* (pp. 143-176). San Francisco: Jossey-Bass.

Jackson, S. E., & Ruderman, M. N. (Eds.). (1995). *Diversity in work teams.* Washington, DC: American Psychological Association.

Jandt, F. E., & Pedersen, P. B. (Eds.). (1996). *Constructive conflict management Asia-Pacific cases.* Thousand Oaks, CA: Sage.

Janis, I. (1982). *Groupthink* (2nd ed.). Boston: Houghton Mifflin.

Janis, I. (1988). Groupthink. In R. Katz (Ed.), *Managing professionals in innovative organizations* (pp. 332-340). Cambridge, MA: Ballinger.

Jehn, K. A. (1995). A multimethod examination of the benefits and detriments of intragroup conflict. *Administrative Science Quarterly, 40*(3), 256-282.

Jewell, L., & Reitz, J. (1988). The role of the group and the organization: Group decision making. In R. Katz (Ed.), *Managing professionals in innovative organizations: A collection of readings* (pp. 247-261). Cambridge, MA: Ballinger.

Johnson, D. W., & Johnson, F. P. (1994). *Joining together: Group theory and group skills* (5th ed.). Englewood Cliffs, NJ: Prentice-Hall.

Johnston, W. B., & Packer, A. H. (1987). *Workforce 2000: Work and workers for the 21st century.* Indianapolis, IN: Hudson Institute.

Jones, G. R. (1995). *Organizational theory, text, and cases.* New York: Addison-Wesley.

Juran, J. M. (1989). *Juran on Leadership for Quality.* New York: Free Press.

Kagitcibasi, C., & Berry, J. W. (1989). Cross-cultural psychology: Recent research and trends. *Annual Review of Psychology, 40,* 493-531.

Kahan, J. P., Webb, N., Shavelson, R. J., & Stolzenberg, R. M. (1985). *Individual characteristics and unit performance.* Santa Monica, CA: RAND.

Kane, J. S., & Lawler, E. E. (1978). Methods of peer assessment. *Psychological Bulletin, 85,* 555-586.

Kane, J. S., & Lawler, E. E. (1980). In defense of peer assessment: A rebuttal to Brief's critique. *Psychological Bulletin, 88,* 80-81.

Kanin-Lovers, J., & Cameron, M. (1993, January-February). Team-based reward systems. *Journal of Compensation and Benefits,* pp. 56-60.

Kanter, R. M. (1982). Dilemmas of managing participation. *Organizational Dynamics, 11*(5), 5-27.

Kaplan, R. S., & Norton, D. P. (1996). *The balanced scorecard: Translating strategy into action.* Boston: Harvard Business School Press.

Katerberg, R., & Blau, G. (1983). An examination of level and direction of effort and job performance. *Academy of Management Journal, 26*(2), 249-257.

Katz, D., & Kahn, R. (1966). *The social psychology of organizations.* New York: John Wiley.

Katzell, R. A., & Thompson, D. E. (1990). Work motivation: Theory and practice. *American Psychologist, 45*(2), 144-153.

Katzenbach, J. R., & Smith, D. (1993a). The discipline of teams. *Harvard Business Review, 71*(2), 111-120.

Katzenbach, J. R., & Smith, D. (1993b). *The wisdom of teams.* Boston: Harvard Business School Press.

Kelly, J. E. (1978). A reappraisal of socio-technical systems theory. *Human Relations, 31*(12), 1069-1099.

Kelly, J. E. (1992). Does job re-design theory explain job re-design outcomes? *Human Relations, 45*(8), 753-774.

Kelly, L., & Reeser, C. (1973). The persistence of culture as a determinant of differentiated attitudes on the part of American managers of Japanese ancestry. *Academy of Management Journal, 16,* 67-76.

Kemp, N. J., & Cook, J. D. (1983). Job longevity and growth need strength as joint moderators of the task design-job satisfaction relationship. *Human Relations, 36*(10), 883-898.

Kent, R. N., & McGrath, J. E. (1969). Task and group characteristics as factors influencing group performance. *Journal of Experimental Social Psychology, 5,* 429-440.

Kichuk, S. L., & Wiesner, W. H. (1996). *Personality and team performance: Implications for selecting successful product design teams* (Working Paper No. 51). Hamilton, Ontario, Canada: Innovation Research Working Group, McMaster University.

Kidwell, R. E., Jr., & Bennett, N. (1993). Employee propensity to withhold effort: A conceptual model to intersect three avenues of research. *Academy of Management Review, 18*(3), 429-456.

Klein, J. (1984, September/October). Why supervisors resist employee involvement. *Harvard Business Review,* pp. 87-95.

Klein, J. (1994). Maintaining expertise in multi-skilled teams. In M. M. Beyerlein & D. A. Johnson (Eds.), *Advances in interdisciplinary studies of work teams: Theories of self-managed work teams* (pp. 145-166). London: JAI Press.

Klimoski, R., & Jones, R. (1994). *Team decision making in organizations: New frontiers. The case for personnel selection.* Part of symposium, Team decision making in organizations: New frontiers, at the Annual Conference of the Society for Industrial/Organizational Psychology, Nashville, TN.

Kohn, A. (1993). *Punished by rewards: The trouble with gold stars, incentive plans, A's, praise, and other bribes.* Boston: Houghton-Mifflin.

Kouzes, J. B., & Posner, B. Z. (1987). *The leadership challenge.* New York: Jossey-Bass.

Kowitz, A. L., & Knutson, T. J. (1980). *Decision making in small groups: Search for alternatives.* Boston: Allyn & Bacon.

Kroeber, A. L., & Parsons, T. (1958). The concepts of culture and of social system. *American Sociological Review, 23,* 582-583.

Kruse, D. L. (1993). *Does profit sharing affect productivity?* Cambridge, MA: National Bureau of Economic Research.

Lamal, P. A. (1991). Aspects of some contingencies and metacontingencies in the Soviet Union. In P. A. Lamal (Ed.), *Behavioral analysis of societies and cultural practices* (pp. 77-85). New York: Hemisphere.

Landy, F. J., & Becker, W. S. (1987). Motivation theory reconsidered. *Research in Organizational Behavior, 9,* 1-38.

Larson, C. E., & LaFasto, F. M. J. (1989). *Teamwork.* London: Sage.

Latham, G. P., & Lee, T. W. (1986). Goal setting. In E. A. Locke (Ed.), *Generalizing from laboratory to field settings* (pp. 101-117). Lexington, MA: Lexington Books.

Lawler, E. E., III. (1973). *Motivation in work organizations.* Monterey, CA: Brooks/Cole.

Lawler, E. E., III. (1986). *High-involvement management.* San Francisco: Jossey-Bass.

Lawler, E. E., III. (1988a). Pay for performance: Making it work. *Personnel, 65*(10), 68-71.

Lawler, E. E., III. (1988b). Substitutes for hierarchy. *Organizational Dynamics, 17*(1), 4-15.

Lawler, E. E., III. (1988c). Transformation from control to involvement. In R. H. Kilman & T. J. Covin (Eds.), *Corporate transformation.* San Francisco: Jossey-Bass.

Lawler, E. E., III. (1988d). Choosing an involvement strategy. *Academy of Management Executives, 2*(3), 197-204.

Lawler, E. E., III. (1989). Substitutes for hierarchy. *Incentive, 163*(3), 39-45.

Lawler, E. E., III. (1992). *The ultimate advantage: Creating the high involvement organization.* San Francisco: Jossey-Bass.

Lawler, E. E., III. (1995). The new pay: A strategic approach. *Compensation and Benefits Review, 27*(4), 14-22.

Lawler, E. E., III, Ledford, G. E., & Chang, L. (1993). Who uses skill-based pay and why. *Compensation and Benefits Review, 25*(2), 22-26.

Lawler, E. E., III, Ledford, G. E., & Mohrman, S. A. (1989). *Employee involvement in America.* Houston, TX: American Productivity and Quality Center.

Lawler, E. E., III, & Mohrman, S. A. (1989). With HR help, all managers can practice high-involvement management. *Personnel, 66*(4), 26-31.

Lawrence, P., & Lorsch, J. (1967). *Organization and environment.* Cambridge, MA: Harvard University Press.

Lee, S. K. (1992). Quantitative versus qualitative research methods—two approaches to organization studies. *Asia Pacific Journal of Management, 9*(1), 87-94.

Lee, S. M. (1971). An empirical analysis of organizational identification. *Academy of Management Journal, 14,* 213-226.

Lefkowitz, J. (1994). Sex-related differences in job attitudes and dispositional variables: Now you see them. . . . *Academy of Management Journal, 37*(2), 323-349.

Lepper, M. R., & Greene, D. (1978). *The hidden costs of reward: New perspectives on the psychology of human motivation.* Hillsdale, NJ: Lawrence Erlbaum.

Lepper, M. R., Greene, D., & Nisbett, R. E. (1973). Undermining children's intrinsic interest with extrinsic reward. *Journal of Personality and Social Psychology, 33,* 25-35.

Lindblom, C. E. (1959). The science of muddling through. *Public Administration Review, 19,* 79-88.

Locke, E. A. (1968). Toward a theory of task motivation and incentives. *Organizational Behavior and Human Performance, 3,* 157-189.

Locke, E. A., & Latham, G. P. (1990). Work motivation and satisfaction: Light at the end of the tunnel. *American Psychological Society, 1*(4), 240-246.

Locke, E. A., Latham, G. P., & Erez, M. (1988). The determinants of goal commitment. *Academy of Management Review, 13*(1), 23-39.

Locke, E. A., Shaw, K. N., Saari, L. M., & Latham, T. P. (1981). Goal setting and task performance: 1969-1980. *Psychological Bulletin, 90,* 125-152.

Lofland, J. (1971). *Analyzing social settings.* Belmont, CA: Wadsworth.

Loher, B. T., Noe, R. A., Moeller, N. L., & Fitzgerald, M. P. (1985). A meta-analysis of the relation of job characteristics to job satisfaction. *Journal of Applied Psychology, 70*(2), 280-289.

Lorsch, J. W., & Morse, J. J. (1974). *Organizations and their members.* New York: Harper & Row.

Lott, A. J., & Lott, B. E. (1961). Group cohesiveness, communication level, and conformity. *Journal of Abnormal and Social Psychology, 62,* 408-412.

Macionis, J. J. (1997). *Sociology* (6th ed.). Upper Saddle River, NJ: Prentice Hall.

Macy, B. A., Peterson, M. F., & Norton, L. W. (1989). A test of participation theory in a work re-design field setting: Degree of participation and comparison site contrasts. *Human Relations, 42*(12), 1095-1165.

Maier, N. R. F. (1963). *Problem solving discussions and conferences: Leadership methods and skills.* New York: McGraw-Hill.

Malott, R. W. (1989). The achievement of evasive goals: Control by rules describing indirect-acting contingencies. In S. C. Hayes (Ed.), *Rule-governed behavior: Cognition, contingencies, and instructional control* (pp. 269-322). New York: Plenum.

Malott, R. W. (1992). A theory of rule-governed behavior and organizational behavior management. *Journal of Organizational Behavior Management, 12*(2), 55-65.

Mann, R. D. (1959). A review of the relationships between personality and performance in small groups. *Psychological Bulletin, 56,* 241-270.

Mannheim, B. (1983). Male and female industrial workers: Job satisfaction, work role centrality, and workplace preference. *Work and Occupations, 10,* 413-436.

Manz, C. C. (1992). *Mastering self-leadership: Empowering yourself for personal excellence.* Englewood Cliffs, NJ: Prentice Hall.

Manz, C. C., & Sims, H. P., Jr. (1987). Leading workers to lead themselves: The external leadership of self-managing work teams. *Administrative Science Quarterly, 32,* 106-128.

Manz, C. C., & Sims, H. P., Jr. (1989). *Superleadership.* New York: Prentice Hall.

March, J. G., & Simon, H. A. (1958). *Organizations.* New York: John Wiley.

Maskell, B. H. (1991). *Performance measurement for world class manufacturing: A model for American companies.* Cambridge, MA: Productivity Press.

Maslow, A. H. (1970). *Motivation and personality* (2nd ed.). New York: Harper & Row. (Original work published 1954)

Mayo, E. (1946). *The human problems of an industrial civilization.* New York: Macmillan.

Maznevski, M. L. (1994). Understanding our differences: Performance in decision-making groups with diverse members. *Human Relations, 47*(5), 531-552.

McAdams, J. L. (1996). *The reward plan advantage: A manager's guide to improving business performance through people.* San Francisco: Jossey-Bass.

McCoy, T. J. (1992). *Compensation and motivation: Maximizing employee performance with behavior-based incentive plans.* New York: Amacon.

McCrae, R. R., & Costa, P. T. (1987). Validation of the five-factor model of personality across instruments and observers. *Journal of Personality and Social Psychology, 52*(1), 81-90.

McEnery, J. M., & Lifter, M. L. (1987). Demands for change: Interfacing environmental pressures and the personnel process. *Public Personnel Management, 16*(1), 61-67.

McGee, G., & Ford, R. C. (1987). Two (or more) dimensions of organizational commitment: Reexamination of the affective and continuance commitment scales. *Journal of Applied Psychology, 72*(4), 638-642.

McGrath, J. E. (1962). The influence of positive interpersonal relations on adjustment and effectiveness in rifle teams. *Journal of Abnormal and Social Psychology, 65,* 365-375.

McGrath, J. E. (1964). *Social psychology: A brief introduction.* New York: Holt, Rinehart & Winston.

McGregor, D. (1960). *The human side of enterprise.* New York: McGraw-Hill.

McSween, T. E. (1995). *The values-based safety process: Improving your safety culture with a behavioral approach.* New York: Van Nostrand Reinhold.

Meeker, L. (1993). *Business foundation for self-managed work teams* (Internal document to managers at Texas Instruments, Dallas, Texas). Dallas: Texas Instruments.

Mento, A. J., Steel, R. P., & Karren, R. J. (1987). A meta-analytic study of the effects of goal setting on task performance: 1966-1984. *Organizational Behavior and Human Decision Processes, 39,* 52-83.

Meyer, C. (1994). Team measures. *Harvard Business Review, 72*(3), 95-103.

Meyer, J. P., Paunonen, S. V., Gellatly, I. R., Goffin, R. D., & Jackson, D. N. (1989). Organizational commitment and job performance: It's the nature of the commitment that counts. *Journal of Applied Psychology, 74*(1), 152-156.

Michalak, B., Fischer, S., & Meeker, L. (1994). *Experiential activities for high performance teamwork.* Amherst, MA: Human Resource Development Press, Inc.

Mickelson, J. S., & Campbell, J. H. (1975). Information behavior: Groups with varying levels of interpersonal acquaintance. *Organizational Behavior and Human Performance, 13,* 193-205.

Mikalachki, A. (1969). *Group cohesion reconsidered.* London: School of Business Administration.

Miles, R. E. (1965). Human relations or human resources. *Harvard Business Review, 43*(4), 148-151.

Mintzberg, H. (1987). Crafting strategy. *Harvard Business Review, 65*(4), 66-75.

Mintzberg, H., Raisinghani, D., & Theoret, A. (1976). The structure of "unstructured" decision processes. *Administration Science Quarterly, 21*(June), 246-275.

Mitchell, D. J. B., Lewin, D., & Lawler, E. E. (1990). Alternative pay systems, firm performance, and productivity. In A. S. Blinder (Ed.), *Paying for productivity: A look at the evidence* (pp. 15-94). Washington, DC: Brookings Institution.

Mohrman, S. A., Cohen, S., & Mohrman, A. M., Jr. (1995). *Designing team-based organizations: New forms for knowledge work.* San Francisco: Jossey-Bass.

Morgan, B. B., Jr., & Lassiter, D. L. (1992). Team composition and staffing. In R. W. Swezey & E. Salas (Eds.), *Teams: Their training and performance* (pp. 57-74). Norwood, NJ: Ablex.

Morgan, E., Jr., & Hiltner, J. (1992). *Managing aging and human service agencies.* New York: Springer.

Morrison, A. M., & Von Glinow, M. A. (1990). Women and minorities in management. *American Psychologist, 45,* 200-208.

Morse, J. J., & Wagner, F. R. (1978). The congruence of employee personality characteristics, job design, and work system variables: Implications for worker productivity and experienced quality of life at work. In A. R. Negandhi & B. Wilpert (Eds.), *Work organization research* (pp. 279-297). Kent, OH: Comparative Administration Research Institute, Kent State University.

Mottaz, C. J. (1988). Determinants of organizational commitment. *Human Relations, 41*(6), 467-482.

Mowday, R. T., Steers, R. M., & Porter, L. W. (1979). The measurement of organizational commitment. *Journal of Vocational Behavior, 14,* 224-247.

Myers, M. S. (1991). *Every employee a manager.* San Diego: University Association.

Neil, C. C., & Snizek, W. E. (1987). Work, values, job characteristics, and gender. *Sociological Perspectives, 30,* 245-265.

Nelson, R. (1994). *1001 ways to reward your employees.* New York: Workman.

Nemeth, C. (1986). Differential contributions of majority and minority influence. *Psychological Review, 93,* 23-32.

Neuhaus, R. H. (1990). *Long-term care administration: Teamwork and effective management.* New York: University Press of America.

Nieva, V. F., Fleishman, E. A., & Rieck, A. (1978). *Team dimensions: Their identity, their measurement, and their relationships* (Final Technical Report for Contract No. DAHC19-78-C-0001). Washington, DC: Advanced Research Resources Organizations.

Nohria, N., & Eccles, R. (1992). Face-to-face: Making network organizations work. In N. Nohria & R. Eccles (Eds.), *Networks and organizations: Structure, form, and action* (pp. 288-307). Boston: Harvard Business School Press.

Nordstrom, R., Lorenzi, P., & Hall, R. V. (1990). A review of public posting of performance feedback in work settings. *Journal of Organizational Behavior Management, 11*(2), 101-123.

Norman, W. T. (1963). Toward an adequate taxonomy of personality attributes: Replicated factor structure in peer nomination personality ratings. *Journal of Abnormal and Social Psychology, 66*(6), 574-583.

Nurick, A. (1982). Participation in organizational change: A longitudinal field study. *Human Relations, 35,* 413-430.

Nutt, P. C. (1984). Types of organizational decision processes. *Administrative Science Quarterly, 29,* 414-450.

O'Leary-Kelly, A. M., Martocchio, J. J., & Frink, D. D. (1994). A review of the influence of group goals on group performance. *Academy of Management Journal, 37*(5), 1285-1301.

Oregon Productivity Center. (1986). *Productivity by the objectives matrix.* Corvalis: Oregon Productivity Center Press.

Organ, D., & Hammer, W. C. (1950). *Organizational behavior.* Plano, TX: Business Publications.

Orsburn, J., Moran, L., Musselwhite, E., Zenger, J. H., & Perrin, C. (1990). *Self-directed work teams: The new American challenge.* Homewood, IL: Business One, Irwin.

Parker, L. D. (1984). Control in organizational life: The contribution of Mary Parker Follett. *Academy of Management Review, 9*(4), 736-745.

Parker, L. E., & Price, R. H. (1994). Empowered managers and empowered workers: The effects of managerial support and managerial perceived control on workers' sense of control over decision making. *Human Relations, 47*(8), 911-952.

Pasmore, W. A. (1988). *Designing effective organizations: The sociotechnical systems perspective.* New York: John Wiley.

Pasmore, W. A., Francis, C., Haldeman, J., & Shani, A. (1982). A sociotechnical systems: A North American reflection on empirical studies of the seventies. *Human Relations, 35*(12), 1179-1204.

Patton, M. Q. (1990). *Qualitative evaluation and research methods.* Newbury Park, CA: Sage.

Pearce, J. A., II, & David, F. R. (1983). A social network approach to organizational design-performance. *Academy of Management Review, 8*(3), 436-444.

Pearce, J. A., & Ravlin, E. C. (1987). The design and activation of self-regulating work groups. *Human Relations, 40*(11), 751-782.

Perrow, C. (1967). A framework for comparative organizational analysis. *American Sociological Review, 32*(2), 194-208.

Perrow, C. (1970). *Organizational analysis: A sociological view.* Belmont, CA: Wadsworth.

Perrow, C. (1986). *Complex organizations* (3rd ed.). New York: Random House.

Peters, T. J., & Waterman, R. H., Jr. (1982). *In search of excellence: Lessons from America's best-run companies.* New York: Warner Brothers.

Peters, W. S., & Champoux, J. E. (1979). The use of moderated regression in hob redesign decision sciences. *Decision Sciences, 10,* 85-95.

Pfeffer, J. (1983). Organizational demography. In L. L. Cummings & B. M. Staw (Eds.), *Research in organizational behavior* (pp. 299-357). Greenwich, CT: JAI Press.

Pfiffner, J. M. (1960). Administrative rationality. *Public Administration Review, 20,* 125-132.

Pinkley, R. L. (1990). Dimensions of conflict frame: Disputant interpretations of conflict. *Journal of Applied Psychology, 75,* 117-126.

Pizam, A., & Reichel, A. (1977). Cultural determinants of managerial behavior. *Management International Review, 17,* 65-72.

Plunkett, L. C., & Fournier, R. (1991). *Participative management: Implementing empowerment.* New York: John Wiley.

Polley, D., & Van Dyne, L. (1994). The limits and liabilities of self-managed work teams. In M. M. Beyerlein & D. A. Johnson (Eds.), *Advances in interdisciplinary studies of work teams: Theories of self-managed work teams* (pp. 1-38). London: JAI Press.

Priem, R., & Price, K. (1991). Process and outcome expectations for the dialectical inquiry, devil's advocacy, and consensus techniques of strategic decision making. *Group and Organization Studies, 16,* 206-225.

Prue, D. M., & Fairbank, J. A. (1981). Performance feedback in organizational behavior management: A review. *Journal of Organizational Behavior Management, 3,* 1-15.

Rakos, R. F. (1991). Behavioral analysis of socialism in Eastern Europe: A framework for understanding the revolutions of 1989. In P. A. Lamal (Ed.), *Behavioral analysis of societies and cultural practices* (pp. 87-105). New York: Hemisphere.

Ray, D. W., & Bronstein, H. (1995). *Teaming up: Making the transition to a self-directed, team-based organization.* New York: McGraw-Hill.

Rees, F. (1991). *How to lead work teams: Facilitation skills.* San Diego: Pfeiffer.

Reichers, A. E. (1985). A review and reconceptualization of organizational commitment. *Academy of Management Review, 10*(3), 465-476.

Rentsch, J. R., & Hall, R. J. (1994). Members of great teams think alike: A model of team effectiveness and schema similarity among team members. In M. M. Beyerlein & D. A. Johnson (Eds.), *Advances in interdisciplinary studies of work teams: Theories of self-managed work teams* (pp. 223-262). London: JAI Press.

Roethlisberger, F. I., & Dickson, W. J. (1939). *Management and the worker.* Cambridge, MA: Harvard University Press.

Rose, R. A. (1988). Organizations as multiple cultures: A rules theory analysis. *Human Relations, 41*(2), 139-170.

Rosen, B., & Jerdee, T. H. (1985). *Older employees: New roles for valued resources.* Homewood, IL: Dow Jones-Irwin.

Sackmann, S. A. (1991). Uncovering culture in organizations. *Journal of Applied Behavioral Science, 27*(3), 295-317.

Salancik, G. R., & Pfeffer, J. (1978). A social information processing approach to job attitudes and task design. *Administrative Science Quarterly, 23,* 224-253.

Salas, E., Dickinson, T. L., Converse, S. A., & Tannenbaum, S. I. (1992). Toward an understanding of team performance and training. In R. W. Swezey & E. Salas (Eds.), *Teams: Their training and performance* (pp. 3-30). Norwood, NJ: Ablex.

Sanchez, J. I., & Brock, P. (1996). Outcomes of perceived discrimination among Hispanic employees: Is diversity management a luxury or a necessity? *Academy of Management Journal, 39*(3), 704-719.

Schein, E. H. (1984). Coming to awareness of organizational culture. *Sloan Management Review, 24*(2), 3-16.

Schindler, P. L., & Thomas, C. C. (1993). The structure of interpersonal trust in the workplace. *Psychological Reports, 73,* 563-573.

Scholtes, P. R. (1987). *An elaboration on Deming's teachings on performance appraisal.* Madison, WI: Joiner Associates.

Scontrino, P. (1995, July/August). An effective productivity and quality improvement tool. *Journal for Quality and Participation,* 90-93.

Scott, S. G., & Bruce, R. A. (1994). Determinants of innovative behavior: A path model of individual innovation in the workplace. *Academy of Management Journal, 37*(3), 580-607.

Scott, W. G., & Mitchell, T. R. (1976). *Organization theory* (3rd edition). Homewood, IL: Irwin.

Seashore, S. (1954). *Group cohesiveness in the industrial work group.* Ann Arbor: Institute for Social Research, University of Michigan.

Selltiz, C., Jahoda, M., Deutsch, M., & Cook, S. W. (1959). *Research methods in social relations.* New York: Holt, Rinehart and Winston.

Seward, R. R., Yeatts, D. E., Seward, J. A., & Stanley-Stevens, L. (1993). Fathers' time spent with their children: A longitudinal assessment. *Family Perspective, 27*(3), 275-283.

Shaw, D. G., & Schneier, C. E. (1995). Team measurement and rewards: How some companies are getting it right. *Human Resource Planning, 18*(3), 34-49.

Shaw, M. E. (1971). *Group dynamics: The psychology of small group behavior.* New York: McGraw-Hill.

Shiflett, S. C. (1972). Group performance as a function of task difficulty and organizational interdependence. *Organizational Behavior and Human Performance, 7*, 442-456.

Shonk, J. H. (1992). *Team-based organizations: Developing a successful team environment.* Homewood, IL: Business One, Irwin.

Simon, J. L. (1969). *Basic research methods in social science.* New York: Random House.

Sims, H. P., Jr., & Lorenzi, P. (1992). *The new leadership paradigm: Social learning and cognition in organizations.* Newbury Park, CA: Sage.

Sink, D. S., & Tuttle, T. C. (1989). *Planning and measurement in your organization of the future.* Norcross, GA: IIE Press.

Skinner, B. F. (1938). *The behavior of organisms: An experimental analysis.* New York: Appleton-Century.

Skinner, B. F. (1974). *About behaviorism.* New York: Knopf.

Snizek, W. E., & Little, R. E. (1984). Accounting for occupational and organizational commitment: A longitudinal reexamination of structural and attitudinal approaches. *Sociological Perspectives, 27*(2), 181-196.

Spence, J. T., & Helmreich, R. L. (1978). *Masculinity and femininity: Their psychological dimensions, correlates, and antecedents.* Austin: University of Texas Press.

Spence, J. T., Helmreich, R. L., & Pred, R. S. (1987). Impatience versus achievement strivings in the Type A pattern: Differential effects on students' health and academic achievement. *Journal of Applied Psychology, 72*, 522-528.

Spitzer, D. R. (1995). *Supermotivation: A blueprint for energizing your organization from top to bottom.* New York: Amacom.

Stanley-Stevens, L. (1994). *Gender and job satisfaction: Test of an integrated model.* Ph.D. dissertation, University of North Texas, Denton.

Steers, R. M., & Spencer, D. G. (1977). The role of achievement motivation in job design. *Journal of Applied Psychology, 62*, 472-479.

Steiner, I. D. (1972). *Group processes and productivity.* New York: Academic Press.

Streufert, S., & Nogami, G. (1992). Cognitive complexity and team decision making. In R. W. Swezey & E. Salas (Eds.), *Teams: Their training and performance* (pp. 127-152). Norwood, NJ: Ablex.

Sundstrom, E., De Meuse, K. P., & Futrell, D. (1990). Work teams: Applications and effectiveness. *American Psychologist, 45*(2), 120-133.

Susman, G. I. (1979). *Autonomy at work: A sociotechnical analysis of participative management.* New York: Praeger.

Swezey, R., & Salas, E. (1992). *Teams: Their training and performance.* Norwood, NJ: Ablex.

Tannen, D. (1990). *You just don't understand: Women and men in conversation.* New York: William Morrow.

Tannenbaum, S. I., Beard, R. L., & Salas, E. (1992). Team building and its influence on team effectiveness: An examination of conceptual and empirical developments. In K. Kelly (Ed.), *Issues, theory, and research in industrial/organizational psychology* (pp.117-153). New York: Elsevier Science.

Taylor, F. W. (1911). *The principles of scientific management.* New York: Harper.

Terborg, J. R., Castore, C., & DeNinno, J. A. (1976). A longitudinal field investigation of the impact of group composition on group performance and cohesion. *Journal of Personality and Social Psychology, 34*(5), 782-790.

Tett, R. P., Jackson, D. N., Rothstein, M., & Reddon, J. R. (1994). Meta-analysis of personality-job performance relations: A reply to Ones, Mount, Barrick, and Hunter. *Personnel Psychology, 47,* 157-172.

Thomas, J., & Griffin, R. (1983). The social information processing model of task design: A review of the literature. *Academy of Management Review, 8*(4), 672-682.

Thomas, M. C., & Thomas, T. S. (1990). *Getting commitment at work: A guide for managers and employees.* Chapel Hill, NC: Commitment Press.

Thompson, J. (1967). *Organizations in action.* New York: McGraw-Hill.

Tindale, J. A. (1991). *Older workers in an aging workforce.* Ontario, Canada: National Advisory Council on Aging.

Tjosvold, D. (1986). *Working together to get things done: Managing for organizational productivity.* Lexington, MA: Lexington Books.

Tosti, D. T. (1986). *Feedback systems: Introduction to performance technology.* Washington, DC: International Society for Performance Improvement.

Trevino, L. K., Lengel, R. H., & Daft, R. L. (1987). Media symbolism, media richness, and media choice in organizations: A symbolic interactionist perspective. *Communication Research, 14,* 553-574.

Triandis, H. C., & Brislin, R. W. (Eds.). (1980). *Handbook of cross-cultural psychology.* Boston: Allyn & Bacon.

Trist, E. L., & Bamforth, K. W. (1951). Some social and psychological consequences of the longwall method of coal-getting. *Human Relations, 4,* 3-38.

Trist, E. L., Higgin, G. W., Murray, H., & Pollack, A. B. (1963). *Organizational choice.* London: Tavistock.

Tsui, A. S., Egan, T. D., & Xin, K. R. (1995). Diversity in organizations: Lessons from demography research. In M. M. Chemers, S. Oskamp, & M. A. Costanzo (Eds.), *Diversity in organizations: New perspectives for a changing workplace* (pp. 191-219). Thousand Oaks, CA: Sage.

Turner, A. N., & Lawrence, P. R. (1965). *Industrial jobs and the worker.* Boston: Harvard Graduate School of Business Administration.

U.S. Bureau of the Census. (1994). *Statistical abstract of the United States: 1994.* Washington, DC: Government Printing Office.

U.S. Department of Defense. (1994). *Self-managed work teams: Master plan.* St. Louis, MO: Defense Contract Management Office.

U.S. Department of Labor. (1989). *Handbook of Labor Statistics, Bulletin 2324.* Washington, DC: Bureau of Labor Statistics.

Varela, J. A. (1971). *Psychological solutions to social problems.* New York: Academic Press.

Varney, G. H. (1989). *Building productive teams: An action guide and resource book.* San Francisco: Jossey-Bass.

Vroom, V. H. (1995). *Work and motivation.* New York: Jossey-Bass. (Original work published 1964)

Vroom, V. H., & Yetton, P. W. (1973). *Leadership and decision-making.* Pittsburgh: University of Pittsburgh Press.

Wagner, J. A., III. (1995). Studies of individualism-collectivism: Effects on cooperation in groups. *Academy of Management Journal, 38*(1), 152-172.

Wagner, J. A., III, & Gooding, R. Z. (1987a). Effects of societal trends on participation research. *Administrative Science Quarterly, 32,* 241-262.

Wagner, J. A., III, & Gooding, R. Z. (1987b). Shared influence and organizational behavior: A meta-analysis of situational variables expected to moderate participation-outcome relationships. *Academy of Management Journal, 30*(3), 524-541.

Wagner, J. A., III, & Moch, M. K. (1986). Individualism-collectivism: Concept and measure. *Psychologica, 28,* 173-181.

Wall, T. D., Kemp, N. J., Jackson, P. R., & Clegg, C. W. (1986). Outcomes of autonomous workgroups: A long-term field experiment. *Academy of Management Journal, 29*(2), 280-304.

Wall, V., & Nolan, L. (1986). Perceptions of inequality, satisfaction, and conflict in task-oriented groups. *Human Relations, 39,* 1033-1052.

Waterman, R. H. (1987). *The renewal factor.* New York: Bantam.

Watson, W. E., Kumar, K., & Michaelsen, L. K. (1993). Cultural diversity's impact on interaction process and performance: Comparing homogeneous and diverse task groups. *Academy of Management Journal, 36*(3), 590-602.

Webb, E. T., Campbell, D. T., Schwartz, R. D., Sechrest, L., & Grove, J. B. (1981). *Nonreactive measures in the social sciences.* Boston: Houghton Mifflin.

Weick, K. E., & Penner, D. D. (1969). Discrepant membership as an occasion for effective cooperation. *Sociometry, 32,* 413-424.

Weldon, E. J. (1993). *Strategy formation in empowered work teams.* Working Paper, Indiana University.

Wellins, R. S., Byham, W. C., & Dixon, G. (1994). *Inside teams: How 20 world-class organizations are winning through teamwork.* San Francisco: Jossey-Bass.

Wellins, R. S., Byham, W. C., & Wilson, J. M. (1991). *Empowered teams: Creating self-directed work groups that improve quality, productivity, and participation.* San Francisco: Jossey-Bass.

Wetherbe, J. C. (1991, March). Executive information requirements: Getting it right. *MIS Quarterly,* pp. 51-65.

Wiersema, M. F., & Bantel, K. A. (1992). Top management team demography and corporate strategic change. *Academy of Management Journal, 35,* 91-121.

Woodward, J. (1958). *Management and technology.* London: Her Majesty's Stationery Office.

Woodward, J. (1965). *Industrial organization: Theory and practice.* London: Oxford University Press.

Yeatts, D. E. (1992). *Network on self-managed teams* (Brochure describing a network of organizations meeting to share knowledge about self-managed teams).

Yeatts, D. E., Hipskind, M., & Barnes, D. (1994, July/August). Lessons learned from self-managed work teams. *Business Horizons,* pp. 1-8.

Yeatts, D. E., Hyten, C., & Barnes, D. (1996). What are the key factors for self-managed team success. *The Journal for Quality and Participation, 19*(3), 68-77.

Yeatts, D. E., Stanley-Stevens, L., & Ruggiere, P. (1992). The self-managed work team: Reasons for failure and potential solutions. *Quality and Productivity Management, 9*(4), 26-32.

Yin, R. K. (1989). *Case study research: Design and methods.* Newbury Park, CA: Sage.

Zaccaro, S. J., & Lowe, C. A. (1988). Cohesiveness and performance on an additive task: Evidence for multidimensionality. *Journal of Social Psychology, 128,* 547-558.

Zander, A. (1994). *Making groups effective* (2nd ed.). San Francisco: Jossey-Bass.

Zenger, T. R., & Marshall, C. R. (1995). Group-based plans: An empirical test of the relationships among size, incentive, intensity, and performance. In *Academy of Management Journal, best papers proceedings* (pp. 161-165). New Brunswick, NJ: Academy of Management.

Zey, M. (Ed.). (1992). *Decision making alternatives to rational choice models.* Newbury Park, CA: Sage.

Zey-Ferrell, M. (1979). *Dimensions of organizations: Environment, context, structure, process, and performance.* Santa Monica, CA: Goodyear.

Zigon, J. (1995). *How to measure the results of work teams.* Media, PA: Zigon Performance Group.

# Other Suggested Readings

Bernstein, P. (1997). *American work values: Their origin and development.* New York: State University of New York Press.

Beyerlein, M., & Bullock, M. (1995). *The International Conference on Work Teams Proceedings: Anniversary collection: The best of 1990-1994.* Denton, TX: The Interdisciplinary Center for the Study of Work Teams.

Boulding, K. (1963). *Conflict and defense.* New York: Harper & Row.

Bureau of Labor Statistics. (1971). *Employment and earnings.* Washington, DC: U.S. Department of Labor.

Bureau of Labor Statistics. (1992). *Employment and earnings.* Washington, DC: U.S. Department of Labor.

Fernandez, J. P. (1981). *Racism and sexism in corporate life.* Lexington, MA: Lexington Books.

Goldberg, A. M., & Pegels, C. C. (1985). *Quality circles in health care facilities: A model for excellence.* Rockville, MD: Aspen Systems Corp.

Goodman, P. S., Ravlin, E. C., & Argote, L. (1986). Current thinking about groups: Setting the stage for new ideas. In P. S. Goodman (Ed.), *Designing effective work groups* (pp. 1-33). San Francisco: Jossey-Bass.

Gross, S. E., & Blair, J. (1995). Reinforcing team effectiveness through pay. *Compensation and Benefits Review, 27*(5), 34-38.

Gunther, J., & Hawkins, F. (1996). *Total quality management in human service organizations.* New York: Springer.

Hall, R. H. (1996). *Organizations: Structures, processes, and outcomes* (6th ed.). Englewood Cliffs, NJ: Prentice Hall.

Hunt, J. G., & Larson, L. L. (Eds.). (1979). *Crosscurrents in leadership.* Carbondale: Southern Illinois University Press.

Kemmerer, F. N., & Thiagarajan, S. (1992). Incentive systems. In H. D. Stolovich & E. J. Keeps (Eds.), *Handbook of human performance technology: A comprehensive guide for analyzing and solving performance problems in organizations* (pp. 312-330). San Francisco: Jossey-Bass.

Loscocco, K. A. (1989). The instrumentally oriented factory worker: Myth or reality. *Work and Occupations, 16,* 3-25.

Mager, R. F., & Pipe, P. (1970). *Analyzing performance problems.* Belmont, CA: Fearon.

Manz, C. C., & Sims, H. P., Jr. (1984). Searching for the "unleader": Organizational member views on leading self-managed groups. *Human Relations, 37*(5), 409-424.

Manz, C. C., & Sims, H. P., Jr. (1986). Leading self-managed groups: A conceptual analysis of a paradox. *Economic and Industrial Democracy, 7,* 141-165.

Manz, C. C., & Sims, H. P., Jr. (1990). *Self-managing teams: Becoming a superleader.* King of Prussia, PA: Organizational Design and Development.

Mohrman, S. A., & Mohrman, A. M. (1997). *Designing and leading team-based organizations: A workbook for organizational self-design.* San Francisco: Jossey-Bass.

Perrow, C. (1977). Three types of effectiveness studies. In P. S. Goodman, J. M. Pennings, & Associates (Eds.), *New perspectives on organizational effectiveness* (pp. 96-105). Washington, DC: Jossey-Bass.

Rummler, G. A., & Brache, A. P. (1995). *Improving performance: How to manage the white space on the organizational chart* (2nd ed.). San Francisco: Jossey-Bass.

Stolovich, H. D., & Keeps, E. J. (1992). *Handbook of human performance technology: A comprehensive guide for analyzing and solving performance problems in organizations.* San Francisco: Jossey-Bass.

Welford, A. T. (1988). Preventing adverse changes of work with age. *International Journal of Aging and Human Development, 27*(4), 283-291.

U.S. Department of Defense. (1990). *Quality and productivity self-assessment guide for defense organizations.* Washington, DC: Author.

Yeatts, D. E. (Forthcoming). Self-managed work teams: What works? *Clinical Laboratory Management Review.*

Yeatts, D. E., Hyten, C., Wagner, M., Maddox, K., & Barrit, R. (1997, February). Systems for work teams: Supporting information systems for teams. *Team Magazine,* pp. 46-49.

# Index

# About the Authors

**Dale E. Yeatts, Ph.D.,** is Associate Professor in the Department of Sociology at the University of North Texas. He has been studying the performance of self-managed work teams since working for the American Society for Training and Development in 1987. He has received grants from the National Science Foundation and Texas Advanced Research Program to study the performance of SMWTs and has published articles on SMWTs in numerous journals, including *Business Horizons* and the *Journal for Quality and Participation.* He has consulted with various organizations, such as Boeing, Texas Instruments, the U.S. Department of Defense, and the General Services Administration, to help them improve their SMWT programs.

**Cloyd Hyten, Ph.D.,** is Associate Professor in the Department of Behavior Analysis at the University of North Texas. He has also published in the area of work teams and has received a grant from the National Science Foundation to study the performance of SMWTs. His research has focused particularly on performance measurement and compensation systems.